NEW DIRECTIONS IN THE SOCIOLOGY OF GLOBAL DEVELOPMENT

RESEARCH IN RURAL SOCIOLOGY AND DEVELOPMENT

Series Editor: Frederick H. Buttel[†]

Volume 1: Focus on Agriculture – H. Schwarzweller

Volume 2: Focus on Communities – H. Schwarzweller

Volume 3: Third World Contexts – H. Schwarzweller

Volume 4: Rural Labor Markets – W.W. Falk and T.A. Lyson

Volume 5: Household Strategies – H. Schwarzweller and D.C. Clay

Volume 6: Sustaining Agriculture and Rural Community – H. Schwarzweller and T.A. Lyson

Volume 7: Focus on Migration – H. Schwarzweller and B.P. Mullan

Volume 8: Dairy Industry Restructuring – H. Schwarzweller and A.P. Davidson

Volume 9: Walking Towards Justice: Democratization in Rural Life – Michael M. Bell, Fred T. Hendricks and Azril Bacal

Volume 10: Nature, Raw Materials, and Political Economy – Paul S. Ciccantell, David A. Smith and Gay Seidman

RESEARCH IN RURAL SOCIOLOGY AND DEVELOPMENT
VOLUME 11

NEW DIRECTIONS IN THE SOCIOLOGY OF GLOBAL DEVELOPMENT

EDITED BY

FREDERICK H. BUTTEL[†]

Department of Rural Sociology, University of Wisconsin-Madison, USA

PHILIP McMICHAEL

Department of Development Sociology, Cornell University, USA

ELSEVIER
JAI

Amsterdam – Boston – Heidelberg – London – New York – Oxford
Paris – San Diego – San Francisco – Singapore – Sydney – Tokyo

ELSEVIER B.V.	ELSEVIER Inc.	ELSEVIER Ltd	ELSEVIER Ltd
Radarweg 29	525 B Street, Suite 1900	The Boulevard, Langford	84 Theobalds Road
P.O. Box 211	San Diego	Lane, Kidlington	London
1000 AE Amsterdam,	CA 92101-4495	Oxford OX5 1GB	WC1X 8RR
The Netherlands	USA	UK	UK

© 2005 Elsevier Ltd. All rights reserved.

This work is protected under copyright by Elsevier Ltd, and the following terms and conditions apply to its use:

Photocopying
Single photocopies of single chapters may be made for personal use as allowed by national copyright laws. Permission of the Publisher and payment of a fee is required for all other photocopying, including multiple or systematic copying, copying for advertising or promotional purposes, resale, and all forms of document delivery. Special rates are available for educational institutions that wish to make photocopies for non-profit educational classroom use.

Permissions may be sought directly from Elsevier's Rights Department in Oxford, UK: phone (+44) 1865 843830, fax (+44) 1865 853333, e-mail: permissions@elsevier.com. Requests may also be completed on-line via the Elsevier homepage (http://www.elsevier.com/locate/permissions).

In the USA, users may clear permissions and make payments through the Copyright Clearance Center, Inc., 222 Rosewood Drive, Danvers, MA 01923, USA; phone: (+1) (978) 7508400, fax: (+1) (978) 7504744, and in the UK through the Copyright Licensing Agency Rapid Clearance Service (CLARCS), 90 Tottenham Court Road, London W1P 0LP, UK; phone: (+44) 20 7631 5555; fax: (+44) 20 7631 5500. Other countries may have a local reprographic rights agency for payments.

Derivative Works
Tables of contents may be reproduced for internal circulation, but permission of the Publisher is required for external resale or distribution of such material. Permission of the Publisher is required for all other derivative works, including compilations and translations.

Electronic Storage or Usage
Permission of the Publisher is required to store or use electronically any material contained in this work, including any chapter or part of a chapter.

Except as outlined above, no part of this work may be reproduced, stored in a retrieval system or transmitted in any form or by any means, electronic, mechanical, photocopying, recording or otherwise, without prior written permission of the Publisher.

Address permissions requests to: Elsevier's Rights Department, at the fax and e-mail addresses noted above.

Notice
No responsibility is assumed by the Publisher for any injury and/or damage to persons or property as a matter of products liability, negligence or otherwise, or from any use or operation of any methods, products, instructions or ideas contained in the material herein. Because of rapid advances in the medical sciences, in particular, independent verification of diagnoses and drug dosages should be made.

First edition 2005

British Library Cataloguing in Publication Data
A catalogue record is available from the British Library.

ISBN-10: 0-7623-1250-5
ISBN-13: 978-0-7623-1250-4
ISSN: 1057-1922 (Series)

∞ The paper used in this publication meets the requirements of ANSI/NISO Z39.48-1992 (Permanence of Paper).
Printed in The Netherlands.

Working together to grow
libraries in developing countries

www.elsevier.com | www.bookaid.org | www.sabre.org

ELSEVIER   BOOK AID International   Sabre Foundation

CONTENTS

LIST OF CONTRIBUTORS   vii

EDITORIAL ADVISORY BOARD   ix

DEDICATION: TO FREDERICK H. BUTTEL   xi

PART I: NEW RESEARCH AGENDAS IN THE ERA OF GLOBAL DEVELOPMENT

NEW DIRECTIONS IN COMMODITY CHAIN ANALYSIS OF GLOBAL DEVELOPMENT PROCESSES
Jane L. Collins   3

TRANS-LOCAL AND TRANS-REGIONAL SOCIO-ECONOMIC STRUCTURES IN GLOBAL DEVELOPMENT: A 'HORIZONTAL' PERSPECTIVE
Sandra Halperin   19

CHANGING RURAL SCENARIOS AND RESEARCH AGENDAS IN LATIN AMERICA IN THE NEW CENTURY
Norman Long and Bryan Roberts   57

CONQUERING, COMPRADOR, OR COMPETITIVE: THE NATIONAL BOURGEOISIE IN THE DEVELOPING WORLD
Andrew Schrank   91

PART II: GLOBAL DEVELOPMENT AND POLICY QUESTIONS

WHAT IS FOOD AND FARMING FOR? – THE (RE)EMERGENCE OF HEALTH AS A KEY POLICY DRIVER
Tim Lang   123

PROMOTING SUSTAINABLE DEVELOPMENT:
THE QUESTION OF GOVERNANCE
  Geoffrey Lawrence   145

'STATELESS' REGULATION AND CONSUMER
PRESSURE: HISTORICAL EXPERIENCES OF
TRANSNATIONAL CORPORATE MONITORING
  Gay Seidman   175

PART III: STRATEGIC QUESTIONS AND GLOBAL DEVELOPMENTS

THE POVERTY OF RESOURCE EXTRACTION
  Stephen G. Bunker   211

FROM COLONIALISM TO GREEN CAPITALISM:
SOCIAL MOVEMENTS AND EMERGENCE OF FOOD
REGIMES
  Harriet Friedmann   227

GLOBAL DEVELOPMENT AND THE CORPORATE
FOOD REGIME
  Philip McMichael   265

SHIFTING STRATEGIES OF SOVEREIGNTY:
BRAZIL AND THE POLITICS OF GLOBALIZATION
  Sara Schoonmaker   301

LIST OF CONTRIBUTORS

Stephen G. Bunker[†]	Department of Sociology, University of Wisconsin, Madison, WI, USA
Jane L. Collins	Department of Rural Sociology and Women's Studies, University of Wisconsin, Madison, WI, USA
Harriet Friedmann	Department of Sociology, University of Toronto, Centre for International Studies, Toronto, ON, Canada
Sandra Halperin	Department of International Relations and Politics, University of Sussex, UK
Tim Lang	Department of Health Management & Food Policy, Institute of Health Sciences, City University, London, UK
Geoffrey Lawrence	School of Social Science, University of Queensland, Queensland, Australia
Norman Long	Department of Rural Development Sociology, Wageningen University, The Netherlands
Philip McMichael	Department of Development Sociology, Cornell University, NY, USA
Bryan R. Roberts	Department of Sociology, University of Texas at Austin, Austin, TX, USA
Andrew Schrank	Department of Sociology, University of New Mexico, NM, USA
Sara Schoonmaker	Department of Sociology and Anthropology, University of Redlands, CA, USA
Gay Seidman	Department of Sociology, University of Wisconsin-Madison, Madison, WI, USA

EDITORIAL ADVISORY BOARD

Norman Long Wageningen University, Wageningen, Netherlands (International Rural Sociology Association)

Max Pfeffer Cornell University, USA (Rural Sociological Society)

Hilary Tovey Trinity College, Dublin, Ireland (European Society for Rural Sociology)

Frank Vanclay University of Tasmania, Australia (International Rural Sociology Association)

DEDICATION:
TO FREDERICK H. BUTTEL[†]

This edition of *Research in Rural Sociology and Development* is dedicated to Frederick H. Buttel, who edited the series from 2002 to 2005. Knowing that he was terminally ill, Fred asked me in the summer of 2003 to co-edit this particular volume. He died in January 2005, unable to see the project through to its completion. Nevertheless, the volume bears the stamp of Fred's clear vision. It grew out of a symposium Fred organized at the XI World Congress for Rural Sociology in Trondheim, July 2004. He named that symposium 'New Directions in the Sociology of Global Development.' Chapters in this volume include papers presented at that symposium, complemented by an additional selection of outstanding papers we commissioned. Together, these chapters constitute a fitting memorial to Fred's unparalleled breadth of contribution to the sociology of development.

Frederick H. Buttel was the William H. Sewell Professor of Rural Sociology, and Professor of Environmental Studies, at the University of Wisconsin, Madison. He was also Co-Director of the Program on Agricultural Technology Studies at UW-Madison, Chair of the Development Studies Program, and a Senior Fellow at the Center of World Affairs and the Global Economy. Elected a Fellow of the American Association for the Advancement of Science (AAAS) in 1987, he was also Past President of the Rural Sociological Society, of the Agriculture, Food and Human Values Society, of the Environment and Society Research Committee (RC24) of the International Sociological Association and former Chair of the Section on Environment and Technology of the American Sociological Association. Co-editor of the journal *Society and Natural Resources*, Fred also sat on numerous editorial boards of a range of other professional journals. He co-authored *Environment, Energy and Society: Toward a New Synthesis* (2002), *The Sociology of Agriculture* (1990), and *Los Movimientos Ecologistas* (1984); and co-edited several books, including *The Rural Sociology of the Advanced Societies* (1980), *Labor and the Environment* (1984), *Towards a New Political Economy of Agriculture* (1991), *Hungry for Profit: The Agribusiness Threat to Farmers, Food and the Environment* (2000), *Environment and Global Modernity* (2000), *Sociological Theory and the Environment* (2002), *The Environmental State Under Pressure* (2002), and *Environment, Energy and Society: Exemplary Works* (2003).

While Fred's scholarly output and professional engagement was unusually prodigious, it is noteworthy that he accomplished much of this while battling ill-health for more than a decade. Nevertheless, during this time he remained steadfastly committed to his personal vision of public social science. His engagement with his craft, his colleagues, his students, and citizens and farmers within the realm of his applied research, was exemplary, and was recognized as such at a day-long, well-attended *Festschrift* at the August 2004 meetings of the Rural Sociological Society in Sacramento. Fred was in attendance, to hear colleagues and ex-students speak to his substantial and outstanding contributions to three areas of research: sociology of agriculture, sociology of the environment, and technology and society. Most of all, they spoke of his remarkable intellectual insight, and foresight, namely, his ability to spot emerging social trends, and his ability to identify and link intellectual currents – whether in the literature or in his colleagues. He had an uncanny ability to match colleagues whose work was either complementary or convergent, and in doing so, to strengthen their own contributions to public social science. This volume bears witness to Fred's dedication to nurturing new research among his colleagues, and so we, his colleagues, dedicate this volume to his extraordinary life.

Philip McMichael
Ithaca, New York

PART I:
NEW RESEARCH AGENDAS IN THE ERA OF GLOBAL DEVELOPMENT

NEW DIRECTIONS IN COMMODITY CHAIN ANALYSIS OF GLOBAL DEVELOPMENT PROCESSES

Jane L. Collins

ABSTRACT

While some researchers have considered commodity chain analysis to be a tool or method that is "innocent of theory," or can be combined with any theory, this paper argues that it has a specific set of theoretical investments. It argues that commodity chain analysis emerged in response to criticisms of the determinism, economism, and western bias in earlier development paradigms. Drawing on recent scholarship, it argues that researchers have turned to the study of commodity chains to provide situated and contingent accounts of global political economy that are historically specific, sensitive to culture and meaning, and attentive to subaltern perspectives.

INTRODUCTION: A METHOD WITHOUT A THEORY?

Commodity chains have always been central to development discourse. Colonial relationships were structured around the flow of sugar and coffee, spices and bananas, and of course, slaves. Early theories of dependency and underdevelopment took the unequal terms of these commodity exchanges, and their legacy in the post-colonial period, to be a key factor explaining the distribution of poverty and underdevelopment in the 20th century. In these early formulations, theorists embedded their discussions of commodities and commodity chains within broader frameworks of class struggle or world systems dynamics. In the 1980s, this changed, however. As post-modern theories and the end of the Cold War posed challenges to these large paradigms, some scholars began to embrace the study of commodity chains as a *methodological* strategy that permitted them to continue empirical work despite loosened theoretical moorings. They sought to disentangle the approach from the theories that had structured its inquiries in the past.

At times, researchers argued that commodity chain analysis was a method or approach that was "innocent of theory." For example, Phillip Raikes and his colleagues, speaking of the French *filières* tradition, claimed that it "is seen by many adherents as a neutral and purely empirical category." They also described it as "less a theory than a meso-level field of analysis" (Raikes, Jensen, & Ponte, 2000, p. 2). Researchers who sought to dis-embed commodity chain analysis from theory referred to it as an "approach," an "analytical tendency," a "heuristic tool," a "framework," and a "model." Many who turned to commodity chain analysis as a data-gathering strategy argued that it was well suited to capturing the complex transactions of an era of globalization and corporate domination of agriculture. For example, Bill Friedland (1984, p. 223) suggested that it was a method that made sense at a time when diversified farming was giving way to specialty production of particular crops or animals. Others held that, with the declining relevance of national accounts data for understanding trade and economic policy, the commodity chain provided a way to encompass the array of actors and institutions involved in what Harriet Friedmann (1993, p. 52) has called "private global regulation." As an analytical tool that did not begin with a presumption that states or particular institutions would be key actors, they argued that it could grasp the evolving organizational aspects of international trade, the linkages that animate it, the coordination that makes it possible, and the new global bodies that regulate it.

These claims created an image of commodity chain analysis as innocent of, or untouched by, theory. Yet, in a related way, some scholars have suggested that it has an opposite tendency – to promiscuously consort with theories of any origin. It could be argued that the method has provided a haven where researchers from disparate paradigms meet and a free space for mixing and matching different theoretical traditions. Friedland (1984, p. 222) has observed that while his version of the method – which he calls commodity systems analysis – owes much to neo-Marxist labor process paradigms, it also had "honorable antecedents in [the] mainstream functionalism [of] industrial sociology." Other researchers, like Jane Dixon (1999) or Peter Jackson (1999), have sought to combine political economic analysis with the study of meaning and cultural value along the commodity chain. A cursory review of studies from the 1980s to the present that have used commodity chain analysis reveals that researchers have combined it with the following theoretical frameworks: institutionalist economics, business theories of competitive advantage, labor process studies, regulation theory, convention theory, actor network theory, political economy of development or agriculture, world systems theory, dependency theory, transaction cost approaches, neo-Marxism, network analysis, social constructionism, and industrial upgrading.

This paper has a primary and a subsidiary purpose. The first is to address the question: "does commodity chain analysis have a theory?" But to answer this question, it will digress to explore the historiographic puzzle of why commodity chains became so popular in the late 20th and early 21st century. The evidence suggests that the analysis of commodity chains helped researchers to resolve, at least provisionally, some deep issues facing modernist development theory. Observing these theoretical maneuvers suggests that the method can never be "innocent" of theory, that researchers have deployed it most effectively in concert with highly sophisticated theory, and that there are ways to do so that are responsive to critiques of modernist development paradigms.

COMMODITY CHAIN ANALYSIS AND THE CRISIS OF DEVELOPMENT THEORY

The rise in the fortunes of commodity chain analysis in the 1980s coincided with a widespread critique of "development" as a practice and of development theory as an ideology. Fueled by new post-structuralist approaches in the humanities and social sciences, and by the beginning of the end of the Cold War, critics expressed skepticism about all grand "theories of everything," but especially about those that celebrated and promulgated western models of "progress." These critics took development theory, both neo-classical and marxist, to task for its economism, its determinism, and its western bias.

The force of these critiques left many development scholars casting about for ways to do research that addressed social and economic change that were not implicated in economism and determinism, did not reify capital and its processes, and did not make western hegemony seem inevitable. As Lourdes Gouveia poignantly formulated the question: "how far can we carry our rejection of all attempts to delineate the contours of a social epoch? Can we avoid exaggerating the solidity of our social structures...and still speak...of relatively durable macro-institutional arrangements...?" (1997, p. 306). Many researchers saw commodity chain analysis, at least initially, as offering an alternative to a modernist development theory – one that dealt with "relatively durable macro-structural arrangements" but that provided more room for contingency and agency as well as for discourse and culture.

Jane Dixon has explicitly suggested that the analysis of commodity chains offers a "way out" of the impasse created by the critique of development. She has argued that it can be adapted to post-modern theoretical perspectives because it "demands an actor orientation and is context and case specific." She suggested that it is consistent with a social constructionist approach and amenable to discussions of "consumers and others responsible for the commodity's social life." (1999, p. 151). In a similar way, Watts and Goodman (1997, p. 13) have noted that commodity chain research avoids the grand generalities associated with discourses of development and globalization by focusing on distinct commodity-specific or sectoral dynamics, and by highlighting what Laura Raynolds and others have called "the multiple trajectories associated with agrarian internationalization." Goodman and DuPuis (2002, p. 13) have asked whether the method might be amenable to the analysis of culture and consumption, and while they remain critical of the degree to which it has incorporated such analysis to date, they point to its *potential* for "looking at the 'life of things' in society, a life that goes beyond the fetishized sphere of exchange...to the reproductive world in which things gain other meanings." So to what extent can commodity chain analysis bear the weight of these expectations? And, more specifically, *how* do researchers see it as resolving the three specific criticisms of development theory mentioned above?

COMMODITY CHAIN ANALYSIS AND DETERMINISM

Critics of development theory frequently have pointed to its reliance on a totalizing logic of capital accumulation that spreads over and colonizes spaces. Julie Graham and Katherine Gibson (Gibson–Graham, 1996) give us a somewhat more poetic version of this claim when they refer to capitalism as the "heroic/tranformative agent of development and modernity; ...the phallus that structures social space and confers meaning upon social practices and positions." The questions these critics raise are about the way in which certain patterns of change appear inevitable in development discourse, in which the activities of different spheres appear to be functionally integrated, and in which the space for innovation, resistance or counter-hegemonic practice is limited or absent altogether.

Even at the pinnacle of political economy's prestige in the sociology of development and sociology of agriculture, researchers who studied commodity chains were always somewhat aberrant in the detailed nature of their accounts of world system dynamics. In their early accounts of California lettuce and tomato commodity chains, Friedland and his collaborators, for example, laid out a Marxist labor process framework. They defined the key categories of mode of production, social relations of production, and the technical division of labor. Then they said that having "set the stage" they would move on to a more concrete analysis of agriculture. It is at this point that Friedland elaborates his well-known "five foci" for commodity systems analysis: production practices, grower organizations, labor markets, science, and marketing and distribution systems. The story that these authors produced, about the complicity between growers and the state in structuring immigration from Mexico to the U.S. through the *bracero* program and the delicate interplay between new technologies and the supply of labor, was not abstract and determinist, but deeply historical and aware of political contingency (Friedland & Barton, 1975; Friedland, Barton, & Thomas, 1981).

Similarly, Heffernan and Constance, working on the U.S. poultry commodity chain in the 1980s, discussed the actions and interests of specific transnational corporations, including Cargill, Tyson, and Mitsubishi. They traced mergers and acquisitions, interconnections between firms, and changing patterns of vertical integration. The actions of these firms are not presented as the unfolding of an inevitable trajectory of expansion and accumulation, but as a process driven by named actors, and one that could be derailed by contingencies such as diminished fossil fuel availability, national policies of food security, or new forms of global regulation. (1994).

More recent proponents of commodity chain research have argued explicitly that it provides an alternative to the totalizing frameworks of development theory. For Gereffi and Korzeniewicz (1994, p. 4) this is because commodity chains are *embedded* in time and space, and analyzing them demands attention to the organizational context. In a recent article, Friedland (2001) has suggested that this is because commodities are linked to the mid-range concept of *communities*, defined both spatially and functionally, and thus require analysis of *local* social institutions. Watts and Goodman (1997, p. 15) have credited the study of commodity chains with offering opportunities to explore "the role of technology, the mediations of the state and the agency of individual actors." In general, proponents have suggested that focusing on commodity chains provides an alternative to development theory's fixation with "production," an antidote to our tendency to see power as flowing in only direction, and a cure for our willingness to attribute change to abstract forces (like globalization or dependency) that have no faces or addresses.

Two examples suggest how researchers have used the study of commodity chains to build contingency, specificity and multiplicity into their accounts. In a widely read edited volume on commodity chains that appeared in 1994, Gary Gereffi, while operating within what is nominally a world systems perspective, has argued for jettisoning concepts of national development and industrialization and replacing them with more open-ended accounts of the networking activities of firms and the competitive dynamics of sectors. Focusing on the global apparel industry, he has created a "network-centered and historical approach that probes above and below the level of the nation-state to better analyze structure and change in the world economy."

Borrowing concepts from institutionalist economics and economic sociology, Gereffi has focused on strategies of industrial upgrading that explore how developing nations – where the least profitable parts of commodity chains have historically been located – might "capture" more profitable nodes. He examines how corporations construct networks to improve their position within commodity chains and how those who gain control over certain nodes in the chain become "lead firms" that drive the entire industry or sector. Mapping these strategies and their changes over time, Gereffi (1994) creates an account of development process that includes both state and corporate actors, is highly contingent and contested, and that captures what he calls the "microfoundations of internationalizing trade networks."

In a similar way, Harriet Friedmann (1978, 1993) has used the tools of regulation theory to describe the construction of the world grain trade in the post-World War II period. Regulation theory as an intellectual project has emphasized the multiple, and historically specific, forms of capitalist accumulation. In the words of John Wilkinson (1997, p. 311), it is indebted to the "Annales school of history, to…institutional analyses of political science and law, to Bourdieu's concepts of 'habitus' and 'field' and to the social science analysis of corporatism and procedures of coordination." Friedman draws on its premises to construct her concept of the food regime, which she uses to link international relations of food production and consumption to forms of accumulation. As Dixon (1999, p. 152) has said, Friedmann's concept of food regimes stands alone, within political economy, in acknowledging gendered consumer practices and norms of consumption.

In a series of articles published in the 1970s and 1980s, Friedmann mapped the set of national policies and international arrangements that led to American grain surpluses from the 1950s to the 1970s, and the way in which the U.S. government used food aid to create new markets for grain in developing nations. This work was notable for the ways that it linked the politics of grain production in the U.S. to the politics of grain consumption in developing countries that received food aid and imported wheat, and for the connections it drew between sales of U.S. wheat, the decline of native grains, and proletarianization in developing nations (1978, 1980, 1987, 1993). In a sense it accomplishes what Goodman and DuPuis (2002, p. 9) have called "the ambitious task of theorizing the ways that practices of food provision and consumption are co-determined."

In later work, Friedmann and McMichael (1989) have described the growth of the post-war agro-food commodity complexes that they call "durable foods" and "intensive meat production." Within these complexes, agricultural products such as soy or corn become part of commodity chains that are "dominated at both ends by increasingly large industrial capitals." Their account of the capture of agriculture by industry and the rise of new forms of agro-industrial capital is macro in scale, but emphasizes contingency and politics. For example, in discussing the growth of "durable foods," Friedmann and McMichael emphasize that sweeteners and protein fillers can be derived from a variety of sources, and that industrial actors choose sources based on relative prices with prevailing techniques. These prices and techniques are themselves political – since agricultural policies determine supplies and prices of grains and soy, while state-funded research determines what technologies are available. There is no pre-determined outcome here, as different branches of capital, distributed across national boundaries, vie for ascendancy. In a similar way, they show that the growth of the meat/soy/maize complex depended on the negotiation of trade rules that permitted the transnational integration of the sector and that were in contradiction with the growth of the state system in the post-World War II period. The picture that emerges is one in which outcomes are contested and uncertain and in which not only capitalism, but the food sector itself, is highly differentiated. As Friedmann and McMichael (1989, p. 112) say, "not only is agriculture no longer a coherent sector, but even food is not."

The work of these researchers does not go as far as some critics have suggested it should in abandoning structural concepts and in specifying actors and processes. Busch and Juska, for example, have complained of a continued tendency, in commodity chain research, to "reify" corporate actors. They have suggested that actor network theory, by focusing on ties between individuals, rather than institutions, offers advantages in accounting for specific instances of corporate behavior and outcomes. Cargill Grain Corporation and national legislatures do not act, they argue, but rather individuals within the firm or the Congress (1997). This call to "deconstruct the institutional actors of political economy" is useful in putting names and faces on sometimes shadowy global actors. But it also skirts close to the edge of methodological individualism in refusing to acknowledge the role of institutional culture and practice, regulatory and legal conventions, and other sets of patterned and somewhat durable social relationships.

COMMODITY CHAIN ANALYSIS AND ECONOMISM

Critics of development theory have also argued that researchers have privileged the economy over other aspects of life, seeing it as the fundamental determinant of social systems and historical events. To quote Graham and Gibson (1996, p. 24) once again, "within political economy and the political movements it has spawned or inspired, economic determinism has reigned." Critics argue that development theorists have paid scant attention to culture (except as an impediment to economic progress) and even less to meaning and to discourse.

For Jane Dixon (1999), the analysis of commodity chains provides opportunities to draw culture and meaning in, because of the nature of the commodity itself. Commodities are not only central to trade, but to human physical comfort, to self-expression and to group representation. They can signify social status and the comforts of home. In her words, "moving beyond the exchange value of a thing to what Marx called its use value, and beyond its production to those who process, advertise, sell, buy, and use it, opens political economy to considerations of meaning and to the unwaged work and play of the sphere of social reproduction" (1999, p. 157). For these reasons feminist analysts, and a variety of post-modern theorists, have seen commodity studies as occupying a ground where the material, the social, and the meaningful meet.

One of the most successful accounts linking production and consumption, culture and political economy in the study of a commodity is, of course, Sidney Mintz's *Sweetness and Power* (1985). In this now classic work, Mintz tracks the meteoric rise in sugar consumption in Europe from 1650 to 1900, problematizing how this "demand" was created, how tastes evolved toward a preference for sweetness, and how sugar moved from "a luxury, a medicine, a spice" to a daily necessity. He shows how these changes depended on the European seizure of colonies and the creation of colonial enterprises based on slavery. He argues that sugar made visible the connection between the will to work and the will to consume, so that new wage earners partly worked to be able to buy it. But also its cheap calories and satisfying properties reduced the cost of feeding European workers. In this way Mintz argues, quoting Marx, "the veiled slavery of wage workers in Europe needed, for its pedestal, slavery pure and simple in the New World."

While in this brief formulation Mintz' account would appear to fall into the category of totalizing explanations, it is full of contingency, agency, and strange historical accident. As he notes "because the whole process – from the establishment of colonies, the seizure of slaves, the amassing of capital, the protection of shipping and all else...took shape under the wing of the states, such undertakings were at every point as meaningful politically as economically" and the outcome of political struggles between industrialists and mercantilists, colonists and metropole were uncertain in each era. Consumer taste is not simply a matter of free will, in his view, which would require us to assume "that each and every Briton, day by day and year by year, chose individually to seek and consume sucrose" in greater and greater quantities. But neither is it simply dictated by those in power; rather, it is the result of a complex interaction between the availability and marketing of goods by capitalist firms and local practices of consumption that include food habits and cuisine. Mintz (1985, p. xvii) has said that "as one attempts to put consumption together with production...there is always a tendency for one or the other to slip out of focus." But in his book, economy and culture are tightly bound together as he shows how the first sweetened cup of tea prefigured both new social relations and new meanings of work and self (1985, p. 214).

A more recent study that illustrates the inseparability of cultural and economic processes in the life of a commodity is Melanie DuPuis' (2002) account of how milk became a staple in the American diet. Her book investigates the changing cultural landscape within which milk drinking became popular, including the portrayal of milk as "the perfect food," which tapped into concepts of perfectability in American public life. She describes the 19th century public rhetoric and debate that created milk as a new, modern food that was complete and brought the purity of farm life to urban consumers, even before pasteurization and refrigeration had rendered milk safe for these populations. Examining why this should have been the case, she shows how this trend was driven by a complex array of factors, including growing numbers of women working outside the home, the loss of family-based "communities of practice" within which knowledge about breast-feeding of infants was transmitted, middle and upper class ideas of genteel femininity, and the industry's development and advertising of new products.

Turning to the production side, she details shifts in the social, political and economic relationships of dairy farming from the late 19th century to the present. She contends that milk is different from many other commodities, such as wheat, rice or orange juice, because people have been unwilling to adopt its concentrated or powdered form, and must be consumed within a short period. This has meant that production continues to be local rather than global, organized in "milksheds" around urban centers. She describes the way in which this organization creates competition among producers from different regions, which in some periods has allowed policy makers or large buyers to control milk prices. But she also shows how policies in each of the three big milk states in the U.S. have evolved differently, as policy-makers and organized public actors weigh the protection of small farms against the provision of cheap milk.

Like Mintz, DuPuis' work shows the interplay between the ways in which milk was used, the ways it was thought about, the transportation systems that moved it, and the interests that profited from it. By focusing on key debates in public institutions, she is able to show how market forces, resources, and culture meet. What links the work done by farm extension agents in New York State with the habits of milk consumers in New York City in her account, is the way that power has structured what they both take for granted about milk, about health, and about proper farming.

COMMODITY CHAIN ANALYSIS AND WESTERN BIAS

A third critique of development theory has argued that while it has pretended to speak from the neutral position of science, it has represented western interests and values and has left no space for subaltern voices. In the words of Akhil Gupta: "The 'modern,' the celebration of western progress, civilization, rationality and development, came to be instituted as a global phenomenon through colonialism.... After the formal demise of colonialism, one of the chief mechanisms by which this self-representation has been promulgated has been through development discourse." Calling it "orientalism transformed into a science for action," Gupta (2000) argues that "development discourses, with their built-in teleologies and spatial hierarchies, created subject positions that reinscribed inequalities after the dismantling of colonial rule." Julie Graham and Katherine Gibson (1996) have concurred. They write: "During the post-World War II period, bourgeois economic development theory installed industrial capitalism at the pinnacle of economic and social evolution, constituting the western experience of capitalist development as the model and measure for all the world." They argued that both mainstream and left development discourses shared this view of capitalist development as the "motor of history," differing principally "in how to read such a change: was it the coming of an earthly kingdom or...a process of devastation and laying waste?"

Here, I will turn briefly to research I conducted in the late 1990s on the global apparel industry as an example, because my use of commodity chain analysis was directly tied to my desire to provide a more open-ended and multi-vocal account of development process (Collins, 2003). The International Labor Organization has called the global apparel industry a "true one-world employer" in the sense that workers in different parts of the world compete to perform the same operations for the same firms and that companies can scan the global landscape in search of the kind of workers that please them. As an anthropologist by training, I wanted to bring an ethnographer's eye to the experience of workers positioned differently within this global labor market and to the question of what unites and divides them.

Given this question, I faced a problem: how do you study a global industry? Anthropologists are trained to go to a particular place and get to know it very well, but how do you do that with a phenomenon that does not happen in a single place, but is scattered around the globe? A phenomenon that geographers say occurs, not in a "space of place," but a "space of flows?" How do you study all of its different manifestations – and what feminists would call its "situated perspectives" – and integrate them into a coherent story?

In order to resolve this problem, I combined commodity chain analysis with multi-sited ethnographic investigation along the commodity chain. In the first, more standard part of the analysis, I read the trade press and the economics journals to figure out the structure of the apparel industry and the competitive pressures it faces. This kind of analysis helped me to trace the economic linkages that join Wall Street and Madison Avenue, the factories that make clothing, the stores that sell them and the consumers that buy them. It allowed me to develop an understanding of the global regulatory environment and the way in which the interests of corporations transcended, and frequently contradicted, the interests of national governments.

In the ethnographic part of the research, my goal was to put names and faces on actors throughout the commodity chain, from the offices of

Liz Claiborne in New Jersey to a factory floor in Aguascalientes, Mexico. I wanted to be able to say something about the decisions and actions, struggles and negotiations that took place in a large number of specific places where people live and work. As George Marcus (1995) has pointed out, the goal of this kind of multi-sited ethnographic investigation is not to provide a holistic representation of a global industry, but to collect a set of partial or situated perspectives relating to the phenomenon in question, juxtaposing views and experiences that have traditionally been kept apart. To quote Jennifer Mendez (2005) "what emerges is a picture, not of a global village, but of a transnational political terrain, rife with conflict and competition" (2005). Then, for the researcher, analysis consists of positing a logic of connection among the sites, developing an argument about their relationships to one another. This seemed to me to be a good way to construct a study of a global industry like apparel.

In many ways, the second part of this approach seems similar to what actor network theory theorists have been calling for, since it explores the way that actors in networks create social relationships and social meaning. But it locates these networks and interactions in a broader framework, situating them within the political economy of the commodity chain and reading their meaning within the political terrain of that location. So this approach names and specifies concrete acts as Latour (1993) or Busch and Juska (1997) urge. But it also examines the policies and procedures that make a given apparel firm more than the sum of its individual employees, as well as the competitive climate of the industry, the laws and rules that govern its labor and trading practices, and the way in which the industry is driven by trends like retail consolidation and the imperative to demonstrate a continually rising share price.

CONCLUSION

I began by suggesting that the growing popularity of commodity chain analysis was fueled by the development critiques of the 1980s, and the desire to find ways of working that continued to address issues of political and economic change while taking these critiques seriously. I have pointed to examples of work that used a commodity chain approach to produce accounts of change that were less deterministic, less economistic and less imbued with western bias than many neoclassical or Marxist accounts of development process. I believe that these examples demonstrate the potential for situated, contingent accounts of global political economy that are historically specific, sensitive to culture and meaning, and attentive to subaltern perspectives.

These accounts are likely to be more fragmentary in their exposition, more tentative in their conclusions, and more aware of gaps and fissures than their predecessors. But they are not all at the micro-sociological level. As Akhil Gupta has said, "the post-modern critique of meta-narratives has too often been extended to any explanation that seeks to account for global phenomena such as capitalism, confusing closure with scale." He continues, while "some scholars have argued that a turn to 'local' events and individual life narratives is a way to evade totalizing explanations...'local' phenomena...are...no less susceptible to totalizing, unsituated and teleological representations than global ones" and "there is no reason that non-teleological explanations about capitalism cannot be advanced (2000, p. 12).

But are commodity chain analyses innocent of theory? Are these accounts purely empirical, drawing on the metaphor of the commodity chain simply as a device to organize the collection of data? I think that this is not, and cannot be the case. Each of the research projects I have described had strong theoretical motivations. In fact, in all of the cases that I cited, researchers were influenced by more than one paradigm. Friedland strategically combined labor process theory with more standard versions of industrial sociology; Gereffi drew together world systems theory with institutionalist economics. The regulationist perspective that Friedmann and McMichael used to craft their concept of the food regimes was already an amalgam or integration of several different theoretical approaches.

As a method, commodity chain analysis appears able to accommodate a variety of different theoretical agendas, but it cannot stand alone. No method or approach is innocent of theory, and commodity chains are no exception. Rather, I would argue that it is a richly promiscuous approach that helps to concretize and situate a broad range of theoretical perspectives, and that doing so makes them skeptical of determinisms, more sensitive to culture, and more aware that the processes we label "development" are experienced, understood and valued differently from locations along the commodity chain.

REFERENCES

Busch, L., & Juska, A. (1997). Beyond political economy: Actor networks and the globalization of agriculture. *Review of International Political Economy*, 4(4), 688–708.

Collins, J. L. (2003). *Threads: Gender, labor and power in the global apparel industry*. Chicago: University of Chicago Press.

Dixon, J. (1999). A cultural economy model for studying food systems. *Agriculture and Human Values*, 16, 151–160.

DuPuis, E. M. (2002). *Nature's perfect food: How milk became America's drink*. New York: New York University Press.

Friedland, W. (1984). Commodity systems analysis: An approach to the sociology of agriculture. In: H. K. Schwarzweller (Ed.), *Research in rural sociology and development: A research annual* (pp. 221–235). Oxfordshire: Elsevier.

Friedland, W. (2001). Reprise on commodity systems methodology. *International Journal of Sociology of Agriculture and Food, 9*(1), 82–103.

Friedland, W. H., & Barton, A. H. (1975). *Destalking the wily tomato: A case study in social consequences in California agricultural research*. Department of Applied Behavioral Sciences, University of California, Davis. Research Monograph No. 15.

Friedland, W. H., Barton, A. E., & Thomas, R. J. (1981). *Manufacturing green gold: Capital, labor and technology in the lettuce industry*. New York: Cambridge University Press.

Friedmann, H. (1978). World market, state and family farms: Social bases of household production in the era of wage labor. *Comparative Studies in Society and History, 20*(4), 545–586.

Friedmann, H. (1980). Household production and the national economy: Concepts for the analysis of agrarian formations. *Journal of Peasant Studies, 7*, 158–184.

Friedmann, H. (1987). The family farm and international food regimes. In: T. Shanin (Ed.), *Peasants and peasant societies* (pp. 247–258). London: Basil Blackwell.

Friedmann, H. (1993). The political economy of food. *New Left Review, 197*, 29–57.

Friedmann, H., & McMichael, P. (1989). Agriculture and the state system: The rise and decline of national agricultures, 1870 to the present. *Sociologia Ruralis, 29*, 93–117.

Gereffi, G. (1994). The organization of buyer-driven global commodity chains: How U.S. retailers shape overseas production networks. In: G. Gereffi & M. Korzeniewicz (Eds), *Commodity chains and global capitalism* (pp. 95–122). Westport: Praeger.

Gereffi, G., Korzeniewicz, M., & Korzeniewicz, R. P. (1994). Introduction. In: G. Gereffi & M. Korzeniewicz (Eds), *Commodity chains and global capitalism* (pp. 1–14). Westport: Praeger.

Gibson-Graham, J. K. (1996). *The end of capitalism (As we knew it): A feminist critique of political economy*. London: Blackwell.

Goodman, D., & DuPuis, E. M. (2002). Knowing food and growing food: Beyond the production-consumption debate in the sociology of agriculture. *Sociologia Ruralis, 42*(1), 5–22.

Gouveia, L. (1997). Reopening totalities: Venezuela's restructuring and the globalisation debate. In: D. Goodman & M. Watts (Eds), *Globalising food: Agrarian questions and global restructuring* (pp. 305–323). New York: Routledge.

Gupta, A. (2000). *Postcolonial development: Agriculture in the making of modern India*. Durham: Duke University Press.

Heffernan, W., & Constance, D. (1994). TNCs and the globalization of food. In: A. Bonnano, L. Busch, W. Friedland, L. Gouveia & E. Mingione (Eds), *From Columbus to ConAgra: The globalization of agriculture and food*. Lawrence: University of Kansas Press.

Jackson, P. (1999). Commodity cultures: The traffic in things. *Transactions of the Institute of British Geographers, 24*, 95–108.

Latour, B. (1993). *We have never been modern*. Cambridge: Harvard University Press.

Marcus, G. (1995). Ethnography in/of the world system: The emergence of multi-sited ethnography. *Annual Review of Anthropology, 24*, 95–117.

Mendez, J. B. (2005). *From the revolution to the maquiladoras: Gender, labor and globalization in Nicaragua*. Durham: Duke University Press.
Mintz, S. W. (1985). *Sweetness and power: The place of sugar in modern history*. New York: Penguin.
Raikes, P., Jensen, M. F., & Ponte, S. (2000). Global commodity chain analysis and the French Filière approach: Comparison and critique. Copenhagen: Centre for Development Research, Working Paper no. 00.3.
Watts, M., & Goodman, D. (1997). Agrarian questions: Global appetite, local metabolism: nature, culture and industry. In: D. Goodman & M. Watts (Eds), *Globalising food: agrarian questions and global restructuring* (pp. 1–35). New York: Routledge.
Wilkinson, J. (1997). A new paradigm for economic analysis? *Economy and Society, 26*(3), 305–339.

TRANS-LOCAL AND TRANS-REGIONAL SOCIO-ECONOMIC STRUCTURES IN GLOBAL DEVELOPMENT: A 'HORIZONTAL' PERSPECTIVE[☆]

Sandra Halperin

ABSTRACT

This chapter explores the trans-national and cross-regional interactions and connections that, beginning in the late eighteenth century, brought about the development of dualistic economies within and outside of Europe; and how this circuit was reconfigured after the world wars by means of decolonization, nationalism, "first" and "second" world development, and globalization. What this perspective brings into view is a horizontal rather than vertical division of the world: the synchronic and interdependent development of dynamic focal points of growth throughout the world shaped, both within and outside of Europe, by trans-local interaction and connection, as well as by local struggles and relations of dominance and subordination.

[☆] A shorter version of this paper will appear in Varieties of World-Making: Beyond Globalization by Peter Wagner and Nathalie Karagiannis ((c) Liverpool University Press 2006). Adapted with permission.

New Directions in the Sociology of Global Development
Research in Rural Sociology and Development, Volume 11, 19–55
© 2005 Elsevier Ltd. All rights reserved.
ISSN: 1057-1922/doi:10.1016/S1057-1922(05)11002-6

INTRODUCTION

Most perspectives on development assume that industrial capitalism was achieved in "the West" through a process of nationally organized economic growth and that, today, its organization is becoming increasingly trans-local or global. However, nationally organized economic growth has rarely been the case: from the start, capitalist development has been essentially transnational in nature and global in scope involving, not whole societies, but the advanced sectors of dualistic economies in Europe, Latin America, Asia, and elsewhere. This paper endeavours, therefore, to explore development from a perspective that analytically shifts the axis of view from the vertical (states, regions) to the horizontal (classes, networks) and, in this way, to bring into view the synchronic and interdependent development of dynamic focal points of growth throughout the world shaped, both within and outside of Europe, by trans-local interaction and connection, as well as by local struggles and relations of dominance and subordination.

Most accounts of the development of capitalism begin with the "rise of Europe." The story they tell is that the "lights went on" in Europe following the European dark ages (or, certainly by the eve of Europe's "industrial revolution") just as, or long after, they had gone out elsewhere in the world; and that, as a result of European exploration, settlement, colonization, and conquest, lights of varied brightness and colour gradually appeared in non-European areas of the world over the course of the next two centuries.

Accumulating evidence of its inadequacies is making this story increasingly unconvincing. As Janet Abu-Lughod (1989) and others have shown, the rise of Europe took place within an already existing system, stretching from western and southern Europe through the Middle East to China, and characterized by a prosperous and far-flung trading network and an active and important network of intercultural exchange. European military expansion into this system did not displace or destroy it: when the "lights went on in Europe" they remained on elsewhere in the world.

Thus, after the "lights went on in Europe", the actual pattern of economic expansion throughout the world resembled (to borrow an image from James Blaut, 1993, p. 171), "a string of electric lights" strung across Asia, the Middle East, Africa, Latin America, and Europe. These lights illuminated small islands of urbanized industrial society and export sectors in Asia, Latin America, Europe, and elsewhere, each surrounded by traditional communities and institutions and underdeveloped, weakly integrated local economies. This pattern developed around the world as elites and ruling groups, seeking to expand production while, at the same time, avoiding the social levelling required for the production of articles for mass local consumption, produced for external markets, instead. As a result, both *within* and outside of Europe, domestic markets remained weak and poorly integrated, and economic expansion proceeded through a trans-local/cross-regional exchange of capital and commodities among governments, ruling groups, and elites.

LOCAL RELATIONS OF POWER IN EUROPE

Distinctions are conventionally drawn between class structures in different European societies and, particularly, between those that were supposedly dominated by an indigenous, independent capitalist bourgeoisie, and those that were not. This distinction is the basis of various schemas that define "two roads" to industrial capitalism and democracy in Europe. One road, exemplified by Britain, is characterized by the emergence of a relatively open political space – the result of a bourgeois revolution having displaced the old landed aristocracy and the absolutist state. The second road, exemplified by Germany and other "late" developers, is distinguished by its relatively closed political space, the result of the continuing dominance of an agrarian class able to block industrialization and resist democracy.[1]

But nowhere in Europe was there a clear division between industrial and landed capital; in fact, everywhere industrial capitalist development was characterized by their fusion. In Britain, as elsewhere, the nature of industrial capitalist development was shaped by the political convergence of a landed aristocracy and large capitalist manufacturers.[2]

Many have argued that this elite had become bourgeoisified by the eighteenth or nineteenth century. However, throughout the nineteenth century, the most effective elites were traditional and aristocratic, land owning and rent receiving, and oligarchic. Rosa Luxemburg got it precisely right: in England, there was no revolutionary changeover from medieval to modern society, but "an early compromise which has preserved [into the twentieth century] the old remnants of feudalism." The old forms of medieval England "were not shattered or swept away, but filled with new content" (Luxemburg, 1976, p. 232).

The ways in which agrarian elites exercised power, and the degree of closure and restriction they succeeded in maintaining varied; but while it is possible to quibble about the extent that these varied, it was not substantial enough to constitute a different "road." Either, the aristocracy absorbed the industrial bourgeoisie and dominated it, protecting land and income structures; or the aristocracy resisted the industrial bourgeoisie and dominated it, protecting land and income structures. Either way, the road that emerges is essentially the same.

The two roads of industrial capitalist development that supposedly emerged in Europe were thought to have resulted from different relationships between the rising capitalist bourgeoisie and absolutism. The road to industrial development and democracy was made possible, it is assumed, by the conflict between the new industrial capitalist classes in Europe and absolutist monarchs; while the road to autocracy emerged as a result of the fusion of these classes with absolutism. However, the conflict between the "new" bourgeoisie and absolutist monarchs involved only selective aspects of absolutism and, specifically, those that scholars have identified as "enlightened" and "liberal" (see, e.g., Gagliardo, 1967). The leaders of the "national" revolutions and revolts against absolutism were opposed to the "liberal" reforms and, particularly, the price and wage controls, labour protections, and national welfare systems that had been introduced in Britain, France, and elsewhere by monarchs beginning in the sixteenth century. Their aim was to seize control of the state in order to preserve their privileges and prerogatives, to privatize new sources and means of producing wealth, to dismantle much of what today we would consider socially enlightened about "liberal absolutism," and retain much of what was not in a new guise. In fact, many of the revolutionary and progressive changes attributed to the nation states established by the "new" capitalist class were aspects of liberal absolutism that survived the nationalist assault; they originated, not with a revolt against the mercantilist systems of "Absolutist" states, but with reforms of land, tax, educational and legal systems introduced by "Absolutist" monarchs.

For instance, the features of France that, in 1815, were thought to resemble a "bourgeois" state, were the work, not of the Revolution, but of the *ancient regime*. It was the *ancient regime* that established the centralized administrative apparatus of the French state, introduced standing armies, national taxation, a codified law, and the beginnings of a unified market. It was France's *ancient regime* that, long before 1789, began the break up of large estates into a multiplicity of small proprietorships. Nor, as de Tocqueville concluded, were the ideas and values supposedly born in the Revolution the product of a new and revolutionary class (1955, p. ix). In sum, "from a strictly French point of view, the balance sheet of the French Revolution is relatively meagre" (Wallerstein, 1996, p. 12).

It is often assumed that, in Britain, the repeal of the Corn Laws marked the end of the power of the traditional landowning elite there. The Corn Laws, however, were not shoring up a declining sector; they were designed to retain the high profits generated during the Napoleonic war years. Wheat prices did not fall until the onset of the Great Depression in the 1870s (Hobsbawm, 1968, p. 197). For most of the nineteenth century, British agriculture remained the biggest branch of the economy by far in terms of employment. In 1891 it still employed more than any other industrial group. Only in 1901, with the growth of the transport industry and metal industries complex, did it cease to be the largest branch of the economy in employment terms (Hobsbawm, 1968, p. 195).

Revolutions in Europe in 1789, in the 1820s, 1830s and in 1848 gave a stronger position to industrialists and bankers, weakened the landlords' influence and, in places, partly replaced the political personnel. However, they failed to bring about a thorough-going transformation of social structures. Except in Russia after 1917, the traditional social structure of Europe remained essentially intact up until 1945.

While the capitalist class or bourgeoisie was a heterogeneous class, with many different elements or "fractions," the circumstances of nineteenth century Europe and, specifically, the revolutionary currents unleashed, first, by the French Revolution and the Napoleonic wars and, later, by the revolutions of 1848, increasingly polarized European society along class lines and, thus, brought about the fusion and unity of various fractions of capital. As a result, the economic divisions among capitalists, and other divisions of various kinds that might have given rise to intra-class conflict, were of far less importance than the issues over which that class as a whole was more or less united. So, for example, while landed and industrial capital in Britain clashed over the Corn Laws, they were united in a struggle to prevent labour from achieving any significant political and economic power; and it was this struggle that dominated the nineteenth and early twentieth centuries in Europe.

In 1848 a class compromise was forged between industrial and landed elites as a result of the willingness of the industrial bourgeoisie to press their demands through mobilizing the masses. After 1848 landlords and industrial capitalists can be seen as fractions of a single class.[3]

During the interwar period, and as a result of World War I, an intra-class division began to open up. In Britain, this was evident by the chasm that, by 1939, divided Chamberlain and Churchill. Confrontation with more powerful and militant working classes as a result of the war, elements of capital began to recognize the limits of the system. It became apparent that far more dire social externalities might be produced by a continuing dependence on methods of increasing absolute surplus value, than those that the U.S. model showed might be produced by a shift to relative surplus value production. The narrowing prospects for increasing overseas markets, and the escalating costs it entailed must have also become increasingly apparent (more on this, below). Moreover, a "second industrial revolution" was occurring, made up of the electrical, chemical, and auto industries comprising relatively large firms with capital-intensive processes. These industries were bound to look upon good labour relations and high and steady levels of production as more important than low wages and mere cheapness. Since their products and production runs demanded a more homogeneous market of high-income consumers, they were also more interested in the domestic and Dominion markets than with those of India and the less developed world or even Europe.[4]

However, though there were differences among fractions of capital during the interwar years, the revolutionary currents unleashed by World War I increasingly polarized European societies and, in this way, worked effectively to keep the capitalist class unified. As a result, the continuing prominence of the traditional elite was evident to 1939, and beyond.

Land in Britain, as elsewhere in Europe, was highly concentrated and, throughout the nineteenth century, the larger landowners continued to enlarge and consolidate their landholdings.[5] Its farming system was among the least mechanized among advanced countries. The majority of farms in England and Wales did not possess either a tractor or a milking machine until World War II, despite their having been available for thirty years or more. They remained relatively small and investment in them relatively low.

Like its agriculture, Britain's financial and industrial sectors were bound by monopoly and restriction.[6] The City of London, in which greater fortunes were made than in the whole of industry, remained "enmeshed in a pseudo baronial network of gentlemanly non-competition."[7] Industry became increasingly penetrated by monopoly and protection during the nineteenth century. Traditional corporatist structures – guilds, patronage and clientelist networks – survived in some places and grew stronger. Elsewhere, new corporatist structures were created. The modern cartel movement began developing in the 1870s and by 1914 pervaded industry throughout Europe. In what David Landes aptly calls "a commercial version of the enclosure movement" (1969, p. 247), Britain answered the cartel with the "combine," which amalgamated in various degrees a sizeable fraction of the productive units of a given trade.

These formed part of the complex of privileged corporations and vested interests in Europe that, by 1914, had become "quite as formidable as those of the Old Regime" (McNeill, 1974, pp. 164–165).

These were neither peripheral aspects of Britain's industrialization, nor ever-diminishing "forces of resistance" to industrial expansion. They highlight the extent to which the traditional landowning elite – which formed the basis of Britain's "capitalist class,"[8] dominated the state apparatus, and led Britain's capitalist development – channelled industrial expansion into dualistic and monopolistic forms. Dualism preserved the political and economic bases of traditional groups by restricting growth to within the constraints posed by the concentration of capital and land ownership. In so doing, it also generated the structural distortions that, collectively, are erroneously associated exclusively with third world "dependent" development. Dominant classes monopolized domestic industry and international trade through cartels and syndicates, tariffs and other controls. They instituted corporatist arrangements of a discriminatory and "asymmetrical" nature to limit competition and they obstructed rising entrepreneurs and foreign competitors. As a result, industrial expansion in Europe was shaped, not by a liberal, competitive ethos, as is emphasized in most accounts; but by feudal forms of organization, monopolism, protectionism, cartelization and corporatism, and by rural, pre-industrial, and autocratic structures of power and authority.

THE TRANS-LOCAL STRUCTURE OF INDUSTRIAL CAPITALIST EXPANSION

Perhaps the most crucial chapter in modern history for understanding the accelerating globalization of capital today is the dismantling of eighteenth century Europe's systems of national welfare and regulated markets, and the social conflicts that emerged as a result. The context of these events was the attack on the regulations of the "Absolutist" (i.e., interventionist) state.

In the eighteenth century, "Absolutist" governments in England,[9] France, and elsewhere in western Europe were regulating local markets, as well as controlling employment, and settlement. "Absolutism" was attacked by its opponents for its over-regulation. However, the aim of much of this regulation was to provision the local community and ensure fair practice, to protect the local population against monopoly and speculation, and against shortages and high prices. In England, official regulations prevented middlemen merchants from bypassing or cornering the market, and ensured quality control, a "just price," and an adequate domestic supply of goods; and market courts enforced them (Lie, 1993, p. 282). Those in England who demanded "freedom of trade" during the eighteenth century were actually demanding freedom from the requirement to trade inside open markets, by means of open transactions, and according to the rules and regulations which ensured fair practices and prices (Lie, 1993, p. 283).

In the eighteenth century Britain, entrepreneurs sought to escape government regulations through long-distance trade and expanded production for export.[10] As a result, competition for labour increased, and this enabled workers to bargain for wages and regulate their work time. Wages rose throughout the century and labourers were able "to take on less work and spend more time at leisure without endangering their traditional standard of living" (Gillis, 1983, p. 41). Economies in Europe at the time were based on local markets and face-to-face relations between seller and consumer, so workers were often able to exercise economic power as consumers, as well.

However, by the end of the eighteenth century these features became the target of a broad campaign to "dis-embed" capitalist development. In order to consolidate and maintain the subordination of labour to capital (the basic relation of capital), dominant classes sought to keep labour poor (political power was based on wealth, not citizenship) and in excess of demand (in "reserve"); gradually but persistently, they worked to destroy the market position of the skilled labourers of previous centuries who were more independent and valuable, and could therefore command higher wages and regulate their own time. By pursuing a strategy of expanding production largely for export, they obviated the need to furnish labourers with sufficient means to buy what they produced and deprived them of the ability to exercise power through consumer choice or boycott, as they had in the eighteenth century. They kept peasants and rural workers poor and weak by blocking land reform; monopolized domestic industry and international trade through the creation of cartels and syndicates, and through tariffs and various other controls; instituted corporatist arrangements of a discriminatory and "asymmetrical" nature to place further limits on competition; and obstructed rising entrepreneurs and foreign competitors. Land and industry became concentrated in fewer and fewer hands in the course of the century; methods of increasing absolute surplus value production, and traditional manufacturing, persisted; and an unprecedented degradation and intensification of labour, both within and outside of Europe, produced an increasing volume of goods and capital for circulation among a trans-national network of property-owners.

Europe's Transnational Industrial Expansion

States in Europe were built up within a pre-existing, region-wide system of social institutions, relationships, and norms. Administration derived from the same principles, political assemblies were composed of the same elements and invested with the same powers. For centuries, and with the Church acting as an international unifying agent, regulating economic life and political and class struggles across the region, political development, class struggles, social change, ideology, and culture remained essentially trans-European.[11]

As many scholars have noted, Europe's elite was more closely tied by culture and concrete interests to an international class than to the classes below them. The pan-regional elite, as Eric Hobsbawm has pointed out, bore something like a family resemblance to one another and was often physically distinct from peasants within their own countries; often they were of a different nationality or religion, or spoke a different language. Even where they had the same nationality and religion, their mode of life had in all respects more in common with elites elsewhere in Europe, than with the lower classes within their own countries.[12]

Because of the essentially transnational nature of European society and the similarities and interdependencies that it created among states, as the various economies of Europe began to expand in the nineteenth century, their advanced sectors were tied more closely to those within the economies of other European countries than to the more backward sectors within their own (see Halperin, 2004, Chapter 3). As a result, Europe's economic expansion took place within, and was crucially shaped by, an increasingly interdependent industrial system. Since interdependent parts must grow in some sort of balance if profitability is to be maintained, the advanced sector in one country had an interest in supporting and maintaining the growth of advanced sectors in other countries,[13] thus, reinforcing and maintaining the uneven and "dual" pattern of economic expansion characteristic of industrial capitalist development everywhere in Europe. In the nineteenth century, and as a result of the structural relations of connection and interaction that constituted the trans-European class, similar relations were established in sites of production; and they were reproduced, in similar ways, by their maintenance throughout the social formation.

The ruling classes of European states were not separate-but-similar classes. Rather, they formed a single trans-regional elite, and their broadly similar characteristics, interests, capabilities, and policies were constituted and reproduced through interaction, connection, and interdependence. While the properties of dominant groups in different parts of Europe may have varied, the connections and interactions among them were rich and concrete and, in themselves, and within the constraints and opportunities present in different contexts, produced a set of common solutions to the problems of organizing production along new lines.

The late eighteenth century "industrial revolution" in Europe did not involve any fundamental change in this trans-European social system. In fact, the reorganization of social relations of production in Europe as a result of the "industrial revolution" brought different groups across states into closer relations of interdependence.

It is generally the case that elites are interested in adopting the most up-to-date methods of multiplying their revenue, wealth, and power. The obvious success of the British elite in this regard would have been expected to inspire elites elsewhere in Europe to emulate British economic, social, administrative, and intellectual trends.

It was, thus, that common problems arising from the establishment of a capitalist labour market and new labour processes were generally resolved throughout Europe in broadly similar ways. Dominant classes have a common interest in exploiting labour (for profit). The ability to exploit labour by paying less for it than the value it produces is a necessary condition for creating surplus value and, thus, of realizing profit. In order to exploit labour, capitalists must maintain an advantageous balance of power. Since it is a necessary condition for realizing profit, it was a task faced by every dominant group seeking to increase profits by expanding production; and, given the numerical inferiority of capitalists, it was a critical one. How it was met by dominant classes, varied across different societies according to the type of goods they produced for sale and their power relative to labour. But similar capabilities, as well as a common Europe-wide context tended to shape their interaction with labour in similar ways. In Britain, dominant classes ensured that the conditions for realizing profit were met by using methods of absolute surplus value production at home (see Halperin, 2004, Chapter 3) and expanding production largely for export to other ruling groups. This became the model for industrial capitalism throughout Europe.

Europe emerged into its first century of industrial capitalism from the crucible of the Great War. A quarter century of war and revolutionary turmoil had made clear the central dilemma for dominant groups tempted by the possibilities of great profits to reorganize production along the lines of industrial capitalism: how to mobilize – train, educate and, in other ways, empower – labour while, at the same time, maintaining the basic relation of capitalism, i.e. the subordination of labour to capital. The Great War had revealed the dangers of a trained and compact mass army: many analogies, in fact, were drawn between the mass army of soldiers created in the Great War and the mass industrial army of workers needed for industrial capitalist production. At the same time socialism had been born in the French Revolution and its focus, in particular, on eradicating private property – something dominant classes had achieved through a century or more of struggle – seemed, in combination with the revolutionary ferment unleashed by the war, to threaten an anti-capitalist revolt of the masses. This was the context within which elites throughout Europe undertook to mobilize labour for industrial production.

Elites were cohesive, had much to gain, controlled immense resources, and were free to deploy these resources in a sustained pursuit of their aims. They either controlled the apparatus of the state directly or had access to political leaders and could trade their political support, or the withdrawal of political opposition, for concessions from them. They were therefore able to carry on a class struggle throughout the nineteenth century by means of a purposive, determined, and essentially coherent legislative, legal, military, and political assault on artisans, labourers, and peasants.

We are permitted to say that policies are "designed" – that they are intended, calculated, planned, premeditated, or deliberate. However, as is often the case, there were unintended consequences of these policies and in this case, there were important ones. By generating imperialist rivalries and conflicts that eventually led to multi-lateral great power war in Europe, external expansion had the unintended consequence of forcing governments and ruling elites to mobilize (and, thus, organize, train and, in other ways, empower) the masses. This is precisely what it seemed a century of external expansion had enabled them to avoid. As a number of scholars have shown, war often produces social levelling, revolution, and shifts in the balance of social forces (e.g., Marwick, 1980, Chapter 11; Andreski, 1954, pp. 33–38; Titmuss, 1958, p. 86; Sorokin, 1927, pp. 338, 348–349, 1969, p. 501; Schumpeter, 1976, p. 419). In the course of the world wars this is what happened in Europe.

*The "European Model" of Industrial Capitalist Expansion:
A Reinterpretation*

Foreign trade was the primary engine of economic growth in England in the nineteenth century; but it was the home market that initially gave the impetus to industrial growth in England between 1750 and 1780 (Eversley, 1967, p. 221; see also Mathias, 1983, pp. 16, 94). Britain's industrial output quadrupled during the eighteenth century, and the bulk of this output mass consumption goods. Thus, during the century, England's breakthrough in production was accompanied by a democratization of consumption at home.[14] In the nineteenth century, however, and long before it had been exhausted as a market for goods and capital, Britain's domestic economy ceased to expand; so much so, that by 1914 it had become under-mechanized and poorly integrated relative to those of other advanced countries.

Numerous scholars have pointed out that British investors under-invested in the domestic economy and, instead, massively exported capital.[15] They point out that funds used for British foreign investment could have been used to improve the technical performance of British industry (Lewis, 1978a, pp. 176–177, 1972, pp. 27–58; see also Trebilcock, 1981); they could have "helped to augment the stock of domestic housing and other urban social overhead projects and, thus, expand the domestic market for the expanded output of the British economy."[16] Not only was investment needed at home but between 1880 and 1914 returns from overseas investment were "far below what presumably could have earned by devoting the same resources to the expansion of domestic industry."[17] Moreover, these investments were generally also exposed to more risk than domestic investments.

Why, then, did investors neglect opportunities for profitable home investment and, instead, pursue investments overseas that were riskier, more difficult and costly to acquire and, in some cases, not as lucrative? The usual explanation is that the domestic market was not yet developed enough to absorb the output of expanded production and to provide profitable investment opportunities for surplus capital and that, as a result, capitalists were forced to seek for larger markets and more profitable fields of investment abroad.[18] But capital exporters did not then, and tend not now, to have capital saturated domestic economies. Britain, and other European economies, did not, as is usually assumed, develop initially on the basis of the expansion of the internal market and then, subsequently, expand into the foreign, colonial, and world markets: they expanded production first and foremost for foreign markets, and long before the opportunities for profitable investment had been exhausted at home.[19]

In fact, the market that was "saturated" in Britain in 1902 and before, as John Hobson made clear, was the one constituted solely by the wealthy classes. Thus, to speak of "saturation" assumes that the mass of the population has no demand for any goods other than those necessary for their own physical reproduction. Hobson argued that if the mass public raised its standard of consumption to keep pace with every rise of productive powers, there could be no excess of goods or capital... . Foreign trade would indeed exist, but there would be no difficulty in exchanging a small surplus of our manufactures for the food and raw material we annually absorbed, and all the savings that we made could find employment, if we chose, in home industries (Hobson, 1902, p. 81).

Therefore, "It is not industrial progress that demands the opening up of new markets and areas of investment," Hobson argued, "but mal-distribution of consuming power which prevents the absorption of commodities and capital within the country" (1902, p. 85). This was a typical consequence of capitalism, Hobson observed; but it was not a necessary one.[20] He argued, in fact, that whatever was produced in England could be consumed in England, provided that their was a proper distribution of "the 'income' or power to demand commodities" (1902, p. 88). But, as Hobson noted, more than a quarter of the population of British towns was living at that time at a standard "below bare physical efficiency" (1902, p. 86).

Some theorists argue that while capital exports may not have been necessary as a means of securing markets for surplus goods, they were necessary to Europe's industrialization as a means of acquiring raw materials and accumulating capital (see e.g., Wallerstein, 1974, p. 38, 51, pp. 93–95, 237, 269, 349). However, this contention has become the focus of considerable dispute. Paul Bairoch has argued that the "core" countries had an abundance of the minerals of the Industrial Revolution (iron ore and coal); they were almost totally self-sufficient in raw materials and, in fact, exported energy to the Third World.[21] Colonialism, Bairoch argues was, therefore, not necessary for industrial growth in Europe.[22] In fact, he argues, it may have actually *hampered* national economic growth and development.

If one compares the rate of growth during the nineteenth century it appears that non-colonial countries had, as a rule, a more rapid economic development than colonial ones. There is an almost perfect correlation. Thus colonial countries like Britain, France, the Netherlands, Portugal, and Spain have been characterized by a slower rate of economic growth and industrialization than Belgium, Germany, Sweden, Switzerland and the United States. The "rule" is, to a certain extent, also valid for the twentieth century. Thus Belgium, by joining the colonial "club" in the first years of the twentieth century, also became a member of the group characterized by slow growth. The loss of the Netherlands' colonial Empire after World War II coincided with a rapid acceleration in its economic development (1993, p. 77). Expanding on this argument, Bairoch suggests that one reason for Britain's relative absence of the "new" industries that emerged at the end of the nineteenth century was because its "ability to sell easily non-sophisticated manufactured goods to its colonies forestalled the need for modernization" (1993, p. 167).

Given the difficulties with standard interpretations of British investment, it seems reasonable to look elsewhere for an explanation.

Production processes, as Alfred Sohn-Rethel has pointed out, are structured in ways that enable capital to retain its control over the class struggle

(1978, p. 163). Decisions about whether and how to increase or restructure production are based on calculations about the conditions necessary for the realization of profit. Disadvantageous social externalities produced by the introduction of new production methods and by an expansion of output would be part of those calculations. Had the "democratization of consumption" of the eighteenth century continued, and had a broad-based industrial growth developed, along with the mass purchasing power and internal market needed to support it, the class, land, and income structures on which the existing structure of social power in Britain rested would have been destroyed.

Britain's consumer revolution in the eighteenth century had important implications for the structure of British society.[23] Mass consumption is associated with democracy. The consumer revolution and the emergence of a domestic market for mass- produced consumer goods, because it worked to undermine class distinctions and increase social mobility, was politically threatening and, thus, was not encouraged. A fully industrialized economy requires mass mobilization. Mass mobilization for industry (as for war) creates, out of the relatively disadvantaged majority of the population, a compact and potentially dangerous force; thus, elites showed little interest in the expansion of industry at home. Marx, as in much of his writing, was here perhaps only reflecting a general perception of his times when he wrote that

> The advance of industry...replaces the isolation of the labourers...by their revolutionary combination, due to association. The development of ModernIndustry, therefore, cuts from under its feet the very foundation on which the bourgeoisie produces and appropriates products (Marx, 1967, pp. 93–94).

It might be argued that owners of wealth were not conscious of the social externalities associated with the application of large masses of labour to production. This seems hardly plausible. The problems of setting to work and controlling masses of labour are not so substantially different in capitalist production as to have made all prior problems and their solutions irrelevant. For centuries landlords had been confronted with the "great fear" of mass peasant uprisings, and had organized production in ways that reinforced the existing relations of power and authority. The difference in capitalist production, and it is crucial, is not the strategic power that workers have – peasants had that too – but that for industry to grow and remain competitive a sizeable portion of the labour force must be educated, skilled, and mobile. If property owners were not conscious of the dangers of mass mobilization for industry, would they not have been after Marx spelled it out for them in the widely read and cited *Communist Manifesto*?

The development of exogenous demand and consumption through the export of capital and goods ensured that the benefits of expanded production would be retained solely by the property-owning classes. In 1914, British industrialization was as sectorally and geographically limited as dualistic colonial economies. Landed and industrial property had become increasingly concentrated. Mechanization, skilled labour, and rising productivity and real wages were found only in sectors producing for export. These sectors had only a limited impact on the rest of the economy. Little attempt was made to expand or mechanize industries producing goods for domestic household consumption. Consequently, the building industries grew by expanding employment, rather than by introducing innovations either in organization or technology. New techniques were introduced "slowly and with considerable reluctance". In the 1930s, half the industry's workforce still practiced "their traditional handicrafts, especially in house building, largely untouched by mechanization" (Benson, 1989, p. 20). Though Britain had pioneered electro-technics, by 1913 the output of the British electrical industry was little more than a third of Germany's (Hobsbawm, 1968, p. 180). Before World War II, less than a third of those employed in the transport sector were employed by the railways (28% in 1931). A majority of those engaged in transport worked for a small employer or were self-employed (Benson, 1989, pp. 22–23). Despite the British origins of the machines and machine tools industry, it was not until the 1890s that automatic machine-tools production was introduced in Britain. The impetus came from the United States, and the desire on the part of employers "to break down the hold of the skilled craftsmen in the industry" (Hobsbawm, 1968, p. 181). Gas manufacture was mechanized late, and as a result of pressure from trade unions.

Even Britain's export industries were slow to adopt new techniques or improvements, not only in textiles, but also in coal, iron, steel, railways and shipbuilding. The supply of coal increased,[24] not by introducing labour-saving techniques, but by increasing the number of coalminers.[25] In the 1930s, "more than 40% of British coal was cut and practically 50% conveyed without the aid of machinery" (Benson, 1989, p. 16). Though Britain was pre-eminent in steel production and had pioneered major innovations in its manufacture, with the exception of the Bessemer converter (1856), Britain was slow to apply the new methods and failed to keep up with subsequent improvements.[26] By the early 1890s, Britain had fallen behind Germany and the U.S. American shipbuilding expanded at a faster rate than British and, by 1860, had almost caught up. Though British industrialization was based on the expansion of capital goods production for railway building, rapid technical improvement came, even here, only when compelled by military competition and the modernizing armaments industry.[27]

The Circuit of Capital: The Nineteenth Century Origins of Contemporary Global Governance

Europe's economy before World War II was based on the development of external markets for heavy industry and high-cost consumption goods. By expanding its shipbuilding, boiler making, gun and ammunition industries, Britain was able to penetrate and defend markets overseas; this, in turn, provided opportunities for Britain to build foreign railways, canals, and other public works, including banks, telegraphs, and other public services owned or dependent upon governments. British exports of capital provided purchasing power among foreign governments and elites for these goods and services, and funded the development and transport of food and raw materials exports to Europe, thus creating additional foreign purchasing power and demand for British goods, as well as decreasing the price of food, and thereby the value of labour, in Britain.[28] At the centre of this circuit was the City of London, which like the advanced sector of a "dependent" economy worked to build strong linkages between British export industries and foreign economies, rather than to integrate various parts of the domestic economy.

The bulk of Britain's capital exports between 1880 and 1913 went to the Dominions, Europe, and the U.S. Almost 70% of it went into docks, tramways, telegraphs and telephones, gas and electric works and, in particular the enormously capital-absorbing railways.[29] Only the production of modern armaments is more capital absorbing (the mass production of armaments in the United States, and their export to Europe's great and small powers, began in the 1860s).[30] Increasing blocs of territory throughout the world became covered with networks of British built and financed railroads, provisioned by British steamships and defended by British warships.

Throughout the circuit, both within and outside of Europe, the same overall pattern of dualistic growth emerged, though with variations according to each country's place in the circuit and the type of goods it produced for sale. France, whose empire, export earnings, and foreign investment were second only to Britain's, exported high-cost textiles and luxury goods (e.g., silks, laces, wines, delicacies), built railroads in Russia with French equipment and capital. Germany's dualistic industrial expansion took off with its "marriage," not of "iron and finance" as in Britain, but of "iron and rye," celebrated, in 1879, along with the enactment of an Anti-Socialist Law and state legal enforcement of cartel agreements to limit production. In Italy and Austria-Hungary, industrial development focused on expanding heavy industry and gaining railway concessions in the Balkans.

Other states – Russia, the United States, Canada, and Australia – were incorporated into the circuit as raw material producers. These increased their production of agricultural and other raw materials exports to pay for railways, iron and steel, armaments and other foreign manufactures. Russia paid for these imports and its interest on its enormous foreign debt, by steadily increasing agricultural exports even during famines (e.g., in 1891; in 1913, 74% of Russian exports consisted of agricultural produce and timber (Munting, 1982, p. 31). Colonial territories that became independent states – as, for instance, states in the Balkans and in Latin America – remained within the circuit. Local elites, whether in colonies, former colonies, or states that had never been colonies, imported British capital and goods, developed mines and raw materials exports, and built railways and ports, in order to extend, consolidate and maintain their power and become wealthy.[31]

Placing European imperialism in the context of this circuit and the overall pattern of dualism that characterized economic expansion in the nineteenth century, it appears that imperialism made it possible for elites to expand production without the redistribution and reform necessary for the further development of the home market. Imperialism was not only proposed and advocated by the aristocracies and nobilities of almost all European countries in the nineteenth century, and the wealthy elites and governmental officials connected with them;[32] they were the most ardent – one might say, even, the only – proponents of imperialism. The most active proponents of imperialism were landowning and industrial elites who saw it as a means of alleviating land hunger.[33]

Financial houses acquired influential newspapers in European cities (e.g., in Berlin, Vienna, and Paris) in order to "popularise the notion of the need for and glory of acquiring access to or ownership of overseas territories" (Hobson, 1902, p. 60). Despite such efforts, however, popular enthusiasm for imperialism remained limited throughout the nineteenth century. In Britain public interest became evident only from 1894, and then it was "a spasmodic reaction to specific overseas issues rather than a consistent expression of nationalist or racialist idealism" (Fieldhouse, 1973, p. 75). The public in Germany regarded imperialism with indifference, though sometimes after a spectacular victory the public flared "into a collective but brief enthusiasm which was quickly doused by irritation over expenses and losses in these far-off places." In France, "[t]here existed no genuine colonial consensus;"

"the extensive and costly empire remained a permanent object of discussion" (Wesseling, 1997, pp. 45, 25).

In Lenin's view, the upper stratum of the working class had been politically corrupted by imperialism (1939, p. 64, 67). However, at least in Britain, this appears not to have been the case. In an investigation of working class attitudes towards imperialism, Henry Pelling found that, of the dozen trade union leaders who were in the House of Commons at the start of the South African War, only one (Havelock, Wilson), took the "imperialist" side; none of the nine trade union leaders in the new Parliament elected in 1900 supported the war (1968, pp. 82–83). Richard Price (1972) concluded, in a later study, that Britain's empire mattered little to the working classes, as did Alfred Williams, in an earlier study (1911, p. 157).

It was the conviction of "many authors" that the prosperity and political and social stability enjoyed by the great colonial powers was connected with their overseas possessions (Wesseling, 1997, p. 41; see also Wehler, 1969). However, by the eve of World War I, the extremes of wealth and poverty created by dualistic economic expansion were generating more or less continual conflicts (see Halperin, 2004, Chapters 4 and 5). Britain, in 1914, "was a divided country, in which extremes of wealth and poverty coexisted, often in a state of mutual fear and incomprehension" (Floud, 1997, p. 7). In 1913, less than 5% of Britain's population over 25 years of age possessed over 60% of the wealth of the country (Clough, 1940, pp. 672–673). Though the population of Britain had become on average nearly three and a half times richer between 1830 and 1914, "the range of incomes around the average did not significantly diminish; the rich remained much richer than the average, the poor much poorer – up to a third of the population in 1914 had incomes which did not provide them with sufficient food to sustain health throughout the year" (Floud, 1997, pp. 3, 15). Moreover, "While 30% lived below the margin, perhaps a further 40% or even more lived so close to the margin that they could be, and often were, forced below it by a variety of life events."[34] Wages rose sharply between 1905 and 1913, but the gain was offset by a strong increase in the cost of living and by a wide range of social and economic factors (Perrot, 1986, p. 104; Benson, 1989, p. 56).

By 1914, tensions were rising not only within European states, but among them, as well. As more and more countries began pursuing dualistic, externally oriented economic expansion, conflict over territories in Africa and Asia increasingly threatened to lead to war. At the same time, expansionist aims began more and more to focus on Europe itself and, as they did, Europe's balance of power and imperialist regimes began to dissolve.

WHAT CHANGED AND WHY

As more and more countries began to pursue dualistic, externally oriented economic expansion, competitive rivalries began to sour relations among European ruling groups. Perhaps the most thoroughly explored instance of this was the dissolution of Germany's relations with other European powers. In the last decades of the nineteenth century, the expansion of the German naval fleet put a strain on Anglo-German relations; while the adoption of tariffs that closed the German market to Russian rye soured relations with Russia. At the same time, and with opportunities to expand overseas quickly diminishing, the expansionist aims of European powers began more and more to focus on Europe itself. Networks of British built and financed railroads already covered overseas territories; but, after 1870, an upsurge in European railway construction began, France built railroads in Russia, German steel and capital built the Baghdad Railway; Italy and Austria-Hungary competed for railroad concessions in southeast Europe so that, as 1914 approached, 'there was something of a railroad war between Italy and Austria-Hungary in the Balkans' (Kurth, 1979, p. 21). Rivalry and rising tensions in Europe led to the dissolution of the "Bismarckian System;" and this, along with the antagonism created by German naval building, led to the reconfiguration and increasing polarization of interstate relations in Europe.[35] The European balance of power and imperialist regimes began to dissolve. By 1914, war appeared to be the only means by which "national" capitals could improve the terms on which they were integrated into the world circuit of capital.[36]

The threat of a multilateral imperialist war in Europe forced governments and ruling elites to do precisely what a century of *overseas* imperialist expansion had enabled them to avoid, mobilize the masses. As a result, the First World War succeeded in bringing into conflict the two central features of Europe's industrial development – internal restriction and external expansion.

In the eighteenth century, governments had relied on the social elite to pay for mercenary troops and to provide military leaders to fight professional wars. The impact of these wars on the social order had been relatively limited, as they tended to reinforce the *status quo* by heightening existing social inequalities. However, the wars fought by Napoleon's mass "citizen" armies and the mass armies mobilized to fight against them, had very different consequences. The participation of the lower classes in the war effort and in areas of work and social life usually barred to them, worked to enhance the power of labour and to strengthen its market position. It also compelled governments to ensure their loyalty by extending to them various rights. Serfdom was abolished in Prussia concurrently with Stein's military reforms, as it was in Russia when Alexander II transformed the army from a professional into a conscript force. In Austria, the adoption of universal military service coincided with reforms that established a constitutional Monarchy (Andreski, 1968, p. 69).

Thus, after the end of the Napoleonic Wars, and despite the difficulty of raising and maintaining large mercenary forces, Europe's use of citizen armies largely ended, and there was a return to old-style armies of paid professionals, mercenaries, and "gentlemen" (Silver & Slater, 1999, p. 190). The new weapon introduced by Napoleon was used in 1870 by France and Germany, also with frightening consequences (the rising of the Paris commune), and then not again until 1914.[37]

In 1914, aggressive imperialist threats on their frontiers forced European states, once again, to use what was then still the most powerful weapon of mass destruction, the *lévee en masse*. The mass mobilizations for World War I set in motion a social revolution that, between 1917 and 1939, swept through all of Europe. The efforts of Western governments and ruling elites to prevent its further spread and escalation led directly to the Second World War. At its end, the region was wholly transformed. Previous regional conflagrations had been followed by restorations (e.g., the Napoleonic Wars, the revolutions of 1830 and 1848, and World War I); however, World War II, by shifting the balance of class power throughout Europe, made restoration impossible. Instead, the vastly increased organizational strength and power of working classes and peasant masses, and the decline of the aristocracy as a result of wartime changes, created the conditions for an historic class compromise and for the achievement in Western Europe of universal suffrage, a relatively more nationally embedded capitalism (i.e., a more balanced and internally oriented development) and, for a time, unprecedented growth and relative peace and stability.

In the years leading up to the war, there had been a marked rise of socialist parties and a steady and dramatic increase in the number of their members, their candidates returned to representative bodies, and their share of the popular vote. By 1914, labour violence was raising alarms in all the capitals of Europe and social polarization and conflict was evident throughout the region.[38] Thus, even as they declared war, European governments were unsure whether workers would voluntarily join the war effort, or whether oppressive measures would be needed to induce them to participate. However, everywhere in Europe, industrial workers and peasants were inducted into national armies and moulded into effective fighting forces. In some places they enthusiastically supported the war. In Britain, large numbers of working-class volunteers signed up before conscription began in January 1916; by the time volunteering ceased, nearly 30% of men employed in industry had volunteered.

Many contemporary observers assumed that working class participation in the war represented a victory of nationalism over Socialist solidarity (see, e.g. Braunthal, 1967, p. 355; Schumpeter, 1976, p. 353; Carr, 1945, pp. 20–21). But labour struggles continued throughout the war and, in many places, increased both in number and intensity; moreover, millions of European workers participated in massive strikes and demonstrations in solidarity with the Russian Revolution in 1917. In fact, the war proved to be a watershed in the development of socialism and of organized labour in Europe.[39] At its end, left-wing parties and movements emerged throughout Europe, and trade union membership skyrocketed as unskilled and agricultural labour and women joined the ranks of organized labour for the first time.

By the end of World War I, labour's wartime mobilization and participation had increased its relative power within European societies. Throughout Europe, the mobilization of urban working classes and peasant masses to fight the war had produced stronger, larger, more united and better organized urban and rural labour movements. Trade union membership doubled in Britain (from 4 to 8 million; Geary, 1981, pp. 151–155); in Italy, it doubled during the war and nearly doubled again by 1920 (Maier, 1975, p. 47). By 1920, Europe had 34 million trade unionists (Ogg, 1930, pp. 759–797). Skilled and unskilled workers, workers of different occupations, anarchists and socialists, Social Democrats and Communists, revolutionaries and reformists closed ranks.[40]

In 1870, the lower classes had constituted some 75% of European society of which, only about 15% were skilled workers (Gillis, 1977, p. 268). But, up until World War I, the great landed families and their allies had been successful in maintaining the social and political isolation of agrarian labour by exempting their resident tenants and other workers from labour legislation and preventing them from securing the right to organize.[41] Thus, unskilled labour had remained outside the ranks of organized protest almost everywhere before the First World War.[42]

Between 1914 and 1921, unskilled labour joined the ranks of organized labour. Trade union membership doubled in Britain during the war. In Germany, unskilled workers became active for the first time during the revolutionary upheavals of the post-war period. In Italy, the rapid expansion of heavy industry in the war and immediate post-war period drew the new factory working class into radical politics. Revolutionary protests and strikes in the Balkans occurred only after World War I, and involved mainly urban unskilled labour in the railway, mining, tobacco, and textile industries. After World War I, revolutionary activity in Poland, Hungary and Czechoslovakia was carried out mainly by unskilled urban labour and by peasants.

After World War I, peasant protest also emerged in new organizational forms throughout Europe. In Germany, Austria, Romania, Yugoslavia, Czechoslovakia, Poland, Hungary, Latvia, Estonia, Bulgaria, Lithuania, and Finland, hordes of peasants who had fought in the war demanded the abolition of large estates and the creation of peasant freeholds.

Given the growth, rather than diminution, of working-class activism and organization after the war, it seems reasonable to assume that when the working classes joined up with national armies, they did so to advance their own struggle for economic and political rights.[43] It was widely acknowledged that the war could not be won if workers did not support it; workers therefore had reason to believe that their patriotism and sacrifices might win them rights for which they had struggled for over a century.[44] Their struggle continued, both during and after the war; and, ironic or contradictory as it might seem, socialist solidarity, as for instance in the strikes and demonstrations throughout Europe in 1917, continued to be a means of advancing it.

Following World War I, leaders and ruling classes in all western European countries were committed to re-establishing the pre-war *status quo*.[45] Thus, despite the profound dislocations that the war brought, it took a second massively destructive European war to make restoration of the nineteenth-century system impossible. It was the demand for labour and need for its cooperation for a second European war that compelled a political accommodation of working-class movements.[46]

A class compromise was concluded in Western Europe after World War II on the basis of social democratic and Keynesian goals and policy instruments. It required that social democrats consent to private ownership of the means of production and that capitalists use the profits they realized from this to increase productive capacity and partly for distribution as gains to other groups (Przeworski, 1979, p. 56). Wages rose with profits, so that labour shared in productivity gains, making higher mass consumption possible for new mass consumer goods industries. States administered the compromise by resuming the welfare and regulatory functions that it had relinquished in the nineteenth century. For the first time parties representing labour became legitimate participants in the political process. Socialists regularly participated in coalition governments in Austria, Switzerland, the Netherlands and the Scandinavian countries. Post-World War II development in Europe was characterized by sustained growth rather than short-lived windfalls, and by a more equitable distribution of income. No longer based on dualistic expansion, it was the outcome of the performance largely of the society itself rather than of foreign islands of capital. In contrast to pre-war economic policies, post-war policies were designed to expand domestic markets through increased production, rather than to divide up and exploit national markets through restrictive practices; to encourage competition rather than cartelization; to raise the level of earnings and of welfare of the working class, and to increase and regulate domestic investment.

THE RECONFIGURED CIRCUIT

The adoption of social democratic policies effectively ended the dualism that once had characterized European economies. As a result, European economies expanded in ways that, after World War II, became associated with "First World" and "Second World" development. However, the circuit of exchange that had produced dualism in Europe endured and continued to reproduce it elsewhere in the world. The survival of this pattern of development was the result of a massive and coordinated campaign by Western, newly independent, and "developing" states to eradicate social democracy and consolidate dualistic structures throughout what became, as a result of their efforts, the vast, global "third world." Once socialism had been destroyed in both the "third world" and the "second world," Western states began a campaign to reverse their own post-World War II social settlements. The emerging trend, therefore, is of re-integration, of both the "second world" and, eventually, the "first world," into a system of local and trans-local relations similar to the one that, in those areas of the world, predated the crisis of the world wars and the great depression.

Nationalism and Dualism in the Third World

Within the circuit of exchange that linked dualistic economies around the world in the nineteenth century, there emerged a struggle for power among European ruling groups that culminated and came to a conclusion in the two-phased war in Europe at the beginning of the twentieth century. The crisis in Europe provided an opportunity for elites in states and territories in other parts of the world to better their position within the circuit. Restricted in their access to benefits enjoyed by European elites and not fully accepted by them, these elites sought to wrest a larger share of political power for themselves. As had been the case with similar intra-elite struggles in Europe, nationalism was used by these contending elites to articulate their demands, win the support of the lower classes, and gain state power. And as had been the case in Europe, in the newly "independent" states established after World War II, these nationalist movements became fused with a program of capitalist expansion that consolidated dualism.[47]

Thus, decolonization and nationalism did not mark the end of the circuit, but rather the emergence of a modernized, more efficient form of it. The nationalist elites who had won "independence" from the imperialist powers were able to more effectively police local labor and consolidate different systems for transnational and local interests and actors. Though they had identified nationalism with national development as a means of legitimizing themselves as a new ruling group, the association of nationalism with development was, in fact part of a broad vision that they shared with retreating colonial administrators and with a wide set of transnational elites concerned with maintaining and reproducing the circuit.

Once in control of state power, nationalist elites continued to build up export industries and continued, within restricted foreign-oriented enclaves, to accumulate wealth and enjoy Western standards and styles of living without transforming their largely traditional and non-industrial economies and societies.[48] They purchased masses of weapons from Britain and the U.S. to protect these enclaves so that local elites could continue to accumulate wealth safe from the mass misery growing up around them. Eventually, in Britain and America, and after they had become the world's two largest weapons exporters, expanding military-industrial complexes began to draw industrial capital from the mass-consumption goods sector and to free it from the need to maintain mass purchasing power. As a result, wage levels and work conditions began to erode, along with other gains which labour had made in those and other Western countries as a result of the post-war social settlements.

The Acceleration of Capitalist Globalization

By the late 1970s and 1980s, the global crusade to contain the spread of socialism around the world had succeeded to a phenomenal degree. Western states then began a forceful campaign to reverse the social settlements that had tied capital to the development of their own national communities.

Central to this campaign was the introduction of a series of measures designed to dis-empower labour and undermine democracy at home.

At the time Keynesian social democratic compromises were concluded in Western Europe, the United States had already adopted fordism. Fordism, which had been introduced in the U.S. during the Great Depression, had required far less of a concession by capital than did the compromise in Europe. The U.S. had already made the shift to mass production and consumption when it adopted fordism, having poured its steel into its own railroads, and then into automobiles;[49] and it had enjoyed a higher level of domestic investment. Consequently, the U.S. economy had grown faster than Western European economies (Schönfield, 1965, pp. 5–6).

As a result of both these factors and of the world wars, U.S. industry had few competitors. Consequently, the higher wages conceded as part of the fordist compromise could be paid for by higher prices. Because it had few competitors, U.S. industry could also add capacity relatively cheaply. Moreover, the Keynesian policies that formed part of the fordist compromise functioned as a welfare program for the mass production of armaments which had begun in the U.S. in the 1860s and, thereafter, had become an increasingly important part of the U.S. economy. However, as international competition from Europe and Japan intensified, profit margins in the U.S. began to narrow, and U.S. business became increasingly committed to escaping the implications of the fordist compromise in a "sealed-off domestic context."[50]

By the late 1970s, and in the context of a new opportunity structure (the combination of the decreased threat of socialism and increased international competition), the U.S. and Western European states began to dismantle the restrictions and barriers on capital mobility that they had imposed after World War II and to restructure or eliminate regulatory agencies and social welfare programs. The result of these measures has been an expansion of the export-oriented growth that characterized the pre-world war international political economy. U.S. capital exports since the late 1970s differ in a number of ways from those that had characterized the outflow of U.S. "productive" capital to Europe and elsewhere after World War II. Before the 1970s, U.S. capital exports were relatively small (British capital exports in the nineteenth century had amounted to 10% of GDP; at their peak, those of the U.S. had been around 2% of GDP). U.S. firms had invested in Europe because it was the only way to access European markets given "[t]he sharp drop in the trade share of GDP that occurred in Europe subsequent to the depression, the persistence of capital and currency controls, and the presence of substantial non-tariff barriers...". Moreover, these investments had supported an overall system of welfare, income equality, and higher wages at home. "While firms fought for market share overseas, they did so in ways that boosted workers' incomes and domestic demand rather than suppressing those incomes" (Schwartz, 2002–2003, pp. 40–41).

The U.S. capital exports that began in the late 1970s, however, are part of an overall shift that involves downsizing work forces and resetting corporate activity "at ever lower levels of output and employment" (Williams et al., 1989, p. 292). In fact, despite the tendency to refer to current trends collectively as *"neo-liberal"* globalization, the expansion underpinning "globalization" has been, as was Europe's nineteenth century expansion, essentially *anti-liberal* in nature. It is characterized by increasing concentration and monopoly, by the increasing tendency of large firms to buy existing assets through mergers and acquisitions rather than to build new ones (Williams et al., 1989; Nitzan, 2002, p. 241).

An economic development process involves accumulation of capital and the employment of more personnel to increase productive capacity. This can be achieved either by expansion – a simple multiplication of the capacity at a given moment – or by intensification, i.e. an improvement in production techniques. Before World War II, economic development in Europe proceeded principally by means of lateral gains, through the acquisition of spheres of interest, rather than intensive gains, through improved organization or productivity. Similarly, U.S. expansion today is proceeding not through the creation of additional capacity, but by lateral gains: by squeezing other countries' firms out of their markets, restructuring those markets and integrating them into U.S. commodity chains; and, increasingly, as Nitzan (2002) has argued, through buying existing assets through mergers.

With the increase in capital mobility and foreign investment, has come the ability to move production to low-wage areas. This has reduced the bargaining power of labor relative to capital in negotiations that determined wages and working conditions, not only in industries experiencing capital outflow, but in related industries, as well (Crotty & Epstein, 1996, p. 131). As a result, methods of absolute surplus value production have returned: intensifying work regimes, reducing real wages, cutting health, pension, and social safety net protections; and restructuring employment away from full-time and secure employment into part-time and insecure work.

The overall trend to which all this points is to a reconfiguration of the circuit of capital, once again. It was reconfigured after World War II to accommodate social democratic concessions in the West. Now it may be in the process of a reconfiguration involving the re-integration of both the "second world" and much of the "first world" into the circuit on the basis of the dualistic growth that characterized their development previously and which, throughout the post-World War II era, had continued to characterize the "development" of the "third world."

CONCLUSIONS

The eminent historical comparativist, Karl Polanyi believed that the great transformation that occurred in the course of the world wars – from free unregulated markets to welfare states – represented a permanent change, both in the nature of the international system, as well as in its constituent states. But Polanyi did not live to see the beginning of the rise, once again, of the "unregulated" market. Had he done so, he perhaps would have seen the rise and demise of Europe's nineteenth-century system, not as a once-and-for-all occurrence, but as part of an on-going struggle over the distribution of costs and benefits of industrial capitalism. It is a struggle, previous sections suggest, that continues today.

Though the free market and the *laissez-faire* state gave way, in varying degrees, to regulated markets and interventionist states after World War II, the liberal international order survived. The hybrid system that this created has been characterized as one of "embedded liberalism" (Ruggie, 1982).

It was, in fact, Polanyi's analysis of Europe's nineteenth century market system (in *The Great* Transformation, 1944) that inspired the notion of markets as embedded and dis-embedded. Polanyi argued that, before the rise of the unregulated market system at the end of the eighteenth century, exchange relations were governed by principles of economic behaviour (reciprocity, reallocation, and house-holding) that were "embedded" in society and politics. At the end of the eighteenth century, however, states began to institute changes that formed the basis of the dis-embedded capitalist development that characterized Europe's nineteenth century industrial expansion.

The collapse of the nineteenth century system and the conclusion of a "compromise" between capital and labour, led to the re-embedding of European economies after 1945. Welfare reforms partially de-commodified labour, and by means of market and industry regulation, investment and production were made to serve the expansion and integration of national markets. Now, however, a campaign to promote the dispersal of capital investment and production to foreign locations – the current "globalization" campaign – is seeking to reverse the post-World War II compromise and to dis-embed national markets, once again.

In the history of capitalism, then, there have been phases of nationally embedded and global free market capitalism – periods when capital is relatively more or less free from national state regulation. Markets were embedded until the end of the eighteenth century; after that, and throughout the nineteenth century, they were dis-embedded; then, after the nineteenth century system collapsed in the course of the world wars, a compromise was concluded which resulted in markets being re-embedded. Today, efforts are being made to reverse this compromise and to return, once again, to the disembedded capitalism that characterized nineteenth-century Europe.

NOTES

1. See, e.g., Coates (2000), van der Pijl (1998) and Moore (1966). Alexander Gerschenkron (1962) argued that the later industrializers in Europe tended to favour authoritarian government as part of an effort to mobilize capital and repress wages.

2. In Britain, an open land market meant that new wealth did not challenge old, but simply bought a landed estate. At the same time the younger sons of landowners were joining the merchants and professional men (Morris, 1979, p. 15).

3. Within this class, landlords remained dominant. Despite all that had been written about industrialists replacing landowners as the dominant element in the ruling elite, as late as 1914 industrialists "were not sufficiently organized to formulate broad policies or exert more than occasional influence over the direction of national affairs" (Boyce, 1987, p. 8). Until 1914, non-industrial Britain could easily outvote industrial Britain (Hobsbawm, 1968, p. 196).

4. Boyce (1987, p. 11). That elements of Britain's capitalist class were beginning to consider the possibilities of the U.S. model was apparent from discussions of the U.S. experience during the 1920s and, in light of that experience, the importance of the home market for British manufacturers, and the need to reconsider Britain's approach to foreign lending and its reliance on overseas markets. On this see, e.g., Boyce (1987, pp. 102–105).

5. In 1897, 175,000 people owned ten-elevenths of the land of England, and forty million people the remaining one-eleventh (Romein, 1978, p. 195).

6. Hobsbawm (1968, p. 169). Friedrich Engels observed that, in the last decade of the nineteenth century,

> [e]verything connected with the old government of the City of London – the constitution and the administration of the city proper – is still downright medieval. And this includes also the port of London [which has] in the past seventy years... been delivered up to a small number of privileged corporations for ruthless exploitation (1971[1889], p. 396).

7. Despite its reputation for cosmopolitanism and the fact that, in the last decades before 1914, "the rare dynamic entrepreneurs of Edwardian Britain were, more often

than not, foreigners or minority groups – Jews, Quakers, Germans, Americans – the City was operated by men of English or Scottish stock and members of the established church" (Boyce, 1987, p. 20).

8. "Far from the bourgeoisie having overthrown the aristocracy, we have instead the aristocracy becoming the bourgeoisie" (Wallerstein, 1991, p. 58).

9. Many historians assume that England did not experience a form of state corresponding to the absolute monarchies of the continent because English monarchs could not take the property of their subjects without their consent in parliament. But continental absolutism was also based on the rights of property.

The term "absolutism" was used by those who opposed state policies and reforms that today we associate with the welfare state and progressive liberalism. Conventional accounts of this history assume that opposition to absolutism was principally concerned with a variety of "freedoms." However, the record of the states that emerged with the defeat of 'absolutism' provides little, if any, support for this view.

10. British exports increased 67%; production for the home market increased only 7%.

11. See, e.g. Mann (1988), Mattingly (1955), Pirenne (1969, 1958), Stubbs (1967), Granshof (1970), Hill (1905), Balch (1978) and Strayer (1970).

12. The French nobility considered itself to be a nation consisting of an international aristocracy and separate from the French lower classes. See, e.g., the Comte de Boulainvilliers, *Histoire de l'Ancien Gouvernement de la France*, 1727, Tome I; Albert Thierry, *Considèrations sur l'histoire de France*, 5th ed. Paris, Chap. II; and the Comte Dubuat-Nançay, *Les Origines de l'Ancien Gouvernement de la France, de l'Allemagne, et de Italie*, 1789. After the outbreak of the French Revolution, the French nobility tried to form an internationale of aristocrats in order to stave off the revolt of those they considered foreign enslaved people.

Eric Hobsbawm writes that in the 1780s and throughout Europe "townsmen were often physically different from peasants... . Even townsmen of the same religion and nationality as the surrounding peasantry looked different: they wore different dress, and indeed in most cases (except for the exploited indoor labouring and manufacturing population) taller, though perhaps also slenderer" (Hobsbawm, 1962, pp. –28). On the eve of World War I, the impoverished masses crowding the slums of London and other European cities were so "stunted and wizened by illness and poverty" as to appear "as another race to upper class observers" (Floud, 1997, p. 14).

13. For much of the nineteenth century, the "advanced sectors" of European and other economies developed, less through direct competition with each, than by means of a mutually reinforcing circuit of investment and exchange. See Halperin (2004, Chapter 3).

14. During the century, there was a marked improvement in the variety and quality of household furnishings, decorations, and "luxury" items among artisans and farmers. In fact, "a greater proportion of the population than in any previous society in human history" was able "to enjoy the pleasures of buying consumer goods" and "not only necessities, but decencies, and even luxuries" (McKendrick, Brewer, & Plumb, 1982, p. 29; see also Thirsk, 1978).

15. In the nineteenth century, Britain devoted a substantially smaller proportion of her national output and savings to home investment than did any of her major

competitors (Floud, 1981, pp. 12–17). In 1913, one-third of Britain's net wealth was invested overseas. "Never before or since has one nation committed so much of its national income and savings to capital formation abroad" (McCloskey, 1981, p. 143). At the height of the Marshall Plan in 1947 the level of U.S. foreign investment as a share of national income was around 3% (McCloskey, 1981, p. 144).

16. Barratt Brown, 1970: x. See, also, Davis and Huttenback, 1988. For similar arguments concerning Germany, see Wehler (1969), for France, see Langer (1931) and Wesseling (1997).

17. Davis and Huttenback, 1988. In some respects London's institutions were more highly organized to provide capital to foreign investors than to British industry. Committee on Finance and Industry, Macmillan Report (1931, p. 171). Capital flowed between London and the far reaches of the Empire, but not between London and the industrial north. As Charles Kindleberger describes it,

> A limited number of firms in a limited number of industries could get access to the London new-issues market – railroads, shipping, steel, cotton (after 1868), along with banks and insurance companies. And some attention was devoted to refinancing existing private companies. For the most part, however, the flow of savings was aimed abroad and not to domestic industries (Kindleberger, 1964, p. 62).

18. Lenin (1939) and John Hobson (1902) contended that Britain's foreign investment and that of other advanced countries was a result of a super-abundant accumulation of capital and the consequent pressure of capital for new fields of investment. The notion that advanced countries had capital-saturated economies, was current at the time they wrote and has since been embraced by a wide variety of theorists and historians.

19. See, e.g., Trebilcock (1981), Lewis (1972, pp. 27–58), Cameron (1961, pp. 123, 152), Cairncross (1953, p. 225), Lévy (1951–1952), p. 228; and Sée (1942, p. 360).

20. Though Lenin recognized that profitable investment opportunities could be provided with an adequate and sustained rise in the consumption of the masses this was, for Lenin, only "a theoretical possibility to be dismissed as utterly incompatible with the real balance of power in any capitalist society" (Strachey, 1959, p. 117).

21. Bairoch (1993, p. 172). The minerals prominent in tropical trade today did not come to the fore until the end of the nineteenth century. In 1913, minerals were prominent in the exports only of Peru and Mexico (Lewis, 1978a, p. 201). Moreover, throughout the nineteenth and early twentieth centuries (until around 1920), terms of trade were unfavourable for Britain (see Strachey, 1959, pp. 149–151) and improved for the less developed countries. It was only after World War II (in the 1950s, and again in the 1980s) that terms of trade in primary goods deteriorated (Bairoch, 1993, pp. 113–114). The exception – and, as Arthur Lewis points out, it is an important one for Latin America (and for arguments to be developed, below, concerning cheap food imports) – is sugar which, relative to manufactured goods, deteriorated by 25–35% between 1830 and 1910.

22. Belgian's King Leopold compared Africa with a "magnificent cake" suggesting, as Wesseling points out, that it was a luxury rather than a necessity (Wesseling, 1997,

p. 92). Bismarck, in a speech to the Reichstag on 26 January 1899, said of the German colonists in Africa: "They cannot prove that it is useful for the Reich. I, however, cannot prove that it is harmful to it, either" (1924–1932, pp. XIII, 386; quoted in Wesseling, 1997, p. 90).

23. That this was widely recognized is evident in the laws regulating consumption that were found throughout history, in Europe and elsewhere, and persist in many places throughout the world, today. Sumptuary laws restricting the personal consumption of goods based on class and income, enacted in Europe between the fifteenth and eighteenth centuries were retained by many states well into the nineteenth century.

24. From 49 million tons in 1850 to 147 million in 1880.

25. There were 200,000 coal-miners in Britain in 1850, half a million tons in 1880, and 1.2 million in 1914 (Hobsbawm, 1968, p. 116).

26. For example, the Siemens–Martin open-hearth furnace (1867), which made it possible to increase productivity; the Gilchrist–Thomas process (1877–1878), which made it possible to use phosphoric ores for steel manufacture. With respect to the latter, Britain continued to import non-phosphoric ores, and failed to exploit her own phosphoric ore deposits until the 1930s.

27. See also Mathias (1983, pp. 373–393). Mathias contends that arguments about differences between earlier and later industrializing countries do not explain the "failure in innovation and development, widespread in the British economy" (1983, p. 375).

28. Britain's industrial wage earners realized 55–60% of their wage in the form of food; the steady fall in prices of staple food imports after 1874 (grain, tea, sugar, lard, cheese, ham, and bacon; Mathias, 1983, p. 345), allowed real wages in Britain to rise until World War I. In Britain, the value of labour was reduced, not only by importing cheap food from abroad, but by forcing workers to consume poorer quality food, as, for instance, in Ireland, where the cost of feeding workers was forced down by making them dependent on the potato crop for sustenance. The use of the potato allowed workers to survive on the lowest possible wage. Thus "for nearly fifty years a regular dietary class-war took place, with potatoes encroaching on bread in the south, and with oatmeal and potatoes encroaching in the north" (Thompson, 1975, p. 145).

29. As did the bulk of French and Belgian foreign investment, 12% of British investment went into extractive industries (agriculture and mining); only 4% went into manufacturing (Edelstein, 1981, p. 73).

30. Dobb (1963, p. 296). Hobsbawm argues that, at least in the short run, railway building in Britain had little to do with developing the domestic market. All industrial areas were within easy access of water transport by sea, river, or canal, and water transport was and is by far the cheapest for bulk goods (coal mined in the north had been shipped inexpensively by sea to London for centuries). Moreover, regularity of flow, and not speed, was the important factor in transporting non-perishable goods; and this was supplied by water transport. In fact, Hobsbawm argues, "many of the railways constructed were and remained quite irrational by any transport criterion, and consequently never paid more than the most modest profits, if they paid any at all. This was perfectly evident at the time...". What was also evident is that investors were looking "for any investment likely to yield more than the 3.4% of public stocks." Railway returns eventually settled down at an average of about 4% (Hobsbawm, 1968, p. 111).

31. Some former colonies did not develop the sharp dualism that characterized industrial expansion in Europe. In Australia, Canada, and New Zealand there was no pre-existing landed elite, and the colonists displaced, overwhelmed or destroyed prior inhabitants. In these countries, revenues were not used solely to enrich a traditional landowning class and their allies as they were in Europe and in Latin America. In the United States, where a strong landowning class developed in the south, a struggle between landowners and industrialists culminated in civil war and the victory of the industrial capitalist bourgeoisie. More on this, below.

32. British, German, Italian, and Russian landowning elites were the most active champions of imperialist expansion. Britain's imperialists were the aristocracy, and later the Tories (Barratt Brown, 1970, pp. 53–54). Italian imperialism was promoted by the church and the landowning nobility. In Germany, the most persistent and zealous champion of imperial expansion were the landowners organized in the powerful *Bund der Landwirte* and other agrarian groups in Germany, as well as the Pan-German League, representing both the great landowners and the large industrialists (see, e.g., Meyer, 1955; Wertheimer, 1924). The Russian nobility and large landowners represented by the pan-Slav movement championed the cause of Russian imperial expansion (Mazour, 1955). Large industrialists also pressed for imperialist expansion. Among the most influential imperialists were representatives of iron and steel and heavy industry (railroads and shipping), like Joseph Chamberlain in Britain and Jules Ferry in France, and the large industrialists in Germany who, after the 1870s, joined with landowners in the Pan-German League (see, e.g., Langer, 1931, Chapter 9).

33. The cause championed by Germany's big landowners and large industrialists in the 1870s of acquiring additional *Lebensraum* in order to offset the land hunger of the German masses, expressed a general theme of landowners and industrialists everywhere in Europe.

34. Floud (1997, p. 24). A number of investigators of working-class life showed that, in the decade leading up to the First World War, a significant proportion of the population of England and Wales were living in poverty without recourse to poor relief. Charles Booth's survey of London's East End in 1886 showed that over 30% of the population had an income that was inadequate for their support (1889). Seebohm Rowntree's survey of York in 1899 found 28% of the population was too malnourished to work a normal day and their children could not be fed enough to grow at a normal rate (1901, pp. 86–87).

35. The dissolution of the Bismarckian system paved the way for the emergence of two camps in Europe: the Triple Alliance and the Triple Entente. This new structure heightened competition and tension and led to an accelerated arms race in Europe. In these conditions, the Balkans took on a new significance: for if either power combination made gains in the Balkans, it would achieve a decisive advantage over the other bloc. In 1914, it was this, many historians argue, that motivated Germany's unconditional support for Austria and Russia's support for Serbia. Backing a potential ally in a war to reacquire Alsace-Lorraine, France gave her support to Russia.

36. The crisis that culminated in a two-phased imperialist war in Europe provided an opportunity for elites in states and territories in other parts of the world to better their position within the circuit. Restricted in their access to benefits enjoyed by European elites and not fully accepted by them, these elites sought to wrest a larger

share of political power for themselves. As had been the case with similar intra-elite struggles in Europe, nationalism was used by these contending elites to articulate their demands, win the support of the lower classes, and gain state power.

37. The new weapon involved "masses raised by universal conscription, armed and equipped by large-scale state-intervention in industry" (Howard, 1961, p. 9). See, for an overview of this issue, Howard (1961, pp. 8–39). Russia conscripted large numbers of men for the Crimean War; but contrast a description of the forces raised for that war (Royle, 1999, pp. 91–92) with the account of the French mobilization in 1870–1871 (and its connection to the rising of the Paris Commune) in Taithe (2001, esp. pp. 6–13, 22–28, 38–47).

38. After the turn of the century, industrial disputes reached unprecedented proportions. Bitter strikes swept France, Germany, Italy, Britain, Belgium, and Russia during the 1900s. In France, the years from 1892 to 1910 were the most militant in the history of the working class. There were over 1000 strikes per year after 1906. The first attempts to organize national stoppages came in 1906. In Germany, the number of industrial disputes escalated from 1,468 strikes in 1900 to 2,834 in 1912 (Geary, 1981, p. 105). There were bloody strikes in Berlin in 1910 and in the Ruhr in 1912. Between 1900 and 1914, strikes, strikers, and workdays lost in Italy were about eight times higher than in the 1880s (Bordogna et al., 1889, pp. 223–224). There were violent strikes in Britain and Belgium in 1911, 1912, and 1913. In Russia, violence escalated throughout the first decade of the century.

39. Socialist parties came to power in Sweden (1920), Denmark (1924) and Norway (1927); a Labour government took office in Britain in 1923; the Left triumphed in France in 1924; in Belgium and Holland, socialists entered the cabinet for the first time in 1939.

40. James Cronin observes that, before the war, the distinction within the working class 'between "rough" and "respectable," between the skilled and organized and the unskilled and unorganized', had been 'very real to contemporaries and was reflected in many aspects of politics and collective action'. Following the war, however, 'a variety of technical, social and economic processes conjoined to produce a working class that was, if not more internally homogeneous, a least less sharply divided within itself, and also more culturally distinct from middle and upper class society than its Victorian analogue had been' (1982a, pp. 121, 139).

41. Peasants who were part-time artisans were often radical in politics. But peasants whose main contact with the outside world was the local church, accepted the traditional order (Zeldin, 1977, pp. 127–139). Unlike liberal capitalists, the feudal lords had always felt an obligation towards their serfs in times of need (as Bismarck pointed out). Moreover, in those places where peasants could hope to buy land, the peasants saw the nobility as allies against the bourgeoisie in the competition for landownership.

42. The July 1830 insurrection in Paris was staged by highly skilled workers in specialist trades (see Pinkney, 1964). It was from the skilled workers, the top 15 percent of the working class, that the trade union leadership in Britain was recruited beginning in the 1860s (Gillis, 1977, p. 269).

43. Hobsbawm has argued this view persuasively (1990, especially pp. 120–130).

44. Workers were probably also motivated to join the war effort for the economic security of army pay (Benson, 1989, p. 162).

45. As Philip Abrams observes, the very term "reconstruction" reflected the ambiguity of official thinking in Britain. Though Ministers spoke "as though the word meant transformation...the original reconstruction committees had been set up...to restore the social and economic conditions of 1914" (1963, p. 58). Socialist and partly socialist governments that came to power in Germany, France, and Austria, were brought down before they were able to effect any change in capitalist institutions.

46. Fascism and the sacrifices entailed in defeating it effectively discredited the old right throughout Europe. Thus, even where workers were not mobilized for the war effort as, for instance, in France, the balance of political power after the war shifted in their favour.

47. The elites who led movements for decolonization and national independence were part of a transnational elite. Their concern was with their role in the overall system – rather than with vertical inequality (exploitation). As in Europe, in the "developing world," elites legitimized their claim of representing the people/nation by asserting that the nation as a whole is locked into a vertical exploitative relationship with other nations.

48. The result, in the Middle East, is that the share of manufacturing in production in 1990 – 13% – was precisely what it was in the mid-1950s.

49. In 1914 there was, in the U.S., about 1 car per 35 persons; a level not reached by European countries until the 1960s. By the 1920s, 30% of American steel went into automobiles. This was an important factor in American "isolationism" before World War II (Kurth, 1979, pp. 27–28).

50. Van der Pijl (1998, p. 119). Wage increases had previously been paid for by higher prices. But when international competition began to act as a constraint on pricing in the 1970s, capitalists were caught in a profit squeeze between labour keeping wages high, and foreign competitors holding prices down (Cox, 1987, p. 280; see also Rupert, 1995, pp. 177–78).

REFERENCES

Abu-Lughod, J. (1989). *Before European hegemony: The world system A.D. 1250–1350.* New York: Oxford University Press.
Andreski, S. (1968). *Military organization and society.* Berkeley: University of California Press.
Bairoch, P. (1993). *Economics and world history: Myths and paradoxes.* London: Harvester.
Balch, R. (1978). The resigning of quarrels: Conflict resolution in the thirteenth century. *Peace and Change, 5,* 33–38.
Barratt, B. M. (1970). *After imperialism* (revised ed.). London: Merlin Press.
Benson, L. (1989). *The working class in Britain, 1850–1939.* London: Longman.
Blaut, J. (1993). *The colonizer's model of the world: Geographical diffusionism and Eurocentric history.* London: The Guilford Press.
Boyce, R. W. D. (1987). *British capitalism at the crossroads, 1919–1932.* Cambridge: Cambridge University Press.
Braunthal, J. (1967). *History of the International, Vol. I: 1864–1914.* New York: Praeger.
Cairncross, A. K. (1953). *Home and foreign investment, 1870–1914.* Cambridge: Cambridge University Press.

Cameron, R. (1961). *France and the economic development of Europe.* Princeton: Princeton University Press.
Carr, E. H. (1945). *Nationalism and after.* London: Macmillan.
Coates, D. (2000). *Models of capitalism: Growth and stagnation in the modern era.* Cambridge: Polity.
Crotty, J., & Epstein, G. (1996). In defence of capital controls. In: L. Panitch (Ed.), *Are there alternatives? Socialist register 1996.* London: Merlin Press.
Davis, L. E., & Huttenback, R. A. (1988). *Mammon and the pursuit of empire.* New York: Cambridge University Press.
Dobb, M. (1963). *Studies in the development of capitalism* (Rev. ed.). New York: International Publishers.
Edelstein, M. (1981). Foreign investment and accumulation, 1860–1914. In: R. C. Floud & D. N. McCloskey (Eds), *The economic history of Britain since 1700*, Vol. 2. Cambridge: Cambridge University Press.
Eversley, D. E. C. (1967). The home market and economic growth in England, 1750–1780. In: E. L. Jones & G. E. Mingay (Eds), *Land, labour, and population in the industrial revolution.* London: Arnold.
Fieldhouse, D. K. (1973). *Economics and empire, 1830–1914.* London: Weidenfeld and Nicolson.
Floud, R. (1997). *The people and the British economy, 1830–1914.* New York: Oxford University Press.
Gagliardo, J. G. (1967). *Enlightened despotism.* New York: Thomas Y. Crowell.
Geary, D. (1981). *European labour protest, 1848–1939.* London: Croom Helm.
Gerschenkron, A. (1962). *Economic backwardness in historical perspective.* Cambridge, MA: Harvard University Press.
Gillis, J. R. (1983). *The development of European society, 1770–1870.* Boston: Houghton Mifflin.
Granshof, F. (1970). *The middleages: A history of international relations.* New York: Harper and Row.
Halperin, S. (2004). *War and social change in modern Europe: The great transformation Revisited.* Cambridge: Cambridge University Press.
Hill, D. J. (1905). *A history of diplomacy in the international development of Europe I.* New York: Longmans.
Hobsbawm, E. (1962). *The age of revolution 1789–1848.* New York: Mentor.
Hobsbawm, E. (1968). *Industry and empire.* London: Weidenfeld and Nicolson.
Hobson, J. A. (1902). *Imperialism: A study.* London: Allen and Unwin.
Howard, M. (1961). *The Franco-Prussian War.* London: Rupert Hart-Davis.
Kindleberger, C. (1964). *Economic growth in France and Britain, 1851–1950.* Cambridge, MA: Harvard University Press.
Kurth, J. R. (1979). The political consequences of the product cycle. *International Organization, 33,* 1–34.
Langer, W. L. (1931). *European alliances and alignments, 1871–1890.* New York: Alfred A. Knopf.
Lenin, V. I. (1939). *Imperialism.* New York: International Publishers.
Lévy, M. (1951–1952). *Historie economique et sociale de la France depuis 1848.* Paris: les Cours de Droit, Institut d'Erudes Politiques.
Lewis, A. (1972). The historical record of international capital movements to 1913. In: J. H. Dunning (Ed.), *International investment: Selected readings.* Harmondsworth: Penguin.

Lewis, A. (1978a). *Growth and fluctuation, 1870–1913*. London: George Allen & Unwin.
Lewis, A. (1978b). *The evolution of the international economic order*. Princeton: Princeton University Press.
Lie, J. (1993). Visualizing the invisible hand. *Politics & Society, 21*, 275–306.
Luxemburg, R. (1976). *The national question*. New York: Monthly Review Press.
Maier, C. (1975). *Recasting Bourgeois Europe*. Princeton: Princeton University Press.
Mann, M. (1988). European development: Approaching a historical explanation. In: J. Baechler, A. Hall & M. Mann (Eds), *Europe and the rise of capitalism*. Oxford: Basil Blackwell.
Marwick, A. (1980). *Image and reality in Britain, France, and the U.S.A. since 1930*. London: Collins.
Marx, K. (1967). *Communist manifesto*. London: Penguin.
Mathias, P. (1983). *The first industrial nation* (2nd ed.). New York: Methuen.
Mattingly, G. (1955). *Renaissance diplomacy*. Baltimore: Penguin Books.
Mazour, A. (1955). *Russia: Past and Present*. New York: Van Nostrand.
McCloskey, D. N. (1981). *Enterprise and trade in Victorian Britain*. London: Allen & Unwin.
McKendrick, N., Brewer, J., & Plumb, J. H. (1982). *The birth of a consumer society*. London: Europa.
McNeill, W. H. (1974). *The shape of European history*. London: Oxford University Press.
Meyer, H. C. (1955). *Mitteleuropa in German thought and action, 1815–1945*. The Hague: Martinus Nijhoff.
Moore, B. (1966). *Social origins of democracy and dictatorship*. Boston: Beacon.
Morris, R. J. (1979). *Class and class consciousness in the industrial revolution*. London: Macmillan.
Munting, R. (1982). *The economic development of the USSR*. London: Croom Helm.
Nitzan, J. (2002). Regimes of differential accumulation: Mergers, stagflation and the logic of globalization. *Review of International Political Economy, 8*(2), 226–274.
Ogg, F. A. (1930). *Economic development of modern Europe*. New York: Macmillan.
Perrot, M. (1986). On the formation of the French working class. In: I. Katznelson & A. Zolberg (Eds), *Working-class formation*. Princeton, NJ: Princeton University Press.
Pirenne, H. (1958). *A history of Europe*. Garden City, New York: Doubleday.
Pirenne, H. (1969). *Economic and social history of medieval Europe*. New York: Harcourt, Brace and Co.
Price, R. (1972). *An imperial war and the British working class*. London: Routledge and Kegan Paul Ltd.
Przeworski, A. (1979). The material bases of consent. *Political Power and Social theory, 1*, 21–63.
Romein, J. (1978). *The watershed of two eras*. Middletown: Wesleyan University Press.
Royle, T. (1999). *Crimea: The Great Crimean War, 1854–1856*. Boston: Little Brown and Company.
Schonfield, A. (1965). *Modern capitalism*. London: Oxford University Press.
Schumpeter, J. A. (1976). *Capitalism, socialism and democracy*. London: Routledge.
Schwartz, H. (2002–2003). Hobson's voice: American internationalism, Asian development, and global macro-economic imbalances. *Journal of Post-Keynesian Economics, 25*(2), 331–351.
Sée, H. (1942). *Histoire Économique de la France II: Les Temps modernes, 1789–1914*. Paris: Colin.

Silver, B. J., & Slater, E. (1999). The social origins of world hegemonies. In: G. Arrighi & B. J. Silver (Eds), *Chaos and governance in the modern world system*. Minnesota: University of Minnesota Press.

Sorokin, P. (1927). *Social mobility*. London: Harper.

Sorokin, P. (1969). *Society, culture, and personality: Their structure and dynamics*. New York: Cooper.

Strachey, J. (1959). *The end of empire*. New York: Praeger.

Strayer, J. (1970). *On the medieval origins of the modern state*. Princeton: Princeton University Press.

Stubbs, W. (1967). *Seventeen lectures on the study of medieval and modern history and kindred subjects*. New York: Fertig.

Taithe, B. (2001). *Citizenship and wars: France in turmoil, 1870–1871*. London: Routledge.

Thirsk, J. (1978). *Economic policy and projects: The development of a consumer society in early modern England*. Oxford: Clarendon Press.

Thompson, E. P. (1975). Standards and experiences. In: A. J. Taylor (Ed.), *The standard of living in Britain in the industrial revolution*. London: Methuen & Co Ltd.

Titmuss, R. M. (1958). *Essays on the welfare state*. Boston: Beacon Press.

Trebilcock, C. (1981). *Industrialization of the continental powers 1780–1914*. London: Longmans.

Van Der Pijl, K. (1998). *Transnational classes and international relations*. London: Routledge.

Wallerstein, I. (1974). *The modern world system I*. New York: Academic Press.

Wallerstein, I. (1991). *Unthinking social science: The limits of nineteenth-century paradigms*. Cambridge: Polity Press.

Wallerstein, I. (1996). *Historical capitalism* (2nd ed.). New York: W. W. Norton.

Wehler, H.-U. (1969). *Bismarck und der imperialismus*. Cologne: Kiepenheuer.

Wertheimer, M. S. (1924). *The Pan-German league, 1890–1914*. New York: Columbia University Press.

Wesseling, H. L. (1997). *Imperialism and colonialism*. Westport: Greenwood Press.

Williams, A. (1911). *Life in a railway factory*. (2nd ed.). London.

Williams, K., et al. (1989). Do labor costs really matter? *Work, Employment, and Society*, 3, 281–305.

CHANGING RURAL SCENARIOS AND RESEARCH AGENDAS IN LATIN AMERICA IN THE NEW CENTURY

Norman Long and Bryan Roberts

ABSTRACT

The chapter identifies key components of the new patterns of farming and rural livelihoods emerging in Latin America in the twenty-first century. By the beginning of the millennium, most rural areas of Latin America had become integrated into global agricultural commodity networks that curtail the opportunities for small-scale, family-based farming and result in two predominant types of production, the corporate large-scale enterprise suited to oils seeds and their derivatives, cattle or vegetables for processing and the smaller commercially oriented farm producing market garden products, fruits and wine. Both types of farms often form part of commodity networks organized by domestic intermediaries, large-scale supermarket chains, such as Wal-Mart and Carrefour, and foreign food marketers. In addition to the multiplication of external commercial linkages, high levels of urbanization have increasingly blurred the distinction between the rural and the urban. Off-farm work, including international labor migration, is now an important source of rural livelihoods. This context means that research needs to address the multiple interfaces that now connect the different types of rural inhabitants with a wide range of external actors.

INTRODUCTION

In this chapter, we aim to identify the key components of the new patterns of farming and rural livelihoods emerging in Latin America in the twenty-first century. We do this conceptually as well as empirically through a review of trends in agricultural production and illustrative case studies. Current rural transformations in Latin America, more strikingly than in the past, blur the distinction between urban and rural, undermine subsistence farming systems and are marked by the absence of major rural development programs, whether initiated by governments or emerging from coalitions of small-scale producers and entrepreneurs. The rural population is now a small minority of the total population of the Latin American region. Agriculture is heavily embedded in national and international commercial circuits and depends on an increasingly high level of technological inputs, including biotechnology. In contrast to earlier periods when agrarian reform, rural social movements and the revitalization of small-scale farming dominated national agendas, today the integrated development of rural areas has become in most countries a secondary political and economic concern.

The preoccupation with planned development was central to the idea of a sociology of rural development, which is rooted in the era of interventionist policies (spanning the mid-1950s until the early 1980s). In this era, national states, supported by international donors, attempted to stimulate economic growth, improve welfare and alleviate poverty through the implementation of planned development. In the countryside, this came to signify a number of intervention measures: the transfer of modern technologies, the introduction of new hybrid crop varieties, community development and cooperatives, land reform and resettlement programmes, and various small-scale agricultural and non-agricultural income-generating projects.

Along with this almost unstoppable march of planned interventions came the demand from donors and implementing agencies for sociologists and anthropologists to provide background data and analysis, to undertake the evaluation of projects in order to establish how far policy goals were achieved and 'target groups' reached, and to advise on issues of local participation. This put rural sociology/anthropology and social development issues squarely on the applied policy map. Examples are the interesting early and continuing 'farmer-researcher' based research carried out at the International

Center for Tropical Agriculture (CIAT), Cali, Colombia (Ashby, 1996) and the International Potato Center (CIP), in Lima, Peru (Rhoades, 1984).

This situation changed, however, following the oil price and national economic crises of the early 1980s, when structural adjustment measures were introduced to promote better management of national economies and to install tighter fiscal and administrative control and accountability by the state. The same policy criteria were, of course, applied at local level to rural development projects, which increasingly looked to the gurus of economics, administrative studies and sound management practice for help and legitimation, rather than to the 'softer' social sciences. Economic efficiency – carefully orchestrated to meet shifting market demand – and improved administrative practice would, it was assumed, generate improved economic returns and 'good governance'; and multiparty democracy and decentralization policies would result in more effective grass-roots participation.

By the 1990s, some new elements had been added to this unfolding neoliberal policy agenda in an attempt to give it a more caring 'human face.' These concerned environmental problems and 'sustainable' livelihoods, issues of human rights and citizenship (including claims on the basis of gender, ethnicity and migrant status) and the central role of 'social capital' in binding together civic groups and networks of trust. The official rationale for such policy additions was that of avoiding or compensating for the excesses and social exclusivity of 'free' market outcomes, and thus of protecting the poor – both rural and urban.

Yet, despite such concessions to social development, the philosophy and economics of neoliberalism has continued to occupy center-stage. Its principles not only penetrate national policies and global concerns but also play a role in shaping the perceptions and strategies of local actors – rural and urban in regard to livelihoods and the organization of economic life (Slater, 2004). Agriculture has become part of a global system of production covering a wider range of foodstuffs than ever before in which less-developed countries are increasingly embedded.

Interwoven with these changes were additional constraints on rural life brought by urbanization and globalization. We begin then with an overview of the main demographic and economic trends affecting rural Latin America at the century's end. We emphasize the diversity of the region and the differences between countries in their involvement in the global agricultural economy. Although urbanization and globalization are radically changing the nature of agriculture and of rural life, they are not doing so in a homogeneous direction. Also, political maneuvering and organization affect outcomes, as do the adaptive strategies of local actors in the face of the opportunities and constraints associated with globalization. We develop these points more fully in subsequent sections.

THE CHANGING CONTEXT AT THE CENTURY'S END

In a previous publication, we reviewed the evolution of the agrarian structures of Latin America from 1930 to 1990 (Long & Roberts, 1994). We emphasized the partial nature of the agrarian transformations amidst a capitalist development in agriculture that affected almost all countries of the region. Plantation production, medium-scale commercial production and peasant semi-subsistence agriculture co-existed in most countries. Only in a few countries or sub-regions, such as Argentina, Uruguay and South-Central Brazil, was production for national consumption or export profitable enough to lead to a thoroughgoing commercialization of agriculture. Elsewhere, peasant households provided temporary labor for the plantations and commercial farms, foodstuffs for the growing cities and served as pioneers in opening up new regions for settlement. In many instances, such as in the south of Mexico and the Amazonian region of Brazil, these new areas were subsequently colonized, often first by small-scale producers who cleared the land, and then by cattle ranchers or plantation agriculturalists.

The context within which these developments occurred was the rapid urbanization of the Latin American region. Because of high birth rates, this initially did little to alleviate population pressure on land in most countries. It did, however, transform the nature of rural livelihood strategies, creating new opportunities as well as new challenges. The creation of a substantial urban market for foodstuffs enabled even small peasant producers to sell, at times, directly in the urban marketplace. The dependence on monetary income in rural areas increased as improved communications and the interrelationships established through rural–urban migration brought industrialized foodstuffs and other industrial products into the village. This made off-farm work, often implying long-distance and even international migration, an increasingly important part of the rural economy. Additionally, state policies in many Latin American countries had an 'urban bias' that favoured urban residents through food subsidies at the expense of rural producers (Lipton, 1977; Grindle, 1986).

The changes in this context at the century's end are largely associated with the adoption in most Latin American countries of neo-liberal economic policies, though these policies have varied in intensity and scope from country to country. The generalized and relatively rapid adoption of these new policies in the 1990s was based on external indebtedness and the consequent dependence of countries on the policy remedies of the multilateral agencies, particularly the International Monetary Fund, the World Bank and the Inter-American Development Bank (see Gwynne & Kay, 1999). Several implications of the new economic and political context are important for the discussion that follows.

Tariffs protected large- and small-scale enterprises from competition during the period of Import Substituting Industrialization (ISI), whereas free trade has brought considerable competition from foreign imports in both manufacturing and agriculture. The resultant emphasis on increasing productivity to meet competitive pressures has tended to displace labor and to make it more insecure in both manufacturing and agricultural enterprises. It has also led to an emphasis on new crops in agriculture that are more competitive on the world market.

Whereas the state during ISI was both economically and politically nationalist, had a national development discourse and often implemented national development plans, particularly for rural areas, current ideology leaves development to market forces, with the state exercising a regulatory role. The state during ISI was highly centralized both in administration and in the provision of key services, such as education, health and social security. However, the dominant contemporary tendency is that of administrative decentralization to provincial and local municipal governments, which are also charged with the administration of health and educational services.

With increasing democratization throughout Latin America in the 1980s and 1990s, local people have acquired more say in local governments, which now have larger revenues and expenditures than in the past, although this gain in resources is often counterbalanced by the withdrawal of central government financial support for local services and infrastructure. As Schuurman (1997) documents, decentralization discourses are rampant and receive positive support from all quarters – international finance agents, governments, the political left, NGOs and people's organizations as well as planners and applied social scientists. The issue remains, however, as to how far such policies effectively empower local groups and strengthen local forms of governance.

These economic and political changes have contradictory implications for rural areas in Latin America. The income opportunities in agriculture are now likely to be more concentrated than in the past, making it more difficult for subsistence-oriented farmers to generate cash incomes. On the other hand, small-scale farmers have more room for political maneuver to the extent that they can influence local government and the allocation of its resources.

A further set of variations arises as a result of demographic changes (Potter & Tuiran, 2005). There is a drop in human fertility throughout Latin America that narrows the previous differences between high fertility countries such as Mexico and Brazil and low fertility countries, such as Argentina and Uruguay. By 2000, Latin America had become a highly urbanized continent with some 75% of its population living in urban places (UNPD, 2004). Though United Nations estimates are based on a minimal definition of urban (2,500+population or the administrative center of a district), Latin American urbanization has been concentrated in large cities (100,000 and over) and continues to be so in the contemporary period. High levels of urbanization have been accompanied by a general decrease in the level of population growth, although the Central American countries of Honduras, Guatemala and El Salvador, and Haiti, remain at a level of 2% growth per annum, and Paraguay and Venezuela in South America retain rates of over 2% per annum. By 2000, most countries are more than 60% urban with Argentina, Chile, Brazil, Uruguay and Venezuela above 80% (UNPD, 2004).

The decline in the proportion of the rural population has been accompanied by a decline in the proportion of the agricultural labor force. Though this decline has been constant throughout the period 1970–2000, it is only in the last years that the absolute numbers of those working in agriculture have in fact declined (Table 1). Excluding Mexico, Central America retains a higher proportion working in agriculture than does South America; but there are major differences between those countries that industrialized early or rapidly and those that possess a weak industrial base.

The countries of the Southern cone fit the category of early or fast industrializing countries, as also does Brazil and Venezuela, and have an agricultural labor force that constitutes less than 20% of the total labor force. The countries with a weak industrial based, mainly those of Central America – excluding Costa Rica, Mexico and Panama (whose development was based on its commercial role vis-à-vis the Canal), but including Bolivia, Ecuador, Paraguay and Peru – still have agricultural labor forces in excess of 30% of the total labor force. The countries that retain a large labor force in agriculture are also, it should be noted, those countries that have substantial indigenous populations: Bolivia, Ecuador, Guatemala, Paraguay and Peru. We will return to this point later when we examine the new ruralities in Latin America.

These demographic changes have the following consequences (Portes & Roberts, 2005). Reduction in fertility, though more marked in urban areas, combined with decreasing proportion of the rural population, results in much less rural–urban migration than in the ISI period, and consequently in

Table 1. Evolution of the Agricultural Labor Force in Latin America, 1970–2000 Selected Countries (000s).

Country	1970 No.	1970 %	1980 No.	1980 %	1990 No.	1990 %	2000 No.	2000 %
Venezuela	829	26.0	751	14.6	874	12.0	805	8.1
Argentina	1,495	16.0	1,384	12.9	1,482	12.1	1,464	9.8
Uruguay	207	18.6	192	16.6	193	14.2	190	12.6
Chile	715	24.1	800	20.9	938	18.8	980	15.8
Brazil	16,066	47.2	17,480	36.7	15,232	23.3	13,211	16.7
Nicaragua	350	51.1	393	39.6	392	28.6	396	20.0
Costa Rica	243	42.9	290	35.2	307	26.1	324	20.2
Panama	211	41.6	197	28.9	245	26.2	251	20.3
Colombia	3,080	45.1	3,776	40.5	3,696	26.6	3,719	20.4
Mexico	6,541	43.8	7,995	36.3	8,531	27.8	8,551	21.4
Ecuador	997	51.5	1,013	39.8	1,201	33.3	1,249	25.9
El Salvador	673	56.8	697	43.6	709	36.4	775	29.1
Peru	1,915	48.3	2,183	40.3	2,654	35.7	2,965	30.4
Honduras	580	67.4	684	57.2	693	41.4	769	31.7
Paraguay	409	49.8	514	44.8	595	38.9	706	34.3
Bolivia	872	55.1	1,064	52.8	1,249	46.9	1,497	44.2
Guatemala	1,106	61.1	1,257	53.8	1,569	52.4	1,916	46.1
Total[a]	36,289	42.1	40,670	34.3	40,560	25.2	39,768	19.5
% Rural	10,6399.2	42.3	11,3679.7	35.2	11,2316.8	28.7	11,2835.4	24.4

Source: FAOSTAT Population data, February 2004.
[a]The percentages are the percentage of the total labor force that works in agriculture.

much lower overall rates of urbanization. The predominant forms of migration become urban-to-urban migration and international migration. Urban growth ceases to be concentrated in one or two major primate cities. There is a growth of intermediate cities and a more dispersed pattern of urbanization. However, new forms of urban agglomeration emerge. These are mega urban regions, such as the basin of Mexico City or the state of Sao Paulo metropolitan constellation. These agglomerations contain a central metropolis, which is the location of the headquarters of large firms and specialized services, several more specialized industrial cities, and a peri-urban hinterland of villages and small towns, which mix agriculture (often market gardening) with crafts, services and outsourced production for foreign and national enterprises.

Urban labor markets appear less able to absorb migrants than in the past. Levels of unemployment and underemployment are higher in the late 1990s in Latin America than they were in the 1970s (Portes & Roberts, 2005). The urban population is likely to be residentially less stable than in the past, moving from city to town, to work abroad or back to rural areas. Urbanization is less hierarchically ordered than in the past, but the countryside is extensively urbanized, even in vast relatively unexploited rural areas, such as the Amazon (Browder & Godfrey, 1997). Most of the rural population now lives in fairly close proximity to towns and transportation. The overall consequence of these demographic changes is that the rural–urban divide becomes even more blurred than in the past, making it necessary to reconceptualize the nature of rural space in Latin America. Yet, the extent of this blurring differs considerably by country and region within country, depending on the extent of urbanization and the nature of the urban system.

What changes, then, have occurred in agricultural and livestock production in these years and how do these create new challenges and opportunities for the rural population? The following analysis is based on data on agricultural production and import/export trade taken from the Food and Agricultural Organization of the United Nations (FAO) statistical database (Faostat, 2004). Though trends vary by country, some central tendencies are apparent. Areas under permanent crops and pastures have increased throughout the region, especially in countries which have expanded their agricultural frontiers, particularly Brazil. Areas under irrigation have also increased throughout the region, most markedly in Mexico, Brazil and Chile. Agricultural output has increased substantially and so has agricultural productivity. The FAO estimate of the per capita production index (baseline 99–01) for food products shows an increase from 79.3 in 1970 to 103.5 in 2002.

At the same time, agriculture contributes a relatively small share to national GDPs, even in those countries that have developed a substantial commercial agriculture such as Argentina, Brazil and Mexico. In Argentina, agriculture contributed 4.9% of value added to the GDP in 2000, down from 5.3% in 1990. In Brazil, agriculture contributed 7.7% of value added in 2000, up from 7.0% in 1990, and in Mexico, agriculture's contribution was 4.5% in 2000, down from 5.5% in 1990. In all three cases, however, agriculture's absolute contribution at constant prices increased between the two years.

The political weight of landowners may thus be less than in the past, particularly amongst those landowners involved in traditional cash-crop production. Those involved in the new export crops, as we will see, have strong links to global financial and distribution interests and continue to be key political actors at national and sub-national levels.

There has been a significant shift in the types of agricultural exports and thus in the contribution of different agricultural products to GDP. In 1970, the two major exports by value were coffee and tea (38.9%) and meats and hides (15.5%), followed by fruit and vegetables, textile fibers and cereals, each of which accounted for just over 10% of export value (Chart 1). By 2000, the two major exports by value were oilseeds and their derivatives (31.6%) and fruit and vegetables (26.8%). The categories of coffee/tea and of meats/hides barely contributed 10% each of export value. Within the category of fruits and vegetables, there is a substantial increase in market garden crops for the urban consumer, such as asparagus, avocados, tomatoes, chilies and peppers, cucumbers, grapes and onions. Non-agricultural products, such as fish products and wood pulp for paper have also increased their contribution to the region's exports. Fish products are significant exports in Chile, Peru, Mexico and Ecuador, while wood pulp for paper is important in Brazil and Chile.

The countries of Latin America differ considerably in terms of the crops and livestock that they export. The major exporters by value are Argentina

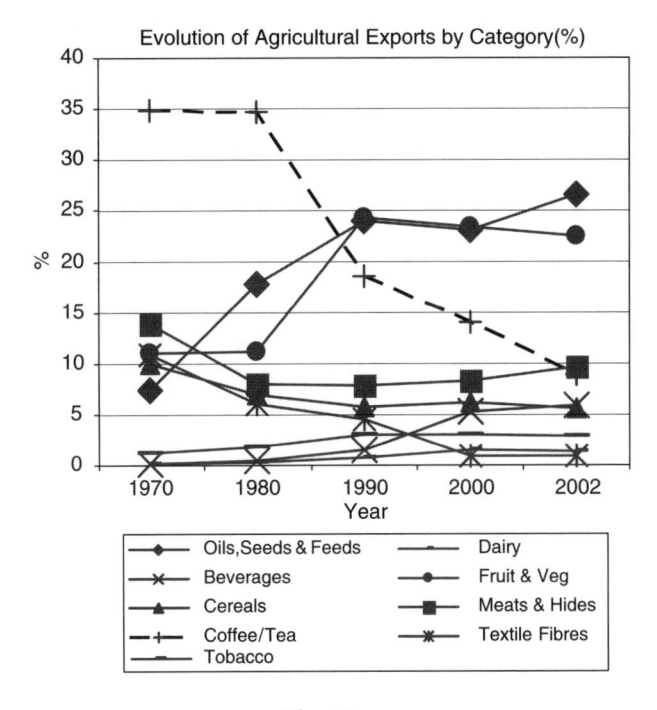

Chart 1.

and Brazil (21.7% and 32.9% of the region's total export value respectively in 2002), both of which have shifted their exports away from their traditional ones, which were meat and cereals in the Argentinean case and coffee in the Brazilian case. In both countries, oil seed and their derivatives, which include vegetable oils and feedstuffs, are now the major exports (54.6% and 36.7% respectively of each country's total exports by value in 2002) with meat increasingly important in Brazil. Chile, in contrast, is an example of a country that has dramatically increased its contribution to the region's exports moving from less than 1% of the region's exports by value in 1970 to 6.8% in 2002, but without substantially changing the profile of its agricultural exports. As in 1970, Chile continues to specialize in the export of wine, fruits and vegetables, taking advantage of tariff reductions to increase its sales to northern markets. In addition, fish products and pulp for paper are important contributors to Chile's exports.

Mexico presents yet another pattern. Overall, Mexico is one of five Latin American countries that import more agricultural products by value than they export (El Salvador, Panama, Peru and Venezuela are the others). Mexico's deficit is accounted for mainly by imports of meat and meat products (17.9% of imports by value), by cereals (15.8%) and by oil seeds and their derivatives (15.8%). Mexico maintains a favorable import–export balance in fruit and vegetables, particularly in crops such as tomatoes, chilies/peppers and other salad crops, most of which are exported to the U.S. Distilled alcoholic beverages and beer have been other export success stories. Peru shows similar tendencies, importing cereals and oilseeds and their derivatives, but increasing their exports of non-traditional vegetables, especially asparagus. Like Chile, Peruvian fisheries make a substantial contribution to exports. In general, then, imports of agricultural products increase in relation to exports in most Latin American countries between 1970 and 2000.

The incidence of these trends differs between Latin American countries, and so too does their impact. However, they point in similar directions. The new forms of internal and external demand for agricultural products foster two very different production systems in agriculture. One is the corporate, large-scale enterprise suited to large-scale agricultural production such as oil seeds and their derivatives, cattle or vegetables for processing. This type is capital rather than labor intensive. The other is small, commercially oriented farms producing market garden products, fruits and wine. This type has a relatively high degree of labor input, technological sophistication and quality control. Both types of farms often form part of commodity networks organized by domestic intermediaries, large-scale supermarket chains, such as Wal-Mart and Carrefour, and foreign food marketers.

The two types of production systems can, and in the case of soybean production in Brazil, do cater for the same crop. Which system predominates often depends on political influence and organization rather than simply on economic viability. These production systems differ in their demand for temporary and full-time labor, including gender and skill composition. They also differ in their local linkages in terms of service provision, transport, manufacturing and processing industries. The linkage issue was first raised by Hirschman (1977) in his analysis of backward and forward linkages and remains as relevant today for understanding the opportunities opened up and the constraints generated at the local level by the new production systems. The nature and extent of linkages are sources of difference in rural livelihoods and affect the room for maneuver that different rural actors have in the face of increasing agricultural globalization.

In researching these issues we should be careful not to operate with a simple model that sees large-scale, often foreign, enterprises as closing off local opportunities, while the smaller commercial production systems are seen as more favorable to local development. In an earlier study, in the Peruvian Andes, of the impact of a mining enclave on its surrounding region, we showed the multiple ways in which the presence of this large-scale foreign enterprise stimulated the rise of smaller-scale local enterprises in agriculture, trade and manufacturing (Long & Roberts, 1984).

The foregoing overview of the macro economic, demographic and political trends suggests that the emerging rural sector in Latin America is far from uniform. It is also sufficiently different from the past in terms of the nature of agricultural production and rural livelihoods to require a rethinking of the analytical concepts needed for researching rural questions. Rural spaces are now much less territorially bounded than in the past, more differentiated, and more closely and diversely linked with external actors, both national and international. The next section offers a preliminary attempt to set out an appropriate conceptual and methodological agenda.

THE RISE OF NEW RURALITIES: CONCEPTUAL AND METHODOLOGICAL ISSUES

Our starting point is the globalization of agriculture, but we emphasize both the diversity and uneven nature of this process (cf. Buttel, 1994). From this perspective, the impact of globalization on agriculture takes place through a series of heterogeneous commodity networks based on different types of food production and associated patterns of distribution and consumption. We prefer the term 'commodity network' rather than 'commodity chain' since our focus is on the multiple sets of actors involved, the differences in their interests and values and the processes of competition and negotiation present in their interaction. The actors in these networks are less circumscribed by territorial boundaries – local, provincial or national – than they were in the past. Moreover, our use of the term, the 'new ruralities,' is intended to underscore the diversity of rural identities and livelihoods that now exists in the countryside, even within the same geographical space. In respect to these changes, there are four distinct components that we single out as priorities for research.

The first component concerns the ill-defined nature of rural space, which nowadays, can no longer be considered coterminous with agricultural space. This situation contrasts with that of the 1970s and 1980s when researchers identified the central problems for analysis as the 'agrarian question,' namely the debate about the significance of proletarianization versus peasantization of the countryside. This was a major preoccupation of agrarian social science, particularly in Latin America, during the 1970s and 1980s (see Kautsky, 1899; de Janvry, 1981; Harriss, 1982; Goodman & Redclift, 1981; and many articles in the *Journal of Peasant Studies*). In the contemporary countryside, agricultural production can no longer be privileged over other income-earning/livelihood activities and we should go beyond agricultural production and resource issues to look more broadly at the utilization of countryside resources. This means a concern for landscape and environmental dimensions, for recreation and leisure time pursuits, and for the management of forest and water resources, and similar amenities.

A second component of the new ruralities is the new limits on the extent to which outside authorities or powerful groups can impose or dictate the transformation of the countryside. The number of significant actors involved in the countryside has grown, making it more difficult for any one interest to predominate. The different actors involved – peasant smallholders, indigenous people, commercial farmers, transnational companies, agricultural bureaucrats, credit banks, various agrarian organizations, property developers, and city folk moving into the countryside to enjoy a more rural lifestyle – all struggle to advance their own particular interests and to have a say in what happens to rural resources in the short and longer term.

The organizational forms that result are complex and varied, since each 'solution' represents a specific configuration of interlocking actors' 'projects' generated by the encounters, negotiations and accommodations that take place between them, even though some may never in fact meet face-to-face

(Long & van der Ploeg, 1994; Long, 2001, pp. 49–72). The influence of actors who are remote from the action–situation is especially pertinent in an age where information technology penetrates more and more into everyday life. Many commercial farmers in poor countries now communicate through walkie-talkies with their farm overseers or foremen in the fields, and possess mobile phones and computers that can directly access foreign commodity markets for up-to-date information on prices and product turnover.

And wage-earning migrants living abroad constitute an important source of information, and their remittances subsidize incomes and livelihood activities in their places of origin. An interesting example is the regular flow of highly skilled shepherds from the remoter areas of highland Peru to work on the sheep ranches of the mid-west of the U.S. They speak no English and often little Spanish, yet their expertise is highly valued since it helps to maintain high levels of reproduction and offspring survival among the sheep. Unlike many international agricultural migrant workers, these workers are legal, have three-year contracts and earn a regular dollar wage, part of which they remit or save to invest in small-scale business and farming ventures on returning home (Altamirano, 1991).

The limits on externally imposed transformations are reinforced by the third component of the new ruralities. This is the importance of value contestation and construction, both socio-cultural and economic, in the operation of new global commodity networks. Here, research should focus especially on the dynamics of these processes at the level of local producers as well as on the transformation of values as commodities pass into the arenas of processing, marketing, retailing and consumption (see Long & Villarreal, 1998; Stanford, 2002 on avocados). For example, the organization of marketing and retailing is not simply a matter of adding value to the commodity. Rather it constitutes a series of interlocking arenas of struggle, as we will illustrate in the Jalisco milk case, in which various parties may contest notions of 'quality,' 'convenience' and 'price.'

Undertaking a commodity flow analysis – in terms of both practice and discourse – gives attention to the ways in which people organize themselves around commodities and ascribe values to them (cf. Appadurai's (1986) notion of 'the social life of things'). These contestations and negotiations usually entail the mobilization of arguments about what constitutes consumer preference, the availability and advantages of particular technologies, and issues relating to the material presentation of the commodity to its relevant audiences (i.e., in relation to the supermarkets, small retailers, 'alternative' food shop owners, and an array of different consumer interests). Language representations and the clashes that they invoke can also segment markets.

This is illustrated in respect to consumption preferences by the often-heated debates that arise concerning food quality and extend to embrace issues of a 'healthy' diet, nutritional 'needs' and 'environmental pollution.'

Hence, as social constructs, commodities contribute to the development of both markets and consumer life styles in contemporary society. A commodity approach, therefore, should give attention to how new alliances are built between producers, distributors, retailers and consumers. These commodity networks can improve the bargaining powers of producer and consumer organizations vis-à-vis corporate global interests as well as those of the often 'disempowered' low- and middle-income nation states.

Emphasizing value contestation and construction also draws attention to the continuing and innovative resistance to absorption into global commodity networks. This occurs when producers, consumers and agricultural workers identify critical interests, both cultural and economic, as being threatened or marginalized by outside markets and institutions. Such interests are often based on existing life styles or local forms of knowledge that are seen as vital to a community's identity and survival. This opens up a related line of enquiry, namely, the exploration of the processes by which people and their 'objects of desire' generate certain cultural identifications that segment markets, create specialized demands for production and even reduce the commoditization of the countryside.

Immigrant populations often generate these specialized demands. An example is the extensive market created for corn husks grown by small-scale farmers in Mexico, packaged by Mexican plants and then transported across the border for the making of *tamales* in California (Long & Villarreal, 1998). We also find cases where farmers opt out of global commodity markets since they judge that the benefits of meeting one's own consumption requirements outweigh any gains made through commoditization. One such case is that of farmers in the Sierra Norte of Oaxaca in Mexico who prefer to consume and exchange locally their native varieties of maize even though the costs of production are above market prices (Appendini et al., 2003). In yet other situations producers and consumers may commit themselves to the idea of finding an alternative way through the formation of non-monetary exchange systems, such as the *trueque* movement in Argentina, which at its highest point in 2002 had an estimated 2.5 million members (Primavera, Covas, & De Sanzo, nd.; Gonzalez Bombal & Luzzi, 2002). On the other hand, local organizing practices and networks may contribute innovatively to the production of high-quality commodities destined for less exploitative external markets, such as, for example, those associated with the principles of 'fair trade' (see Whatmore & Thorne, 1997; Fisher, 1997). One further general observation is that if intervening parties, such as multinational firms, the state or retail organizations, fail to take seriously the ways in which people mobilize and use resources through existing social networks and cultural commitments, then they run the risk of being rejected by, or distanced from, the life experiences and priorities of local producers. Hence, the importance of studying how external market demands are internalized or modified by local populations (Pottier, Bicker, & Sillitoe, 2003).

The fourth component of the new ruralities follows from the previous one. This relates to the fact that 'nature,' more than in the past, has come to mean quite different things to different actors. It can no longer, therefore, be considered the taken-for-granted backdrop to agriculture and rural life. Recent research has documented the extent that local actors (e.g. peasants and traders) and outsiders (e.g. agricultural extensionists, pollution officers, conservationists and research scientists) differ in their assessments and priorities, and in the way they represent 'nature–man' relations and the 'environment.' And some researchers now call for the abandonment of the commonplace distinction between the nature/man or nature/culture divide in favor of the composite notion of 'social nature' (Braun & Castree, 1998; also see Ingold, 1986; Croll & Parkin, 1992; Ellen & Katsuyoshi, 1996).

Underlying these discussions is the more pragmatic question of what measures to use in the management of so-called natural resources. Here, the focus is on how the state attempts to control people and territory as against how people *in situ* go about utilizing and conserving resources and biodiversity. Indigenous social movements, as we will see, have quite different conceptions of their rights and relationships to territory than do national governments, particularly when it comes to water, forest and subsoil resources. In the current international context, governments are frequently faced with the choice of implementing what are called 'centralized' or 'decentralized' modes of resource control – the latter usually implying some community involvement in natural resource management or the creation of relatively autonomous national parks that cater for ecological tourism. It remains an open question as to whether such decentralized modes of control are, as Schuurman (1997) is inclined to conclude, a part of neoliberal discourse that contributes to the 'hollowing out of the state' and to the furtherance of global forms of capitalist exploitation. Or is it a way of increasing empowerment among local people in the management of their own resources?

Nowadays environmental policies are hedged round with a host of regulatory prescriptions of a global kind (for example, the Convention on International Trade in Endangered Species (CITES) and the Convention on Bio-Diversity (CBD), and subject to pressures from powerful conservationist lobbies. As many studies have shown, the protection and conservation of wildlife through the setting up of national parks or protected areas does not necessarily ensure the continued preservation of natural resources and endangered species. These environmental and biodiversity conservation issues – coupled as they are with a booming eco-tourism – are critically important for the future livelihoods of many rural inhabitants.

These components of the new ruralities raise a central methodological issue. This concerns the need to bridge the evident disjuncture between the sociology of rural development and ecological/environmental anthropology. Whereas the sociology of rural development has generally focused on issues of production, consumption and commodity values in the context of globalization, ecological anthropology has principally concerned itself with the conceptual issue of how to relate social-to-natural phenomena and has explored the epistemological understandings and cultural meanings associated with social and environmental relationships. Clearly, there is a need to synthesize these contrasting perspectives so as to achieve greater insight into questions of diversity and change in the countryside.

As a preliminary exploration of these new ruralities and the research challenges they pose, we now present three illustrative case studies to highlight the changes in rural landscapes and the options available to rural inhabitants.

RECONFIGURING RURAL SPACE:
THREE CASE STUDIES

The three cases analyzed below are illustrative of what we see as key issues facing policy makers, researchers and the many other actors involved in the new ruralities of Latin America. The cases highlight the conceptual issues outlined in the previous section, namely the importance of value construction and contestation in the operation of new global commodity networks, the limited extent to which transformations can be imposed externally, the ill-defined nature of rural space and the multiple meanings attributed to nature and countryside resources. All three cases illustrate the complexity and multifaceted nature of the changes in rural livelihoods that result, directly or indirectly, from globalization. Despite similar external pressures, the cases show that the direction of change is neither homogeneous nor predictable. The play of politics, at both local and national levels, affects outcomes, as also do the adaptive strategies of local actors and fluctuations in the global economy.

This is true even in the first case, soybean production in Brazil, which is an example of one of the most radical reconfigurations of rural landscapes and livelihoods brought by large-scale export-oriented production. The second case, milk production in Jalisco, Mexico, illustrates the increasing importance of international standards of quality and safety for the survival of even those enterprises that supply a domestic market. The third case looks at the apparently paradoxical case of the revival of indigenous identities in the face of economic liberalization and globalization so that they become an important element of the new ruralities in Latin America.

The Case of Brazilian Soybeans

The major Latin America soybean producer is Brazil, whose 2003 production of 51 billion metric tons approximated that of the USA at 66 billion tons. Argentina is the second largest producer in Latin America, but, in recent years, several Latin American countries have considerably extended their soybean production, notably Uruguay, Bolivia, Colombia, Ecuador, Guatemala, Honduras and Paraguay (Faostat data, 2004).

The impact of the change to soybean production on rural livelihoods is both direct – on the areas in which it is implanted – and indirect through the expulsion of existing rural populations. In Brazil, the conversion to soybean production of large areas of Southern Brazil, such as the state of Paraná, resulted in an estimated net migration of 2.5 million displaced rural workers in the 1970s (Martine, 1988; Mahar, 1989, p. 31; both quoted in Browder & Godfrey, 1997, p. 168). Since 1980, the area under soybean cultivation has risen from 8.8 million hectares to 18.5 million hectares, extending into the Center-West states of the Brazilian Amazonia, such as Mato Grosso and Mato Grosso do Sul (Flaskerud, 2003). By 2002–2003, soybean production and soybean farms were larger in the Center-West of Brazil than in the traditional Southern area of production.

Large-scale soybean production in Brazil is usually based on a no-till system, particularly in areas of poor soil, which accounts for some 50% of production, in which herbicides are used to limit weed growth. Though in comparison to U.S. production systems, the large-scale farms in Brazil are more labor intensive, they need only a fraction of the labor used in small-scale farms. One estimate put the labor needs of a 30 ha ecological soybean farm at 147 h/ha/year compared with 40.5 h for a 3,000 ha herbicide farm (Ortega, Miller, Anami, & Beskow, nd). A 50,000 ha soybean farm in the Center-West employs between 200 and 300 workers on a year round basis

(Flaskerud, 2003). Large-scale producers are closely allied to multinational companies, such as Monsanto, for seeds and herbicides, or food and feedstuff companies, such as Archer Daniels Midland (ADM), for sales and processing. Though Brazil has been one of the few countries to ban genetically modified (GM) seeds, their use has grown in recent years and in 2004 they were permitted on a limited scale by the government (Rohter, 2003). Monsanto produces GM seeds that are resistant to herbicides, facilitating no-till production systems.

Nevertheless, small-scale soybean farming can survive in the face of large-scale production. In fact, the small labor-intensive soybean producing farms of between 30 and 300 hectares can be more profitable per hectare than the large farms (Ortega et al., nd, Table 4). However, the scale of production of the large farms drives down prices. The small soybean farmer gains little advantage from the innovations in seed and herbicides since their production systems usually include intercropping, which makes herbicide use inappropriate. In this situation, the introduction of genetically modified seeds and the expansion of large-scale soybean farming have become a divisive political issue in Brazil.

The Brazilian Landless Worker Movement (Movimento dos Trabalhadores Rurais Sem Terra (MST)) was first organized from the state of Paraná, and has become one of the major opponents of the introduction of organically modified soy seed, lobbying government to prohibit their use and taking direct action against Monsanto experimental stations (MST website). The MST is also engaged in the resettlement of landless agricultural workers and the development of production cooperatives. It produces organic soy seed and runs soybean farms in Parana that produce high yields using conventional seed. The MST supported the Worker's Party candidate, Lula, in the 2002 Presidential elections in Brazil, but has since become an opponent of his agricultural policies, including permitting the use of GM seed for soybean production. Lula's justification has been the priority he gives to producing food cheaply for the poor in Brazil and the role of soybeans not only in generating export earnings but of providing feed for cattle and poultry production. The MST does, however, cooperate with some of Lula's government agencies, notably the Institute for Colonization and Agrarian Reform (INCRA).

Brazil's agrarian landscape is being substantially changed by its 'new' major agricultural products – oilseeds & derivatives and meat & meat preparations. Whereas the old agrarian heartland of Brazil, the states of the Center-South and South of Brazil, account for a steadily declining proportion of Brazilian agricultural production, those of the Center-West and

North, the Brazilian Amazonia, are expanding production and production areas rapidly, increasingly at the expense of the Amazonian forest. Originally, the colonization of the Amazonia region was conceived by the military governments of 1960s and 1970s as part of enhancing national security by developing the frontier, providing land for migrants displaced from the South and as a means of relieving land-pressure in the North-East (Browder & Godfrey, 1997, pp. 67–71). The transport networks established to facilitate colonization together with land grants and low land prices made the Amazonia attractive to extractive activities, particularly lumber, but increasingly to cattle-raising and subsequently to soybean production, creating a sequence in which small-scale farmers, timber extraction and roads prepare the way for pasture, which when degraded, can be turned over to soybean production. This sequence is a dynamic one since large-scale livestock producers sell their lands to soy production and move further northwards to new frontiers (Castro, 2004).

The small-scale farmers that first colonized the area were often displaced by the larger operators, either forcibly, by being bought out, or through the failure of their enterprises. Poor soils, poor communications and lack of local markets made small-scale farming relatively unprofitable. Even the basic foodstuffs sold in small town stores in Amazonia were imported from the Center-South of the country (Browder & Godfrey, 1997, pp. 281–285). However, as Browder and Godfrey (1997) point out, these processes did not result in rural landscapes totally dominated by large-scale farming and by surplus extraction entirely for the benefit of national and international corporate interests. Rather, the development of the frontier gave rise to two distinct patterns of urbanization – a corporate and a populist urbanization (*ibid.*, p. 100). In states like Rondônia, the influx of landless farmers from the South coupled with the support of the Brazilian Institute of Colonization and Agrarian Reform (INCRA) ensured that small-scale agricultural colonization predominated. Timber extraction and small-scale mining helped power the colonization process, but, from the beginning, it was based on a network of small urban settlements closely integrated with agricultural and extractive activities, often by the ownership of both urban and rural properties.

The pattern of populist development described by Browder and Godfrey is one of a shifting and chaotic pattern of urbanization as old frontiers are exhausted and new ones opened up leading to the decline of old urban centers and the rise of new ones. However, it is a pattern of agrarian development that appears able to sustain a relatively large population, of whom few are specialized agricultural producers. Decentralization in Brazil also supports this pattern of urbanization by mandatory transfers of revenue from federal government to state and municipal government. These transfers increase local revenues, giving local authorities more say in the allocation of jobs in the social services and public administration.

Corporate urbanization, which Browder and Godfrey see as predominating in the state of Pará, is based on large-scale projects – construction, mining and agriculture. These brought not only the workers needed for the project, but a large number of migrants attracted by the prospect of the economic opportunities being created. Currently, the driving force of corporate urbanization is soybean production. Initially, this concentrated in the non-forest areas, but with the expansion in demand, the new areas being cleared in Matto Grosso are forest. The governor of Mato Grosso is a member of one of Brazil's largest soybean producing companies and advocates increased deforestation of the state to improve production (Rohter, 2003). Small and medium size towns arise to service the projects, such as the town of Campo Verde in Mato Grosso, a center for soybean production, storage and agricultural vehicle dealerships, with a population in the municipality that grew from nothing to 30,000 in 15 years. The soybean production and distribution system is also the basis for several intermediate size cities in Mato Grosso, such as its capital Cuiabá with a population of some 500,000, and the nearby city of Rondonopolis with a population of 150,000. These towns often have a dualistic structure in which the purpose-built housing of the workers in the projects contrasts with the informal housing of temporary and service workers.

The Brazilian soy bean case shows the power but also the limits of economic globalization. The rising worldwide demand for soy is an interesting case of a newly valued food very popular as both a direct and indirect (through animal feed) source of protein that originated in East Asia and now is used worldwide. The demand for soy is transforming vast tracts of the Brazilian countryside, including the deforestation of part of the Amazonian forest. Note, however, that the triumph of large-scale production systems in the Amazonian region is as much political as economic. The profitability of soybean farming in Amazonia depends on government support in terms of the provision of cheap land and transport infrastructure, as well as allowing deforestation and the use of genetically modified seeds. Party politics flourish in Brazil and play an important part in shaping outcomes, namely through the struggles of the landless workers' movements (MST) and the political maneuvering of the soybean lobbies at national, state and municipal levels.

Even in the case of large-scale soybean production, the transformations produced are uneven and partial because of the shifting and provisional nature of soybean farming. This situation generates a variety of small-scale opportunities. Poor transport infrastructure and the need to transport products, such as soybeans, over large distances generate a demand for small-scale commerce, repair, and food and lodging services. Entrepreneurial opportunities emerge which can be combined with small-scale farming to provide livelihoods. This Brazilian case also shows the analytic inappropriateness of the rural–urban divide. The Amazonian population is highly urban, and even those extracting a living from agriculture maintain houses in towns and more basic shelter in the rural hinterland.

Mexican Dairy Industry: The Case of Jalisco

Mexico provides a striking example of a Latin American country with a marked deficit in the export of agricultural products. This trend has continued with the implementation of North American Free Trade Agreement (NAFTA) and Mexico now imports large amounts of grains (even maize), animal foodstuffs and milk products due principally to lower U.S. prices. Mexico is presently the world's leading importer of powdered milk: the devaluation of the peso in 1994 and the economic crisis that followed led to an overnight doubling of domestic market prices (Garcia-Hernández, 1998). One recent study argues (Rodríguez-Gómez, 1999, pp. 339–340) that this trend toward globalization brought about three contradictions in the internal market: the dairy industries preferred, because of cost factors, to use imported powdered milk and milk derivatives; farmers' had to face the issues of high production costs and low wholesale milk prices; and the dairy industries justified their use of imported goods in terms of the low quality of Mexican products which did not meet international standards. In general, the farmers blamed government and its incapacity to regulate imports and to provide support for domestic producers for this deteriorating situation. Another factor was that milk prices were kept at an artificially low level to benefit urban consumers rather than farmers and rural consumers. After 1994, government policy vis-à-vis milk consumption shifted from a system based on price control to a social program aimed at supplying subsidized milk to lower income groups (Lara-Covarrublas et al., 2003, p. 86). Rodríguez-Gómez (1999) goes on to look in detail at the dynamics of these processes in the state of Jalisco (see also the studies by Cervantes Escoto & Soltero Beltrán (2004) and Lara-Covarrublas et al. (2003)).

Jalisco leads the production of Mexican milk production (18% of the total during the period 1990–1998). Most of this comes from the region of

Los Altos, which accounts for an incredible 13% of national production. Early in the 1990s, the ministries of Agriculture and Commerce, together with the social compensation programme (*Solidaridad*) joined forces with the Los Altos-based regional and transnational dairy industries (e.g. Nestlé, Lechera Guadalajara, Parmalata) to encourage the formation of small- and medium-scale farmers' associations for the cooling and marketing of milk cooperatively. A principal aim was to improve milk quality throughout the region, but 90% of the dairy producers lacked the material and technological basis for achieving this. The role of the dairy processing industries was to persuade these farmers' associations to purchase cooling tanks and market the milk collectively. They also introduced a new graduated pricing system based on a hierarchy of quality levels. In this way they sought to get farmers to adhere to the standards of production set by international trading companies in accordance with their established quality criteria. This entailed two processes: increased vertical integration of production units with milk suppliers, and the production of so-called 'better quality' and 'safe' milk at lower prices (Cervantes Escoto & Soltero Beltran, 2004, p. 208). Yet, although these various industries collaborated with each other, thus giving the impression that they were operating with the same concept of 'quality,' a whole series of discourses developed that favored specific definitions, commercial practices, and power relations between farmers, traders, agro-industrial enterprises and government agencies.

The issue of quality standards stimulated the organization of legally recognized dairy producers' associations (*sociedades de producción*) that had ongoing contracts with particular processing companies for marketing their total milk production. In return the industry promised to facilitate farmers' access to cooling tanks, either by providing them on loan or by offering group credit for their purchase, but the companies retained the right to reject milk that did not meet their quality standards and to determine the prices they would pay. The state agencies also offered access to tanks and credit, and in some cases assumed up to 40% of the costs of building the tank and installing electricity and other utilities. However, despite all this external investment in the promotion of quality-controlled milk production, farmers' in Los Altos initially showed a reluctance to opt for these new arrangements.

The reasons for this were several. In the first place, producers and entrepreneurs in this region have a reputation for fiercely defending their independence vis-à-vis central government and other outside interests (Gonzalez, 1974). This attitude is deeply embedded in the history of the struggles of the *Cristeros* – conservative Catholic rebels, based in Los Altos, who fought both the *agraristas* (i.e. protagonists of agrarian reform) and the Mexican state in the 1920s (Meyer, 1974). This socio-political stance is still evident in the contemporary politics and culture of Los Altos where everyday life and trust revolve around family and personalistic ties, and not joint ventures with government or large corporate institutions. Hence farmers were skeptical about the advantages of joining farmers' associations and shouldering collective and financial and other arrangements. They reasoned that this could endanger their own individual and family enterprises, and perhaps the other economic activities in which they were involved. Nevertheless, many farmers' associations came into existence, some effectively combining both smallholder *ejidatarios* and private land owners. In the end, while acknowledging the many difficulties and insecurities that such changes might bring, a majority of farmers voiced the opinion that they had little alternative but to form these associations along the lines proposed by the dairy processing industry, otherwise they stood to lose an important growing market for their milk.

On the other hand, farmers continue to sell in a wide variety of local markets. For instance, fresh milk is sold on a door-to-door basis in the towns of the region as well as to local cheese, butter, cream and local sweet processors. The latter operate a variety of quality requirements that fit their own particular technologies. For the small-scale industrial consumers of warm milk, such as the various artisanal creameries, quality simply means the absence of water in fresh milk, whereas larger scale processors equate quality with a certain milk temperature, approved levels of solids and fat contents, absence of harmful bacterial materials, and levels of acidity. The majority of dairy producers in Los Altos, therefore, adopt a diversified production and marketing strategy that enables them to supply 'modern' quality-controlled milk for the dairy industry, while continuing to provide fresh, less standardized, varieties for the local processing of cheese, butter, creams etc. Indeed, many farmers adamantly refuse to acknowledge that the cooling of milk adds to its quality. As Rodríguez-Gómez (1999, p. 351–352) points out, "But, farmers' responses are as contradictory and ambiguous as are the processes of social, material, cultural and power transformation brought by the standardization of this cultural form."

Nowadays Jalisco boasts more than 330 dairy farmers' associations, but this does not imply that 'modern' quality-controlled milk production now constitutes the central dynamic of family farming in Los Altos. In addition to dairying activities, these same farmers are involved in a variety of on- and off-farm work, including that of national and international migrant labor.

The family and regional economy is thus both diversified and flexible. One interesting dimension concerns the reconfiguring of roles within the families of small and medium-scale farmers. Children now take charge of delivering the fresh milk to the shared cooling tank; young men and women milk and feed the cows, while the wives are required to wash the farm's milk containers. In many cases, this results in the releasing of adult males from dairying to work on other tasks on the farm or they seek farm or off-farm work in neighboring areas and even as far afield as the U.S.

Another element that has significantly changed the agrarian situation concerns the way in which the newly founded farmers' associations have undermined the position of local commercial traders who previously acted as intermediaries between the dairy producers and the older processing companies. Now, of course, it is the farmers' associations that are directly responsible for negotiating with the dairy industries the terms and details of the milk contracts. Much of this process relates to quality standardization, which from the farmers' point of view entails the necessity of gaining as much autonomy as possible in the production process and achieving greater control over the profits generated in the marketing chain. Many similar processes pertain to other 'globalized' commodities and to a wide range of food products. The farmers' of Jalisco have made certain advances in these respects through collective actions spearheaded by their associations, but have not gained as much ground as their counterparts in Aguascalientes. The latter, it seems, have succeeded in strengthening their associations through the formation of a single overarching organization which allows for greater room for maneuver and negotiation with the dairy industry and state agencies. In Michoacán, in contrast, local systems of power and patronage have run counter to the goal of creating viable, profitable producer organizations (McDonald, 2003). As in the Jalisco case, milk 'quality' became a critical issue in Michoacán that was fiercely contested by the different actors: the small-scale dairy farmers, the larger producers, the milk processing firms and the government technical 'experts.'

The case of the Jalisco dairy industry underlines the degree of maneuver possessed by small-scale producers even in the face of the standardization imposed by international agreements and adopted by state agencies and large-scale distributors. This occurs, in part, through contestation over the differing definitions of quality used by local producers and consumers as opposed to those promoted by technical experts employed by government and large-scale distributors. Also important is the increasing political organization and clout possessed by small-scale producers in part advanced by democratization and political decentralization.

The Resurgence of Ethnicities

Our third illustrative case is the apparently paradoxical one of the resurgence of collective indigenous identities in the face of the triumph of liberalism. In the nineteenth century in Latin America, political and economic liberalism was the explicit foe of corporate identities, particularly with respect to collective property, whether of the church or indigenous communities (De la Peña, 1998). In the mid-twentieth century, the study of indigenous communities was mainly the speciality of anthropologists concerned to document the cultural practices and peculiarities of what, at the time, seemed like a disappearing world. Rural sociologists tended, in contrast, to view indigenous populations, particularly those of the Andean highlands, Mexico and Central America, as peasants, whose customs and practices, including agriculture, could best be understood in terms of the constraints and strategies of family-based farming. The predominant view of Latin American governments tended to be that indigenous cultures were a barrier to modernization. Indigenous languages were prohibited in schools and in the work of government. In Peru, the government renamed the previously designated 'indigenous communities' as 'peasant communities' as an explicit step in their progress to modernization. In the case of Mexico, the indigenous past was revered, but the indigenous present was treated as a living museum and placed under the tutelage of the National Indigenous Institute. Thus any group that spoke an indigenous language and manifested a distinctive culture was separated from the mass of the rural population, whether 'peasant' or 'proletarian'.

By the end of the twentieth century, indigenous social movements had become some of the most active and consequential movements in Latin America (Kearney, 1996; De la Peña, 1998; Langer & Muñoz, 2003; Van Cott, 2000; Varese, 1996; Hale, 2004). They have gained political power in both Bolivia and Ecuador. They are even active and influential in countries, such as Argentina and Chile, whose governing elites, for long, resolutely denied that their countries had indigenous populations.

The nature and impact of indigenous identities and movements reflect the two facets of neo-liberal reforms in the region, one economic and the other political and social. The former brings increasing economic pressure on the rural and urban poor, whereas the latter promotes rights, democracy and what Hale (2004) calls 'neoliberal multiculturalism.' Democratization in the region has created spaces within which indigenous movements can develop and make their demands heard. In this, they have been supported by national and international networks of NGOs that work on human rights issues (Deere & León, 2000). The United Nations and most governments of the developed world have also supported indigenous rights through sponsoring conferences, making grants-in-aid to indigenous organizations and, at times, through insisting that respect for indigenous rights and identities be part of multilateral loan and grant agreements.

The demand-making capacity of indigenous groups and their self-awareness as social actors have also increased with better communications, including the use of the internet, increases in levels of education of indigenous people and the mobilizing impact of migration and urbanization. At the same time, indigenous populations remain the poorest segment of the population with pressing necessities, which have been aggravated by the economics of neoliberalism, such as competition from cheap imported foodstuffs. Strengthening indigenous culture as a means of eliminating the marginality and powerlessness of indigenous people is a major platform for indigenous social movements and the organizations that support them (Iturralde & Krotz, 1996).

The aspect of indigenous identities and social movements that concerns us in this paper is their rural character. Not all those who identify themselves as indigenous live in rural areas. Indeed, in Chile, for example, a majority of the Mapuche live in large cities, predominantly Santiago. However, in most indigenous movements fundamental aspects of the construction of their identities are embedded in the culture and practices of agricultural, pastoral and forest activities. Also, some of the most important demands of indigenous movements are for agricultural and forest land, including the return of ancestral land (Alwyn, 2002). They claim the right to live according to their traditional laws and practices, as in the case of communal work arrangements, collective tenure, household relations or community rituals (De la Peña, 1998; Iturralde, 2001). These are most compatible with rural not urban life. Likewise, the demands of indigenous movements for cultural rights, such as multicultural education, are most easily implemented in rural rather than urban settings. Their emphasis on territorial autonomy and a return to a traditional rural life may, at times, be more political and ideological than a practical plan, but the consequent emphasis on the importance of agriculture to indigenous people is an important component of the new ruralities in Latin America.

In reviewing the resurgence of Black and indigenous collective movements in Central America, Charles Hale (2004) argues that the imagined and occupied spaces that these movements create are essentially rural ones. As Hale points out, there have been substantial achievements in extending and recognizing Black and indigenous rights in Central America, partly as a result of the strength of grass-roots organizations, but also because of external backing from multilateral agencies and foreign governments. Hale shows how the multiculturalism that is promoted is mainly limited to the cultural sphere and rarely reaches migrants or city dwellers. It creates in Hale's words "contaminated spaces, where the hand of the state is already present in the very efforts conceived to contest state oppression." The material gains of the movements are usually over land rights, which in the past had been sources of bitter conflict between the landed elites of Central America and the Black and indigenous populations. Conceding land rights is now easier for elites because of the decline in the importance of agriculture in the Central American economies and a shift of investments from traditional export crops to financial, commercial and industrial activities. Land grants have little economic cost for governments since they are not accompanied by the economic and infrastructural aid needed to make local production commercially viable. Indeed, the greater control that Black and indigenous movements have won over local municipal administrations can be a pyrrhic victory in the context of the administrative decentralization fostered by neoliberal reforms. It shifts responsibility for alleviating poverty and providing services from national to the local level of government.

The resurgence of indigenous identities thus represents an unpredictable face of the changing ruralities that accompany globalization. They have led to a series of conflicts with the state and private interests (Arce, 2003b; Namuncura, 1999). Indigenous movements have often limited the expansion of large-scale projects in ranching, plantations, lumber or hydroelectric dams. The state's conception of preserving ecology, as in the case of national parks, can conflict with what indigenous people see as their traditional rights and farming practices.

Yet, the greater international visibility of indigenous movements gives them more clout than non-indigenous small-scale farmers in resisting encroachment. They are also a potential force behind the revitalization of small-scale, family-based farming and craft activities in many areas of Latin America. This revitalization often includes using traditional knowledge and farming practices alongside those of modern technology (Albó, 1996). In Chile, for example, we interviewed a young Mapuche professional, who was a computer technician in the regional capital of Temuco. He was active in one of the Mapuche movements and had returned to his family's small farm in the surrounding countryside. There, with the help of small loans from the German overseas development agency (GTZ), he was practicing organic farming, including the production of worms to make organic fertilizer. He, with several other local small farmers, sent their organically produced wheat directly to Santiago, where they could obtain twice the price of that offered in the local Temuco market.

A further aspect of the resurgence of indigenous identities concerns the importance of 'social capital' and building trust relations within the new ruralities. We noted earlier how top-down central state development projects have been replaced in the contemporary period by a policy of decentralizing services and by placing more emphasis on community and other non-state contributions to rural development projects. In the 1990s, social investment funds in many Latin American countries provided relatively small amounts of money for local community development that required communities to bid competitively for the projects and to provide inputs into them. Durston's (1999, 2004) studies in Guatemala and Chile have shown that fundamental to the success of these projects is the degree of trust and communal organization present at the local level – what he labels, 'community social capital.'

In his studies, it is indigenous communities with a strong tradition of collaboration and a sense of identity that are often most able to make a success of the project. Equally important to the success of such community development projects, as Tendler (1997) shows in her studies in Ceara in Brazil, is the quality and effectiveness of the relationships established at the interfaces between the community and external actors, whether agencies of government or NGOs. One of the most common obstacles to achieving this arises from the mind-set of 'facilitators' who often undervalue local knowledge and view indigenous people and other rural groups as lacking in appropriate skills (Spink, 2000; Arce, 2003a).

Urbanization and globalization have also economically revalued traditional practices and cultures, making them an important part of the new ruralities. Tourism provides a clear example. Despite the importance of enclave-type tourist development, such as the beach resorts of Mexico and the Caribbean, there has been a growing emphasis on small-scale tourist development. A main aim has been to spread more widely the economic benefits of the increasing numbers of national and international tourists in the Latin American region. In those countries with strong indigenous cultures, these are increasingly being capitalized in terms of tourism, as in the case of the city of Cuzco, the Sacred Valley and the Inca trail in Peru. These tourist experiences include visits to traditional villages and fiestas, the employment of local guides and the purchase of traditional crafts. While the Cuzco area is a dramatic example of this new form of rural development, the Peruvian government development agency, FONCODES, has been promoting small tourism projects throughout the Andean area and into the

Peruvian Amazon. In Chile, the Mapuche have also been developing small-scale tourist enterprises at the local level, which create for the visitor something of the experience of 'traditional' Mapuche lifestyles.

CONCLUDING REMARKS

A central theme of this chapter has been the contemporary diversity of rural areas in Latin America, based on differences in the ways that producers, large and small, accommodate to the demands of the global economy. We should be clear, however, that there are important differences between the diversity that exists today in rural areas and that which existed in the past. In the period of ISI, rural diversity was based on the uneven and partial nature of the capitalist transformation of the rural economy with peasant farming and traditional estates coexisting with modern commercial farming. In that period, the processes of transformation had a distinctly national character with marked differences between the agrarian structures of different countries that reflected their degree of urbanization and industrialization, and the actions of individual states.

Contemporary rural diversity in Latin America reflects the direct impact of global flows of trade, investment and information that are, in contrast with the past, unmediated by national governments. Furthermore, these global processes envelop rural economies whose capitalist transformation is, in most cases, far from complete. Even small-scale family farmers in Latin America are increasingly part of these processes, whether in terms of increased international migration or through being directly affected by the changing priorities for foodstuffs in the world market. Free trade brings with it more competition for the small-scale, family-based rural producer and demands more of that producer in terms of product standards. The growing urban markets of Latin America threaten to further marginalize the situation of the small-scale producer, creating demands for a wider range of foodstuffs that are met through large-scale national and international distributors and retailers who deal directly with large-scale producers.

Bleak as this situation may appear for the survival of small-scale family agriculture, we have chosen to emphasize the possibilities still open in rural areas for people to adapt to the new situation and create spaces for their own endeavors. Transnational companies and their national allies cannot completely monopolize control over rural production and labor, especially when agricultural yields are critically affected by changes in climatic and ecological conditions. Also, there is no guaranteed market for a country's agricultural products in the face of changing consumer preferences and competition at the world level over major export agricultural commodities. With increased democracy and administrative decentralization, there are now more political opportunities at the local level for small-scale farmers, other small-scale entrepreneurs and farm workers to further their interests. The possibility of alliances with non-farm social groups across the rural–urban divide increases as the countryside begins to serve the short-term and long-term recreational and residential needs of city dwellers, both foreign and national.

National and transnational migrant networks connect up many rural areas of Latin America with labor markets in the large cities of Latin America, Europe and the United States. Remittances and information flow back to rural families and communities, facilitating improvements in services, supplementing incomes and, at times, becoming a basis for new entrepreneurial ventures. Some of the poorer communities can only survive because of remittances. These processes entail that rural spaces are neither discrete nor self-contained. In this context, research needs to address the multiple interfaces that now connect the different types of rural inhabitants with a wide range of external actors. With this comes a clash of cultural perspectives and practices, but also the possibility for negotiation and accommodation.

Contributing to the reconfiguration of the rural is the diminished role of the state in rural development. The state has relinquished many of its tasks to non-state bodies, such as NGOs, private companies and bilateral aid organizations. In rural areas, many NGOs and private consultancies are now actively providing technical inputs into agriculture and facilitating the capacity of better-endowed farmers to supply markets at comparative advantage. Existing policy rhetoric and politico-economic circumstances have opened up new spaces for interest groups to contest these 'realities' – in some cases, successfully resorting to the use of information technologies and global networks to galvanize public opinion and to press their particular claims.

These conditions and dilemmas make it increasingly difficult to design models for promoting specific development trajectories, for identifying alternative scenarios, or for predicting the side effects of mainstream development policies. Indeed these various side-effects and the breakdown of many well-intentioned development efforts have become the central predicaments of international aid, as witnessed by the failure to foresee or effectively deal with ecological disasters, civil strife, severe imbalances in local economies, and the dislocations brought by the now huge transnational migration process. The complicated mixture of intended, unintended, and unanticipated outcomes of development policy compounds this situation.

The research challenge is considerable, but is best met by combining, as Buttel (2001) argues, both political economy and actor-oriented perspectives. We would add to Buttel's review of late twentieth century agrarian political economy by emphasizing the increasing importance of urbanization in shaping and, at times, destroying rural space. The increasing importance of off-farm work among rural inhabitants, as well as their family and work links with urban areas at home and abroad, means that rural areas cannot be analyzed as discrete economic and social spaces. The challenge for both political economy and actor–oriented perspectives is, then, to avoid using a fixed spatial idea of the 'rural' or the 'agrarian,' while still retaining a sense of the difference that the distinctive geographies of rural areas make to outcomes.

REFERENCES

Albó, X. (1996). Poverty, development and indigenous identity. In: D. Iturralde & E. Krotz (Eds), *Indigenous development: poverty, democracy and sustainability* (pp. 33–45). Washington, DC: Inter-American Development Bank.

Altamirano, T. (1991). Pastores Quechuas en el Oeste Norteamericano. *América Indígena*, (Vol. 50(2–3)). Mexico: Instituto Indigenista Interamericano.

Alwyn, J. (2002). Politica Publicas y Pueblos Indígenas: El Caso De La Política de Tierras del Estado Chileno y el Pueblo Mapuche. CLASPO Website Document, University of Texas at Austin. (http://www.utexas.edu/cola/llilas/centers/claspo/networkdocuments.htm).

Appadurai, A. (Ed.) (1986). *The social life of things: Commodities in cultural perspective*. Cambridge: Cambridge University Press.

Appendini, K., Garcia Barrios, R., & de la Tejeda, B. (2003). Seguridad alimentaria y 'calidad' de los alimentos: Una estrategia campesina? *European Review of Latin American and Caribbean Studies, 75*, 65–83.

Arce, A. (2003a). Value contestations in development interventions: Community development and sustainable livelihoods approaches. *Community Development Journal, 38*(3), 199–212.

Arce, A. (2003b). Re-approaching social development: A field of action between social life and policy processes. *Journal of International Development, 15*(7), 845–861.

Ashby, J. (1996). What do we mean by participatory research in agriculture? In: CIAT (Centro Internacional de Agricultura Tropical), *New frontiers in participatory research and gender analysis* (pp. 15–22). Cali, Colombia: Centro Internacional de Agricultura Tropical (CIAT), Publication No. 294.

Braun, B., & Castree, N. (1998). *Remaking reality: Nature at the millennium*. London and New York: Routledge.

Browder, J. O., & Godfrey, B. J. (1997). *Rainforest cities: Urbanization, development, and globalization of the Brazilian Amazon*. New York: Colombia University Press.

Buttel, F. H. (1994). Agricultural change, rural society, and the state in the late twentieth century: Some theoretical observations. In: D. Symes & A. J. Jansen (Eds), *Agricultural restructuring and rural change in Europe* (pp. 13–31). Wageningen: Wageningen Studies in Sociology WSS 37.

Buttel, F. H. (2001). Some reflections on late twentieth century political economy. *Sociologia Ruralis, 41*(2), 165–181.

Castro, C. P. (2004). Plantio de Grãos em Áreas de Fronteira, Ação Antrópica e Desmatamento. Grupo de Trabalho 6, II Encontro da Associação Nacional de Pós-Graduação e Pesquisa em Ambiente e Sociedade.

Cervantes Escoto, F., & Sotero Beltrán, E. (2004). Escala calidad de leche, y costos de enfriamiento y administración en termos lecheros de los Altos de Jalisco. *Téc Pecu Méx., 42*(2), 207–218.

Croll, E., & Parkin, E. (Eds) (1992). *Bush base: Forest farm.* London: Routledge.

Deere, C. D., & León, M. (2000). Neo-liberal agrarian legislation: Gender equality, and indigenous rights: The impact of new social movements. In: A. Zoomers & G. van der Haar (Eds), *Current land policy in Latin America: regulating land tenure under Neoliberalism* (pp. 75–92). Amsterdam: KIT Publishers.

De Janvry, A. (1981). *The agrarian question and reformism in Latin America.* Baltimore and London: Johns Hopkins University Press.

De la Peña, G. (1998). Etnicidad, ciudadania y cambio agrario: apuntes comparativos sobre tres paises latinoamericanos. In: C. Dary (Ed.), *La Construcción de la Nación y la Representación Ciudadana en México, Guatemala, Perú y Bolivia* (pp. 27–86). Guatemala: FLACSO.

Durston, J. (1999). Building community social capital. *CEPAL Review, 69,* 103–118.

Durston, J. (2004). *Capital social campesino y Clientelismo en chile: Análisis de interfaz en una comunidad mapuche.* Working Paper, CLASPO Website, University of Texas at Austin (http://www.utexas.edu/cola/llilas/centers/claspo/durstoncapitalsocial.pdf).

Ellen, R. F., & Katsuyoshi, F. (Eds) (1996). *Redefining nature: Ecology, culture and domestication.* Oxford and Washington, DC: Berg.

Iturralde, D. (2001). Land distribution and the politics of race relations in Latin America. *UNRISD document for racism and public policy conference,* Durban, South Africa, 3–5th September.

Iturralde, D., & Krotz, E. (Eds) (1996). *Indigenous development: Poverty, democracy and sustainability.* Washington, DC: Inter-American Development Bank.

Faostat. (2004). Faostat data on agricultural production, last updated in December 2004. (Faoaostat.fao.org/faostat/collections?subset = agriculture).

Fisher, E. (1997). Beekeepers in the global 'Fair Trade' market: A case from Tabora region, Tanzania. *International Journal of the Sociology of Agriculture and Food, 6,* 109–159.

Flaskerud, G. (2003). Brazil's soybean production and impact. North Dakota State University Extension Service Web Manuscript EB-79. (http://www.ext.nodak.edu/extpubs/plantsci/rowcrops/eb79w.htm).

Garcia-Hernández, L. A. (1998). Skim milk powder imports and the role of CONASUPO. Paper presented to the North American forum workshop on the role of the state in agricultural trade, Stanford University, California, November 20–21st.

Gonzalez, L. (1974). *San Jose de Gracia: Mexican village in transition.* Austin, TX: University of Texas Press.

Gonzalez Bombal, I., & Luzzi, M. (2002). Redes de Trueque: su expansion a los sectores populares en la lucha en contra de la Pobreza. Universidad Nacional General Sarmiento, Argentina.

Goodman, D., & Redclift, M. (1981). *From peasant to proletarian: Capitalist development and agrarian transitions.* Oxford: Blackwell.
Grindle, M. S. (1986). *State and countryside: Development policy and agrarian politics in Latin America.* Baltimore, MA: Johns Hopkins University Press.
Gwynne, R. N., & Kay, C. (Eds) (1999). *Latin America transformed: Globalization and modernity.* London and New York: Arnold and Oxford University Press.
Harriss, J. (Ed.) (1982). *Rural development: Theories of peasant economy and agrarian change.* London: Hutchinson.
Hale, C. R. (2004). Central American cultural politics after the structural break. Paper presented to the Walker symposium on The crisis of the state in Latin America Colby College, 10th April.
Hirschman, A. O. (1977). A generalized linkage approach to development with special reference to Staples. In: M. Nash (Ed.), *Essays on economic development and cultural change in honor of Bert F. Hoselitz* (pp. 67–98). Chicago: University of Chicago Press.
Ingold, T. (1986). *The appropriation of nature: Essays on human ecology and social relations.* Manchester: Manchester University Press.
Kautsky, K. (1988 [1899]). *The agrarian question.* London: Zwan Publications.
Kearney, M. (1996). Introduction: Ethnicity and Class in Latin America. *Latin American Perspectives, 23*(2), 5–16.
Langer, E. D., & Muñoz, E. (Eds) (2003). *Contemporary indigenous movements in Latin America.* Wilmington, DE: SR Books.
Lara-Covarrublas, D., Mora-Flores, J., Martínez-Damián, M. A., García-Delgado, G., Omaña-Silvestre, J., & Gallegos-Sánchez, J. (2003). Competitiveness and comparative advantages of milk production systems in Jalisco state, México. *Agrociencia, 37*, 85–94.
Lipton, M. (1977). *Why poor people stay poor: Urban bias in world development.* Cambridge, MA: Harvard University Press.
Long, N. (2001). *Development Sociology: Actor Perspectives.* London and New York: Routledge.
Long, N., & Roberts, B. (1984). *Miners, peasants and entrepreneurs.* Cambridge, UK: Cambridge University Press.
Long, N., & Roberts, B. (1994). The agrarian structures of Latin America: 1930–1990. In: L. Bethell (Ed.), *The Cambridge history of Latin America* (Vol. VI, pp. 325–390). Cambridge: Cambridge University Press.
Long, N., & van der Ploeg, J. D. (1994). Heterogeneity, actor and structure: towards a reconstitution of the concept of structure. In: D. Booth (Ed.), *New directions in social development* (pp. 62–89). London: Longmans.
Long, N., & Villarreal, M. (1998). Small product, big issues: Value contestations and cultural identities in cross-border commodity networks. *Development and Change, 29*(4), 725–750.
Mahar, D. (1989). *Government policies and deforestation in Brazil's Amazon region.* Washington, DC: The World Bank.
Martine, G. (1988). Changes in agricultural production and rural migration. Manuscript. Brasilia: Instituto de Planejamento Econômico e Social.
McDonald, J. H. (2003). An exploration in the veiling of power: The politics of development in rural West Mexico. *Mexican Studies/Estudios Mexicanos, 19*(1), 161–185.
Meyer, J. (1974). *La Cristiada.* Mexico: Siglo veintiuno editors.
MST Website. www.mstbrazil.org/background.html

Namuncura, D. (1999). *Ralco: Represa o pobreza?* Santiago, Chile: Lom Ediciones.
Ortega, E., Miller, M., Anami, M. H., & Beskow, P. R. (Nd). From energy analysis to public policy: Soybean in Brazil. Laboratorio de Engenharia Ecológica e Informática Aplicada. Brazil: State University of Campinas (www.unicamp.br/fea/ortega/soja/soybean-ortega.pdf).
Portes, A., & Roberts, B. (2005). Free market city: Latin American urbanization in the years of neoliberal adjustment. *Studies in Comparative International Development, 40.*
Potter, J., & Tuiran, R. (2005). Demographic change and development. In: C. Wood & B. Roberts (Eds), *Rethinking Latin American development* (pp. 249–268). University Park, PA: Penn State University Press.
Pottier, J., Bicker, A., & Sillitoe, P. (Eds) (2003). *Negotiating local knowledge: power and identity in development.* London: Pluto Press.
Primavera, H., Covas, H., & De Sanzo, C. (Nd.). Reinventando el mercado: la experiencia de la Red Global de Trueque en Argentina. Document on Redlases Website. www.redlases.org.ar
Rhoades, R. E. (1984). *Breaking new ground: Agricultural anthropology.* Lima: International Potato Center (CIP).
Rodríguez-Gómez, G. (1999). Weaving quality and power: The domestication of global conventions among dairy farmers in Western Mexico. *Urban Anthropology, 28*(3–4), 327–371.
Rohter, L. (2003). Hard realities: Brazil drops resistance to genetically altered crops. *New York Times*, September 28th.
Rohter, L. (2003). Increased soybean production in Brazil threatens Amazon. *New York Times*, September 17th.
Schuurman, F. J. (1997). The decentralization discourse: Post-Fordist paradigm or neo-liberal cul-de-sac? *The European Journal of Development Research, 9*(1), 150–166.
Slater, D. (2004). *Geopolitics and the post-colonial.* Oxford, UK: Blackwell.
Spink, P. (2000). The rights approach to local public management: Experiences from Brazil. *Revista da Administração de Empresas, 40*(3), 45–65.
Stanford, L. (2002). Constructing Quality: The political economy of standards in Mexico's avocado industry. *Agriculture and Human Values, 19*, 293–310.
Tendler, J. (1997). *Good government in the Tropics.* Baltimore, MD: Johns Hopkins University Press.
United Nations Population Division (UNPD). (2004). *World urbanization prospects, 2003 Revision.* New York: United Nations.
Van Cott, D. L. (2000). *The friendly liquidation of the past: The politics of diversity in Latin America.* Pittsburgh, PA: University of Pittsburgh Press.
Varese, S. (1996). The Ethnopolitics of Indian Resistance in Latin America. *Latin American Perspectives, 23*(2), 58–71.
Whatmore, S., & Thorne, L. (1997). Nourishing networks: Alternative geographies of food. In: D. Goodman & M. Watts (Eds), *Globalising food* (pp. 287–304). London and New York: Routledge.

CONQUERING, COMPRADOR, OR COMPETITIVE: THE NATIONAL BOURGEOISIE IN THE DEVELOPING WORLD

Andrew Schrank

ABSTRACT

This paper documents and accounts for the globalization of the so-called national bourgeoisie in the late twentieth century. A substantial and growing body of sociological literature holds that firms and investors from the developing world have been denationalized, neutered, or destroyed by their efforts to penetrate international markets – and that cross-national economic competition is therefore giving way to transnational class conflict over time. By way of contrast, I hold that not only peripheral capitalists but their elected and appointed representatives are compelled to undertake large-scale, fixed investments, exploit their competitive advantages, and challenge foreign firms – and their respective representatives – on their own soil by the very logic of capitalist competition, and that the aforementioned challenges will occur on political as well as economic terrain.

INTRODUCTION

This paper reconsiders the role of the so-called national bourgeoisie in the developing world. By national bourgeoisie, I mean native-born (or naturalized) members of the capitalist class. I ask why otherwise discordant liberal and radical development theories portray the national bourgeoisie as the *primum mobile* of social and economic development (Evans, 1982, pp. S210–S211). What is distinctly national – and, therefore, potentially developmental – about the national bourgeoisie? And I defend a supply-side alternative to the traditional demand-side answer. While the demand-side approach holds that indigenous firms and investors rely upon local product markets and customers, and therefore tend to view the wage bill as a valuable source of aggregate demand as well as a worrisome variable cost (Chibber, 2005, esp. pp. 227–228). The supply-side view holds that indigenous firms and investors rely upon "place-specific" (Harvey, 1982) inputs, investments, and assets including – but not limited to – political influence, and are therefore more "developmentally nutritious" (Helleiner, 1990) than their foreign counterparts regardless of demand-side considerations.

Obviously, the two perspectives part company over the implications of the national bourgeoisie's growing dependence upon foreign customers and allies in the twenty-first century. While the demand-size view treats peripheral capital's overseas ambitions and ventures as threats to "peripheral Fordism" (Lipietz, 1984; see also Robinson, 2001, p. 168), and is therefore rather pessimistic about the prospects for national development in the current era, the supply-side approach holds that joint ventures, strategic alliances, and developing country exports of both manufactured goods and skill-based services reflect not the abdication but the ascendance of the national bourgeoisie (Harris, 1991), and is therefore agnostic – if by no means optimistic – about the future.

Consider, for example, India's storied software suppliers. While Peter Evans bemoans their dependence upon low value added service exports, or "bodyshopping," in his by now classic account of information technology (IT) policy in the newly industrializing countries (Evans, 1995), firms like Wipro, Infosys, and Tata Consultancy Services are not only beginning to compete with the "big five" (Accenture, Cap Gemini Ernst & Young, Deloitte, KPMG, and Pricewaterhouse Coopers) in the market for skill-based software services but are also beginning to develop new products and procedures of their own – and their move up in the global value chain is apparently both a cause and a consequence of rising real wages in their country's IT sector (Mehta, 2004; Engardio & Einhorn, 2005; NASSCOM, no date).

Nor are India's IT firms unique. A significant number of developing country enterprises have overcome their inauspicious origins and surroundings by exploiting – rather than succumbing to – the process of globalization. Brazil's EMBRAER (Empresa Brasiliera Aeronáutica) has transformed itself from a publicly owned military aircraft manufacturer into the world's fourth largest private manufacturer of commercial aircraft by utilizing an innovative combination of production and marketing tactics (Goldstein, 2002; Wheatley, 2004). Argentina's Techint has assumed a dominant position in the international market for seamless steel pipe by pursuing an aggressive approach to mergers and acquisitions (Kock & Guillén, 2001; Etchemendy, 2001; Salmon, 2002b). And Thailand's CP Group (Charoen Pokphand) has maintained revenues in excess of $6 billion per year – as well as the jobs of approximately 80,000 agribusiness, petrochemical, and allied manufacturing workers in more than 20 different countries – by pursuing an equally aggressive approach to consolidation and divestment in the aftermath of the East Asian financial crisis of 1997 and 1998 (Pananond, 2001, pp. 47–48).

The point is most assuredly *not* that developing country firms and investors are *pari passu* propelling their countries and compatriots upward in the international division of labor. After all, the world economy is decidedly dynamic and most – if not necessarily all – peripheral economies are running faster to stay in place (Arrighi, 1990; Kaplinsky, 2001; Wade, 2003a). But the globalization of peripheral capital is nonetheless worthy of reconsideration for at least three reasons. First, it will almost inevitably influence the distribution of roles and places within the admittedly sticky international division of labor and issues of mobility and immobility have traditionally been central to sociological theory. Second, it has already transformed the production profiles of the more developed countries (MDCs) and the resultant patterns of employment and income distribution are not only important in their own right but will also influence the broader politics of the "globalization project" for years to come (McMichael, 2004). And, third, it is likely to affect the interests of – and the opportunities available to – peripheral governments in the World Trade Organization (WTO) and similar international institutions and to thereby influence their long-term evolution and perhaps even their modification or transformation.

In fact, the WTO's disciplines on trade, investment, services, and intellectual property, are arguably *designed* to constrain the growth and dynamism of peripheral capital. Ha-Joon Chang suggests that policymakers in the developed north are using the WTO (and related agreements) to "kick away the ladder" their own forebears used to scale the international hierarchy of nations more than a century ago (Chang, 2002; see also Wade, 2003a, b), and the maturation of the peripheral bourgeoisie is arguably being taken far more seriously by the northern policymakers and trade negotiators who are defending the interests of northern capital from the southern threat than by academic commentators who – by assuming that the material interests of northern and southern capital are compatible with each other now and for the foreseeable future – tend to deny that a threat exists (Radice, 1999; Robinson & Harris, 2000; Robinson, 2001, 2001–2002, 2004; Chimni, 2004; Desai, 2004; Panitch & Gindin, 2004).

I have divided my effort to reconsider the role and reputation of the national bourgeoisie in the developing world into three distinct sections. First, I trace contemporary sociology's apparent indifference to the growing dynamism and belligerence of peripheral capital to the continued influence of the demand-side approach to the national bourgeoisie. By distinguishing the national bourgeoisie from the comprador bourgeoisie at the point of sale rather than the point of production (Vitalis, 1990, p. 305; Embong, 2000, esp. p. 995; Chibber, 2005, p. 230), I argue, contemporary sociologists rule out the possibility of a cosmopolitan-yet-combative capitalist class by assumption and thereby wrongly portray the growing ambition and ability of peripheral capital as the failure rather than the flowering of the national bourgeoisie. Second, I trace the growth of cosmopolitan-yet-combative capitalists in three different sectors and countries – forestry and forest products in Chile, pharmaceuticals in India, and cement in Mexico – to the behavior of *indigenous* entrepreneurs and investors who hold *place-specific* investments and assets and therefore have distinct *national* or *territorial* interests whether they serve domestic or foreign markets (see Polanyi, 1944, p. 152; as well as Harvey, 1982). Thus, the national bourgeoisie's "home country bias" and corresponding behavior derive not – *contra* the existing literature (Lipietz, 1984; Robinson, 1999, 2001, 2002; Chibber, 2005) – from an anachronistic or outdated "Fordist" pact with local workers and consumers (Robinson, 2001, p. 168; see also Lipietz, 1984) but from immobile investments in land, physical capital, and human relationships, which are no less important in the contemporary era of globalization than they were in the admittedly bygone era of "nationalist" development projects. And, finally I discuss my conclusions and their implications for future research. Ultimately, my goal is neither to overestimate the power of firms and states in the periphery nor to underestimate the power of transnational corporations from the core but to acknowledge and account for the persistence of conflict between core and periphery and to thereby underscore the inherently *contested* – if by no means anodyne – nature of the globalization project.

ABDICATION OR ASCENDANCE? THE GLOBALIZATION OF THE NATIONAL BOURGEOISIE

The late twentieth century has frequently and accurately been characterized as an era of "globalization." By eliminating the many physical and institutional barriers which had previously served to slow the crossborder flow of trade, investment, and to an admittedly lesser degree migration, the end of the Cold War, the demise of Third World nationalism, and the rapid growth and diffusion of information, communications, and transportation technologies conspired to create "a single, integrated economy which is worldwide or global in scope" (Kurth, 2002, p. 6284; see also Stallings, 2003; McMichael, 2004).

The data in Table 1 confirm the validity of the conventional wisdom by underscoring the depth and pace of both the procedural and substantive integration of the international economy in recent years. The data speak for themselves: Flows of trade and investment are accelerating. Tariffs are falling. And regional and multilateral trade and market harmonization agreements are growing in size as well as in number.

Both the procedural changes and their substantive impacts have been particularly pronounced in the developing world. For example, the ratio of trade to GDP has grown by a mere 15 percent in the developed countries – which already featured relatively open product markets at the beginning of the decade – and by almost 50 percent in developing countries. And the

Table 1. Indicators of Globalization.

Indicator	1990	2000
Trade in goods as a percentage of world product	32.4	40
Trade in goods as a percentage of developed country product	32	37.1
Trade in goods as a percentage of developing country product	34.6	51.6
Gross direct foreign investment as percentage of world product	2.7	8.8
Average developed country tariff (%)	7.9	4
Average developing country tariff (%)	23.2	11.3
Number of regional trade agreements	31	156
Number of World Trade Organization (WTO) members	0	148

Sources: World Bank (2002), Table 6.1; World Bank, unpublished data on average tariffs (dates may not correspond to exact year); WTO (www.wto.org); and Global Policy Forum (http://www.globalpolicy.org/globaliz/charts/rta.htm).

developing country share of inward foreign direct investment (FDI) has grown as well, for transnational corporations have used the processes of trade liberalization and deregulation to integrate their global production and distribution networks to a heretofore unprecedented degree. "In turn," writes Diana Tussie, "big firms from developing countries have seized the moment and are also adopting an accelerated strategy of internationalization." (Tussie, 1998, p. 187; see also Martin, 1997). Tussie invokes a number of Latin American examples including Mexico's Cemex (Cementos Mexicanos), Argentina's YPF (Yacimientos Petroliferos Fiscales), and Chile's Luksic (1998, p. 187; see also Garrido & Peres, 1998; Financial Times, 1998).[1] They are by no means unique, however, for a host of Asian, African, and Eastern European firms have rationalized their operations, upgraded their human and physical capital, and moved into international markets as well, and Leslie Sklair and Peter Robbins have therefore gone so far as to argue that "globalizing corporations are emerging all over the world" (Sklair & Robbins, 2002, p. 97).

The consequences are astounding. First, the worldwide distribution of economic activity has shifted markedly over the course of the last decade. The developing country share of world manufacturing value added has grown from 16.7 to 24.1 percent (United Nations Industrial Development Organization (UNIDO), 2004, p. 184). The nominal value of developing country manufactured exports has grown by a factor of three. And the developing country share of world-manufactured exports has therefore grown from 16.6 to 26.8 percent (UNIDO, 2004, p. 186). While the exports in question are frequently – if by no means invariably – marketed by foreign firms under their own brand names, they are usually produced by local firms and managers in their own factories, and they invariably and necessarily meet international standards for price and quality (see Keesing & Lall, 1992, esp. pp. 178–179). Nor are the developing country gains limited to low technology sectors. On the contrary, they have been higher in high-technology goods like pharmaceuticals, office machinery, and transportation and telecommunications equipment than in middle and low-technology commodities like iron and steel, petrochemicals, and textiles, clothing, and footwear (UNIDO, 2004, p. 188; see also Amsden, 2003, p. 34; Lall, 2004, pp. 193–195). And they threaten to obscure unprecedented – albeit all but unmeasurable – growth in a variety of skill-based service exports (see, e.g., Mehta, 2004; Engardio & Einhorn, 2005).

Second, the higher income countries have acted to defend their markets and interests from the developing country threat. The recently rescinded United States steel tariffs are by far the best known but by no means the only example of northern commercial hypocrisy (Watson, 2003; Lipietz, 2003). The European Union (EU) has imposed a surcharge on Brazilian iron exports, challenged South Korean shipbuilders before the WTO, and retained a decidedly protectionist approach to agriculture for well over a decade (see, e.g., Gazeta Mercantil, 2001; Ward, 2003; Song, 2004). And the more developed countries as a whole have pioneered the use of so-called antidumping measures to "safeguard" their vulnerable domestic industries from foreign competition (Finger, Ng, & Wangchuk, 2001).

And, finally, the developing countries have responded in kind. They have not only used the WTO to resist northern protectionism (e.g., the steel, iron, and shipbuilding cases) but have simultaneously taken antidumping measures of their own. In fact, the developing countries are by now the most frequent users of antidumping initiatives (Finger et al., 2001, p. 6) and have also managed to "create a balance of power," according to some observers, in the WTO (Christian Science Monitor, 2004; McLaughlin, 2004). Therefore, the so-called north–south conflict is alive and well – if perhaps being waged on fresh terrain with new weapons – in the twenty-first century.

The depth of north–south discord is not entirely obvious, however, for the contemporary sociological literature tends to subordinate the reality of international conflict and competition to a myth of transnational consensus and cooperation. A *tour d'horizon* of the recent literature would therefore reveal extensive disquisitions on the allegedly "transnational" state epitomized *by* the multilateral institutions and very little evidence of north–south conflict *at* the multilateral institutions (see, e.g., Robinson & Harris, 2000; Robinson, 2001; Chimni, 2004; as well as McMichael, 2001 for an important exception). Take for example, William Robinson's myriad contributions to the globalization debate. While he all but derides hypothetical executives who "strategize at the annual Davos meeting of the World Economic Forum over what proposals to bring to the WTO" (Robinson, 2001, p. 182), Robinson ignores the very possibility of irresolvable differences at the WTO and thereby assumes what needs to be proven: that the national bourgeoisie has indeed been absorbed into a "transnational capitalist class."

In fact, the problem of bourgeois extrusion is particularly acute among radical sociologists like Robinson. While Marx and Engels portrayed trade in manufactures as the death knell of feudalism and the dawn of bourgeois rule (see Marx, 1978 [1850]; Marx & Engels, 1888 [1848]), and therefore welcomed the globalization of the industrial capitalist class in nineteenth century Europe, Robinson treats globalization as the death knell not of the precapitalist elite but of the national bourgeoisie itself, and therefore worries (see Robinson, 1998, 1999, 2001, 2001–2002, 2002). By pursuing foreign markets and courting foreign allies, he argues, developing country firms and investors abandon not only their "reciprocal obligations to labor" (Robinson, 2002, p. 1063) but their "national affiliations" (Robinson, 1998, p. 581) more generally – and thereby "contribute to the demise of the diverse alliances between subordinate classes and national ruling classes that characterized the old national development processes and pave the way for the new class relations of global capitalism" (Robinson, 2002, p. 1064).[2]

Nor is Robinson alone. A substantial and growing body of literature treats the transcendence of the domestic market as a threat to the role and identity of the national bourgeoisie in the developing world. For example, Alain Lipietz holds that protected manufacturers forged "Fordist" pacts with their respective popular sectors in countries like Brazil, Mexico, and South Korea in the late 1970s (Lipietz, 1984). Roger Burbach worries that "these elites now view their interests in an international context and are increasingly opposed to national, protectionist policies" (Burbach, 1997, p. 16). And David Moore therefore bemoans the passing of "Keynesian compromises" designed "to bring states, their subsidised national bourgeoisies, and civil societies to developmental heights" (Moore, 2004, p. 93; see also Dietz, 1989; Radice, 1999; Sklair, 2000; Thomas, 2000; Desai, 2004).

Indeed, Hugo Radice holds "exporting, outward investment, technology imports, or whatever" responsible for the emergence of "new comprador bourgeoisies" in the developing world (Radice, 1999, p. 18), and thereby provokes an interesting question: Are entrepreneurs and investors who defend their local markets more "national" (or nationalist) than entrepreneurs and investors who hope to penetrate foreign ones? The answer is in part definitional, for twentieth century Marxists not only described but *defined* the "national bourgeoisie" as "the segment of local capitalists who are oriented to the domestic market, seek autonomy from metropolitan control, and ally with the state around industrialization" (Chibber, 2005, p. 230), and their descendants therefore exclude the more cosmopolitan representatives of the peripheral private sector from the term's compass.

The issue is not entirely semantic, however, for not only Marxist but non-Marxist scholars frequently posit an *objective* relationship between market orientation and capitalist behavior. While firms and investors who pursue local markets treat wages as a desirable source of aggregate demand as well as an undesirable variable cost, and are therefore amenable to Fordist wage bargains, their more cosmopolitan counterparts treat abor costs as nothing more than a source of competitive advantage, and are therefore openly hostile to working class demands for improved wages and working conditions. Therefore, the national bourgeoisie's absorption into the allegedly transnational capitalist class (TCC) is expected to contribute to the "downward leveling" of wages, working conditions, and ultimately living standards at home and abroad (Robinson, 2001, p. 170; see also, e.g., Robinson, 2002, p. 1064; Sklair & Robbins, 2002, p. 98; Harris, 2005, p. 9).

The downward leveling thesis is at best controversial, however, and the posited causal mechanism is almost certainly incorrect (see, e.g., Amsden, 2003). After all, the most serious threats to labor and the environment derive not from TNCs and internationally competitive firms but from smaller producers who target local markets (see, e.g., Shadlen, 2004, pp. 23–25). Therefore, Judith Tendler describes "a kind of unspoken deal between politicians and their constituents – myriad small firm owners, many in the informal sector. If you vote for me, according to this exchange, I won't collect taxes from you; I won't make you comply with other tax, environmental, or labor regulations; and I will keep the police and inspectors from harassing you" (Tendler, 2002, p. 2). By way of contrast, larger, more competitive firms not only have the wherewithal – if not always the willingness – to pay taxes and comply with regulations but frequently view adherence to internationally recognized labor and environmental standards as the price to be paid for labor peace, public and investor relations, or market access more generally.[3]

In fact, the best historical evidence suggests that "the rise of mass production does not require, but rather issues in, mass consumption – that the latter has depended upon the former, even though, in some important ways, facilitating it" (Brenner & Glick, 1991, p. 66; as well as Brenner, 1999). By undertaking large-scale fixed investments, and thereby raising their rates of productivity to historically unprecedented levels, the largest and most dynamic northern firms not only rendered themselves vulnerable to working class – and at times government – demands for improved wages and working conditions but simultaneously generated the resources necessary to accede to the demands in question and thereby facilitated the eventual growth of mass consumption. The principal problem in developing countries is therefore not an abundance but a paucity of domestically owned, large-scale, internationally competitive firms and suppliers – and the members of the allegedly transnational capitalist class who are currently portrayed as obstacles to the realization of the periphery's goals and aspirations are therefore, in all likelihood, their last, best hope.

ACTING GLOBALLY, THINKING LOCALLY: THE NATIONAL UNDERPINNINGS OF INTERNATIONAL COMPETITION

Nobody denies that the largest and most dynamic peripheral enterprises are forming strategic alliances, undertaking foreign direct investments, and entering world markets. Observers part company, however, over the implications. A number of sociologists hold that the national bourgeoisie has been denationalized, neutered, or absorbed into a transnational capitalist class – and that cross-national economic competition is therefore giving way to transnational class conflict over time (Sklair & Robbins, 2002; Robinson, 2002). Indeed, William Robinson has not only eulogized the national bourgeoisie but anticipated the eventual "dissolution of the historic affinities between capital accumulation, states conceived of in the Weberian sense as territorially based institutions, and social classes and groups" (Robinson, 1998, p. 580; see also Burbach & Robinson, 1999). By way of contrast, I hold that not only peripheral capitalists but their elected and appointed representatives are *compelled* to undertake large-scale, fixed investments, exploit their competitive advantages, and challenge foreign firms – and *their* respective representatives – by the very logic of capitalist competition (see, e.g., Brenner & Glick, 1991, p. 106) and that the aforementioned challenges will occur on political as well as economic terrain. "In a way," writes Ellen Meiksins Wood, "the whole point of 'globalization' is that competition is not just – or even mainly – between individual firms but between whole national economies. And as a consequence, the nation-state has acquired new functions as an instrument of competition" (Wood, 1998, p. 13; see also Brenner, 1999). By exploring public and private sector responses to globalization in three different countries and sectors – forestry and forest products in Chile, pharmaceuticals in India, and cement in Mexico – I hope to validate Wood's assertion, rehabilitate the national bourgeoisie, and bring the globalization project's myriad internal contradictions to the forefront of contemporary sociological analysis.

Forestry and Forest Products in Chile: From Denationalization to Renationalization

The Chilean forestry and forest products industry is a behemoth. The country plays host to more than 2 million hectares of radiata pine and eucalyptus plantations, exports almost $3 billion worth of forest products per year, and is expected to double the value of exports by the end of the decade (McLean, 2003). Furthermore, the industry is dominated by local rather than foreign firms. According to Simon Adamson, New Zealand's trade commissioner for South America, Chile's principal forestry concerns "are all large, local, and long term" (Adamson quoted in McLean, 2003). They are linked backward into wood planting, harvesting, and processing technology; forward into the production of wood chips, pulp, paper, plywood, fiberboard, and furniture; and laterally into transportation and logistics. While the modern forestry and forest products industries have *always* relied upon mass production (Cronon, 1991, Chapter 4), Chilean firms like Compania Manufacturera de Papeles y Cartones (CMPC) and Celulosa Arauco are by all accounts particularly sophisticated, and raw logs therefore constitute no more than 1 percent of the value of their exports (McLean, 2003; see also Gwynne, 1996; Financial Times, 1997; Wood Based Panels International, 1998; Timber and Wood Products, 1998a–c on Arauco and CMPC).

The Chilean forestry and forest products industry rests on a combination of natural or geographic advantages, low labor costs, and human and organizational ingenuity. After all, Chile's climate ensures a short growing cycle. The country's narrow shape means that internal transport costs are relatively low. The rural labor force is largely underemployed. And the Chilean state has been actively sponsoring the industry's development for almost a century (Clapp, 1995; Gwynne, 1996; Ramos, 1998; Timber and Wood Products, 1998a; Kurtz, 2001).

Private foresters first planted non-native pine and eucalyptus in Chile in the late nineteenth century. They used pine in construction and paper making and eucalyptus to fortify mine shafts. And they convincingly demonstrated the untapped potential of the country's forest products sector (Clapp, 1995; Timber and Wood Products, 1998a).

By the early 1930s, therefore, the Chilean government had not only adopted a variety of targeted promotional measures – including tariffs on imported timber and tax holidays on private plantations – but had also invested capital drawn from the public pension fund in a series of publicly owned plantations (see Clapp, 1995, pp. 278–279). While import-substituting industrialization engendered the overvaluation of the peso, the imposition of tariffs on key inputs, and the taxation of raw log exports, and thereby circumscribed the growth of exports in the middle of the twentieth century, it simultaneously encouraged the development of new plantations and ancillary industries like sawmills, pulp plants, and paper mills, and thereby fostered the overall growth of the sector. Nevertheless, Salvador Allende's Popular Unity regime "made the forest industry the most socialized sector of the economy" (Clapp, 1995, p. 280) in the early 1970s and his downfall therefore "left an industry almost entirely in state hands" (Clapp, 1995, p. 280).

The military rulers who deposed Allende hoped to accelerate the industry's development by privatizing public holdings, legalizing the export of raw logs, and resuscitating the aforementioned tax holidays and subsidies for new plantations. By 1980, therefore, the pace of reforestation had accelerated; the percentage of reforestation performed by the state had fallen from a 1973 high of 91 percent to almost zero; the value of wood and cellulose exports had grown by a factor of four; and the industry's principal patrons had for the most part deterred foreign takeovers (see Clapp, 1995, p. 283; Kurtz, 2001, p. 5).

The forestry sector's more ambitious firms found themselves in need of foreign partners in the mid-1980s, however, for the arrival of the debt crisis had all but foreclosed traditional sources of finance and placed a premium on joint ventures and FDI. Therefore, Arauco sold a 33 percent stake to New Zealand firm Carter Holt Harvey (CHH) in 1987 and "benefited from the joint venture due to the capital inputs and international marketing outlets provided" (Gwynne, 1996, pp. 349–350). And CMPC formed a smaller joint venture with a family owned North American firm named Simpson Paper and achieved similar results (Gwynne, 1996, p. 352; see also Clapp, 1995, p. 288).

The joint ventures would not lead to the denationalization of the Chilean forestry sector, however, for both CMPC and Arauco would buy out their foreign partners in the late 1990s (see Timber and Wood Products, 1998b, c; Wood Based Panels International, 1998; *New Zealand Forest Industries*, 2002). CMPC's purchase of Simpson's plantation and processing interests followed the North American firm's decision to divest from pulp and paper and occurred on cordial terms (Mapes, 1997). However, Arauco's purchase of CHH's Chilean interests followed a power grab by the managers of International Paper, who had assumed control of the New Zealand firm in 1995, and represented an unambiguous – as well as an unexpected – victory for Chilean capital (see Gwynne, 1996; Financial Times, 1997; McNabb, 1997, 1999 for details). Arauco's Chilean owners, the Angelini group, paid CHH approximately 20 percent more than the book value for their assets and have nonetheless continued to expand on the basis of their low cost production methods (Torres, 1999). They recently opened a $1.2 billion pulp mill and expect to open several more in the next few years (*New Zealand Forest Industries*, 2002).

Nor is Arauco alone, for CMPC has expanded as well. They purchased assets from Royal Dutch Shell as well as Simpson (Timber and Wood Products, 1998b), and the two companies therefore control 60 percent of their country's commercial tree plantations, additional forest land in Argentina, and a host of upstream and downstream capacity. Anacleto Angelini, Arauco's nonagenarian director, unabashedly describes his former partners, CHH and International Paper, as rivals (Gwynne, 1996, p. 351), and the forestry sectors in both New Zealand and North America angrily decry the growing threat from Chile (McLean, 2003; Peart, 2004; Paul, 2004).

Nevertheless, Chilean foresters confront at least two serious threats of their own: antidumping measures (and related trade barriers) in northern markets (Gonzalez, 1997); and competition from new, lower cost producers in the south (Clapp, 1995, p. 293). The largest Chilean firms have the ear of their government (McLean, 2003), however, and together they have designed a more or less successful two-track response. On the one hand, they have used a series of bilateral and regional trade agreements – as well as the WTO's dispute settlement procedures – to guarantee ongoing market access (Fidler, 1997; Latin America Weekly Report, 2000; Baxter, 2001; Peart, 2004).[4] On the other hand, they have increased productivity and moved into higher value added lines and products (Timber and Wood Products, 1998b; Wood Based Panels International, 1998; McLean, 2003).

In other words, the Chilean state has moved from the direct production and protection of forest products – akin to the roles of *demiurge* and *midwife* described by Peter Evans (Evans, 1995, Chapter 4) – to the indirect support of forestry via "big-business diplomacy" (Amsden, 1989, p. 16) and the provision of public goods. Chilean universities graduate more than 300 foresters every year and human resources are therefore abundant (McLean, 2003). The Fundación Chile, a publicly sponsored technology incubator, is undertaking research and development on information and biotechnology for the forestry sector (Woods, 2002; UNFAO, 2003). And private firms are collaborating with the foundation as well as undertaking R&D efforts of their own (see Timber and Wood Products, 1998b; Untied Nations Food and Agriculture Organization (UNFAO), 2003). The Chileans already design, develop, and distribute world-class forest management software (Press, 1993; Baeza-Yates et al., 1995; UNFAO, 2003), and at least one former Monsanto official believes that they "will be the first to market a transgenic tree" as well (Duncan quoted in Woods, 2002). "They have the tightest focus of anyone and, just as important, they have a government relationship and infrastructure that will be most conducive to supporting a commercial deployment of such a tree" (Duncan quoted in Woods, 2002). A number of experts therefore argue that Chilean public officials and their private interlocutors have transformed a more or less typical extractive industry into a high technology, "natural resource-based production cluster" (Ramos, 1998) with low costs and high – if admittedly uncertain – potential.

Of course, the Chilean forestry industry is not idyllic. While timber is for the most part "cultivated rather than extracted" and forest products are "industrially processed before they leave the country" (Schurman, 2001, p. 9), they rest on a historical foundation of not-so-primitive accumulation. Native peoples have been dispossessed of their land and incorporated into a low-wage, low-skill, and increasingly redundant plantation labor force (Mulligan, 2001; Rohter, 2004). Native forests have been clear-cut by rapacious loggers and timber companies (Clapp, 2001). And the native environment has been despoiled by industrial tree farms (Brown, 2000). The repression, exploitation, and desecration have been carried out by native firms, however, and therefore reflect the ascendance rather than the abdication of the national bourgeoisie.

Pharmaceuticals in India: From Copycats to Innovators

The Indian pharmaceutical industry plays host to approximately 10,000 firms, employs a substantial number of the 12,000 chemistry PhDs who graduate from Indian universities every year, and is the fifth largest in the world by volume (Kripalani, 2005; Pfeifer, 2004; Rai, 2005). According to Saradindu Bhaduri and Amit Ray, the Indian government's active efforts to promote indigenous technological development in the immediate aftermath of independence not only "allowed India to achieve self-reliance in drugs" but also set the stage for a "significant export drive in the last two decades" (Bhaduri & Ray, 2004, p. 88; Grace, 2004, p. 17). Indian firms like Dr Reddy's, Cipla, Nicholas Piramal, and Ranbaxy are not yet household names outside of the subcontinent but are nonetheless gaining market share (Kripalani, 2005; Sridharan, 2005; Wilson, 2005). And Sankar Krishnan, a consultant for McKinsey in Bombay, therefore expects the country's pharmaceutical exports to "more than quadruple to $6.5 billion by 2010" (Tanzer, 2001).

Nevertheless, the industry's image and prospects have recently been transformed by the Indian government's efforts to bring the country's 1970 Patent Law into compliance with the WTO's agreement on trade-related aspects of intellectual property rights (or TRIPS). While the process patents recognized by the original legislation allowed different inventors to patent "the same product as long as it was created by a novel process," and therefore allowed "copycat" drug makers like Cipla and Ranbaxy to "drive the annual price of antiretroviral treatment down from $15,000 per patient a decade ago to about $200 now" (McNeil, 2005; Shadlen, 2005a), the product patents recognized by the WTO-compliant amended legislation are likely to disable the country's copycats, breathe new life into western drug monopolies, and cripple the country's campaigns against HIV/AIDS and other diseases. Thus, Yusuf Hamied, the chairman of Cipla, declared that the passage of the legislation would ensure "a predictable, long term tragedy for the country" (Rai, 2005).

Neither Hamied nor his compatriots are ready to surrender, however, and the larger, more dynamic Indian exporters are therefore responding to the new legislation by forming joint ventures, pursuing R&D, and mining their country's enormous and growing human resource base for new competitive advantages (Kripalani, 2005; Sridharan, 2005; Wilson, 2005). While the largest Indian drug companies invest no more than 8 percent of their sales revenue in R&D, their western rivals invest about 15 percent (Grace, 2004). However, the Indian firms face a decidedly lower cost structure and therefore expect to come up with their own intellectual property (IP) in the medium-term future. According to Cheri Grace, US bench scientists are paid anywhere from five to eight times more than their Indian counterparts. US laboratory leaders are paid about three times more than their Indian counterparts. US clinical trials cost about ten times more than their Indian counterparts. And US manufacturing facilities cost approximately four times more than their Indian counterparts (Grace, 2004, p. 18; see also Tanzer, 2001; Wilson, 2005). Consequently, the cost of developing a new drug "from scratch" in India is "as low as $100 million" or one-tenth the cost in the US (Kripalani, 2005).

The leading Indian firms are therefore *increasing* their R&D expenditures in an effort to develop "blockbuster" drugs of their own. For example, Ranbaxy plans to elevate R&D spending to 10 percent of sales by 2007 and thereby expects to quintuple revenues to $5 billion – almost half from IP – by 2012 (Pfeiffer, 2004; Sahad, 2005). Nor is Ranbaxy alone. Half of the leading Indian drug companies increased their R&D spending between 2002 and 2003 and the average level of R&D spending grew by almost one-third in percentage terms (Grace, 2004, p. 23, 38). "The increased R&D activity is due in part to IP changes and the strategic reorientation they induce, in part to the increasing technological capacity of the top Indian firms, and in part to other domestic policies" including not only the impending amendments to the Patent Law but a series of tax holidays and pricing policies designed to "improve the rewards for R&D" (Grace, 2004, p. 38).

The results are already apparent. While all Indian pharmaceutical firms ignored the patenting process under the old IP regime, they filed 855 patent applications in anticipation of the onset of the new regime in the 2003–2004 fiscal year (Kripalani, 2005). Ranbaxy therefore expects to have four investigational new drug applications in the R&D pipeline by 2007 (Sahad, 2005). Nicholas Piramal expects to have at least five new-patented drugs ready for clinical trials by 2008 (Kripalani, 2005). And Dr Reddy's already owns seven US patents and has eight more chemical compounds ready for clinical trials (Pilling, 1999; Wilson, 2005).

What are the implications of their efforts? Ironically, India's effort to comply with the TRIPS agreement may well redound to the detriment of northern pharmaceutical producers as well as southern pharmaceutical consumers. "If an Indian company makes a drug whose development costs are under $50 million, compared with a billion-dollar-plus development cost in the West," suggests Nicholas Piramal's director of strategic alliances and communications, "we will be able to change the paradigm of drug discovery" (Swati Piramal quoted in Rai, 2005).

Nevertheless, the principal Indian firms would appear to need at least 5 more years to build a blockbuster drug from scratch (Sridharan, 2005) and in the meantime they are pursuing a wide variety of complementary profit-making activities. For example, Ranbaxy and Cipla are pursuing new drug delivery research (Grace, 2004; Sahad, 2005; Sridharan, 2005). Dr Reddy's is outlicensing chemical compounds to western firms (Pilling, 1999). Nicholas Piramal is undertaking contract research as well as contract manufacturing (Sridharan, 2005). And Indian firms as a whole are vying for the unprecedented opportunity created by the near-simultaneous expiration of patents on $60 billion worth of blockbuster drugs over the course of the next 2 years – and will almost certainly exploit their unparalleled cost advantage by continuing to serve the low-margin/high-volume "markets that have been their bread-and-butter for several decades" (Grace, 2004, p. 8).

Ultimately, however, India's pharmaceutical firms have to go beyond their traditional market segments and compete with the big boys head-to-head if they are to survive. They have no choice in the matter. "If companies don't change," says Hamied, "they'll get wiped out" (Hamied quoted in Sridharan, 2005). And Hamied is certainly correct. But he could be speaking of *any* company in *any* industry in *any* country and, in so doing, explaining why they will continue to defend their interests and investments in the face of foreign competition. India's pharmaceutical firms are undergoing a *particular* transformation but they are no more immune from the *general* laws of capitalist competition than Chile's forestry firms or, as (we shall soon see) Mexican cement makers, and they will therefore do their level best to turn necessities – like compliance with the WTO's admittedly draconian IP provisions – into virtues for the foreseeable future.

Cement in Mexico: Branding and Trading a Nontradable Bulk Commodity

Cementos Mexicanos has apparently done the impossible. While cement is easy to produce, it is difficult to transport, all but interchangeable, and therefore almost impossible to "brand," Cemex has transformed cement into an internationally traded, branded product and has thereby transformed itself into the third largest – and by all accounts the most profitable – player in the international industry (Piggott, 2001). In fact, Cemex currently employs 26,000 people, operates in more than 30 different countries on five different continents, and earns revenues of about $8 billion a year (Latin America Weekly Report, 2003; Authers, 2004; Economist, 2004; Moody, 2004).

Cemex's rise is particularly surprising against the backdrop of the North American Free Trade Agreement. After all, the company entered the late twentieth century as an inefficient, diversified, family-owned conglomerate with interests in mines, chemicals, and hotels in addition to cement and ready-mix concrete. By opening the country's market to foreign competition, the Institutional Revolutionary Party (Partido Revolucionario Institucional) placed Mexico's industrial groups at risk. And many sold out or surrendered to their foreign rivals (Arroyo, 2003, p. 21).

Nevertheless, Lorenzo Zambrano, the US-educated chairman of Cemex, pursued a different strategy. First, he sold the company's ancillary operations and concentrated his efforts on the production and distribution of cement and ready-mix concrete (Gascoigne, 1995; Moody, 2004). Second, he used modern information and communications technology to guarantee customers same-day delivery within a half an hour of schedule – improving on the industry average of 3 h and achieving an unprecedented 98 percent rate of reliability in the process (LaFranchi, 1996; Walker, 2001; Barwise & Meehan, 2004; Ruelas-Gossi & Sull, 2004). And, finally, he expanded into world markets via direct investment as well as exports – and thereby lowered the cost of borrowing, raised market access, and mitigated the risk engendered by the cyclical nature of cement demand.

Zambrano believes that Cemex is selling "timeliness and quality" rather than cement per se (Zambrano quoted in Romero, 2000), and he and his managers have therefore modeled their operation not on other manufacturing enterprises but on service providers like Federal Express and police dispatch units. They own a fleet of specialized ships and an army of trucks (Hall, 1994). They communicate with their drivers through a proprietary satellite network and the Global Positioning System. They take pride in their ability to reach "places that lack highly developed road systems, solid telephone networks, and legions of well-educated workers – where surviving in the construction business is like keeping one's head above water in a raging sea" (Katel, 1997, p. 98; see also Dombey, 1996). And they command a substantial price premium on every delivery (Latin America Weekly Report, 2003; Authers, 2004; Moody, 2004). In fact, Cemex is not only the most efficient cement corporation in the world (LaFranchi, 1996) but is also an information technology powerhouse, and Zambrano has recently transformed his IT division into a freestanding, multimillion dollar technology consultancy, Neoris, that targets Fortune 500 companies from offices in Europe, the US, and Latin America (Piggott, 2001).

Nevertheless, Zambrano's achievements are hard won. Cemex originally paid an enormous premium for Mexico's subpar credit ratings and the cost of borrowing actually threatened to impede the company's growth in the late 1980s. By acquiring Spain's two largest cement producers in 1992, however, Zambrano began to generate a hard currency cash flow, reassure his creditors, and gain access to credit on more desirable terms (Gascoigne, 1995; Colitt, 2000; Salmon, 2002a). In fact, the move into world markets served as an alternative – rather than a prelude – to redomiciling the company (O'Brien, 2003). Therefore, Zambrano continued to expand by purchasing a number of different firms and plants in Central and South America and Southeast Asia in the mid to late 1990s. He integrated every newly acquired enterprise into Cemex's global logistics system; upgraded manufacturing capacity; and thereby transformed his company into the largest trader and fourth largest producer of cement in the world (LaFranchi, 1996).

Zambrano had difficulty penetrating the valuable US market, however, for the Department of Commerce had imposed prohibitively high antidumping duties on Mexican cement in 1990 and North American manufacturers had been campaigning against their repeal ever since (Johns, 1990; Economist, 1995). The country's second-largest producer, Southdown, launched a massive public relations campaign against Mexican "dumping" at the dawn of the NAFTA era and the Clinton Administration responded by actually *increasing* the duties on Mexican cement—in spite of GATT and subsequently WTO findings in favor of Mexico—in 1996 (Dunne, 1995; Houston Chronicle, 1996, 1997; Beachy, 1996). While Zambrano answered the North American challenge by serving the US market from his Spanish and Venezuelan plants in the mid- to late 1990s (Gascoigne, 1995), he ultimately *acquired Southdown outright* for $2.6 billion in 2000 – and thereby transformed Cemex into the largest producer in the US market, silenced his loudest critic, and undermined the logical foundations of the Department of Commerce's case all at once. The director of Cemex's US operations therefore notes that his firm has more invested in the US market than any other company and says "it's a little bit ridiculous for anybody to think that Cemex would do anything to harm this market" (Perez quoted in Moreno, 2005).

Nor is the US atypical. Cemex has invested enormous sums in a host of countries including Egypt, Thailand, and most recently England, for Zambrano acquired London-based RMC, the world's largest ready-mix concrete producer, for $4.1 billion in 2005. Cemex hopes to use RMC's unparalleled production capacity to consolidate control over existing markets in Western Europe and North America and to penetrate new markets in places like Eastern Europe as well (see, e.g., Economist, 2004). By diversifying into multiple markets in different world regions, according to Zambrano, Cemex mitigates the risk imposed by the cyclical nature of the construction industry (Dombey, 1996; Katel, 1997). Whereas the old Cemex diversified into multiple sectors in one country, the new Cemex diversifies into multiple countries in one sector. The underlying logic is the same but the economic consequences are radically different, for Cemex is now the world's most efficient producer and the company therefore generates an enormous volume of hard currency and investment capital every year. In fact, the company's cash flow is "devastatingly huge" in the words of one market analyst. "Cemex is printing money" (Uglow quoted in Fritsch, 2002).

A vastly disproportionate share of the company's profit, however, derives from domestic operations (Barham, 2004). According to Elizabeth Malkin, the Mexican market accounts for one-third of Cemex's sales but two-third of the company's operating income (Malkin, 2004; Authers, 2004). While US manufacturers attribute the differential to dumping (i.e., selling cement below the cost of production) in the US market, it is in all likelihood a reflection of the differences between developed and developing country market structures and Mexico's deliberately flaccid antitrust regime. On the one hand, US construction firms are larger than their Mexican counterparts and are therefore able to bid down the cost of cement (Fritsch, 2002; Silver,

2004). Consequently, Cemex's highest profit rates are neither in the US nor in Mexico but in countries like Colombia and Venezuela (Authers, 2004). On the other hand, the Mexican market is almost entirely closed to imports. Cemex controls almost two-thirds of the domestic market. And Mexican consumers – who pay double what US consumers pay – are therefore "paying an export subsidy on each and every ton of cement exported from Mexico" (Mastel, 1999, p. 9; see also Aguilar & De Jong, 2004).

The subsidy is not entirely accidental, however, for the Mexican government has deliberately used antitrust and competition policy to defend native industry in the face of foreign competition, and Cemex is particularly well connected to the government. In fact, the company's directors have always believed that "you can't compete internationally if you don't have a dominant position in domestic markets" (Prieto quoted in Hall, 1994) and Zambrano's willingness to stay rooted in Monterrey rather than to redomicile himself in pursuit of better credit ratings is in all likelihood a product of continued reliance upon political support – not only in the realm of foreign affairs but in antitrust policy as well. Zambrano accompanied Mexico's President Vicente Fox on his trip to the White House in 2001 and continues to seek (and receive) government support whenever necessary. The tools have changed from tariffs, quotas, and export credits to antitrust (non) enforcement and big business diplomacy but the ties between the public and private sectors are no less important now than in the bygone era of explicit industrial policy.

In fact, the cross-subsidization of exports with rents from the domestic market is a time-honored development strategy. By conditioning access to the lucrative domestic market on exports to more perilous foreign markets, notes Alice Amsden (see Amsden, 1989, 2001), late developers in the Global South have tried to steal a march on their northern rivals. While the late developer's traditional weapons of tariffs and subsidies have for the most part been outlawed by the WTO and related agreements, Mexico's experience suggests that new weapons are available. And insofar as they render the domestic market a means to an end – i.e., international competition – rather than an end in itself, they strengthen rather than enervate the national bourgeoisie.

DISCUSSION

The firms I have examined are national champions. They control the commanding heights of their respective national economies. They are owned and operated by leading members of their respective capitalist classes. And they are growing and prospering in spite of the withdrawal or transformation of their respective government subsidies. They are not at all typical, however, for most LDC firms are neither large enough nor sophisticated enough to conquer world markets and are therefore condemned to compete for table scraps in an increasingly cutthroat international economy. While radical social scientists tend to portray large, competitive peripheral firms as the problem, and at the very least imply that their more parochial neighbors offer a solution, they overlook the manifold costs of parochialism – including labor repression, environmental degradation, and political corruption – and simultaneously underestimate the potential benefits of competition.

In fact, the contemporary sociological literature, in general, and proponents of the TCC thesis, in particular, bemoan the immiserizing consequences of accelerating international competition but, like their neo-Marxist predecessors, ignore what historian Robert Brenner and economist Mark Glick have referred to as "the equally obvious counter-tendencies for competition among accumulating, cost-cutting firms on the product and labor markets to stimulate the growth of mass consumption, not only by bringing about the increased employment of wage workers and growing wages, but also by stimulating cost-cutting technical changes that themselves widen the market by making for reduced prices" (Brenner & Glick, 1991, p. 109). Are the so-called counter-tendencies visible in the countries and cases I have examined? The history of the Chilean forestry sector would appear to counsel an affirmative answer. After all, the notoriously abusive industry employs approximately 120,000 workers including about 50,000 temporary or casual workers in silviculture and harvesting (ILO, 2000; Stewart, 2004). While wages and working conditions are at best inadequate, they are almost certainly improving and are particularly high in the downstream processing activities dominated by Arauco and CMPC (Schurman, 2001; Morales, 2003). Nor are the Chileans alone. India's more dynamic pharmaceutical firms pay far less than their western counterparts but far more than their more parochial neighbors. Cemex's Mexican workers make seven times the legal minimum wage (LaFranchi, 1996). And the bivariate correlation between the ratio of trade to GDP – a standard proxy for openness to competition – and an index of real per capita income produced by Bart van Ark and Robert McGuckin for 19 developing countries including Chile, India, and Mexico in 1996 is a staggering 0.81 ($p<0.001$).

The point is most assuredly not that globalization leads always and everywhere to rising living standards and sustainable human development but that the competitive dynamic underlying globalization – that is, the competitive dynamic imposed by capitalist property relations – exposes peripheral workers and their communities to opportunity as well as risk. After all, the competitive dynamic *forces* entrepreneurs and investors to undertake large-scale investments in relatively immobile assets with long maturation periods *on pain of bankruptcy or buyout*. "To remain an independent company meant growing in Mexico," says Zambrano, "plus being elsewhere" (Zambrano quoted in Gascoigne, 1995). And he is almost certainly correct. The Chilean forestry firms paid billions of borrowed dollars to maintain their independence from their North American "partners." And Yusuf Hamied anticipates similar incursions – and hopes for parallel responses – in the Indian pharmaceutical sector. By undertaking costly investments in relatively immobile assets, however, peripheral capitalists like Zambrano, Angelini, and Hamied render their firms vulnerable to the demands of their workers and consumers and duty-bound to pursue further productivity increases.

The likely result is neither an inexorable "race to the bottom" (Robinson, 1999, p. 51; Sklair & Robbins, 2002, p. 98) nor a worldwide "climb to the top" (Crotty, Epstein, & Kelly, 1998) but a political and economic conflict engendered by overcapacity and overproduction. "By virtue of their lower costs," writes Robert Brenner, "firms from the later developing bloc are able to take market share, even while maintaining at least the average rate of profit, by reducing the price for their output" (Brenner, 1999, p. 65). On pain of bankruptcy, however, members of the original bloc counterattack by purchasing new fixed capital and accelerating the process of innovation – often with the implicit or explicit support of their "states or financiers" (Brenner, 1999, p. 65) – and new market entrants from still later blocs follow suit. "Just as the mere oversupply of a line of production cannot be counted on to force enough exit to restore its profitability," writes Brenner, "that same oversupply is insufficient to deter further entry that could bring down its profit rate further" (Brenner, 1999, p. 66).

On the contrary, the growing oversupply of manufactured goods and services tends to foster political as well as economic conflict between the representatives of incumbent and challenger firms. Antidumping initiatives and safeguards in the north, beggar-thy-neighbor macroeconomic policies in the south, discord at the WTO, and the Bush administration's "increasingly protectionist thrust" (Brenner, 2004, p. 97) would all seem to underscore the continued – and arguably growing – importance of the nation-state and nationality in the current era of globalization. "Behind every transnational corporation," writes Ellen Meiksins Wood, "is a national base that depends on its local state to sustain its viability and on other states to give it access to other markets and other labor forces" (Wood, 1998, p. 12).

What is the likely outcome of the struggle for market share? While the MDCs – and the US in particular – are utilizing implicit and explicit subsidies, coercive diplomacy, and draconian restrictions on intellectual property rights to lock in the current international division of labor (see Chang, 2002; Shadlen, 2005b), their success is by no means a foregone conclusion. After all, the newly industrializing countries feature an abundance of skilled and unskilled labor, significant cost advantages, and the motivational power of nationalist – or at times even Third World – ideologies. "There is an effect that is not quantifiable for us," explains Zambrano, "which is to be an example, to be one of the first companies from a developing country to have an international presence" (Zambrano quoted in O'Brien, 2003). The owners and managers of the principal Chilean forestry firms express similar sentiments (McLean, 2003). And Hamied begins his public addresses by immodestly asserting that he represents not only Cipla but the "needs and aspirations of the Third World" (Hamied quoted in Specter, 2001).

While nationalist or Third World ideologies offer their adherents a convenient veil or public relations measure, they are not entirely disingenuous, for peripheral capitalists are not obviously immune from the pull of nationalism. Thus, Jamaican economist Norman Girvan perceptively notes that the mere fact that peripheral capitalists are "weak dependent and junior" need not imply that they are "objectively satisfied" with their position (Girvan, 1980, p. 451), and when they discover opportunities to challenge or perhaps mitigate their dependency by exploiting their myriad advantages they will do so – sometimes to great effect. What if Indian firms design and manufacture the next generation of blockbuster drugs? Or Chilean biotechnology triumphs over timber scarcity? Or Mexican IT becomes the industry standard for logistics and transportation? Who will capture the returns? How will the MDCs react? And what will the world-system look like afterward? The point is *not* that these outcomes are likely but that they are possible and that they are all but completely and indefensibly ignored by a sociology of development that posits – but fails to prove – the eclipse of the nation-state and the demise of the national bourgeoisie.

NOTES

1. The YPF case merits additional commentary in light of the Argentinean oil company's recent purchase by Spain's Repsol. Sebastián Etchemendy notes that

YPF's share of Argentinean oil production had actually diminished and that "Pérez Companc, a national company and a private contractor of YPF since the Ongania dictatorship, had almost doubled its market share and displaced the U.S. company Amoco as the largest private producer of petroleum in Argentina after YPF" in the 1990s (Etchemendy, 2001, p. 13). Therefore, Etchemendy concludes that "in times of economic internationalization, it was, paradoxically, the national bourgeoisie traditionally protected by the state that obtained the best market positions in the subsector, displacing international capital." While Repsol's recent purchase of YPF and Petrobras's acquisition of a controlling interesting in Pérez Companc call the viability of Ethcemendy's conclusion into question, and cast doubt upon the Argentinean bourgeoisie's ability to withstand their country's recent financial crisis, they arguably underscore rather than undercut the growing power of the *peripheral* bourgeoisie more generally – since the respective domiciles of both Repsol and Petrobras (Brazil) lie outside of the "organic core" (Arrighi, 1990) of the world economy.

2. Robinson's collaborators are arguably more perceptive but no less skeptical of the peripheral bourgeoisie. While Jerry Harris welcomes the arrival of assertive public officials and aggressive private sectors in newly industrializing countries like Brazil, China, India, and South Africa, and acknowledges their self-conscious effort to "readjust globalization by developing a power bloc of developing nations" (Harris, 2005, p. 21), he portrays their apparent commitment to "trickle-down" economics as a necessary and all but insurmountable obstacle to more thoroughgoing structural transformation, and therefore calls their antisystemic *bona fides* into question (Harris, 2005, pp. 24–25; cf. Robinson & Harris, 2000).

3. Tendler briefly examines five cases of "upgrading" in small firm clusters; in every case, the upgrading process occurred as a response to foreign or international pressures. Her basic findings are consistent with the results of my own research on labor law enforcement in the Dominican Republic (Schrank, 2005).

4. For example, Chile has been a complainant in the recent controversy over the Byrd Amendment at the WTO. The U.S. congress passed the legislation in 2000 and thereby agreed to transfer antidumping duties to the affected industries – including lumber. Nevertheless, the WTO has ruled that the legislation constitutes an illegal subsidy and has therefore granted Chile and a number of other complainants the right to impose retaliatory sanctions on the U.S. (see Vrana, 2004). I would like to thank María del Carmen Domínguez of the Chilean mission to the WTO for insight into Chile's role in the Byrd conflict.

REFERENCES

Aguilar, D., & De Jong, F. (2004). Cementogate: La gran estafa. *Expansion*. 18 de agosto.
Amsden, A. (1989). Third world industrialization: "Global fordism" or a new model? *New Left Review*, *182*(July–August), 5–32.
Amsden, A. (2001). *The rise of 'The Rest': Challenges to the west from late-industrializing economies*. Oxford: Oxford University Press.

Amsden, A. (2003). Goodbye dependency theory, hello dependency theory. *Studies in Comparative International Development, 38*(1), 32–38.
Arrighi, G. (1990). The developmentalist illusion: A reconceptualization of the semiperiphery. In: W. Martin (Ed.), *Semiperipheral states in the world economy* (pp. 11–42). Westport: Greenwood.
Arroyo, A. (2003). NAFTA in Mexico: Promises, myths, and realities. In Development GAP (Ed.) *Lessons from NAFTA: The high cost of "free" trade.* Hemispheric Social Alliance.
Authers, J. (2004). Why the Mexicans mix cement with football. *Financial Times.* July 8.
Baeza-Yates, R. A., Fuller, D. A., Pino, J. A., & Goodman, S. E. (1995). Computing in Chile: The jaguar of the pacific rim? *Communications of the ACM, 38*(9), 23–28.
Barham, J. (2004). The haves and the have nots. *Latin Finance.* June.
Barwise, P., & Meehan, P. (2004). The benefits of getting the basics right. *Financial Times.* October 8.
Baxter, J. (2001). Canada ponders lumber fight in U.S. courts. *Ottawa Citizen.* August 24.
Beachy, D. (1996). Cemex again loses dumping ruling. *Houston Chronicle.* October 1.
Bhaduri, S., & Ray, A. (2004). Exporting through technological capability: Econometric evidence from India's pharmceutical and electrical/electronics firms. *Oxford Development Studies, 32*(1), 87–100.
Brenner, R. (1999). Reply to critics. *Comparative Studies in South Asia, Africa, and the Middle East, 19*(2), 61–83.
Brenner, R. (2004). New boom or new bubble: The trajectory of the US economy. *New Left Review, 25*(January–February), 57–100.
Brenner, R., & Glick, M. (1991). The regulation approach: Theory and history. *New Left Review, 188*(July–August), 45–119.
Brown, G. (2000). *The woods aren't deep.* Latin Trade, April.
Burbach, R. (1997). Socialism is dead, long live socialism. *NACLA Report on the Americas, 31*(November–December), 15–20.
Burbach, R., & Robinson, W. (1999). The Fin-de-Siecle debate: Globalization as epochal shift. *Science & Society, 63*(Spring), 10–39.
Chang, H. J. (2002). *Kicking away the ladder: Development strategies in historical perspective.* London: Anthem.
Chibber, V. (2005). Reviving the developmental state? The myth of the national bourgeoisie. In: L. Panitch & C. Leys (Eds), *Socialist register 2005* (pp. 226–246). New York: Monthly Review Press.
Chimni, B. S. (2004). International institutions today: An imperial global state in the making. *European Journal of International Law, 15*(1), 1–37.
Christian Science Monitor. (2004). Trade talks back on track. *Christian Science Monitor,* August 2.
Clapp, R. A. (1995). Creating competitive advantage: Forest policy as industrial policy in Chile. *Economic Geography, 71*(3), 273–296.
Clapp, R. A. (2001). Tree farming and forest conservation in Chile: Do replacement forests leave any originals behind? *Society and Natural Resources, 14,* 341–356.
Colitt, R. (2000). Financing costs curb expansion. *Financial Times.* December 20.
Cronon, W. (1991). *Nature's metropolis: Chicago and the great west.* NY: Norton.
Crotty, J., Epstein, G., & Kelly, P. (1998). Multinational corporations in the neoliberal regime. In: D. Baker, G. Esptein & R. Pollin (Eds), *Globalization and progressive economic policy.* Cambridge: Cambridge University Press.

Desai, R. (2004). From national bourgeoisie to rogues, failures, and bullies: 21st century imperialism and the unraveling of the third world. *Third World Quarterly, 25*(1), 169–185.
Dietz, J. (1989). The debt cycle and restructuring in Latin America. *Latin American Perspectives, 16*(1), 13–30.
Dombey, D. (1996). Financial blocks dog Cemex empire building. *Financial Times.* May 17.
Dunne, N. (1995). A concrete case for a dumping dispute. *Financial Times.* May 30.
Economist. (1995). Set in concrete. *Economist.* June 3.
Economist. (2004). Mexico's biggest cement-maker plans to buy Britain's biggest. *Economist.* October 2.
Embong, A. R. (2000). Globalization and transnational class relations: Some problems of conceptualization. *Third World Quarterly, 21*(6), 989–1000.
Engardio, P., & Einhorn, B. (2005). Outsourcing Innovation. *Business Week.* March 21.
Etchemendy, S. (2001). Constructing reform coalitions: The politics of compensations in Argentina's economic liberalization. *Latin American Politics and Society, 43*(3), 1–35.
Evans, P. (1982). Reinventing the bourgeoisie: State entrepreneurship and class formation in dependent capitalist development. *American Journal of Sociology, 88*(Suppl.), S210–S247.
Evans, P. (1995). *Embedded autonomy: States and industrial transformation.* Princeton: Princeton University Press.
Fidler, S. (1997). Chile stresses bilateral accords. *Financial Times.* July 15.
Financial Times. (1997). Angelini plays waiting game. *Financial Times.* February 28.
Financial Times. (1998). Latin America's emerging multinationals. *Financial Times.* April 3.
Finger, J. M., Ng, F., & Wangchuk, S. (2001). *Antidumping as safeguard policy.* Washington: World Bank.
Fritsch, P. (2002). Hard profits. *Wall Street Journal.* April 22.
Garrido, C., & Peres, W. (1998). Big Latin American industrial companies and groups. *CEPAL Review, 66*(December), 129–150.
Gascoigne, C. (1995). Nationality proves a weight for Cemex. *Financial Times.* September 26.
Gazeta Mercantil. (2001). Brazil to resist US and EU in WTO next week. *Gazeta Mercantil.* November 30.
Girvan, N. (1980). Economic nationalists vs. multinational corporations: Revolutionary or evolutionary change? In: H. Sklar (Ed.), *Trilateralism: The trilateral commission and elite planning for world management.* Boston: South End Press.
Goldstein, A. (2002). EMBRAER: de campeón nacional a jugador global. *Revista de la CEPAL, 77* (agosto), 101–121.
Gonzalez, G. (1997). Chile-trade: Business sector accuses U.S. of playing dirty. *Interpress Service.* July 9.
Grace, C. (2004). *The effect of changing intellectual property on pharmaceutical industry prospects in India and China.* London: DFID.
Gwynne, R. N. (1996). Direct foreign investment and non-traditional export growth in Chile: The case of the forestry sector. *Bulletin of Latin American research, 15*(3), 341–357.
Hall, K. (1994). Mexican cement giant flourishes overseas. *Journal of Commerce.* October 31.
Harris, J. (2005). Emerging third world powers: China, India, and Brazil. *Race & Class, 46*(3), 7–27.
Harris, N. (1991). *City, class, and trade: Social and economic change in the third world.* London: I.B. Taurus.
Harvey, D. (1982). *The Limits to Capital.* Oxford: Blackwell.

Helleiner, G. K. (1990). Trade strategy as medium-term adjustment. *World Development.*
Houston Chronicle. (1996). Panel upholds tariff on Mexican cement. *Houston Chronicle.* September 17.
Houston Chronicle. (1997). Dumping to cost Cemex $48 million. *Houston Chronicle.* April 5.
International Labour Organization (ILO). (2000). *Approaches to labour inspection in forestry: Problems and solutions.* Geneva: ILO.
Johns, R. (1990). US dumping charges dash Mexican hopes. *Financial Times.* September 4.
Kaplinsky, R. (2001). Is globalization all it is cracked up to be? *Review of International Political Economy, 8*(1), 45–65.
Katel, P. (1997). Bordering on chaos: The cemex story. *Wired, 5*(July), 98–107.
Keesing, D., & Lall, S. (1992). Marketing manufactured exports from developing countries: Learning sequences and public support. In: G. K. Helleiner (Ed.), *Trade policy, industrialization, and development: New perspectives* (pp. 176–193). Oxford: Clarendon.
Kock, C., & Guillén, M. (2001). Strategy and structure in developing countries: Business groups as an evolutionary response to unrelated opportunities for diversification. *Industrial and Corporate Change, 10*(1), 77–97.
Kripalani, M. (2005). Copycats no more. *Business Week.* April 18.
Kurth, J. (2002). Globalization: Political aspects. In: N. Smelser & P. Baltes (Eds), *International encyclopedia of the social and behavioral sciences* (pp. 6234–6237). Amsterdam: Elsevier.
Kurtz, M. (2001). State developmentalism without a developmental state: The public foundations of the "Free Market Miracle" in Chile. *Latin American Politics & Society.*
LaFranchi, H. (1996). Concrete can't weigh down Cemex. *Christian Science Monitor.* March 13.
Lall, S. (2004). Industrial success and failure in a globalizing world. *International Journal of Technology Management and Sustainable.*
Latin America Weekly Report. (2000). How the Chileans assess prospects. *Latin America Weekly Report.* December 5.
Latin America Weekly Report. (2003). The Cemex way to be a multinational. *Latin Finance.* July.
Lipietz, A. (1984). How monetarism has choked third world industrialization. *New Left Review, 145*(May–June), 71–87.
Lipietz, A. (2003). Steeled to reality. *London Times.* December 6.
Malkin, E. (2004). Mexico antitrust chief seeks stronger laws. *New York Times.* November 11.
Mapes, L. (1997). Simpson sells share of Chile pulp mill. *Seattle Times.* December 3.
Martin, P. (1997). New rivals rush to join the fray. *Financial Times.* October 3.
Marx, K. (1978 [1850]). Class struggles in France. In: R. Tucker (Ed.), *The Marx–Engels reader* (pp.XXXX). NY: Norton.
Marx, K., & Engels, F. (1888 [1848]). *On the Question of Free Trade.*
Mastel, G. (1999). Hit by a load of dumped cement from Mexico. *Journal of Commerce.* November 12.
McLaughlin, A. (2004). "Global South" flexes its trade muscle in Brazil. *Christian Science Monitor.* June 18.
McLean, V. (2003). Country focus switching on to South American forestry. *New Zealand Forest Industries.* December 10.
McMichael, P. (2001). Revisiting the question of the transnational state: A comment on William Robinson's "Social theory and globalization". *Theory and Society, 30*(2), 201–210.
McMichael, P. (2004). *Development and social change: A global perspective.* Thousand Oaks: Pine Forge.

McNabb, D. (1997). Pulp and paper empires spin Latin American web. *The Wellington Dominion.* May 7.
McNabb, D. (1999). Carter Holt sale ends long legal wrangle. *The Wellington Dominion.* December 21.
McNeil, D. (2005). India alters law on drug patents. *New York Times.* March 24.
Mehta, K. (2004). Moving up the value chain. *Global Agenda, 2*(January), 236–239.
Moody, J. (2004). Mexican cement maker with a worldview. *New York Times.* April 15.
Moore, D. (2004). The second age of the third world from primitive accumulation to global public goods. *Third World Quarterly, 25*(1), 87–109.
Morales, E. (2003). *Changing ownership and management of state forest plantations: Chile.* International Institute for Environment and Development.
Moreno, J. (2005). Five questions with Gilberto Perez: Cement firm plans big expansion. *Houston Chronicle, February 23*, p. 2.
Mulligan, M. (2001). Violence soars as Mapuches battle to recover a lost idyll. *Financial Times.* June 2.
NASSCOM. (No date). *Indian software products: Can India emerge as a product development hub?* India Software Products Fact Sheet.
New Zealand Forest Industries. (2002). Export markets: Thinking big in Chile. *New Zealand Forest Industries.* November.
O'Brien, M. (2003). Globe trotting – slowly. *Latin Finance.* July.
Pananond, P. (2001). The making of Thai multinationals: A comparative study of the growth and internationalization process of Thailand's Charoen Pokphand and Siam Cement Groups. *Journal of Asian Business, 17*(3), 41–70.
Panitch, L., & Gindin, S. (2004). Global capitalism and American empire. *Socialist Register 2004: The New Imperial Challenge.*
Paul, P. (2004). Foresters decry trade encounter. *Atlanta Journal-Constitution.* April 6.
Peart, M. (2004). Taking off the tariffs: What prospects for New Zealand forestry at Doha? *New Zealand Forest Industries Magazine.* March.
Pfeifer, S. (2004). India's drug upstarts give big pharma headache. *Sunday Telegraph.* October 24.
Piggott, C. (2001). *Cemex's stratospheric rise.* Latin Finance, March.
Pilling, D. (1999). Doctor in search of patents. *Financial Times.* August 30.
Polanyi, K. (1944). *The great transformation: The political and economic origins of our times.* Boston: Beacon Press.
Press, L. (1993). Software export from developing nations. *IEEE Computer.* December.
Radice, H. (1999). Taking globalisation seriously. In: L. Panitch & C. Leys (Eds), *Socialist register 1999: Global capitalism versus democracy* (pp. 1–28). London: Merlin.
Rai, S. (2005). India adopts patent law covering pharmaceuticals. *New York Times.* March 24.
Ramos, J. (1998). A development strategy founded on natural resource-based production clusters. *CEPAL Review, 66*(December), 105–127.
Robinson, W. (1998). Beyond nation-state paradigms: Globalization, sociology, and the challenge of transnational studies. *Sociological Forum, 13*(4), 561–594.
Robinson, W. (1999). Latin America in the age of inequality: Confronting the new "Utopia." *International Studies Review, 1*(3), 41–67.
Robinson, W. (2001). Social theory and globalization: The rise of a transnational state. *Theory and Society, 30*(2), 157–200.

Robinson, W. (2001–2002). Global capitalism and nation-state-centric thinking – What we *don't* see when we *do* see nation-states: Response to critics. *Science & Society, 65*(1), 500–508.
Robinson, W. (2002). Remapping development in light of globalization: From a territorial to a social cartography. *Third World Quarterly, 23*(6), 1047–1071.
Robinson, W. (2004). Global crisis and Latin America. *Bulletin of Latin American Research, 23*(2), 135–153.
Robinson, W., & Harris, J. (2000). Toward a global ruling class: Globalization and the transnational ruling class. *Science & Society, 64*(1).
Rohter, L. (2004). Mapuche Indians in Chile struggle to take back forests. *New York Times.* August 11.
Romero, S. (2000). Mexican cement giant plans internet emphasis. *New York Times, September 13*, p. 6.
Ruelas-Gossi, A., & Sull, D. (2004). The art of innovating on a shoestring. *Financial Times.* September 24.
Sahad, P. V. (2005). Ranbaxy laboratories: The alchemist who saw tomorrow. *Business Today.* March 27.
Salmon, F. (2002a). Time to deploy the arsenal. *Latin Finance.* March.
Salmon, F. (2002b). Small is bountiful. *Euromoney.* December.
Schrank, A. (2005). Professionalization and probity in the patrimonial state: Labor law enforcement in the dominican republic. Paper presented to the Institute for work and employment research, Sloan School of Management, Massachusetts Institute of Technology, Cambridge, MA. February.
Schurman, R. (2001). Uncertain gains: Labor in Chile's new export sectors. *Latin American Research Review, 36*(2), 3–30.
Shadlen, K. (2004). *Democratization without representation: The politics of small industry in Mexico.* University Park: Pennsylvania State University Press.
Shadlen, K. (2005a). Patents, India, and HIV/AIDS treatment. *LSE AIDS Update 4.* April.
Shadlen, K. (2005b). China, the WTO, and the search for better-than-MFN access to the US: The global politics of regional integration in the Americas. Mimeo. London: LSE/DESTIN.
Silver, S. (2004). Cemex waits to cement its gains. *Financial Times.* November 18.
Sklair, L. (2000). The transnational capitalist class and the discourse of globalisation. *Cambridge Review of International Affairs, 14*(1).
Sklair, L., & Robbins, P. (2002). Global capitalism and major corporations from the third world. *Third World Quarterly, 23*(1), 81–100.
Song, J. (2004). South Korea expects subsidies victory. *Financial Times.* November 30.
Specter, M. (2001). India's plague. *New Yorker.* December 17.
Sridharan, R. (2005). Indian pharma's mid-life crisis. *Business Today.* February 27.
Stallings, B. (2003). Globalization and liberalization: The impact on developing countries. In: A. Kohli, C. Moon & G. Sørenson (Eds), *States, markets, and just growth: Development in the 21st century* (pp. 9–38). NY: UN University Press.
Stewart, D. (2004). A tree grows in Uruguay. *Latin Trade.* September.
Tanzer, A. (2001). Pill factory to the world. *Forbes.* December 10.
Tendler, J. (2002). Small firms, the informal sector, and the devil's deal. *IDS Bulletin, 3*(3), 98–104.

Timber and Wood Products. (1998a). The heart of South America. *Timber and Wood Products.* June.
Timber and Wood Products. (1998b). A paper chain with a heart of wood. *Timber and Wood Products.* June 27.
Timber and Wood Products. (1998c). Chile's gentle giant. *Timber and Wood Products.* June 27.
Thomas, P. (2000). Bringing poulantzas back in. *Innovation, 13*(2), 199–206.
Torres, C. (1999). Chile squeezes last drop from factories – Pulp maker Arauco shows how nation can prosper amid low export prices. *Wall Street Journal.* November 24.
Tussie, D. (1998). Multilateralism revisited in a globalizing world economy. *Mershon International Studies Review, 42*(1), 183–193.
United Nations Food and Agriculture Organization (UNFAO). (2003). *State of forestry in the Latin American and Caribbean region 2002.* Santiago: FAO.
United Nations Industrial Development Organization (UNIDO). (2004). *Industrial development report 2004.* Vienna: UNIDO.
Vitalis, R. (1990). On the theory and practice of compradors: The role of 'Abbud Pasha in the Egyptian political economy. *International Journal of Middle East Studies, 22*(August), 291–315.
Vrana, D. (2004). WTO clears penalty for US. *Los Angeles Times.* November 27.
Wade, R. (2003a). What strategies are viable for developing countries today? The World Trade Organization and the shrinking of "development space". *Review of International Political Economy, 10*(4), 621–644.
Wade, R. (2003b). *Governing the market: Economic theory and the role of government in East Asian industrialization* (2nd ed.). Princeton: Princeton University Press.
Ward, A. (2003). Europe fires WTO flare as S. Korea yards steam ahead. *Financial Times.* June 25.
Walker, L. (2001). Plugged in for maximum efficiency. *Washington Post.* June 20.
Watson, R. (2003). Bush set to end steel tariffs and avert a trade war. *London Times.* December 2.
Wheatley, J. (2004). Embraer hits the stratosphere. *Business Week.* April 19.
Wilson, C. (2005). Voyage of discovery. *New Scientist.* February 19.
Wood, E. M. (1998). Labor, class, and state in global capitalism. In: E. M. Wood, P. Meiksins & M. Yates (Eds), *Rising from the ashes? Labor in the age of 'Global' capitalism.* New York: Monthly Review Press.
Wood Based Panels International. (1998). A league of its own. *Wood Based Panels International.* August 1.
Woods, C. (2002). Here come the super trees. *Latin Trade.* May.
World Bank. (2002). *World development report 2002:* Washington: Oxford/World Bank.

PART II:
GLOBAL DEVELOPMENT AND POLICY QUESTIONS

WHAT IS FOOD AND FARMING FOR? – THE (RE)EMERGENCE OF HEALTH AS A KEY POLICY DRIVER

Tim Lang

ABSTRACT

The restructuring of food systems over recent decades has rightly received social scientific analysis. This paper argues that the public health implications of the cultural and production changes have received less attention. Yet, new health-oriented analyses offer a rich understanding of how societies have changed – in what they eat, why and how food is produced, whose health is affected and by what diseases. Health should be at the heart of social scientific thinking about food and farming. The case for a more integrated approach to food and farming, linking health, environment and society is strong.

☆This chapter is based on the talk prepared for Trondheim 2004. It draws on papers presented to the Fairtrade Foundation in London, March 2004; the European Public Health Association 10th Congress, Oslo, October 2004; and the City Insights lecture in London, May 26, 2004.

INTRODUCTION: HEALTH THE FORGOTTEN DIMENSION?

This paper focuses on one policy strand – public health – in the web of emerging thinking about the future of food and farming. It argues that health ought to be more central in analysis of the re-framing of food policy that is occurring worldwide, not just in developed countries. It is widely understood that, worldwide, both farming and the use of the land are being restructured. A period of great change is underway in which the nature of production and distribution is being altered in a fundamental and rapid fashion. Farming is poised to intensify still further; food's very nature is being moulded to suit processing; the logistics revolution enabled by computers and satellites is transforming distribution; diets are no longer bound by seasonality; off-farm processes as diverse as marketing and packaging frame how food looks. Dynamics between and within sectors are being changed dramatically by new technologies and management.

Over the last two decades, rural sociologists and geographers have been particularly active in mapping how these changes are manifest on the land and up the supply chain, and in exploring what drives those changes. They have pointed to the depth and extent of the restructuring process underway. This social science contribution to analysing modern food systems has been rich and complex but, at the same time, comparatively silent on the role of health in farm and food policy. Social scientists who address the interplay of food and health are rare – if anything, they refer to nutrition at best sketchily or they focus on developing countries cultural change. With good reason, the existence of hunger amidst plenty continues to receive attention. But the case for a rethink about health-food dynamics argued here requires more than a focus on hunger, continuing policy sore though that is the nightmare now stalking the world's health stems from the coincidence of under-, mal- and over-consumption in both developed and developing worlds, albeit in different patterns. Health and ill-health are heavily associated with food in a new, complex and important way. The change in modes of cooking, for instance, (and whether there is cooking at all) in developed societies has both a cultural and health impact that surely warrants attention. The unleashing of vast advertising budgets to undermine staple diets is another feature binding north and south.

This paper argues therefore that a new, interdisciplinary and holistic social scientific analysis of the relationship between food, farming and health is overdue. Further, it proposes that existing social scientific appreciation of environmental, consumer and primary producer complexities means the social sciences are well placed to help frame the emerging analysis known as ecological public health. This is one of the two paradigms which, has been argued (Lang & Heasman, 2004; Lang, Barling, & Caraher, 2001; Barling, Lang, & Caraher, 2002), and are emerging to replace the 'old' productionist food policy framework that focused on raising production and productivity in the second half of the 20th century.

FOOD POLICY IN FLUX

Policy goals such as health, efficiency and environment are fraught with debate. They are reminders that food policies, institutions and debates are contested space within a contextual 'holy triangle' of State, Food Supply and Civil Society (see Fig. 1). This triangle encapsulates an enduring feature of food, its contested nature. Throughout history, in all societies, as food is fought over – consider issues such as land ownership, affordability, quality, trade and health – the three power blocs of state, supply chain and society emerge as foci for interest battles. But this simple triangle is itself a problem. The three power groupings, we know, are fragmented, internally divided, subject themselves to ebbs and flows of power, capital, influence and history.

Despite its simplification, the Triangle model (State – Supply Chain – Civil Society), like most models, has value in pointing to the main tensions over the shape and direction of food. Each 'corner' of the triangle is itself fractured. The supply chain, for example, is internally dynamic; farmers, manufacturers, retailers, logistics, catering/foodservice all vie for consumer spending. Food service in many countries is poised to rival retailer power for direct access to the consumer's money. Some farmers have responded by returning to markets and selling direct to consumers: the farmers' markets and organic movements, notably.

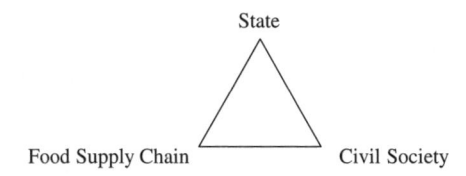

Fig 1. Food as Contested Space between State, Food Supply Chain and Civil Society.

In all food sectors, there are unprecedented levels of concentration. Giant food corporations straddle borders and have immense purchasing power, which enables them to buy already large national champions. Wal-Mart (USA), Tesco (UK), Carrefour (Fr) and Ahold (NL) are striding the globe, emulating a globalisation pioneered by food processors for decades even a century ago. These retail giants set their own standards, separately and in alliances (such as EUREP (www.eurep.org)), sometimes in competition with the State and have long lines of accountability, auditing and controls (Marsden, Flynn, & Harrison, 2000b). They walk a fine line between controlling and servicing consumers (Lang, 2003). Prior to EU enlargement, a study by CAP Gemini showed how in the 15 member states, there were 3.2 million farmers feeding 250 million consumers, via 170,000 outlets, from 88,600 processors and manufacturers, but this supply and demand was funnelled through only 600 supermarket chains with 110 key buying desks (Grievink, 2003). The fewer number of buying desks reflects the purchasing alliances that have grown between retail chains, as they share specifications. This pattern of concentration is repeated, with differences, in some commodity regimes; for instance, just three companies have over 50 per cent of the Brazilian Soya feed trade to Europe too (Vorley, 2004).

To aggregate the complexities of the modern 'State' as Fig. 1 does is also an over-simplification. The State is now multi-level – local, sub-national, national, regional and global. At all levels, there are para-state organisations, through which national governments relate and contest food and farm policy. It is hard to understand the consumer interest without appreciating how arcane issues such as food standards now get fought over – lengthily and sometimes bitterly – at the various levels. Notions of policy competence and subsidiarity are fought over between the levels. Although the 'local' is important, for service delivery, most decision-making now tends to be made in complex negotiations between national, regional and global levels of governance.

The third corner of the triangle, civil society, is the consuming public, with all the diversity that entails – class, gender, age, society, etc. In addition, vast numbers of civil society organizations voice and vie for leadership of the consumer interest. Within this non-governmental organization (NGO) sector, distinctions must be made between Business Interest NGOs (BINGOs), Government-ordained NGOs (GONGOs) and Public Interest NGOs (PINGOs). Civil society is further fractured by class, demographics, culture, rich world/poor world consumer interests, and so on.

Some food and farm sector analysts argue that the role of the state is or ought to be declining. Economists pronounce as to state distortions, notably through unwarranted subsidies. Some realism is due. Even the neo-liberal domination of policy in the last quarter of the 20th century never quite managed to take the state out of food and farm policy discourse. Even within market theory, whose purest ideologues propose that food is or ought to be subject to market forces, and whose policy central tenet is to restrict the role of the state or remove it altogether, the relationship between the supply chain and civil society/consumers is in fact mediated or framed by the state. Even the triumph of the neo-cons in early 21st century USA politics actually used the state to shape the state, not just 'markets'. This heightened ideology in and about food should not surprise us; agriculture and food have always invited state, not just corporate or civilian contestation.

In a 1981 treatise on food policy – the only one with the term in its title – the Agriculture working party of the Organisation for Economic Co-operation & Development (OECD) defined food policy as the actions of the state: those policies affecting food – its supply and impact – which reflect "the dominant priorities and objectives of governments..." (Organisation for Economic Co-operation and Development, 1981). Food policies, argued the OECD, govern the food economy. They defined them as "the set of activities and relationships that interact to determine what, how much, by what method and for whom food is produced." Creating public policy on food is a "dynamic [process] in which there is continual interaction and reaction." Most state attention was assumed to be on just two areas: nutrition and agriculture, a framework shared with the World Bank at that time too.

With regard to agriculture, the policy mission was clear and had been widely agreed by the mid century. A leading World Bank text of the 1980s, too, argued that food policy's goals were to deliver more food. "Food policy encompasses the collective efforts of governments to influence the decision-making environment of food producers, food consumers and food marketing agents in order to further social objectives. These objectives nearly always include improved nutrition for inadequately nourished citizens and more rapid growth in domestic food production" (Timmer, Falcon, & Pearson, 1983, p. 9). Such policies were overwhelmingly pitched in econ-omistic terms, with central attention on farm prices, and, therefore, market access. Efficiency in agricultural systems would improve farm incomes and in turn deliver gains in nutritional status and food security, via low prices (Timmer et al., 1983, p. 14).

For nutrition, the impact of this policy equation was clear: more output would yield more food, reduce insecurity and restrict the vagaries of seasons, terrain and distribution. Nutrition, for the OECD, like all thinking within the dominant productionist paradigm from the 1940s, centred on managing the food chain to deliver more food, more efficiently, more effectively, less wastefully and using 'steered' market forces (Lang & Heasman, 2004). Nutritional health was central to policy mainly because the world had come to realise the extent and structural nature of hunger and that human action was a factor in whether it was tackled. This was a lesson learned by the 1930s, not least by the League of Nations (League of Nations, 1936). The League's quaintly named Mixed Committee on the Problem of Nutrition acknowledged that countries' nutrition status varied by circumstance; some affected by macro-economics and others by the legacy of poor understanding of how nutrition could improve physical performance. Even the well-to-do could be improved by better nutrition, the Committee concluded.

The political implications of the arrival of this modern science-based understanding of nutrition were considerable. The 19th century liberal and even mercantilist schools, which judged food as best left to market forces – the triumph of free traders over protectionists – finally recognised that such economic policy packages could not adequately address the problem of hunger. This was not just a problem for what now we term the developing world – then shaped by colonial reach – but for the rich heartlands also. Entering World War II, for example, Britain, then a world power that only produced 30 per cent of its food and was instead fed by its empire, was accumulating evidence of hunger. The British Medical Association, the doctor's professional body and hardly radical, hosted a conference in 1939 to review food and health. Lord Horder, the President of the BMA, commented in the final report in unashamed radical if patrician terms:

> A short time ago I was so bold – even so impertinent – as to express the wish that the Ministers of Health, of Agriculture and of Transport, with the Governor of the Bank of England, might be locked in a room together and kept there until they had solved the problem of food production and of food distribution in this country. This was only another way of saying that I believed the problems of malnutrition, of food, and of poverty in the midst of plenty – that is surely not an overstatement – could never be solved if dealt with compartmentally, but that they could be solved if taken together and dealt with by a long-term policy. (British Medical Association, 1939, p. 5).

The case for policy intervention and co-ordination with health had moved centre stage. Solutions being mooted included:

- a focus on children with direct provision of welfare services such as for school meals and milk;
- financial and policy support for women such as through direct payments or 'family allowances';

- a concerted focus on food supply;
- controls on trade to make it meet need; and
- a strategy to rebuild national agriculture.

In many developed countries, such debates and policy shifts occurred, within national terms and conditions, with a widely shared experience of agricultural depression, hunger, social dislocation and trade uncertainty. World War II consolidated this experience. Using Britain again, we can note how a conservative doctor such as Sir John Boyd Orr could capture mainstream thinking. He had conducted an oft-cited study of food poverty and ill-health in Scotland in 1936 and had earlier created the Rowett Research Institute, a large agricultural research body in Aberdeen, to improve agricultural output (Boyd Orr, 1936). In 1943, he was arguing on behalf of the state and civil society that war had:

> forced us to adopt a food policy based on the nutritional needs of the people. Soldiers and munitions workers have to be maintained in the highest possible state of fighting and working efficiency, and for the maintenance of the morale of the nation, the people has to be as well fed as possible. [...] Then the available food was distributed in accordance with physiological needs, special measures being taken to ensure that the higher needs of mothers and children and of heavy workers would be met. (Boyd Orr, 1943)

He observed with admiration how the USA was setting targets to increase output: for fruit and vegetables to rise by 75 per cent, milk rise by 39 per cent, eggs by 23 per cent, and so on. This was responsible, health-informed food governance. At the war's end, he became Director General of the newly created Food and Agriculture Organisation (Boyd Orr, 1966). These arguments had captured not just national but international policy space. The productionist paradigm or policy framework had replaced the old order. This new paradigm may be represented as a social 'equation':

> Science + Capital + State Support (Finance + Policy) = Increased production, which if distributed appropriately = Health + Well-being

Productionism (see Table 1) promoted and institutionalised:

- a drive for efficiency, with new indicators such as higher yields, and rational use of labour;
- the triumph of 'scientific farming';
- the appliance of science and technology to reduce waste and increase productivity;
- a good return on capital;
- the demise of so-called 'dog and stick' (i.e. old-fashioned) farming;
- concentration of herds and land-holdings;

Table 1. The 'Upside' of the Productionist Paradigm.

Category of Success	Evidence on	Examples
Technical advance	Increased yields	Hybrid cereals
Efficiency	Mechanisation	Labour replacement
Affordability	Price drops	Drop in pig/poultry prices
Availability	Range of foods	Hypermarkets stock 2–30 k items
Beating hunger	Drop in percentage of population experiencing hunger	FAO estimates of decline in world food insecurity 1960–2000

- a decline of labour directly employed on the land;
- an expansion of infrastructural services such as fertilisers and pesticides to increase crop yields;
- state support through extension schemes;
- intensification – the systematic attempt to achieve more throughput from capital, land, equipment, labour, animals, crops; and
- a reduction of the price of food for mainly urban consumers.

This last issue was particularly important. The productionist paradigm had rightly noted that the health problems of pre-World War II populations were a combination of lack of availability, affordability and price. A policy package that reduced prices by improved efficiencies, would benefit public health it followed. Thus, the close relationship forged in the war between the food industry, particularly food manufacturers, and the government was enshrined in subsidy-welfare packages in the developed world and a package of extension, aid and technology transfer in the developing world. Ministries and departments of agriculture became famously associated with 'agency capture'. The distinction was blurred between national and agricultural interests (Self & Storing, 1971).

It should be acknowledged that the productionist paradigm was in its own terms very effective: introducing remarkable engineering, chemical and biological technologies, improving efficiency, driving down prices, filling supermarket shelves in the West, increasing output in the South, reducing the percentage of humanity suffering hunger (see Table 1). But this has come at a cost to the environment, public health, consumer confidence, animal welfare, terms of trade and social justice (see Table 2). Current policy now has to grapple with these externalities (Pretty, 2002).

Today, the paradigm is under strain because it cannot satisfactorily address the complexities of modern supply. Policy-makers have to grapple with a far wider range of issues than merely under-nutrition or poor

Table 2. The 'Downside' of the Productionist Paradigm.

Category of Concern	Evidence on	Examples
Environment	Residues in food, soil structure and water use	Residues of pesticides and nitrates; biodiversity loss.
Public health	Diet-related degenerative diseases	Spread of coronary heart disease, diabetes, strokes, some cancers, obesity worldwide
Food safety	Contaminants and microbiological	*E. coli*, Salmonella and BSE
Consumer rights	Information	Weak and complex labelling
Animal welfare	Factory farming	Prophylactic antibiotic use
Social justice	Continuation of food poverty	Growth in absolute numbers of food insecure 1960–2000

Table 3. Key Policy Goals and Problems under the 'Old' Food Policy Régime.

Policy Goal to…	And Address the Problem of…
Deliver more food	Under-production
Ensure more food gets to consumers	Poor distribution
Raise efficiency	Reduce waste, increase
Increase productivity	Reduce costs to improve affordability
Tackle under-consumption	Food poverty
Improve skills	Poor farmer knowledge

agricultural supply. Productionism cannot cope with pressing demands formed by evidence on environmental damage or over-consumption. As Maxwell, Slater and co-workers have argued, there is now a transition from an old to a new food policy agenda (Maxwell & Slater, 2004). This policy transition has been driven by structural change in all corners of the Triangle presented in Fig. 1. Table 3 gives some food/nutrition goals and problems the old Productionist paradigm sought to address. Table 4 gives, by contrast, 'new' food policy challenges for the food supply chain in the early 21st century.

The 'old' policy framework assumed that farming's contribution to health was by securing affordable food supply, yet by the 1970s epidemiology was suggesting how, even in developing countries, diet-related ill-health was manifest in a new triple burden: over-, mal- and under-consumption. The deepening food and environment crisis – resource use, access to land,

Table 4. Key Policy Goals and Problems under the 'New' Food Policy Régime.

Policy Goal to...	And Address the Problem of...
Produce more equitable consumption	Inequalities and malnourishment
Reduce over-consumption	Non-communicable diseases: Heart disease, cancers, obesity and diabetes
Make supply chains sustainable and long-term food secure	Environmental damage and cost externalities
Build a more appropriate food culture	Warped information and food cultures weakened by marketing
Ensure high quality	Consumer confidence and vulnerability of long supply chains
Inject real competitiveness to markets	Oligopolies and concentration; domination by retailers

supply, biodiversity, climate, water, etc. – underlines the urgent need for scrutinising ecological public health. Population health goals and environmental health can and should go hand in hand (McMichael, 2001). Good human health requires ecological viability and, vice versa, what is good for ecology – diversity, low impact farming, sustainability – can be good for health. Yet this is not necessarily being delivered.

In this scenario, health – as a policy goal – underpins and transforms the food supply chain's drivers and dynamics, providing an accurate, evidence-led policy framework for food and farming, which it lacks currently. How else could the world's food supply be so centrally implicated in the current main causes of global premature death – hunger and malnutrition on the one hand and over- and mal-consumption leading to the degenerative diseases on the other? For those who fear or resist the injection of a new health perspective into food supply policy, it should be restated that the 20th century production-led revolution in the supply chain – altering what is produced and how – was also based on a health case. This case, in place by the late 1930s but adopted in the 1940s, had proposed that human ill-health was heavily framed by under-consumption and social inequalities, neither of which were natural or necessary states. Production could be raised by science and capital, heralding a world of plenty in place of hunger and insecurity. Industrialisation and intensification were solutions to a real, not imagined, package of policy problems: mal-distribution, waste, under-supply, hunger, and ill-health.

Today, although this productionist approach to health has been hugely successful in reducing the proportion of food insecurity, the world's health profile is now more complex. The co-existence of under-, over- and malconsumption adds policy complexity, which partly explains why systems of governance at national, regional and global levels are not coping with the need to produce a new integrated policy framework; they are locked into segmented modes of policy analysis. A key illustration of this multidimensional challenge is the impact of what is called the nutrition transition, a change in what foods are consumed, tastes, the range of food, not just how food is produced. The shift in nutrient mix received has implications, which ought to be more central to social scientific formulations of rurality, food and farming. Indeed, the new public health challenge posed by changed consumer preferences and regionalisation and globalisation of supply chains requires a return to some basic policy questions. Where does health come from? Land or supermarket? Or put it differently, what good is the land for health?

WHAT IS THE LAND FOR?

Land is natural capital, a resource owned and fought over, a foundation not just for wealth, but also (ill) health. Land is a key to employment, environmental goods, welfare, civic space, identity, amenity for relaxation, tourism and sports, and of course food. With the decline in political power of farmers, the significance of land has been diminished, but oil insecurity or climate changes are likely to herald its return to centre stage in policy. The UK, my own country, illustrates contemporary policy's ambivalent relationship with the land. As the first industrial nation, it was the first to shed its people en masse from the land, the first to require mass and routinised food supply chains to the majority of the population in towns and cities. Britain, as the world's pre-eminent imperial power then took that human experiment to lengths still not emulated by other comparable nations. After a bitter policy fight between the 'old' landed aristocracy and the fledgling 'new' industrial and urban professional classes, in which the latter triumphed, the UK parliament repealed the tariff system that supported homegrown production.

By passing this Repeal of the Corn Laws Act in 1846, the UK began a de facto experiment in what the effects might be of reducing any foodproducing demands on its rural landmass. The implications of this policy experiment have been much analysed and debated, mostly for its impact on farming, food culture and political formation, but also for its impact on health; who more than the British turned food from a pleasure into fuel?

(Driver, 1983). Less attention has been accorded to the impact on English food culture, but even those who argue that England has been unfairly pilloried as home of a restricted, poor-quality diet (Spencer, 2002) agree that the debasement of working class diets and the abandonment of any national or local links with the land coincided.

Others have argued that this poor quality, unhealthy diet was framed by employers whose interest in pursuing the cheap food policy was driven by a desire to constrain wages, food being then a heavy factor in the cost of living. If imported food could be cheaper than home-produced, so much the better. As a result by the time Britain declared war on Nazi Germany in 1939, it had only a third of its food nationally produced. The so-called 'food front' was therefore not just a strategic priority – the British Isles' food trade routes are and were horrendously vulnerable to air and naval blockade – but it highlighted the lesson others had noted, that food has, in modern European parlance, multi-functional characteristics. If one needs secure lines of food supply, as in wartime, that supply has to be able to guarantee health, affordability and all-year round deliveries. At such times, the question posed earlier – 'what is the land for?' – is easily answered, even if less easily delivered. Food remains central, therefore, to the purpose and social value of the land.

These issues are not just of import for a historically peculiar and wet post-imperial power, off the northwest coast of mainland Europe. What emerges is an important recognition that even in a country which pushes the theoretical possibility of abandoning a viable farming to its near limits, history suggests that a central, if not the central purpose of the land has to include a food production function. The policy issue is not so much, *pace* the British, whether to produce food but how, on what terms and for whom/what?

Citizens groups are beginning to engage with this agenda, not least because they have confronted the nature of farming and its impact on the environment and public health. They have supported the new critical analysis of what drives change in the food supply chain (Maxwell & Slater, 2004; Lang, 2003; Marsden, Flynn, & Harrison, 2000a). A combination of new technologies, investment, inter-sectoral restructuring and change in market rules, among other drivers, have led to a shift of power along food supply chain and a period of remarkable concentration throughout. Restless consumers have expressed unease at the worst aspects of modern techniques. This new consumer critique – what might be called a food citizenship – has brought up awkward questions about ethics, prices, global reach and other manifestations of how food is grown, processed, distributed and (not) consumed.

Public health is now (re)joining these issues as a key factor in critical debate after decades of relative silence. Although evidence has mounted as to food's impact on health (WHO, 1990, 2002; WHO/FAO, 2003; WHO/IARC, 2003), there has been less concerted or well-organised championed of policy intervention in the name of health. This period of marginalisation is now coming to a close. The WHO and FAO, notably, have united to show, how dietary change is necessary and how food and farming industries need to produce differently. The Productionist paradigm must alter (Lang & Heasman, 2004).

THE DIET AND NUTRITION TRANSITION: THE EVIDENCE FOR POLICY CHANGE

Food is now the Western world's major cause of pre-mature death. The old North-South/Developed – Developing country dichotomy no longer adequately describes or explains what is happening in food in relation to health. What Prof. Barry Popkin has termed the Nutrition Transition is now evidenced almost worldwide (Popkin, 1999; Caballero & Popkin, 2002). The Nutrition Transition is associated primarily with rising wealth and changed circumstances. The thesis, now extensively supported by country and regional studies (Popkin, 2001) argues simply that diet-related ill-health previously associated with the West and with affluence is increasingly manifest in developing countries (Popkin, 1994; Drewnoski & Popkin, 1997). Populations are shifting diet from one pattern to another – from traditional diets with restricted range and intakes to a diet involving more snacking, more western-style fast foods and soft drinks. Rapid urbanisation and changed patterns of work, in North and South, mean not just a new relationship with the land, but also a redefinition of cultural rules – what to eat, when and how. Sugary soft drinks replace water. Malls, large portion sizes, snacking and 'grazing', 'Americanisation,' supermarketisation – all illustrate the emergence of new urban cultures.

In nutrition terms, this dietary change means there is excessive consumption of fats, salt and sugars and under-consumption of fruit and vegetables. An excess of intake over energy expenditure leads to obesity, which in turn heralds other diseases. One 'quick' indicator is consumption of soft drinks, which replaces water or indigenous drinks. In the UK, consumption of ready-to-drink soft drinks rose from 100 g per person per week in 1975 to over 500 g in 2001. Low-calorie (artificially sweetened) soft drinks have not added to this market, merely expanded it, as has mineral water. At such rates of growth, it may not be too long before the dream comes true held by a late 20th century head of Coca-Cola to have the 'C' on the water tap (faucet) indicate that what gushes forth is not 'cold' water, but Coca-Cola.

At the global level, policy for the last 60 years has centred on combating mal-nutrition. Despite huge advances in output, the UN's Food and Agriculture Organisation estimates around 800 millions are still malnourished, even though the proportion of humanity in hunger has dropped. This is a considerable success, against rising populations. But there are now far more people clinically overweight or obese than hungry. By 2003, the WHO and International Association for the Study of Obesity (IASO), calculated that up to 1.7 billion people were overweight or obese. Extreme forms of obesity are rising even faster than the overall epidemic. In 2003, 6.3 per cent of U.S. women were morbidly obese, with a body mass index of 40 or more.[1] The U.S. Center for Disease Control estimates the cost of obesity and overweight in the USA as about $117 billion (Centers for Disease Control, 2002).

Obesity and overweight levels in the South are rising alarmingly. Countries such as India, China and Brazil to name just three of the South's most populous and influential countries now experience rapid growth of diseases previously associated with the rich North. Yet these countries lack the health infrastructure to be able to deal with them. They cannot afford either the by-pass operations, the stomach-tuck operations or the diabetes treatment that even a rich country like the UK is baulking at, according to two reports produced for the UK Treasury by former banker Derek Wanless (Wanless, 2002, 2004; Hunter, 2003). The 100,000 stomach operations in the USA cost the equivalent of the entire health budget of Vietnam, a country of 70 million people (Rayner, 2003). By any ethical yardstick, this is gross and a distortion of services.

The nutrition transition has immense policy implications. While delivering sufficient calories to feed all reasonably, there is now oversupply and continuing misallocation within and between national food supply chains. The range of foods and their nutrient mix is warped: too much dairy produce and meat, sugars and cereals for animal food; not enough fruit and vegetables and biodiversity coming from the field to the plate (Lang & Heasman, 2004). The cultural shift that accompanies this change is considerable. The capacity of giant food and (soft) drink companies to frame culture with their large marketing budgets should not be underestimated. The top two spenders alone spend around $1.7 billion each per year. Worldwide, an estimated $40 billion is spent annually on food marketing. This is 500 times more what the WHO has to spend on promoting healthy diets (Dalmeny, Hanna, & Lobstein, 2003). In the UK, the food industry spends £750 million per year, yet the entire UK government spends only £7 million on health promotion, i.e. less than 1 per cent of what industry spends (Department of Health, 2004). If one looks at what the industry spends its money on in countries such as the USA or UK, it is hardly a roll call of health-enhancing products. They tend to be high value-added products and/or processed products with relatively high fat, sugar and salt contents (Lang & Heasman, 2004; Nestle, 2002). The impact such spending has on lowincome society is hard to calculate, but the shift from indigenous to externally sourced high-status foods is now seen to carry a health cost.

Dietary change is nothing new. Food cultures have always been in a state of transition. What marks the current era out as special is the pace, extent and global reach of this process. Within marketing circles, it has been common for two decades to talk of the need to create global brands, but modern food Transnational Corporations are more cautious. Nestlé, for instance, the world's largest food company which sells 1–2 per cent of all food sold on the planet prefers a 'glocalised' rather than a globalised approach (Simonian, 2005). Consumers, it argues, are different by region and country. But, while pursuing this 'glocalised' strategy, transnational realities are coming to haunt the world's big players. The obesity pandemic in particular has disciplined and chastened the food giants; threats of litigation and of state action to curb marketing or internalise externalised healthcare costs are encouraging them to rush out new products and to encourage sports activity among the young.

Such corporate action is interesting, not least for how puny it is in effect of the macro-drivers such as the considerable gap between rich and poor both within and between societies; these differentials have a direct impact on public health. The UN's oft-cited statistics are sobering: the richest 1 per cent of the world's population, around 60 million, receive as much income as the poorest 57 per cent, while the income of the richest 25 million Americans is equivalent of almost 2 billion of the world's poorest people (UNDP, 2003). The policy response is underwhelming; income differentials are increasing. In 1960, 20 per cent of the world's population living in the richest countries had 30 times the income of the poorest 20 per cent; by 1997, the richest 20 per cent had 74 times the income of the poorest 20 per cent. The 1999 UNDP report called for tougher rules on global governance, including principles of performance for multi-nationals on labour standards, fair trade and environmental protection, arguing that these are needed to counter the negative effects of globalisation on the poorest nations (UNDP, 1999). By 2003, the tone being taken by UNDP was harsher. In its 2003 Human

Development Report, the 1990s were viewed as a lost decade, a period when inequalities widened rapidly. Fifty countries suffered falling living standards in the 1990s. UNICEF calculates that 800 million go hungry worldwide annually. Understandably, policy activists have tended to concentrate on the indignity and gross hunger that results. But the challenge laid down by the diet and nutrition transition requires a different order of policy than just redistribution, north to south.

Even in rich countries like Britain, food poverty exists. In 1977, Walker reviewed the (in)adequacy of welfare benefits and showed that the key British welfare programme (Supplementary Benefit) was inadequate to cover the nutritional needs of the largest 8–10-year-old children, however efficient their mothers' food purchasing behaviour (Walker & Church, 1978). In his study of 231 at-risk children in poor areas of London between 1973 and 1976, Nelson found a close relationship between restriction of income, poor diet and small size of child (Nelson & Naismith, 1979). He concluded that "at least 11 percent of the children in this study are mildly to moderately malnourished" and called for dietary intervention. In a later study, despite showing that school meals failed to provide the nutritional targets set for them by government, Nelson showed that they were the most important nutritional support outside the home for low-income families (Nelson & Paul, 1983). The impact on health is considerable. The British National Food Survey, a comprehensive annual governmental survey since the 1940s, suggests how the food gap between rich and poor has widened in some areas. On vegetable consumption, for instance, over the quarter century since 1975, the more affluent have eaten more, while the poor have consumed less. The rich eat much more fruit, fish and vegetables than the poor. In 2000, the UK National Diet and Nutrition Survey found only one in five male young people aged 4–18 years ate any green vegetables in a week, and one in five children ate no fruit in a week and three in five ate no leafy green vegetables (Caraher & Anderson, 2001).

Such studies are reminders that supposedly 'modern' debates about consumers, food and class are not new, nor has the problem necessarily been dissipated by rising national wealth (Riches, 1997). In the USA, hunger has been a persistent cause of concern for decades. A mid-1960s study reported that 9 million Americans had deficient diets. By the mid-1990s, after decades of argument about how to measure hunger, the U.S. Census Bureau calculated that 11 million Americans lived in households which were 'food insecure' with a further 23 million living in households which were "food insecure without hunger" (Eisinger, 1998). U.S. surveys estimated that at least 4 million children under age 12 were hungry and an additional

9.6 million were at risk of hunger during at least 1 month of the year preceding the survey.

A 2003 assessment by the Economic Research Service of the United States Department of Agriculture (USDA) is that 11 per cent of American households were food insecure at least some time in 2002, meaning that they did not have "access, at all times, to enough food for an active, healthy life for all household members" (Nord, Andrews, & Carlson, 2003). According to ERS, the prevalence of food insecurity in the USA rose from 10.7 per cent in 2001 to 11.1 per cent in 2002, and the prevalence of food insecurity with hunger rose from 3.3 to 3.5 per cent of the population – this in the richest nation on earth. The findings of such surveys provokes vitriolic criticism from U.S. conservative political groups; they have particularly focused on such studies often determining hunger through self-reports (Sidel, 1997). Proper scientific (weighed and measured) studies are expensive and tend to be low on the research agenda of rich countries. The UK's Food Standards Agency initiated a rare exception in 2004 (due to report in 2006–2007). Pending results, studies using self-reported hunger measures, at least for adults, are probably valid surrogate measures for low intakes of required nutrients. It should be remembered that if there was not a problem, why did a country like the U.S. spend over $25billion on federal and state programmes to provide extra food for 25 million citizens? (Eisinger, 1998). Some welfare programmes have indeed been framed by the need to dissipate stocks.

While income and socio-economic class are still key determinants of food consumption patterns, class formations are no longer bounded within nations alone. As has been noted for marketing earlier, there are other factors at play such as ethnicity, and family experience. Sociologically, it might be more meaningful to conceive of emerging global consuming classes (see Table 5) (Durning, 1992). These fit alongside another three broad categories of poorly consuming food classes worldwide (see Table 6) (Gardner & Halweil, 2000).

THE SOCIAL SCIENCE CONTRIBUTION TO THE FARM-FOOD-HEALTH NEXUS

A more serious social scientific look at the relationship between farming, food and health is long overdue. Public health is the sleeping giant of the new critical literature on food and farming. The health dimension helps to illustrate the cultural and economic drivers of modern food systems.

Table 5. World Consuming Classes.

Category of Consumption	High	Middle	Poor
Population	1.5 billion	3 billion	1.5 billion
Diet	Meat, packaged food and soft drinks	Grain and clean water	Insufficient grain and unsafe water
Transport	Private cars and air	Bicycles and bus	Walking
Source	Long-distance foods; hypermarket and delicatessen/specialist shops	Some long-distance food; local shops and markets	Local food; local shops and markets
Materials	Throw-aways	Durables	Local biomass
Choice	Big choice; global horizons	Sufficient and regional horizon	Limited or absent and local horizon
Environmental impact	High	Considerable	Low

Source: Adapted from Durning (1992).

Table 6. Types and Effects of Malnutrition.

Type of Malnutrition	Nutritional Effect	Number of People Affected Globally (Billion)
Hunger	Deficiency of calories and protein	At least 1.2
Micronutrient deficiency	Deficiency of vitamins and minerals	2.0–3.5
Over-consumption	Excess of calories, often accompanied by deficiency of vitamins and minerals	At least 1.2–1.7

Source: Worldwatch Institute (Gardner & Halweil, 2000) based on WHO, IFPRI, ACC/SCN data.

Conscious of the sheer weight of data of the spread of degenerative diseases in the developing world, and the lessons from the developed world of just how costly they can be, a policy debate is now at last emerging in global forums such as the WHO and FAO as well as in regional and national bodies. The Nutrition Transition concept has informed much of the formulation of the Global Strategy on Diet, Physical Activity and Health, approved at the World Health Assembly in May 2004 (WHO, 2004). This Strategy has been highly sensitive, with strong lobbying against it from sugar, fat and highly processed food interests. Their sensitivity is apt, as a new paradigm is emerging in which health would once again shape what farming does, and what the land is for. A shift from fat to fruit, monoculture to biodiversity promises health not just environmental gains. A study (funded by threatened sectors) into what would happen if the WHO-FAO 916 report was applied to world agriculture worldwide suggested considerable dislocation of current investment. Pig meat production would have to drop by 5 per cent, Butter by 13 per cent, Cream by 18 per cent, Animal fat by 31 per cent, Soybean oil by 14 per cent and Rapeseed oil by 30–35 per cent, and so on (Irz, Shankar, & Srinivasan, 2003). A similar study pointed to major threats to the sugar industry if there was a drop in sugar-based foods (Irz, 2003). Interestingly, no one has funded what opportunities for farming lie in a shift to grains for humans (rather for than animal feed) or to fruit and vegetables, or for simpler rather than more value-added processing.

A tense policy engagement is now underway between WHO and large food corporations, to which social science, with its understanding of the realities of food production and corporate reach, could usefully contribute. The stakes are high, not just for public health, but for governance and the legitimacy of governments to act on the citizens' behalf; the (im)balance between corners of the holy triangle is at stake. Large companies have strong grounds for resisting any regulation or impediments on their right to trade. Equally, others see an opportunity for new 'niche' products, although it is uncertain whether such alterations in product mix will deliver the major dietary change required for health. Profits and market share are at issue. But so too is a narrow conception of consumerism. Major rather than minor changes in daily food purchases are needed to accompany changes in how and why food is produced, what the land is for, what our bodies require to perform optimally? Can any sensible theorising of the new world-food order seriously accept the kind of rubric that marketers and economists offer, such as that consumers are in command? If consumers only know at best around 100 Known Value Items (KVIs), out of say 25,000 on offer, how discriminating can consumers really be? The issue at stake is how to weigh up what consumers really want in relation to what they need for bodily (and cultural) health.

A food and farming system that focuses on choice in the marketplace, but marginalises public health does not deserve intellectual let alone societal support. Policy-makers are already aware of the urgent need to build environmental protection into how food is produced and sold. The arrival of the new public health evidence and analysis could and should alter how policy-makers conceive of future food and farming policy. But, whether they make this mental leap, history suggests, will not just be a matter of evidence.

Crises such as climate change, water shortage, soil erosion, and over-reliance on oil as the 'motor' of the food system – all these are candidates to be straws that finally break the current dominant policy's back. Unfortunately, if the back breaks, it will not just be a system but lives and ecology that fails too. The need for social scientists working in food and farming to engage with this policy, reality has never been stronger. But the importance of health in this unfolding policy dynamic cannot be underestimated.

NOTES

1. BMI is a simple index of weight-for-height: a person's weight (in kilos) divided by the square of the height in metres (kg/m2). BMI provides in the WHO's words "the most useful, albeit crude, population-level measure of obesity." A BMI of between 25 and 29.9 is considered overweight – giving the global figure above of 750 m. Obesity is a BMI of 30 and above – giving the 300 m global figures. A BMI of less than 17 is considered underweight. Another relevant indicator is body fat distribution, often assessed by the waist's circumference or the waist–hip ratio. There is some argument about whether the definition of overweight as being a BMI within the 25–29.9 range should be lowered. A WHO consultation in Singapore in July 2002 considered lowering the threshold from 25 to 23, in which case billions more people would be considered overweight. It was this re-classification, which contributed to the radical upward revision of world obesity figures.

REFERENCES

Barling, D., Lang, T., & Caraher, M. (2002). Joined-up food policy? The trials of governance, public policy and the food system. *Social Policy & Administration, 36*(6), 556–574.
Boyd Orr, J. (1936). *Food, health and income: Report on adequacy of diet in relation to income.* London: Macmillan and Co.
Boyd Orr, J. (1966). *As I recall: The 1880's to the 1960's.* London: MacGibbon and Kee.
Boyd Orr, S. J. (1943). *Food and the people.* London: Pilot Press.
British Medical Association. (1939). *Nutrition and the public health: Proceedings of a national conference on the wider aspects of nutrition. (April 27-28-29).* London: British Medical Association.
Caballero, B., & Popkin, B. M. (Eds) (2002). *The nutrition transition: Diet-related diseases in the modern world.* New York: Elsevier.
Caraher, M., & Anderson, A. (2001). 'An apple a day...'. *Health Matters, 46,* 12–14.
Centers for Disease Control. (2002). *Physical activity and good nutrition: Essentials elements to prevent chronic diseases and obesity 2002.* Atlanta, GA: Department of Health and Human Services, Centers for Disease Control and Prevention.
Dalmeny, K., Hanna, E., & Lobstein, T. (2003). *Broadcasting bad health.* London: International Association of Consumer Food Organisations (IACFO).

Department of Health. (2004). *Choosing health: Making healthy choices easier.* London: Department of Health.
Drewnoski, A., & Popkin, B. M. (1997). The nutrition transition: New trends in the global diet. *Nutrition Reviews, 55,* 31–43.
Driver, C. (1983). *The British at table 1940–1980.* London: Chatto & Windus.
Durning, A. T. (1992). *How much is enough?* Washington DC & London: Worldwatch Institute/ Earthscan.
Eisinger, P. K. (1998). *Towards an end to hunger in America.* Washington DC: Brookings Institute Press.
Gardner, G., & Halweil, B. (2000). *Underfed and overfed: The global epidemic of malnutrition.* Washington, DC: Worldwatch Institute.
Grievink, J.-W. (2003). *The changing face of the global food supply chain.* The Hague: OECD.
Hunter, D. (2003). The Wanless report and public health. *British Medical Journal, 327,* 573–574.
Irz, X. (2003). *Impact of WHO dietary recommendations on World Sugar Consumption, Production and Trade.* Report prepared for the World Sugar Research Organisation. Reading: University of Reading Department of Agriculture & Food Economics.
Irz, X., Shankar, B., & Srinivasan, C. (2003). *Dietary recommendations in the report of a joint WHO/FAO expert consultation on diet, nutrition and the prevention of chronic diseases (WHO Technical Report Series 916, 2003): Potential impact on consumption, production and trade of selected food products: Report for the international federation of agricultural producers & institute for European food studies.* Reading: University of Reading Dept. Agricultural and Food Economics.
Lang, T. (2003). Food industrialisation and food power. *Development Policy Review, 21*(5), 30–39.
Lang, T., Barling, D., & Caraher, M. (2001). Food, social policy and the environment: Towards a new model. *Social Policy & Administration, 35*(5), 538–558.
Lang, T., & Heasman, M. (2004). *Food wars: The global battle for mouths, minds and markets.* London: Earthscan.
League of Nations (1936). *The problem of nutrition (Vol. 1): Interim report of the mixed committee on the problem of nutrition.* Official No. A.12. 1936.II.B.3, 24 June 1936. Geneva: League of Nations.
Marsden, T., Flynn, A., & Harrison, M. (2000a). *Consuming interest: The social provision of foods.* London: UCL Press.
Marsden, T., Flynn, A., & Harrison, M. (2000b). *Consuming interests.* London: UCL Press.
Maxwell, S., & Slater, R. (2004). Food policy old and new. In: S. Maxwell & R. Slater (Eds), *Food policy old and new.* Oxford: Basil Blackwell.
McMichael, A. J. (2001). *Human frontiers, environments and disease. Past patterns, uncertain futures.* Cambridge: Cambridge University Press.
Nelson, M., & Naismith, D. (1979). The nutritional status of poor children. *Journal of Human Nutrition, 33,* 33–45.
Nelson, M., & Paul, A. (1983). The nutritive contribution of school dinners and other mid-day meals to the diets of schoolchildren. *Human Nutrition: Applied Nutrition, 37A,* 128–135.
Nestle, M. (2002). *Politics of food.* Berkeley: University of California Press.
Nord, M., Andrews, M., & Carlson, S. (2003). *Household food security in the United States 2002.* Washington, DC: Economic Research Service, U.S. Department of Agriculture.
Organisation for Economic Co-operation and Development. (1981). *Food policy.* Paris: Organisation for Economic Co-operation & Development.

Popkin, B. M. (1994). The nutrition transition in low-income countries: An emerging crisis. *Nutrition Reviews, 52*, 285–298.
Popkin, B. M. (1999). Urbanisation, lifestyle changes and the nutrition transition. *World Development, 27*(11), 1905–1915.
Popkin, B. M. (2001). An overview on the nutrition transition and its health implication: The Bellagio meeting. *Public Health Nutrition, 5*(1A), 93–103.
Pretty, J. (2002). *Agri-Culture*. London: Earthscan.
Rayner, G. (2003). The big issue. *Public Health News*. November 24, 10–13.
Riches, G. (1997). *First world hunger: Food security and welfare politics*. London: Macmillan.
Self, P. S., & Storing, H. J. (1971). *The state and the farmer*. London: George Allen & Unwin.
Sidel, V. W. (1997). Annotation: The public health impact of hunger. *American Journal of Public Health, 87*(8), 1921–1922.
Simonian, H. (2005). Business life. Chef assumes control of the executive recipe. *Financial Times*. February 22, London, p. 16.
Spencer, C. (2002). *British food*. London: Brub Street.
Timmer, C. P., Falcon, W. P., & Pearson, S. R. (1983). *Food policy analysis*. Baltimore, Maryland: World Bank & Johns Hopkins University Press.
UNDP. (1999). *Human development report*. New York: Oxford University Press & United Nations Development Programme.
UNDP. (2003). *Human development report 2002*. New York: Oxford University Press & United Nations Development Programme.
Vorley, B. (2004). *Food inc.: Corporate concentration from farm to consumer*. London: UK Food Group.
Walker, C., & Church, M. (1978). Poverty by administration: A review of supplementary benefits, nutrition and scale rates. *Journal of Human Nutrition, 32*, 5–18.
Wanless, D. (2002). *Securing our future health: Taking a long-term view*. London: HM Treasury.
Wanless, D. (2004). *Securing good health for the whole population*. London: HM Treasury.
WHO. (1990). *Diet, nutrition and the prevention of chronic diseases*. Geneva: World Health Organisation.
WHO. (2002). *World Health Report 2002: Reducing risks, promoting healthy life*. Geneva: World Health Organisation.
WHO. (2004). *Global strategy on diet, physical activity and health*. Geneva: World Health Assembly.
WHO/FAO. (2003). *Diet, nutrition and the prevention of chronic diseases. Report of the joint WHO/FAO expert consultation*. WHO Technical report series, no. 916 (TRS 916). Geneva: World Health Organisation & Food and Agriculture Organisation.
WHO/IARC. (2003). *World Cancer Report World Health*. Geneva: World Health Organisation/ International Agency for Research on Cancer.

PROMOTING SUSTAINABLE DEVELOPMENT: THE QUESTION OF GOVERNANCE☆

Geoffrey Lawrence

ABSTRACT

Despite continuing disagreement about the meaning of 'sustainable development', the so-called triple-bottom-line trajectory – which would see economic advancement being achieved alongside social equity and environmental security – is viewed as one of the promises for future progress regionally, nationally and globally. At the regional level we are witnessing various experiments in governance that cut across, challenge and undermine existing decision-making structures. They are being developed and implemented because of the perceived failure of older forms of governance to deliver sustainable development. This chapter will examine the 'regional experiment' that is occurring within the advanced societies, identifying the general features of the schemes, policies and programmes that are being promoted to bring about sustainable development. From a policy perspective, it will seek to identify the elements, and forms, of regional governance that appear to provide the best options for sustainable development.

☆This chapter is an extended version of a plenary paper presented at the *XI World Congress of Rural Sociology*, Trondheim, Norway, 25–30 July 2004.

INTRODUCTION

Throughout the world – and at a time when sustainable development is being viewed as a medium term imperative rather than some nebulous, hoped-for, long-term, goal – attention is being given to the improvement of natural resource management and to the livelihoods of people outside the metropoles. New policies and new forms of governance have emerged, including new institutions and policy frameworks. In Australia – as in so many countries around the world – voluntarism and self-help strategies have gone hand-in-hand with regional priority setting and decision-making in the area of environmental protection. There is an effort to address the so-called 'triple bottom line' of economy, society and environment so that economic ambitions are tempered with a respect for social equity and environmental integrity, with the economy being forced to take its place as only one of three 'elements' in the calculus of sustainable development.

Some sociologists such as Archon Fung and Erik Olin Wright, whose work forms a part of the creatively named Real Utopias Project ('embracing the tension between dreams and practice' – see Fung and Wright (2003, p. 7)), consider that what we are witnessing is the emergence of empowered participatory governance. They argue that traditional modes of political representation are frustrating the democratic ambitions of citizens, and that a radical egalitarianism may be possible if the newlyemerging participatory opportunities afforded by such initiatives as neighbourhood councils, administrative and fiscal devolution and stakeholder involvement in habitat conservation planning are supported (Fung & Wright, 2003, p. 5).

This chapter argues that what we are witnessing throughout the so-called advanced world are experiments in sub-national regional governance that are themselves a response to wider problems in managing global capitalism. Rather than solving the problems that are emerging, and rather than unequivocally producing a dynamic that leads to sustainable development, they appear to be generating their own tensions and contradictions – some of which will not be readily resolved within, and indeed may be exacerbated by, the structure of global neoliberalism. What, however, might represent a progressive response – abandoning notions of sustainability and regionality because of the inherent problems and difficulties, or seeking to support sustainable development by improving structures of governance at the regional level?

SUSTAINABLE, AND UNSUSTAINABLE, DEVELOPMENT

One does not need to sit through the 2004 disaster film *The Day After Tomorrow* to recognise the environmental problems that the planet faces as a result of modernisation and industrialisation. We see the signs around us. It is widely acknowledged that industrial pollution, species decline, loss of habitat, increasing demands on fresh water, the erosion of beaches and coastal lands and global warming are directly attributable to human activity (Held, McGrew, Goldblatt, & Perraton, 1999; IPCC, 2001). Just as importantly, we can see a parallel in human devastation in the wasted lives of those who are the victims of global change (Bauman, 2004).

The first popularly accepted definition of sustainable development arose from the report of Norwegian Gro Harlem Brundtland who, with her Commission members, suggested in 1987 that the world should be 'meeting the needs of the present without compromising the ability of future generations to meet their own needs' (World Commission on Environment and Development, 1987). It was a profound statement at the time and a strong reminder to the disposability-is-progress generation that profligacy and disregard for the environment would lead to intergenerational inequities and eventual ecosystem collapse. Of course, as a rather slippery term, sustainability can mean the maintenance of intergenerational well-being; ensuring the continuation of human life indefinitely; maintaining the productivity of economic systems; maintaining biodiversity; and a combination of these (and other) things (see Gowdy, 1999, p. 164). It can be 'weak' or 'strong', or 'reformist' or 'radical' or be about intragenerational equity as much intergenerational equity (see Eichler, 1999; Gowdy, 1999; Gray & Lawrence, 2001). Ironically, sustainability is also seen as a 'grand narrative' in a post-modern era that, itself, rejects grand narratives (Myerson & Rydin, 1996).

The three elements of sustainability – the economy, society and environment – have been, and continue to be, treated separately in academic writings and in public policy. Yet, sustainable development is premised on a new balance being achieved between the three elements – with an effective integration of those elements in public and private decision-making processes (Bates, 2003). But how might these elements be interconnected? As some writers (Giddings, Hopgood, & O'Brien, 2002) have argued, that each is multi-layered, fractured and must, as well, be considered at different spatial levels. As a further complicating issue, in differentiating countrysides there may be a number of alternative trajectories for sustainable development (Marsden, Murdoch, & Abram, 1997).

In rural regions of the so-called advanced societies we have witnessed the entrenchment of productivist or 'high tech' farming systems. This is despite growing recognition that productivist agriculture is largely unsustainable (Altieri, 1998). Its persistence is logically consistent with global neoliberal or free-market policies as they are applied to farming. Hoping to survive in an increasingly competitive international marketplace farmers obey market signals and adopt the behaviour required to ensure their futures in farming. This generally means specialising in production, intensifying and expanding farm operations and purchasing the latest products of agribusiness to gain a competitive edge through increases in productivity and efficiency (see Ilbery & Bowler, 1998). Yet, the pursuit of this has devastating effects on the environment. The clearing of vegetation to bring land into production for agriculture and grazing results in topsoil loss and very often – as water tables rise – to salinisation. There is also evidence, worldwide, of overcropping and overgrazing as farmers seek to secure increases in production in the face of declining prices and poor seasons (O'Connor, 1994; Martinez-Alier, 1999; Lawrence, Cheshire, & Richards, 2004). We also know that the products of agribusiness – in concert with management regimes that endorse or demand monocultural practices and blindly obey world market forces – are implicated in widespread environmental destruction (Magdoff, Foster, & Buttel, 2000). When this is applied to Third World settings, we see how jaundiced a green revolution is for the poor of the world (McMichael, 2004). Finally, it has been argued that the current rules of global trade set by the World Trade Organisation (WTO) promote harmonisation as an important part of liberalisation. This translates, however, into a narrowing of choice for nation states in their attempts to deal with environmental outcomes of economic activity (Levidow, 2005).

Some sociologists and geographers have detected the emergence of a post-productivist and multi-functional countryside – particularly in Europe where there are pressures for continued protection of agriculture, support for local communities, along with the 'greening' of the Common Agricultural Policy (Holmes, 2002; Tilzey, 2003). But others (Wilson, 2001; Argent, 2002; Walford, 2003) have argued that there are only slight traces of such positive change being observed in many of the countries where environmental pollution from farming is at its worse. Nevertheless, pressured by consumers anxious about food quality, animal welfare and a host of environmental matters, there is discernable political pressure for the move to what Marsden (2003, p. 4) has termed a paradigm of rural sustainability, or what we have termed in Australia as 'sustainable regional development' (Lawrence, 1998; Dore & Woodhill, 1999; Lawrence, 2003) – a form of organisation that would seek to secure sustainable livelihoods at the regional (sub-national) level.

The basic argument in this chapter is that the dynamic of productivism can be challenged – and potentially replaced – by triple bottom line approaches, and that these approaches might be best achieved at the regional level on the basis of partnerships between the state and communities. But a second, less optimistic, assertion is that new contradictions are beginning to appear that threaten to undermine the emerging inclusive, adaptive, partnership approach to regional sustainability.

EXPERIMENTS IN REGIONAL GOVERNANCE AND THE GOVERNANCE OF NATURAL RESOURCES

From North America to Europe to the Antipodes there has been an enormous 'shift' towards decision-making at the regional level. Governance is about structures and processes that allow for strategic decision-making outside the traditional institutions and agents given power to govern (Jessop, 1998). The new governance framework is based upon the reinvention of government through multi-level partnerships, knowledge exchange, devolution of decision-making and 'joined up' inter-institutional arrangements. Bureaucratic and technical accountability is being steadily replaced by the building of coalitions and networks at the local level (Reddel, 2002). There is a blurring of the boundaries between the public and private spheres as various 'partnerships' evolve (Head & Ryan, 2003) and as state activities are supplemented by a network of self-governing actors capable of redefining relations between institutions (Stoker, 1998). As Lovering (1999, p. 390) has noted, whereas in the decade of the 1980s there were over 400 regional development agencies worldwide, at the end of the 20th century there were more than 4,000. He is also quick to note that the new regionalism has all the elements of global neoliberalism (with its concerns for competition, the marketplace and business integration) rather than embodying an agenda for comprehensive regional development (Lovering, 2001).

In Europe, the devolution of authority from central governments to sub-national bodies has been a logical extension of the subsidiarity principle – that decision-making should occur at the lowest appropriate level – and it has fostered regionalism through the reliance on multi-level governance

(Gleeson, 2003). Recent regional policy initiatives are concerned with sustainability of regions rather than with the more narrow concern for income and trade performance (Gleeson, 2003, p. 232). In the US, new alliances are forming across existing legislative boundaries with habitat conservation planning now occurring at ecosystem scales and so bypassing statutory standards and procedures, and involving a multiplicity of people and agencies in a new arrangements of power (Karkkainen, 2003).

With the EU's LEADER Programme, a 'new localism' (that is, the creation of integrated plans for local development and the attempt to enlist the participation of the socially marginalised) has been viewed as a direct response to rural socio-economic decline (Moseley, 1999). Although it has been based upon rural development rather than sustainability, per se, LEADER during the 1980s and 1990s sought to create through its Local Action Groups, and in hitherto marginalised areas, an enterprise culture, better service delivery, community empowerment and social inclusion in decision-making (Westholm, 1999) – thereby anticipating what would evolve, in the new millennium, into new governance models in Europe.

In Europe, documents such as the *White Paper on Governance*, the *Environmental Action Programme* and the *EU Sustainable Development Strategy* (see CEC, 2001a, b, c) embrace the need for various tiers of government to interface in a manner that promotes opportunities for integrated approaches to decision-making at the regional level and for citizen empowerment via capacity building (Berger, 2003). The EU is concerned that people are showing increasing distrust for 'distant' and faceless institutions making decisions about their lives. Local and regional bodies and governments are therefore to be involved in partnership arrangements – as part of a different set of 'policy tools' aimed at reducing the alienation and powerlessness that is perceived to be a current feature within the Union (CEC, 2001a, p. 7). It is asserted that inclusiveness and accountability will be achieved through the reform of governance arrangements (CEC, 2001a, p. 8). The two basic elements of EU policy are the inclusion of wider sections of society, and multi-level government (Berger, 2003, p. 231). Of course, the preoccupation with the structures of governance over process-related concerns can gloss over the politically sensitive issue of who holds power, and how – and for what purposes – that power is used.

According to Harriet Bulkeley and co-workers at the University of Durham in the UK, the development of multi-level governance (that is, involving actors and institutions from the public agencies, private businesses and civil society – and at local, state and global levels) can be seen in the emergence of what are being termed transnational municipal networks or

TMNs (Bulkeley et al., 2003). Another example is that of the so-called 'joining up' of decision-making bodies at a multi-level scale with partnerships rather than hierarchies being the new organisational framework (Geddes, 2003).

Leaving aside these examples, it is instructive to consider the experiment in sustainable regional development that is occurring in Australia. Australia has a very large landmass, but is the second driest continent (after Antarctica) in the world. In the last 200 years of white settlement, European-style agriculture, and grazing, together with tree clearing and reliance upon irrigation from unreliable river systems has created major environmental problems. The latter have included soil erosion, waterlogging, the salinisation and acidification of pastures, agro-chemical pollution of waterways, species decline and the uncontrollable spread of weeds. Perhaps, not surprisingly, many of the so-called 'weeds' have been introduced in earlier decades as the supposed solutions to productivity losses in Australian agriculture and grazing (see Gray & Lawrence, 2001).

Although State governments had been charged with the development of agriculture and the management of the environment, the Federal government recognised that if the nation were to address the quite severe problems of environmental degradation in the regions it would need to intervene. But intervention in recent times has not taken a form of top-down regulation. Rather, in consultation with the States, the National Farmers' Federation and the Australian Conservation Foundation, the so-called Decade of Landcare was born in 1989, with the introduction of the National Landcare Programme. The aim was to stimulate the creation of locality-based community landcare groups that would take responsibility for on-the-ground actions to address environmental problems (Lockie, 2004). The Federal government provided funding to underpin group formation, to inspire a higher level of knowledge of the environment and for such activities as tree planting, catchment planning and demonstrations of environmentally sound practices (Campbell, 1994). The landcare programme has exceeded expectations of government, with more than 4,000 groups comprising some 120,000 volunteer workers being established throughout the nation (see Mues, Chapman, & Van Hilst, 1998; Lockie, 2004, p. 43). This represents approximately one third of Australia's farms, with many other regional stakeholders also becoming actively involved. Its success is viewed in terms of: developing 'robust' relations between state agency officials and local communities; increasing the awareness throughout the rural community of environmental issues; improving landholder skills; and enhancing best management practices (Curtis, 2003, p. 447). Featuring ideals of consensus and partnership, the landcare movement is viewed by some as an example of a successful participative democratic structure that is a successful way of promoting more sustainable development (Alexander, 1995).

As part of the new direction in community-based natural resource management, and based upon the success of landcare, Australia's Federal government endorsed the community-partnership model as greatly beneficial for Australian natural resource management (Standing Committee on Environment, Recreation and Arts, 2001, p. 24). In 1997, the Natural Heritage Trust (NHT) was initiated with $1.5 billion in funding having been assigned to projects up until mid-2001, and with another $1 billion being allocated to extend the scheme for another 5 years. This represents one of the biggest environmental investments by the government in Australia's history, with its Landcare, Bushcare, Rivercare and Coastcare programmes relying upon regional delivery as the primary mechanism.

Under these various schemes regional communities (comprising landowners, businesses, NGOs, local, State and Territory governments) are formulating the so-called Accredited Natural Resource Management Plans. These plans define the most important activities for state investment and, therefore, for action at the regional or catchment level.

Catchments are viewed as natural geographical structures that do not conform to State or local government boundaries. The aim, then, is to promote an environmental 'identity' across existing political boundaries and within the catchments. Limited powers are being given to regional bodies (catchment management groups and authorities) to provide leadership in natural resource management issues, undertake regional and local planning, undertake on-ground management and monitoring and to initiate extension and capacity building exercises. While State and local governments are still required to administer land and water legislation and regulation, it is individuals, companies and various 'stakeholders' who are viewed as those who will be responsible for on-ground actions to improve the environment, and to promote regional sustainability (Standing Committee on Environment, Recreation and Arts, 2001, p. 27).

What can be said of these Australian attempts to promote sustainable development through community?

They do represent an attempt to:

- Mobilise community and stakeholder participation and foster wider partnerships with government.
- Identify the sub-state (catchment) region as the most important scale for delivery of sustainability outcomes – thereby moving beyond the

structures of representative democracy (federal, state and local government).
- Highlight the need to see environmental integrity as an essential component of regional progress – thereby moving from regional economic development as the key focus to sustainable regional development as the 'future'.
- Seek to have communities develop frameworks for action that go well beyond the short-term cycles of federal and State budgets (Curtis, 2003; Lawrence, 2003).

But, as we might expect, the success of the Australian experiment in governing sustainability must be tempered with some critical assessment. There have been five main criticisms of the voluntary governance approach to sustainability in Australia:

- Landcare was deemed a 'success' with one-third of primary producers being involved. Some have asked – 'who are these people' and 'what about the other two-thirds'? In some cases, landcare groups formed to block the entry of environmental, and other, stakeholders in decision-making. In other words, some people and groups were deliberately excluded from landcare activities (Morrissey & Lawrence, 1997). In some areas, the majority of producers could be involved in quite profound soil, water and biodiversity destruction, with their involvement in landcare no more than an ideological shield to help protect them against the widespread criticism that might otherwise have ensued.
- There is evidence that governments, through the new natural resource management (NRM) initiatives, are devolving responsibility, rather than *power*. Some NRM groups devise regional plans and priorities only to be told by central government that these are not the main concerns at the federal level. Powerlessness – rather than community capacity – is fostered in such circumstances. The so-called purse strings are held very tightly by central administration.
- The move to partnership arrangements and the winding back of top-down forms of planning can only occur if new support structures (and people) are in place to support the new arrangements. The progress is slow and very frustrating for regional bodies that have been told they will be given a licence to create a new sustainable future. The time that they are able to devote to community activities is also quite limited, with 'burnout' being a major problem (Curtis, 2003).
- Without coordination of government services in natural resource management, regional resource-use planning is being viewed as another 'level'

of bureaucracy one which has the potential to duplicate (rather than to support and complement) current planning activities.
- Finally, Landcare has as one of its mottos 'the right environment to do business'. It is premised on the view that sustainability can be achieved within a system of agricultural productivism. Interestingly, a number of companies in its sponsorship list are implicated in some of the worst environmental destruction in Australia. It is no wonder then, that some consider Landcare and its contemporary equivalents a 'greenwash', allowing environmental degradation to continue while giving corporate entities public credibility in the environmental arena (see discussions in Lockie & Vanclay, 1997; Gray & Lawrence, 2001; Curtis, 2003).

It has been posited that protests against the impacts of neoliberalism and the backlash against globalisation have prompted governments to seek more participatory means of governing (Paterson, Humphreys, & Pettiford, 2003). This is seen as a deliberate means of counteracting opposition by embracing dissent (Paterson et al., 2003) and has, at its heart, the necessity to secure long-term legitimacy. The globalisation of capitalism is a polarising process, creating wealth in some regions and poverty, unemployment, marginalisation and exclusion in others (Sanderson, 2000; Gray & Lawrence, 2001; Bauman, 2004). And, under policies of neoliberal marketisation, the state is no longer willing or able to place a generous safety net under those disadvantaged by change (Geddes, 2003).

WHAT MIGHT BE GOING ON HERE?

Globalisation represents a re-ordering of the world, with market rule as the dominant discourse (Peine & McMichael, 2005). Neoliberalism is generating a series of economic rationalist policy settings that are fostering freemarkets, global flows of finance and socio-economic integration. If the 1940s General Agreement on Tariffs and Trade embraced the ideal of national sovereignty, then the new century's WTO can be viewed as a global governing entity prioritising the needs of the corporation over the community (Peine & McMichael, 2005). Although mediated by the nation state, regional locales are interacting with global firms in a manner that supports those advantaged by access to information technology, skilled labour and so forth. But, at the same time that global flows of capital, products, technologies and knowledge are accelerating, so are concerns about the sustainability of those activities. The so-called 'greening' of western society has, as one of its prominent features, the growing demand by citizens for environmental security (see Brand, 1997). This is becoming something that the state is struggling to achieve through conventional regulatory mechanisms. For this reason, the shift from top-down 'government' to new forms of governing represent not the demise of state authority but a form of re-regulation which attempts to resolve some of the contradictions inherent in capitalist expansion and its consequent impacts upon the ecosystem. A governance model accepts that subsystems – like bioregions – are the site for networking and other arrangements that might allow global processes to be 'managed' in a manner that if not ultimately protecting the environment, at least provides new options for longer term environmental security. The regions are an experiment in the promotion, and governing, of sustainability.

The work of Nicholas Rose (1996) is useful to consider here. He has argued that statist ideologies based on notions of 'society' are being replaced by those of 'community' with the subsequent growth of a new territory of administration being the locale (neighbourhood group, community – for the purposes of argument here, the region), necessitating a re-conceptualisation of the relationship between the state, the market and civil society. Elected governments, in his view, identify and promote the interaction between various stakeholders, rather than impose top-down decisions. Neoliberalism appears to have endorsed and fostered the self-regulation of individuals and communities which, at the regional level, equates to the acceptance of programmes, techniques and procedures that support market rule, productivism and global competition (Higgins, 2002; Herbert-Cheshire, 2003) while, at the same time, seeking to promote sustainable development. The partnership approach that is part of contemporary governance is infused with ideals of community and empowerment. Under advanced liberal rule, the conduct of individuals and communities is shaped by notions of entrepreneurialism and capacity building with those electing to oppose these discourses and policy settings marginalised and, indeed, blamed for their own demise if they and their communities fail to thrive (see Higgins, 2002; Herbert-Cheshire, 2003, p. 280). State agencies are viewed as exerting 'action at a distance', with self-assessment and self-regulation replacing state coercion through regulatory mechanisms.

As Karkkainen (2003, p. 220) reports, decision-making about environmental matters is moving to a model of collaborative problem solving at 'multiple, nested spatial scales'. He considers 'the driving ambition of ecosystem management is to create new human institutions matched to the scales of crucial ecological processes' (Karkkainen, 2003, p. 221). The result is the emergence of hybrid institutions featuring collaborative arrangements between a host of government, business and community entities creating a 'complex web of institutional reconfigurations' in which the state continues to play an important role in the provision of resources. This is broadly consistent with Fung and Wright's (2003) assessment of what they term 'empowered participatory governance' which is typified by: the devolution of decision-making powers to empowered local entities; linkages of accountability to superordinate bodies; and transformations in current forms of representative government.

Fung and Wright (2003) argue that this new model is not that of the New Left where the devolution of power would manifest itself in autonomous decentralisation (or even regional government). Rather it is viewed as coordinated decentralisation where partnership arrangements allow for multi-level power re-alignments. Fung and Wright implicitly believe that empowered participatory democracy has a more radical potential than the earlier revolutionary notions of 'capturing the state'. Why? Because local citizens, in new decision-making networks where there is some semblance of equality of power, have the capacity to make changes and challenge the structures of bureaucracy that were, in the past, barriers to social change. Importantly, they do so with the 'blessing' of the state which is eager to see the mobilisation of popular participation and the resolution of complex local problems through the process of reasoned deliberation (Fung & Wright, 2003, p. 24).

While accepting that there might be 'damning flaws' in their model, Fung and Wright (2003, pp. 29–38) consider that empowered participatory democracy should be readily embraced as an alternative to the failures of earlier statist policies that relied upon mechanisms of representative governance and bureaucracy to deliver fair and equitable solutions to regional problems. While we might question the ability of rural citizens to become engaged, reflexive, participants in the new arrangements from a position of social disadvantage (see Gray & Lawrence, 2001; Cheshire & Lawrence, 2004) – one in which many in rural and regional areas experience social isolation, exclusion and deprivation and where environmental problems remain largely unsolved – it is nevertheless important to note that many regional people have embraced this change as representing a genuine attempt to give them a voice and to achieve action in regional development matters (AFFA, 1999).

THE TENSIONS AND CONTRADICTIONS OF DEVOLVED GOVERNANCE

Not surprisingly, many writers who have examined the emergence of new forms of governance have not been wholly convinced of their capacity to deliver outcomes that challenge current trajectories or that provide for a sustainable future. There appear to be five major concerns:

Regional Bodies Challenge the Power of the Entities that have Created them, yet they Rely upon that Central Power for their Existence

While it is claimed that the movement from government to governance is something innovative, dynamic and empowering for citizens, the regional bodies have tended to exist alongside existing tiers of government, rather than replace them. The regional bodies therefore must deal with the current tiers. There is evidence to suggest that for many people in regional decision-making bodies the experience in dealing with existing state and other bureaucracies is frustrating and, indeed, disempowering and that they are beginning to challenge the legitimacy of the very state entities that approved of their formation. The claim is often made that there is an institutional incapacity in the older structures of representative government that must be overcome for progress to be made at the regional level. Will these new bodies wrest power from the 'centre'? If not, will they be content to remain as the poor cousins of one or more existing level of government?

Local level coalitions and partnerships act upon and transform institutional structures of government (Goodwin, 1998). What if this directly challenges current power structures and arrangements? Because the new forms of governance move within and between current forms of authority, their functions can be readily questioned. And, because they are dependent upon central funding, they can disappear with a withdrawal of that funding (Westholm, Moseley, & Stenlas, 1999). As Shortall and Shucksmith (1998) remind us, if funding is a main stimulus for the creation of partnerships, it is quite likely that those partnerships will collapse if and when funding is withdrawn. Furthermore, 'ephemeral' arrangements neither inspire commitment from stakeholders, nor give hope that longer-term options will be either discussed or pursued by partnerships. There is an assumption that partnerships will be a better (that is more efficient, inclusive and transparent) way of delivering outcomes at the local level. However, as Geddes (2003, p. 15) has argued:

Most partnerships are only weakly constituted in organisational terms, and the great majority have only very limited dedicated staff and financial resources. It is asking a great deal for such weak local organisations to achieve the kind of joined up deliverythat government itself finds very difficult.

Rather than Being Inclusive, Regional Bodies can Exclude Key Stakeholders

There are often elaborate attempts made in the regions to ensure that all key stakeholders are represented on the new bodies. There are some problems here. First, groups have differential power and resources with some having the capacity to lobby within groups, and – behind the scenes – to promote their positions on particular issues. In Australia, many of the stakeholders on catchment management committees are farmers, graziers, local government officials and small business owners with the financial wherewithal to travel long distances and stay – often for several days – at distant venues within the catchments. Younger people, and indigenous Australians are usually notable by their absence. Second, even if representation were equitable at the local level, it could readily be argued that some of the main stakeholders in sustainable development are those outside the regions – those whose livelihoods are strongly affected by those living in, and making decisions about, the catchment. When rounds of priority setting occur in the formulation of catchment management or regional development plans where is the voice of the city environmentalist, the overseas consumer or, as Actor Network theorists would remind us, where is the voice of nature? Indeed, some have criticised the current construction of sustainability for its anthropocentric bias – for interpreting the environment as primarily a resource for human use, rather than being valued for its own integrity (Doyle, 1998).

Partnerships between a multiplicity of actors increasingly allow individuals and groups from business and community sectors to take what are, in essence, political decisions in regard to policy and funding. Although it is believed that transparency and visibility of decision-making processes might help to overcome this problem, it nevertheless remains that local elites – often politically savvy and financially advantaged – can increase their power while at the same time denying it to already marginalised and excluded groups in the community (Westholm, 1999; Walker & Hurley, 2004). Participative processes do not guarantee that decision-making will escape an already-entrenched power regime.

The New Arrangements for Sustainable Development may Embrace and Foster Productivism Rather than Replace it

Citizen power might boost the confidence of local people, without really addressing the wider system of productivism and its unsustainable trajectory.

On many regional bodies charged with sustainable development sit primary producers whose modus operandi is to harness the latest products of science and agribusiness to increase productivity. The need for a radical re-assessment and re-alignment of production regimes is literally off the agenda. Indeed, in the Australian context, producers have – in the face of new knowledge about environmental degradation – been found to deny the evidence; contest the evidence; or, even where they accept the evidence, either blame governments, or maintain that they do not have the financial wherewithal to alter their current production regimes (see Lawrence, Richards, & Herbert-Cheshire, 2003). Some are, of course, adopting 'best management' and other restorative practices (Lockie, 2001). The question is: will incremental change, rather than radical change, be enough to bring about sustainability? There is evidence, worldwide, that the problem will get worse before it gets better, with critics calling for the emergence of an entirely new global system of production and distribution as the only means of achieving sustainability (see Davies, 2004).

Part of the problem is that when left to orthodox economists, the problems of environmental degradation and regional socio-economic degeneration are conceived as market failures. All that is apparently needed is better mechanisms to 'cost' environmental problems, and to allow better market access so that there will be increased trade in environmental goods, and – in relation to regional development – the removal of labour market restraints so that wages become cheaper and business is attracted into the regions (see a critical discussion in Gray and Lawrence (2001)). It could be argued that justifications for the continuation of neoliberal policy settings as the basis for sustainable development empty the latter of any real transformative potential.

In Europe's so-called 'lagging regions' there is a very strong pressure for economic development over environmental concerns (Berger, 2003). While this might seem reasonable (a 'jobs first' strategy) it nevertheless reinforces the claim that in the more marginal regions there is a preoccupation with economic growth, to the detriment of any 'triple bottom line' approach. Significantly, in an era of globalisation, local production sites are integrated into global markets by supranational agribusiness firms, often deliberately by-passing the legislative mechanisms established by the nation state and aimed at protecting the environment (Held et al., 1999). Will the regions compromise environmental security for the short-term economic benefits of investment? Will regional governance arrangements secure the best future for the regions? In Australia, for example, the emerging framework of regional governance has emphasised competition over cooperation – with 'bidding wars' occurring as regional bodies seek to capture as much funding as possible, and within limited federal and State budgets. The 'beggar thy neighbour' approach that has seen the States out manoeuvring each other for private and public funding is being imposed at the regional level, raising the spectre of further unevenness of development as regional options are pursued (Stilwell, 2000).

The Enthusiasm for Participation is Likely be Quelled by the Reality of Accountability

We do not need Max Weber to remind us that voluntary structures can readily transmogrify into bureaucracies and that one of the reasons for this is the perceived need for accountability. Overlapping layers of participative regional governance in the context of the structures of representative government are confusing enough. When multi-layered levels of federal and state agency responsibility and business interactions are also introduced, the result can be total incomprehensibility. And, on top of this, when the public funding is injected into the equation, there are often grave fears that the funds will be either misspent – or will disappear without trace.

In some regions there are literally hundreds of separate entities charged with delivering programmes, often working across a number of regional and sub-regional boundaries, and having no immediate connection with each other. Part of the problem has to do with the so-called 'stove piping' of government activity – a Department of Natural Resources, a Department of Agriculture, a separate Agency for Environmental Protection, another Department of Regional Development, and so forth – where, rather than serving the interests of the community via regional bodies, they compete for funding and 'status' within government. The regional bodies often find it difficult to wend their way through thickets of legislation, forests of paperwork and the jungles of competing responsibilities. But, another part of the problem is that public monies are being delivered to non-democratically elected regional entities. As Gerry Stoker (1998) has reminded us, the emergence of self-governing networks creates the problem of accountability. It is one that is supposedly 'fixed' by central agencies creating a complex set of rules for the procurement and expenditure of funds. However, the outcome is that the regional organisations begin to behave more like regional business organisations or local governments, robbing the organisation of its fluid and dynamic character and ultimately containing expenditures to those activities approved by central bureaucracies. Here, we experience what Eshuis and Van Woerkum (2003, p. 393) refer to as the 'vicious circle of bureaucratic monitoring and distrust'. The irony here is that the move to more participative forms of decision-making activity was motivated, in the first place, by the need to escape the more rigid, technical forms of planning that were seen to be the products of aloof, city-based, government departments (see Lawrence, 2001).

It has been observed that the desire for much stronger integration through 'joined up' governance has led to ever-increasing controls by central administrations as they scrutinize the priorities and performance of local and regional agencies (see Cowell & Martin, 2003). This has been the experience in Australia (Lawrence, 2003) and, it appears, in the US, UK, New Zealand, Canada and many EU states (such as Sweden and the Netherlands) (see Geddes, 2003). In other words, centralised managerialism can readily accommodate a rhetoric of local involvement and capacity building – making something of a mockery of community empowerment. Central power can and does undermine local initiative at the same time as it renders harmless any attempts to develop alternative policy at the local level (Geddes, 2003). If stakeholders believe that a decision-making process is flawed – especially if they don't trust in their ability to have the outcomes of participative decision-making endorsed and 'delivered' – they will be reluctant to participate further and often withdraw their support (Eshuis & Van Woerkum, 2003). They will – ultimately – be disempowered. As Head and Ryan (2004, p. 20) have emphasised:

> Models based on participative governance emphasise the role of trust and mutual adjustment in sustaining policy and delivery networks that are substantially reliant on nongovernment actors. The challenges in building such arrangements in the long term are becoming evident to stakeholders.

It is one thing to accept that the appropriate governing structures for sustainable development will be 'multi-level' and 'multi-stakeholder' (European Communities, 2003) but quite another to conclude that such structures, or what results from deliberations within those structures, might have widespread legitimacy. According to Bulkeley et al. (2003) although the EU supports 'bottom-up' governance to enable people at the grassroot level to participate in decision-making (and to promote transparency, inclusivity and accountability), the ideal of participative democracy is compromised by 'patterns of power and legacies of past relationships that can obscure processes and complicate decision making' (Bulkeley et al., 2003, p. 250). In fact, multi-level governance entities can sidestep the political and institutional structures of the nation state and bring 'global' policies to bear on their local actions (Bulkeley et al., 2003, p. 251). This may further global governance but fail to do so in ways that would enhance sustainable development – particularly when the global agenda is one of extending the influence of free trade and corporate expansionism (Stiglitz, 2003; McMichael, 2004). We have to ask: will 'bottom-up' governance ultimately be compromised by a lack of democratic legitimacy? (Bulkeley et al., 2003).

Finally, partnerships often rely upon a slow accumulation of social trust: this tends to reduce the ability of groups to undertake action in short time periods and, indeed, when decisions are made they tend to be about incremental, not radical, change (Westholm, 1999, p. 21).

Rural People are Expected to Act to Save the Planet, but their Ability to do so is Proscribed by their Liminality

'Progress' in capitalist agriculture is usually typified by the following: under demands of competition: farm numbers decline; farm size increases; labour is replaced by technology; off-farm inputs (machinery, agrichemicals, fertlizers and capital) are purchased in ever larger volumes; and, farm output burgeons (Stirling, 2001; Lawrence et al., 2004). Farm output enters the marketplace where – in the context of slowly growing demand – it fails to provide the level of profit needed to sustain the economic base of farming, placing pressure on farmers to leave the land, increase farm size, purchase more inputs – and so forth. It is not without good reason that this has been termed the 'treadmill of production' (Schnaiberg, 1980). It is a treadmill that has – as one of many unintended consequences – environmental degradation.

Given that much of the degradation of natural resources is a by-product of productivist agriculture, it would therefore seem appropriate that rural producers are progressively enrolled in schemes to alter their on-farm activities. What must be recognised, however, is that a large proportion of farmers – particularly so-called 'family farmers' – are economically marginalised, failing to obtain sufficient income from agricultural endeavours to maintain their livelihoods (Barr & Cary, 2000; Almas & Lawrence, 2003). Many have to pursue off-farm work options to maintain a cash flow. Should we expect that they would have the funds or time to devote to correcting environmental degradation, despite the various incentives offered by the state?

Apart from the farmers, many of those living in rural communities have been progressively disempowered and detraditionalised under neoliberal policies that remove the social services and infrastructural platforms that might enhance community action (see Gray & Lawrence, 2001). And, as people leave farming and rural regions, the extent of social participation and level of trust and scale of community activity are all curtailed and threatened (Pretty, 2002). 'Self-help' and partnership initiatives look to be going only part-the-way to addressing the mistakes of the past and of the converting natural resource managers to a new sustainable development trajectory.

It is recognised that globalisation and the accompanying restructuring of the state have produced major regional disparities (Gleeson, 2003). As Fung and Wright (2003, p. 33) acknowledge 'empowered participation may demand unrealistically high levels of popular commitment, especially in contemporary climates of civic and popular disengagement'.

There is also a very interesting notion that if 'family farm' producers have limited ability to change, that if supermarkets are becoming more demanding of the products that they put on their shelves, and that if the majority of agricultural production is really being provided by a very small minority of producers, that it might be that the future for a more sustainable agriculture lies in the closer ties of supermarkets to producers, and under the auspices of informal global regulatory 'audit cultures' such as that of the European Retailers Working Group (known as EUREP – see Campbell, 2004). It is not fanciful to suggest that the corporate food sector might see market advantage in sourcing foods and fibres from farms adhering to clean-and-green guidelines, banning genetically modified organisms from the products they place on their shelves, and imposing very strict sustainability-related standards on their suppliers. Would this not lead to the intriguing conclusion that the faster the smaller producers leave agriculture – and have the remainder linked to a progressive supermarket-based system that took voluntary regulation seriously – the more likely we are to achieve sustainability? (see Burch, Lyons, & Lawrence, 2001; Burch & Lawrence, 2004).

HOW THEN ARE WE TO GOVERN SUSTAINABILITY?

The shift from government to governance (Berger, 2003) is that of a move from a linear, top-down, state-directed system of decision-making to one of non-hierarchical arrangements involving a complex network of both state and non-state players (see Bulkeley et al., 2003, p. 237). Citizen engagement strategies of participatory governance are emerging to challenge the centralised approaches to public administration. What appears to be occurring is that some of the functions of the state are shifting 'upwards' to transnational institutions and organisations, 'downwards' to the regions, and 'outward' to a host of non-state actors (see Bulkeley et al., 2003, following Pierre & Peters, 2000) as part of the hollowing out of the nation state (but see, for an alternative view, Deas & Ward, 2000). Yet, this too gives the impression of a hierarchy of governance when what appears to have emerged is decision-making within 'overlapping and interconnected spheres of authority' (Bulkeley et al., 2003, p. 239). Governance in the EU, for example, is no longer conceived of as the bargaining and negotiation between nation states but, rather, as the outcome of fluid interactions between multiple spheres (supranational institutions, nation states, transnational networks, sub-national governments, place-based partnerships and civil society) (Bulkeley et al., 2003). Europe's Transnational Municipal Networks, for example, not only help in the articulation between various tiers of government but also seek – in their own right – to govern the environment. They do so by disseminating knowledge, lobbying governments and implementing EU policies (Bulkeley et al., 2003). The US's Habitat Conservation Planning and Australia's catchment management strategies are emblematic of the shift from command-type and fragmented government to that of collaborative, integrated, regional ecosystem governance arrangements where recognition is given of the complexity of environmental issues and the need to cross traditional, political and administrative boundaries in an effort to address those issues (Everingham, Cheshire, & Lawrence, 2003; Karkkainen, 2003).

In Australia, my colleagues and I have identified three periods of regional governance since the Second World War. The first was an old-style regionalism that existed until the 1980s. This was associated with decentralisation, exogenous development, the industrialisation of agriculture and welfarist and protectionist policies. A second phase – a form of 'new localism' – arose in the mid-1980s and was typified by an emphasis on individual and community empowerment and action, endogenous development and small government – all endorsed and fostered by neoliberalism. What we believe we are seeing today is something quite different. It is the emergence of the bioregion as the basic delineation for local decision-making, the development of state/community partnerships, the flexible coordination of government activities, some alteration to (rather than a complete escape from) productivist agriculture and strategic state investment in regionally based natural resource management (Everingham et al., 2003). This could be considered a variant of the 'new regionalism' that has been identified in Europe (see commentaries by Rainnie, 2002; Rainnie & Grobbelaar, 2005), although we believe it is really closer to what Marsden (2003, p. 4) considers to be a 'rural development dynamic' that highlights the re-embedding of food supply chains, a focus on rural livelihoods, an agro-ecological approach to farm management and rural sustainability as the goal of development. It is, what is termed in Australia 'sustainable regional development' – a community/government partnership approach that goes beyond the strict neoliberalist-inspired self-help models of the 1990s. While it falls short of a radical sustainability that would be marked by bioregionalism and a shift of power (rather than simply responsibility) to new institutions (see Gray & Lawrence, 2001, p. 153), it represents a positive move to understand the complexity and fragility of ecosystems and to stress the necessity of integrated and multi-level strategies. As Head (2004) has argued, it provides an opportunity for the differences between stakeholders to be discussed, assessed and potentially resolved. It appears to be much more ambitious, for example, than the EU's Eco-management and Audit Scheme that is concerned primarily with governance of the environment (see Heinelt & Smith, 2003). Importantly, sustainable regional development anticipates that the new partnership arrangements must be supported by a long-term commitment by governments and by considerable public funding (Lawrence, 2003).

The question could still be raised, however, of the desirability of moving from known systems of government to untested systems of governance based upon the deliberations of unelected representatives. As Everingham et al. (2003, p. 11) have argued, the broadening of the mandate and accountability for such institutions:

- allows the long-term perspective necessary for environmental sustainability, thereby overcoming the short-term planning timeframe linked to 3- or 4- year election cycles
- provides an opportunity to restore trust between citizens and government departments...with a move beyond rigid one-way forms of public consultation to more diverse, flexible and open systems of engagement that involve a broad spectrum of the regional population and encourage deliberative and discursive participation
- gives legitimacy to local knowledge and the sharing of values, with local people not only having a voice in regional planning, but also helping to shape the process of change.

Social networks are the foundations of society and provide the basis for more formal arrangements of government (Taylor, 2004). As such, they are to be nurtured and promoted to harness social capital and to foster social inclusion (Crow, 2004).

Notwithstanding the potential for a regional renaissance based on 'triple bottom line' approaches, we should nevertheless recall John Lovering's (2001, p. 350) assessment of the present regional agenda:

Portrayals of (regionalism) or devolution as if they represent the triumphant culmination of struggles to empower distinctive regional identities are at best romantic readings...(that) obscure the fact that regionalism can also be a key component of a strategy of state restructuring aimed at realizing a broadly neo-liberal model of globalization.

To sum up the earlier discussions, there are several pointers to success in sustainable regional development:

- Acknowledgement that regional development is about sustainable development and that all plans for development must treat the economy, society and environment on an equal footing.
- An increased devolution of power (not just responsibility) to regional entities, with a real recognition of the potential of these groups to make a difference in terms of long-term natural resource management and social justice.
- Emergence of a structure of governance that ensures that institutional arrangements are conducive to regional decision-making. Government agencies must come behind community initiatives to provide technical support for sustainable development: this will mean a re-organisation of government activities so that holistic approaches are adopted over single departmental priorities.
- Commitment of sufficient financial and other resources to regional groupings to ensure that on-ground activities are undertaken, monitored and improved.
- Acceptance of a long-term time-line to ensure that the regional arrangements are accepted as legitimate and can survive the election timeframes of politics.

CONCLUSION

To paraphrase and update Karl Marx, social scientists have been content to interpret the world when the point, however, is to move it towards a more sustainable trajectory. What sociological insights can we bring to bear on this?

In this chapter I have raised a series of questions about the regional delivery for sustainable development and have argued that while there is evidence of success, this is not to say that it is challenging the framework of current (unsustainable) production, or that it is not a contradictory process at the local level.

What will happen with the regional experiment in sustainability? It has been initiated at least in part because of: the perceived lack of progress being made in fighting environmental degradation; the assumption that if local people 'own' problems they will be more willing to invest time and effort in their solution; and, recognition that long-term environmental progress should not be tied to 3- or 4- year cycles of parliament (in which the environment can be used each time as a political football).

Along with recognition of the failure of the structures and processes associated with representative government to deal with the complexities of sustainability, the five discernable characteristics of regional governance, as it relates to sustainable development, are:

- A so-called 'bottom-up' approach to decision-making, with local communities being encouraged to take ownership of development and natural resource management problems.
- The devolution of responsibility to the regional level. As an element of this, the desire to 'empower' citizens both to understand the issues and to act collectively to overcome them – that is, to raise their capacity to act for themselves.
- A more responsive bureaucratic response to community plans and needs particularly 'whole of government' approaches and an alteration to the organisational culture of 'stove piped' government agencies. The state becomes an 'enabler'.
- Creation of a community-initiated action plan, with clear goals and timelines.
- A series of (often complex) measures for accountability in the expenditure of funds, and in the monitoring and evaluation of sustainability applications (Westholm et al., 1999; Cavaye, 2004).

The real question is: can we trust – and should we endorse – regional partnerships to deliver sustainable development? We know that previous arrangements based upon top-down legislative sanctions have largely failed. We know that sustainability is a long-term goal that must live beyond both parliamentary terms and the lives of the current generation of people in existing communities. We also know that the current arrangements are an experiment: they are hybrid, fragile, uncertain and contingent.

So, why might we want to endorse the emergence of governance structures to foster something called 'sustainable regional development'? Without wanting to be too prescriptive, the answer I will give is pragmatic and eclectic. There is little else that – at this time – appears to provide a genuine option for the future. Should we look to the WTO and other supranational governance bodies for leadership in sustainable development? The answer would seem to be 'no'. As Howard Newby (1996, p. 214) reminded us last decade, most global agencies seeking to govern resources lack legitimacy and respond 'slowly and imperfectly' to the demands of local people. Might, then, we trust the global corporate sector's embracing of 'self-regulation' as the key to sustainability? In some instances yes but in general, certainly no. There are good reasons, then, to look to support the regional 'experiment' in sustainable development. It is community based, government supported and has – at its core – a framework that represents the interests of community/ government partners in triple bottom line action. Why, though, should we place any faith in collaborative arrangements to deliver sustainable outcomes?

We should perhaps recall the words of Christopher Lasch (1995, p. 8) in his book *The Revolt of the Elites* and *the Betrayal of Democracy* when he argued:

> Self-governing communities, not individuals, are the basic units of democratic Life...(Their demise)...calls the future of democracy into question.

In a world of individualisation, detraditionalisation, economic polarisation and environmental degradation, it would seem that social scientists can play an important role in understanding the contours of current regional development and its potential for strengthening democracy. This does not mean a blanket endorsement of regional policy but, rather, the careful evaluation of structures and processes of governance, an understanding of the forces that foster unsustainable practices and an appreciation of the social, economic and institutional mechanisms that might move rural regions further along the path toward sustainable development.

ACKNOWLEDGMENTS

I thank the Australian Research Council for funding several projects that assisted in the production of this chapter. I also thank my colleagues Dr. Lynda Cheshire, Dr. Vaughan Higgins and Dr. Stewart Lockie and post-graduate students Jo-Anne Everingham and Carol Richards for their input into discussions and into earlier papers that I have drawn upon in fashioning this chapter.

REFERENCES

Agriculture, Fisheries and Forestry – Australia (AFFA). (1999). *Managing natural resources in rural Australia for a sustainable future*. A discussion paper for developing a national policy. Canberra: AFFA.

Alexander, H. (1995). *A framework for change: The state of the community landcare movement in Australia*. Canberra: National Landcare Program.

Almas, R., & Lawrence, G. (Eds) (2003). *Globalization, localization and sustainable livelihoods*. Aldershot: Ashgate.

Altieri, M. (1998). Ecological impacts of industrial agriculture and the possibilities for truly sustainable farming. *Monthly Review*, 50(3), 60–71.

Argent, N. (2002). From pillar to post? In search of the post-productivist countryside in Australia. *Australian Geographer*, 33(1), 97–114.

Barr, N., & Cary, J. (2000). *Influencing improved natural resource management on farms: A guide to understanding factors influencing the adoption of sustainable resource practices*. Canberra: Bureau of Rural Sciences.

Bates, G. (2003). Legal perspectives. In: S. Dovers & S. Wild River (Eds), *Managing Australia's environment* (pp. 255–301). Australia: The Federation Press.

Bauman, Z. (2004). *Wasted lives: Modernity and its outcasts*. Cambridge: Polity Press.

Berger, G. (2003). Reflections on governance: Power relations and policy making in regional sustainable development. *Journal of Environmental Policy and Planning*, 5(3), 219–234.

Brand, K. (1997). Environmental consciousness and behaviour: The greening of lifestyles. In: M. Redclift & G. Woodgate (Eds), *The international handbook of environmental sociology* (pp. 204–217). United Kingdom: Edward Elgar.

Bulkeley, H., Davies, A., Evans, B., Gibbs, D., Kern, K., & Theobald, K. (2003). Environmental governance and transnational municipal networks in Europe. *Journal of Environmental Policy and Planning*, 5(3), 235–254.

Burch, D., & Lawrence, G. (2004). Supermarket own brands, supply chains and the changing agri-food system: The UK experience. Paper presented to the XI annual meeting of the Australasian Agri-food Research Network. 9–11 June, Canberra.

Burch, D., Lyons, K., & Lawrence, G. (2001). What do we mean by green? Consumers, agriculture and the food industry. In: S. Lockie & B. Pritchard (Eds), *Consuming foods, sustaining environments* (pp. 33–46). Brisbane: Australian Academic Press.

Campbell, A. (1994). *Landcare: Communities shaping the land and the future: With case studies by Greg Siepen*. Sydney: Allen and Unwin.

Campbell, H. (2004). Green protectionism part 2: EUREP–GAP, agri-food systems governance and the decline of organic exporting from New Zealand. Paper presented to the XI World Congress of Rural Sociology. 25–30 July, Trondheim, Norway.

Cavaye, J. (2004). Governance and community engagement: The Australian experience. In: W. Lovan, M. Murray & R. Shaffer (Eds), *Participatory governance: Planning, conflict mediation and public decision making in civil society* (pp. 85–102). Aldershot: Ashgate.

Cheshire, L., & Lawrence, G. (2004). From protest to partnership: Rethinking local responses to change and restructuring in Australia. Paper presented at the XI World Congress of Rural Sociology. Trondheim, Norway: 25–30 July.

Commission of the European Communities (CEC). (2001a). *European governance: A white paper*. http://europa.eu.int/eur-lex/en/com/cnc/2001/com2001_0428en01.pdf

Commission of the European Communities (CEC). (2001b). *Environment 2010: Our future, our choice – the sixth environmental action programme.* http://europa.eu.int/comm/environment/newprg/

Commission of the European Communities (CEC). (2001c). *A sustainable future for a better world: A European union strategy for sustainable development.* http://europa.eu.int/eurlex/en/com/cnc/2001/com2001_0264en01.pdf

Cowell, R., & Martin, S. (2003). The joy of joining up: Modes of integrating the local government modernisation agenda. *Environment and Planning C: Government and Policy, 21*, 159–179.

Crow, G. (2004). Social networks and social exclusion: An overview of the debate. In: C. Phillipson, G. Allan & D. Morgan (Eds), *Social networks and social inclusion: Sociological and policy perspectives* (pp. 7–19). Aldershot: Ashgate.

Curtis, A. (2003). The landcare experience. In: S. Dovers & S. Wild River (Eds), *Managing Australia's environment* (pp. 442–460). Sydney: The Federation Press.

Davies, G. (2004). *Economia: New economic systems to empower people and support the living world.* Sydney: ABC Books.

Deas, I., & Ward, K. (2000). From the 'new localism' to the 'new regionalism'? The implications of regional development agencies for city-regional relations. *Political Geography, 19*, 273–292.

Dore, J., & Woodhill, J. (1999). *Sustainable regional development: Executive summary of the final report.* Canberra: Greening Australia.

Doyle, T. (1998). Sustainable development and agenda 21: The secular bible of global free markets and pluralist democracy. *Third World Quarterly, 19*(4), 771–786.

Eichler, M. (1999). Sustainability from a feminist sociological perspective: A framework for disciplinary reorientation. In: E. Becker & T. Jahn (Eds), *Sustainability and the social sciences: A cross-disciplinary approach to integrating environmental considerations into theoretical reorientation* (pp. 182–206). London: Zed Books.

Eshuis, J., & Van Woerkum, C. (2003). Trust and monitoring in governance processes: Lessons from landscape management by farmers in a Dutch municipality. *Journal of Environmental Policy and Planning, 5*(4), 379–396.

European Communities. (2003). *A say for the citizens in global governance.* http://europa.eu.int/comm/environment/wssd/governance_en.html

Everingham, J., Cheshire, L., & Lawrence, G. (2003). Regional renaissance? New forms of governance in non-metropolitan Australia. Paper presented to the annual conference of the Australian Sociological Association. 4–6 December, University of New England, Armidale.

Fung, A., & Wright, E. (Eds) (2003). *Deepening democracy: Institutional innovations in empowered participatory governance.* London: Verso.

Geddes, M. (2003). Local governance, partnerships and social inclusion – international perspectives and policy issues. Keynote Address, Colloquium on Local Government and Social Inclusion. September, The University of Queensland, Brisbane.

Giddings, B., Hopgood, B., & O'Brien, G. (2002). Environment, economy and society: Fitting them together into sustainable development. *Sustainable Development, 10*, 187–196.

Gleeson, B. (2003). Learning about regionalism from Europe: 'Economic normalisation' and beyond. *Australian Geographical Studies, 41*(3), 231–236.

Goodwin, M. (1998). The governance of rural areas: Some emerging research issues and agendas. *Journal of Rural Studies, 14*(1), 5–12.

Gowdy, J. (1999). Economic concepts of sustainability: Relocating economic activity within society and environment. In: E. Becker & T. Jahn (Eds), *Sustainability and the social sciences: A cross-disciplinary approach to integrating environmental considerations into theoretical reorientation* (pp. 162–181). London: Zed Books.

Gray, I., & Lawrence, G. (2001). *A future for regional Australia: Escaping global misfortune*. Cambridge: Cambridge University Press.

Head, B. (2004). Participation or co-governance? Challenges for regional natural resource management. Paper presented at the workshop on participation and governance in regional development. Centre for Rural and Regional Development, Hamilton, Victoria.

Head, B., & Ryan, N. (2003). Working with non-government organisations: A sustainable development perspective. *Asian Journal of Public Administration, 25*(1), 31–56.

Head, B., & Ryan, N. (2004). Co-governance or co-option? Regional natural resource partnerships in a federation. Paper presented at the Eighth international research symposium on public management. 31 March–2 April, Budapest University of Economics and Public Administration, Hungary.

Heinelt, H., & Smith, R. (Eds) (2003). *Sustainability, innovation and participatory governance: A cross-national study of the EU eco-management and audit scheme*. Aldershot: Ashgate.

Held, D., McGrew, A., Goldblatt, D., & Perraton, J. (1999). *Global transformations: Politics, economics and culture*. Cambridge, UK: Polity Press.

Herbert-Cheshire, L. (2003). 'Changing people to change things': Building capacity for self-help in natural resource management – a governmentality perspective. In: G. Lawrence, V. Higgins & S. Lockie (Eds), *Environment, society and natural resource management: Theoretical perspectives from Australia and the Americas* (pp. 270–282). Cheltenham: Edward Elgar.

Higgins, V. (2002). Self-reliant citizens and targeted populations: The case of Australian agriculture in the 1990s. *ARENA Journal, 19*, 161–171.

Holmes, J. (2002). Diversity and change in Australia's rangelands: A post-productivist transition with a difference? *Transactions of the Institute of British Geographers, 27*, 362–384.

Ilbery, B., & Bowler, I. (1998). From agricultural productivism to post-productivism. In: B. Ilbery (Ed.), *The geography of rural change* (pp. 57–84). Harlow: Addison, Wesley, Longman.

Intergovernmental Panel on Climate Change (IPCC). (2001). *Climate Change 2001: Synthesis report*. http://www.ipcc.ch/pub/un/syreng/spm.pdf

Jessop, B. (1998). The rise of governance and the risks of failure: The case of economic development. *International Social Science Journal, 155*, 29–46.

Karkkainen, B. (2003). Toward ecologically sustainable democracy? In: A. Fung & E. Wright (Eds), *Deepening democracy: Institutional innovations in empowered participatory governance* (pp. 208–224). London: Verso.

Lasch, C. (1995). New York: Norton.

Lawrence, G. (1998). The institute for sustainable regional development. In: J. Grimes, G. Lawrence & D. Stehlik (Eds), *Sustainable futures: Towards a catchment management strategy for the central Queensland region* (pp. 6–8). CQU, Rockhampton: Institute for Sustainable Regional Development.

Lawrence, G. (2001). *'Self help' in natural resource management: The way forward for regional Australia?* Keynote address to the Western Australian State Landcare Conference. 11–14 September, Mandurah, Western Australia.

Lawrence, G. (2003). Sustainable regional development: Recovering lost ground. In: B. Pritchard, A. Curtis, J. Spriggs & R. Le Heron (Eds), *Social dimensions of the triple bottom line in rural Australia* (pp. 157–170). Canberra: Bureau of Rural Sciences.

Lawrence, G., Cheshire, L., & Richards, C. (2004). Agricultural production and the ecological question. In: R. White (Ed.), *Controversies in environmental sociology* (pp. 221–237). Cambridge: Cambridge University Press.

Lawrence, G., Richards, C., & Herbert-Cheshire, L. (2003). The environmental enigma: Why do producers professing stewardship continue to practice poor natural resource management? Xth Agri-food Research Network Conference. 21–24 April, Akaroa, New Zealand.

Levidow, L. (2005). Governing conflicts over sustainability: Agricultural biotechnology in Europe. In: V. Higgins & G. Lawrence (Eds), *Agricultural governance: Globalization and the new politics of regulation* (pp. 98–117). London: Routledge.

Lockie, S. (2001). Agriculture and environment. In: S. Lockie & L. Bourke (Eds), *Rurality bites: The social and environmental transformation of rural Australia* (pp. 229–242). Sydney: Pluto Press.

Lockie, S. (2004). Collective agency, non-human causality and environmental social movements: A case study of the Australian 'Landcare Movement'. *Journal of Sociology*, 40(1), 41–58.

Lockie, S., & Vanclay, F. (Eds) (1997). *Critical landcare.* Key paper series, No. 5. Wagga Wagga: Centre for Rural Social Research, Charles Sturt University.

Lovering, J. (1999). Theory led by policy: The inadequacies of the 'New Regionalism'. *International Journal of Urban and Regional Research*, 23, 379–395.

Lovering, J. (2001). The coming regional crisis (and how to avoid it). *Regional Studies*, 35(4), 349–354.

Magdoff, H., Foster, J. B., & Buttel, F. H. (Eds) (2000). *Hungry for profit: The agribusiness threat to farmers, food, and the environment.* New York: Monthly Review Press.

Marsden, T. (2003). *The condition of rural sustainability.* The Netherlands: Van Gorcum.

Marsden, T., Murdoch, J., & Abram, S. (1997). Rural sustainability in Britain: The social bases of sustainability. In: M. Redclift & G. Woodgate (Eds), *The international handbook of environmental sociology* (pp. 467–478). Cheltenham: Edward Elgar.

Martinez-Alier, J. (1999). The socio-ecological embeddedness of economic activity: The emergence of a transdisciplinary field. In: E. Becker & T. Jahn (Eds), *Sustainability and the social sciences: A cross-disciplinary approach to integrating environmental considerations into theoretical reorientation* (pp. 112–139). Paris: UNESCO.

McMichael, P. (2004). *Development and social change: A global perspective* (3rd ed.). Thousand Oaks: Pine Forge.

Morrissey, P., & Lawrence, G. (1997). A critical assessment of landcare: Evidence from central Queensland. In: S. Lockie & F. Vanclay (Eds), *Critical landcare* (pp. 217–226). Wagga Wagga: Centre for Rural Social Research.

Moseley, M. (1999). The new localism as a response to rural decline. In: E. Westholm, M. Moseley & N. Stenlas (Eds), *Local partnerships and rural development in Europe: A literature review of practice and theory* (pp. 25–43). Sweden: Dalarna Research Institute.

Mues, C., Chapman, L., & Van Hilst, R. (1998). *Landcare: Promoting improved land management practices on Australian farms.* Canberra: Australian Bureau of Agricultural and Resource Economics.

Myerson, G., & Rydin, Y. (1996). Sustainable development: The implications of the global debate for landuse planning. In: S. Buckingham-Hatfield & B. Evans (Eds), *Environmental planning and sustainability* (pp. 19–34). Chichester: Wiley.

Newby, H. (1996). Citizenship in a green world: The global commons and human stewardship. In: M. Bulmer & A. Rees (Eds), *Citizenship today: The contemporary relevance of T. H. Marshall* (pp. 209–221). London: UCL Press.

O'Connor, M. (1994). Introduction: Liberate, accumulate – and bust? In: M. O'Connor (Ed.), *Is capitalism sustainable? Political economy and the politics of ecology* (pp. 1–21). New York: The Guilford Press.

Paterson, M., Humphreys, D., & Pettiford, L. (2003). Conceptualising global environmental governance: From interstate regimes to counter-hegemonic struggles. *Global Environmental Politics, 3*(2), 1–10.

Peine, E., & McMichael, P. (2005). Globalization and global governance. In: V. Higgins & G. Lawrence (Eds), *Agricultural governance: Globalization and the new politics of regulation* (pp. 19–34). London: Routledge.

Pierre, J., & Peters, G. (2000). *Governance, politics and the state*. Basingstoke: Macmillan.

Pretty, J. (2002). *Agri-culture: Reconnecting people, land and nature*. London: Earthscan.

Rainnie, A. (2002). New regionalism in Australia – limits and possibilities. Paper delivered at the workshop on social inclusion and new regionalism. The University of Queensland, Brisbane.

Rainnie, A., & Grobbelaar, M. (Eds) (2005). *New regionalism in Australia*. Aldershot: Ashgate.

Reddel, T. (2002). Beyond participation: Hierarchies, management and markets: 'New' governance and place policies. *Australian Journal of Public Administration, 61*(1), 50–63.

Rose, N. (1996). The death of the social? Reconfiguring the territory of government. *Economy and Society, 25*(3), 327–356.

Sanderson, I. (2000). Access to services. In: J. Percy-Smith (Ed.), *Policy responses to social exclusion: Towards inclusion?* (pp. 130–147). Buckingham: Open University Press.

Schnaiberg, A. (1980). *The environment*. Oxford: Oxford University Press.

Shortall, S., & Shucksmith, M. (1998). Integrated rural development: Issues arising from the Scottish experience. *European Planning Studies, 6*(1), 73–88.

Standing Committee on Environment, Recreation and the Arts. (2001). *Co-ordinating catchment management – inquiry into catchment management*. www.aph.gov.au/house/committee/environ/cminq/cmirpt/contents.htm

Stiglitz, J. (2003). Globalization and development. In: D. Held & M. Koenig-Archibugi (Eds), *Taming globalization: Frontiers of governance* (pp. 47–67). Cambridge: Polity Press.

Stilwell, F. (2000). *Changing track: A new political economic direction for Australia*. Sydney: Pluto Press.

Stirling, B. (2001). Work, knowledge and the direction of farm life. In: R. Epp & D. Whitson (Eds), *Writing off the rural west: Globalization, governments and the transformation of rural communities* (pp. 247–261). Alberta: The University of Alberta Press.

Stoker, G. (1998). Governance as theory: Five propositions. *International Science Journal, 155*, (March), 17–28.

Taylor, M. (2004). Community issues and social networks. In: C. Phillipson, G. Allan & D. Morgan (Eds), *Social networks and social inclusion: Sociological and policy perspectives* (pp. 205–218). Aldershot: Ashgate.

Tilzey, M. (2003). *A framework for conceptualising agricultural multifunctionality*. EPMG working papers. London: Imperial College.

Walford, N. (2003). Productivism is allegedly dead, long live productivism: Evidence of continued productivist attitudes and decision making in South-East England. *Journal of Rural Studies, 19*(4), 491–502.

Walker, P., & Hurley, P. (2004). Collaboration derailed: The politics of 'community-based' resource management in Nevada county. *Society and Natural Resources, 17*, 735–751.

Westholm, E. (1999). Exploring the role of rural partnerships. In: E. Westholm, M. Moseley & N. Stenlas (Eds), *Local partnerships and rural development in Europe: A literature review of practice and theory* (pp. 13–24). Sweden: Dalarna Research Institute.

Westholm, E., Moseley, M., & Stenlas, N. (Eds) (1999). *Local partnerships and rural development in Europe: A literature review of practice and theory.* Sweden: Dalarna Research Institute.

Wilson, G. (2001). From productivism to post-productivism...and back again? Exploring the (un)changed natural and mental landscapes of European agriculture. *Transactions of the Institute of British Geographers, 26*, 77–102.

World Commission on Environment and Development. (1987). *Our common future.* Oxford: Oxford University Press.

'STATELESS' REGULATION AND CONSUMER PRESSURE: HISTORICAL EXPERIENCES OF TRANSNATIONAL CORPORATE MONITORING

Gay Seidman

ABSTRACT

Can market-based regulation based on consumer pressure and 'independent monitoring' serve as the basis for transnational corporation regulation? In an increasingly integrated global economy, many scholars and policy makers fear that mobile capital may force a 'race to the bottom'; can independent non-governmental organizations and ethical consumers provide a counterweight to cost-cutting pressures? This paper compares three of the best known examples of transnational monitoring – the Sullivan Principles in South Africa, the Rugmark social labeling program in India, and the Commission for the Verification of Codes of Conduct's monitoring experiences in the apparel industry of Guatemala – to consider some common features of transnational monitoring.

At the turn of the twenty-first century, a new global social movement was making itself heard. As the world's economy became increasingly integrated, as global trade patterns revealed themselves in the labels sewn in cotton t-shirts and in dominant discourses, activists decried the apparently ever-growing power of transnational corporations. From street protests in Seattle, to sit-ins in university offices, to heated discussions about the erosion of national sovereignty in international institutions, angry voices began to insist that new patterns of trade and globalization demanded new forms of engagement.

Fueled by factory fires in Thailand, by testimonies from under-age workers in Central America, or by toxic chemical spills in India, concerns about the conditions under which workers in developing countries lived and worked began to permeate discussions about globalization from the early 1990s. Activists argued that multilateral agencies like the World Trade Organization and the International Monetary Fund were dominated by conservative economic policy-makers and corporate leaders, whose concern for greater profit margins led them to ignore spreading misery. It was time, they insisted, to develop a new approach: there had to be some way to shape 'globalization from below,' to avoid the 'race to the bottom' as developing countries competed for foreign investment.

As concern about global sweatshops to spread beyond small activist networks, that new approach began slowly to emerge. Building on examples of earlier transnational anti-corporate campaigns – especially the divestment campaign against corporations involved in South African apartheid and the international boycott of Nestle's sparked by its promotion of baby formula in developing countries – transnational activists began to see consumers in North America and Europe as a new site of potential mobilization. Gradually, they hoped, ethical consumers would learn to use their buying power to punish or reward corporations, and a new kind of market-based activism would make itself felt at the supermarket and in the shopping mall. It was, perhaps, the perfect response to market-based globalization: as 'fair trade' activists quipped, 'Don't get mad, go shopping.'

Business ethicists were quick to join in. Alert consumers, they argued, could use new access to information through the internet to question the conditions under which goods were produced – even if the goods were produced thousands of miles away, in far-off continents by workers so desperate for a job they could not complain about toxic chemicals, long hours, or low pay. Globalization and its discontents, ethicists warned, would soon be a problem for business profitability: consumer concerns about working conditions and environmental degradation would soon become so important that they could affect the corporate bottom line. To avoid boycotts and demonstrations, wise corporations would incorporate codes of conduct and ethical principles into their basic structure, or risk tarnishing their reputations and reducing their market share (Sethi & Steidlmeier, with contributions by Paul & Shrivastava, 1991; Williams, 2000; Waddock, 2002).

Activists and ethicists could point to some real evidence to support the market-based approach. Ethical trading schemes claimed real impact: individual consumers responded to widespread reports of global exploitation by creating an ever-growing market for 'fair-trade' products. In Europe, ethical trading initiatives in food and clothing grew by some 40% annually between 1997 and 2004 (Vidal, 2004). In the United States, telephone surveys found that consumers cared about the conditions under which products were made, and said they would willingly pay more for goods produced under ethical rules (University of Maryland, 2000). In an experiment attempting to test American consumers' behavior, a slight majority of customers at a Michigan department store paid more for socks carrying labels claiming that the socks were produced under good working conditions. True, no consumer questioned the labels' claims (which were in fact entirely fictitious), but the experiment suggested that when a choice was offered, consumers might take the ethical route – at least as long as the price difference remained relatively small (Prasad, Kimeldorf, Meyer, & Robinson, 2004).

Why have global activists turned to visions of labeling and independent monitoring as a new approach to global regulation, especially for workplaces? What are their underlying assumptions about the character of global activism, about the nature of sweatshop production, and the limits of state regulation in a neoliberal era? More importantly, perhaps, what are proponents' assumptions about stateless regulation and social activism, and how do they see these schemes emerging and persisting? Following is a brief discussion of the general approach. I briefly describe three examples, widely cited in the literature as successful examples of transnational corporate monitoring. Then, in comparing the similarities and differences across the three cases, I look for patterns in the way these schemes were constructed and implemented, in order to get a better sense of the possibilities and limits embodied in this approach.

TRANSNATIONAL PRESSURE AND LABOR MONITORING

As countless analysts have noted, through the late twentieth century, transnational corporations expanded beyond the reach of national governments or even international agencies, undermining national sovereignty and local identities as they aggressively spread investments around the world

(Greider, 1997). Over the past 40 years, new technologies and new production strategies have spread industrial production across the globe, often coordinated by large multinational corporations. At the same time, the idea that international trade will serve as the motor of economic growth everywhere has become increasingly accepted by academic economists and policy-makers alike, an apparently seamless consensus backed by the power of international financial institutions (Stiglitz, 2002). Combined, these trends – the globalization of industrial production, and the context of increasingly unfettered international trade – prompted a search for new ways to regulate workplace conditions.

As global trade expanded apace, activists, journalists, and academics suggested that mobilized consumer pressures offered new possibilities for persuading corporations to respect workers' rights. As the world seems increasingly dominated by a global assembly line linking together both producers and consumers around the world, many analysts suggest that a global social movement based in civil society – what Naomi Klein (2002) calls a "bad mood rising" – could use networks of information, purchasing power, and cultural pressure to challenge corporate control.

Of course, proponents generally acknowledge important limits to the strategy, both in terms of target goods, and in terms of consumer audiences. Appropriate targets for transnational boycotts are limited: most goods – including most goods produced in rural areas – are never exported, and thus are not subject to transnational campaigns, no matter how bad the condition in which they are produced. Further, consumer pressure tends to be most effective when applied to well-known logos, easily identifiable products, or goods produced in specific countries; most goods produced in any export-processing zones are not identifiable, and thus not vulnerable to transnational boycotts. Finally, even ethical consumers will balk at boycotts involving goods they consider necessities; it is much easier to persuade consumers to support a boycott if the goods involved are luxuries, or for which there are easy substitutes, than to ask for consumers to engage in real sacrifice.

Successful boycotts appeal to very specific consumers. Ethical consumers form only a small portion of global markets, primarily located in advanced industrial countries and generally concentrated among university students and others with enough disposable time to observe boycotts, and enough disposable income to choose products by ethics rather than by price and quality. Most consumers pay little attention to ethical appeals: Dana Frank's (1999) lively history of 'buy American' campaigns suggests that consumers are not always as responsive as activists might wish. And, of course, as developing country unionists have repeatedly warned, transnational consumer boycotts carry the risk that the wealthy consumers of North America and Europe, rather than workers in developing countries, make key decisions about which labor rights matter, and which factories will be targeted – and while wealthy consumers lose nothing if a company goes bankrupt, workers risk losing their jobs (cf. Ali, 1996).

Nevertheless, to optimistic observers, the new social activism offered hope for restructuring global politics: through transnational networks of mobilized consumers, attentive to ethical violations and insistent on global equity, perhaps it would be possible to 'name and shame' corporate violators, to punish companies who exploited workers and communities in far-flung parts of the world, to use consumer pressure, shareholder resolutions, and international boycotts to police and regulate the transnational corporations which seem so fundamental to globalization. By the late 1990s, social movement theorists began to ask whether transnational social movements represent a new kind of activism: has globalization spawned transnational social movements of a qualitatively different kind than the social movements that came in an earlier, more nation-centered era (Della Porta, Kriesi, & Rucht, 1999; Guidry, Kennedy, & Zald, 2000; Khagram, Riker, & Sikkink, 2002; Smith & Johnston, 2002). Arguing that consumer pressure would push corporations to adopt new codes of conduct, it became increasingly common for scholars to suggest that activists should promote a transnational framework of corporate monitoring, using transparency and publicity to develop new approaches to global corporate conduct (Fung, O'Rourke, & Sabel, 2001; Ruggie, 2003; Ayres & Braithwaite, 1992; Braithwaite & Drahos, 2000).

Building on the Human Rights Example

Whether or not its proponents recognize it, this vision of transnational activism generally builds on the example of the international human rights movement of the last quarter century. In the discursive redefinition of labor rights as human rights, rather than citizenship rights, however, activists have subtly reoriented their appeal, and redefined their targets. Historically, national labor campaigns have mobilized local constituencies to demand that national states enforce citizenship rights; by contrast, transnational labor advocates work on a broader canvas. Local activists provide information about working conditions or environmental degradation to transnational activists; that transnational network uses information to mobilize audiences across international boundaries, hoping to put pressure on perpetrators and persuade them to change their practices.

But whereas the human rights movement sought to mobilize international opinion against the behavior of states, hoping to change the behavior of local states toward their own citizens, the transnational labor movement seeks primarily to mobilize international pressure against corporations and manufacturers, by appealing to consumers – a shift that is more problematic than activists frequently recognize. The ease of this discursive transformation – from targeting states, to targeting multinational corporations – obscures the tensions contained with it, between claims articulated in terms of citizenship, and claims articulated in terms of universal human rights and morality. The philosophical underpinnings of citizenship rights and human rights have very different histories, and different epistemologies: as Shafir (2004) cogently argues, citizenship reflects participation in bounded communities, while human rights discussions evoke a universal human experience, reflecting transcultural, transnational commonalities. Long before the emergence of the modern notion of the nation-state, Shafir notes, citizens addressed their claims to, and expected policies to be implemented by, local states – even if that state might be an undemocratic one.

By contrast, the human rights perspective invokes a set of universal rights based on common human needs and concerns; claims-making occurs not within the framework of domestic law, but through appeals to fundamental, universal human rights within a universal community, especially since the United Nations adopted the international charter of human rights in 1948. Although labor rights are sometimes discussed in similarly universalistic terms – for example, when the history of the global anti-slavery movement is linked to the rise of labor unions (Braithwaite & Drahos, 2000) – most discussions of labor rights focus more explicitly on the role of domestic activism, states, and domestic legal frameworks, with far less reference to a changing and evolving international consensus. Labor rights, as a key component of citizenship rights, have been viewed as rights that have been won through struggle: they vary in different contexts, depending on locally specific histories. By contrast, human rights are generally discussed in more universalistic terms, and human rights discourse tends to explicitly reject local variation – just as global codes of corporate conduct are framed by universalistic concerns, blurring local distinctions.

Targeting Corporations and Consumers

But even aside from this epistemological shift, a consumer-based approach also involves a shift in mechanisms: transnational consumer pressure, rather than state regulation, becomes central to discussions of corporate compliance. How might consumer pressure be built into a system of global corporate regulation? Most proposals for alternative ways to control global sweatshops and environmental degradation remain sketchy, but they share some key features. In general, they replace a state-centered vision of workplace regulation with international codes of corporate conduct, monitored by private agencies and enforced by engaged consumers. As privatized, voluntary commitments, codes of conduct represent promises on the part of major corporations that they will seek to avoid egregious violations while they shift production to parts of the world where governments are too weak or too dependent to enforce labor codes or environmental standards. Conceptualized in terms roughly parallel to the international human rights movement, business ethicists suggest that alert consumers will force corporations to improve the conditions under which their goods are produced, using codes – described by one ethicist as "an idea whose time has come" (Williams, 2000) – as a benchmark against which corporate behavior will be judged.

To all these proposals, the threat of consumer pressure is key. Discussions of corporate codes of conduct generally assume that socially irresponsible behavior will carry real costs: Companies which behave ethically will be rewarded by discriminating consumers, while corporations guilty of producing goods in sweatshop conditions will be exposed, 'shamed,' and boycotted (Sethi et al., 1991; Waddock, 2002; Williams, 2000; Fung et al., 2001). Although this pressure is often exaggerated, there is an increasingly vocal discussion about how to involve multinational corporations in monitoring themselves – essentially, invoking widespread management practices of 'benchmarking,' 'continuous assessment,' and 'self-study' in efforts to raise workplace standards.

Much as activists and ethicists predicted, the movement to mobilize transnational consumer pressure began to have real impact within only a few years, after a few highly successful campaigns targeting high-profile corporations – Gap, Nike, and Starbucks among them – seemed to get results in the mid-1990s. For corporations, the first response was frequently to adopt a code of conduct, promising to make sure the goods they sold in Europe and North America were produced under conditions that were environmentally sound and which did not harm workers. Drafting codes of conduct became an art in itself: by 2001, literally scores of corporate codes of conduct had been published, by individual corporations, by groups of corporations collaborating on setting standards for desirable behavior, and by multilateral organizations like the United Nations' Center on Transnationals (*Bulletin of Comparative Labor Relations* 37, 2000).

On their own, corporate codes of conduct are unlikely to improve working conditions: as most observers note, simply publishing a code for consumers to read in North America hardly guarantees that corporations will enforce their own standards, much less that they will ensure that their sub-contractors – producing in far-flung factories in developing countries, where weak states and corrupt labor inspectors have little interest in enforcing private codes of conduct – will meet the headquarter's standards. All too often, corporate codes of conduct boil down to a public relations exercise, "a lunch, a launch and a logo" (Blowfield, 1999). The fact that a corporation has printed up a code of conduct does not, in fact, offer any real assurance to consumers that goods are produced under safe working conditions, without polluting the local environment, or that the workers who made them were paid even the legal minimum wage, offered any kind of protection from harassment or discrimination, or allowed any rights to free association. Without any systematic process of monitoring, even the most ethical consumer is left choosing between labels, with little hope that those labels reflect real efforts to improve working or environmental conditions around their factories. When Oxfam launched a campaign to promote ethical consumption in 2004, it warned consumers that labels could not be considered accurate indicators of corporate behavior; nevertheless, Oxfam advised, consumers should seek out fair-trade labeled goods, "to send a loud signal to retailers that consumers care and are willing to pay for decent labor standards" (Oxfam, 2004, p. 89).

To be effective, the 'naming and shaming' strategy requires some external system of monitoring corporate conduct. Internal company monitoring processes are not enough: the pressures to reduce labor costs, and the sense that violations tend to occur far from the final point of sale, tempt even companies known for their civic commitment, and few internal monitors can withstand the pressures of the bottom line. Many companies employed either internal monitors or accountants – hardly known for their expertise in identifying safety hazards at work – to police working conditions, but neither approach was likely to ensure great improvements (O'Rourke, 2000). As one observer noted, "Policing of the codes has often been a travesty... Usually the codes are intended to improve public relations rather than industrial relations." (Wells, 1999, p. 500). Given competitive pressures in the global marketplace, most corporate executives – perhaps especially those who rely on sub-contractors to produce elements of their products in export-processing zones around the world – are probably more concerned about price and quality than about working conditions. Without external monitoring, codes may reflect a vision of corporate goals, but they carry no reliable promise that anyone outside the public relations office is paying any attention (Compa, 2001; Compa & Darricarrere, 1996; Posner & Nolan, 2003).

As codes of conduct proliferated, then, so have calls for independent monitoring. Activists increasingly suggest that companies should open their doors to outside observers, allowing outside inspectors into the factory. To ensure that corporations live up to their published codes of conduct, activists, ethicists, and business leaders regularly argue that companies should submit their factories to outside inspectors, who could alert concerned consumers to any violation – or, conversely, could guarantee to consumers that the products were produced under conditions that met the code's requirement. Instead of asking consumers to accept corporate promises on good faith alone, activists argue that corporations should admit independent monitors into their factories and those of their sub-contractors; these outside monitors could then guarantee to head offices and consumers alike that goods had been produced under acceptable conditions (Compa, 2001; Gould, 2003; Rodriguez-Garavito, 2003).

Independent Monitoring

Independent monitoring emerged in the late 1990s as the gold standard of the transnational corporate conduct debate: if corporations were willing to submit to outside monitoring, they would be permitting the kind of information-gathering that would enable consumers and activists to implement 'naming and shaming' mechanisms of global control. While debates persist over who should monitor companies, and how, there is increasing consensus in policy-making circles that a new form of private voluntary initiative holds real promise as a way to hold corporations accountable for the conditions of workers around the world (Gereffi, Garcia-Johnson, & Sasser, 2001; Ottaway, 2001; Schrage, 2004).

Indeed, several distinguished scholars go so far as to suggest that corporate codes and monitoring schemes might provide a foundation for larger global regulatory schemes. Recognizing that individual company codes are neither public enough nor extensive enough to improve global working conditions, proponents of 'soft regulation' often argue that managements and international agencies together could develop larger codes and monitoring frameworks – replacing national labor laws with a cooperative transnational effort to prevent a 'race to the bottom' (Fung et al., 2001; Ruggie, 2003).

With few exceptions, however, discussions of such private, voluntary systems of regulation remained abstract and general: neither activists nor policy-makers tend to look carefully at actually existing independent monitoring schemes. Instead, they refer to historical or existing cases in passing, rarely going into detail or acknowledging important differences between global campaigns, even as they argue that consumer pressure worked to change corporate behaviors. Thus, the 'Sullivan Principles' governing American companies in South Africa under apartheid were likely to be mentioned in the same breath as the global boycott against Nestles for its advertising practices, or a more recent campaign linking Nike's athletic footwear to sweatshops and labor violations. Similarly, there has been little effort to tease out the conditions under which monitoring had worked, the kinds of industries and issues that seemed likely to mobilize broad consumer support, or the different approaches embodied in existing monitoring arrangements. Even discussions of more recent efforts tended to blur important distinctions: a campaign to promote 'fair-trade' coffee, grown by smallholders using environmentally sound practices, is often discussed in the same breath as Rugmark, a social label approach designed to eliminate child labor in India's hand-woven carpet industry.

Discussions of monitoring display an unfortunate tendency to overlook failure. Whenever journalists or researchers have suggested that specific cases of monitoring had proved less than successful, activists and policy-makers tend to drop them from their repertoire, continuing to list only those cases where independent monitoring and consumer pressure seemed to have been successful in changing corporate behavior. Thus, for example, early discussions of consumer pressure frequently cited the efforts by the British-based Body Shop to involve indigenous people of the Amazon in collecting environmentally sustainable ingredients in their products; but when journalists published more critical accounts, those references disappeared from activist and academic discussions alike, apparently dropped in favor of more positive – or less problematic – examples.

In the remainder of this paper, I hope to avoid that trap, by comparing three of the most frequently cited examples of 'successful' independent transnational monitoring in an effort to explore some basic questions about transnational monitoring without ignoring its limitations. I focus on three well-known cases, each involving a slightly different approach to monitoring and labor conditions. In each case – the Sullivan Principles in South Africa, the Rugmark social labeling system in India, and the Commission for the Verification of Codes of Conduct's (COVERCO) monitoring of the apparel industry in Guatemala – I examine the underlying dynamics of a transnational movement as well as the independent monitoring framework. Under what circumstances have transnational social movements emerged around labor conditions? What is the role of local activists in initiating exposes of labor conditions, and under what circumstances have transnational audiences responded? To what kinds of appeals do transnational consumers respond, and what kinds of products are involved? What role is played by local states, and how do export markets feature in the rise of independent markets? What can we learn from a comparison of existing schemes, and what are the implications of these lessons for a broader understanding of transnational movements and labor activism? By considering constraints as well as promise, failures as well as success, I hope to develop a more balanced sense of the promises and pitfalls involved in 'soft regulation' and voluntary codes of corporate conduct, and perhaps a sense of what kinds of policies and processes have worked for transnational labor regulation.

THE SULLIVAN PRINCIPLES

Perhaps the most frequently cited of all efforts to monitor multinationals, the Sullivan Principles in South Africa represents an important historical antecedent to corporate codes of conduct; I argue that it may have altered corporate culture in important ways, changing discussions around corporate responsibility, but its impact on actual conditions was remarkably limited. Between 1977 and 1994, American companies with investments in South Africa submitted to outside monitoring, and today, proponents of such schemes frequently invoke this system as one of the early examples of corporate self-regulation. Although the anti-apartheid campaign is obviously distinct from most transnational labor movements, its focus on corporate involvement in the apartheid economy included close scrutiny of workplace issues and discussions of how to promote 'good corporate citizenship' – to such an extent that the Sullivan system is frequently credited with changing corporate culture, both in South Africa and on the wider global scene (Massie, 1997; Sethi & Williams, 2000). While it is an unusual case, it is an important one: the effort to monitor and transform corporate behavior in South Africa helped shape subsequent discussions about corporate codes of conduct, and the experience illustrates the dynamics through which monitoring schemes are created. It can be argued, I think, that the Sullivan framework is the closest experience we have with full-scale transnational monitoring, and so it is worth exploring in some detail.

What, precisely, was the Sullivan system? From the early 1970s, institutional shareholders in the United States demanded that American companies leave South Africa rather than comply with apartheid legislation; in response, American companies with South African holdings submitted to a voluntary code of conduct, and were subject to independent monitoring. Managers faced real consequences for failing to comply with the code, often including salary penalties and bonuses linked to their Sullivan rating; further, as proponents of 'soft regulation' note, the code was regularly 'ratcheted up,' shifting from an initial focus on workplace integration, to gradually requiring companies donate to local community groups, challenge government repression, and finally, support political change. The Sullivan signatories included a wide range of products, from pharmaceuticals to automobiles, computers to agro-industry; the code was applied in a relatively accessible site, where information about corporate behavior was relatively available (Spence, 1998).

Perhaps, Sullivan's main contribution was in changing corporate discourse about social responsibility. Before Rev. Leon Sullivan introduced his principles, corporate leaders regularly rejected the idea that they could or should use their economic clout to push for reform, in South Africa or anywhere else. Corporate discourse emphasized profits as the only business of business, and rejected the very idea that corporations had social responsibilities beyond the balance sheet. Through its growth spurt of the mid-1960s, South Africa proved irresistible to foreign investors; by 1972, nearly 300 American corporations had established subsidiaries or affiliates there, with a combined investment totaling over $900 million (Blashill, 1972, p. 42; see also Sampson, 1987). By the time the Sullivan system had been in place for a decade, however, South African business leaders were willing to accept some degree of social responsibility – and they regularly pointed to compliance with the Sullivan Principles as an indication of their efforts to take that responsibility seriously (Relly, 1986).

It is also widely acknowledged that no corporate leaders would have agreed to Sullivan's principles, much less submit to independent monitoring, without pressure from the larger anti-apartheid movement. Protestors sought complete withdrawal from South Africa, insisting that companies that complied with South African segregationist laws and paid South African taxes were supporting apartheid (Danaher, 1984; Schmidt, 1980); even Sullivan himself acknowledged that companies acceded to monitoring in order to avert more significant pressure from U.S. institutions (Seidman, 2003). Schoenberger (2000, p. 28) concludes, "The effectiveness of the campaign was based on Milton Friedman's classic model of corporate responsibility, whereby external pressures on a corporation define its societal obligations, not the moral instincts arising from within. The solution in South Africa was achieved not by voluntary self-regulation, but by bashing heads."

But what do we learn from Sullivan's monitoring system? The Sullivan framework represents the first large-scale experiment in independent monitoring of multinationals, and it also set the pattern: Sullivan turned to Arthur D. Little, an accounting firm with no prior monitoring experience, for 'independent' monitoring. But as anti-apartheid activists and business ethicists noted in the early 1980s, ADL did no research of its own on signatories' behavior, nor did it evaluate companies' claims. Although ADL required signatories to confirm some data, like payroll information, with companies' local auditors, most of the responses went directly from local South African managers to ADL, with no outside check on companies' claims. Items that might have helped investors or monitors evaluate claims about increasing black employment – data such as the number of job openings, total number of trainees positions, and total number of black employees – were entirely self-reported. In fact, compliance with only one of the principles – expenditure on corporate contributions to local community projects, such as schools or clinics – was evaluated entirely through verified data (Paul, 1987).

Accountants, of course, are hardly trained to evaluate community programs, but the history of Sullivan's code and ADL's monitoring suggests a prior issue that continues to plague corporate codes of conduct today: who wrote the code, with what questions in mind? The questionnaires were drawn up by American accountants, and throughout entire life of the Sullivan system, they blurred categories that did not translate well from South Africa to the United States. Thus, for example, ADL charts describing signatories' behavior consistently left undefined the corporate understanding of 'black' employees – a category that in South Africa can mean either African workers alone, or African, Asian, and Indian (Massie, 1997) – creating a remarkable vagueness in discussions of hiring practicesin Sullivan signatories, in a context where apartheid's educational segregation and the racial stereotypes embedded in South African racial ideology means that these three groups have faced very different forms of discrimination at work. This vagueness serves as an acute reminder of the pitfalls involved in designing codes that will appeal to American and European consumers and investors, while still addressing local problems: if the monitors could not measure racial integration in South Africa, what happens when monitors try to evaluate compliance with a single global code, designed for use across many different contexts, in places as different as Sri Lanka, Guatemala, or Lesotho?

RUGMARK

Like the Sullivan code, Rugmark – an effort to use social labeling to eliminate child labor in the Indian carpet industry in the 1990s – was initiated as a corporate response to activist concerns. Since its founding in 1994, Rugmark has been viewed internationally as a remarkable experiment. In response to international pressure, Indian carpet exporters agreed to submit to independent monitoring, earning the right to attach a 'child-labor-free' label to carpets in return. Local non-governmental organizations linked to transnational networks of activists support a team of monitors and inspectors, who regularly monitor registered looms, removing children when they are found and punishing weavers who have employed them (Harvey, 1996; Gay, 1998). A decade after its creation, Rugmark was one of the most widely cited cases of transnational consumer pressure, considered as an international success story both for its impact on debates around child labor in India, and for the example it offers for labeling and independent monitoring (Chowdhury & Beekman, 2001; Hilowitz, 1998; ILO, 2004; Voll, 1999).

At home in India, however, Rugmark's approach is more controversial: by the time the program was several years old, many of the activists and organizations originally associated with the program, including UNICEF, distanced themselves from its creation, insisting that their involvement with the program at its inception had been experimental, tangential, or overstated (Pinto interview, 2003; Agnivesh interview, 2003). UNICEF had officially, if quietly, ended its rather limited involvement with Rugmark by 2003. But while many Indian child labor activists had become far more skeptical about the project – in some cases, going so far as to denounce it as a misleading, misguided effort (Agnivesh, 1999a) – Rugmark continued to stand as an international example of a model voluntary labeling scheme, in which 'good' weavers who eliminated child labor and submitted to monitoring by independent outsiders, would be rewarded by gaining privileged access to international consumers.

What prompted the use of social labels in the Indian carpet industry, and to what extent have these labels contributed to a decline in the use of child labor? The focus on child labor in the carpet industry came about almost by accident, when social activists trying to publicize the persistence of bonded labor relations in rural India in the early 1980s conducted several highly publicized raids on carpet sheds in the Mirzapur–Varanasi region, where they found kidnapped children as well as bonded adults. In one dramatic press conference in 1984, activists introduced a group of recently freed children who described their experiences in what the *Times of India* termed the 'torture camp of Mirzapur': children aged 5–12 had been kidnapped from a village in Bihar and sold to a weaver in Uttar Pradesh, living under medieval conditions until their rescue. Ill-fed, beaten, and mistreated, they showed journalists the small burn marks all over their bodies, where their employer had prodded them with red-hot pokers if they fell asleep during 16-hour days at the loom (Agnivesh, 1999b, p. 148; Whittaker, 1988, p. 5).

Rugmark emerged as a transnational response to stories such as these. Inspired by local activists, promoted by trade union and church groups in Germany, and supported by ethical importers in Europe and the United States, Rugmark appears to offer a perfect example of transnational labor monitoring. An activist movement linking social activists in India with conscientious consumers abroad, Rugmark was designed to deploy international consumer pressure to change labor practices in an export-oriented industry. In the absence of Indian enforcement of its own laws, Rugmark's independent monitoring offers a widely lauded example of voluntary corporate self-regulation, an example of how labels might be deployed to improve conditions in far-flung parts of the world, where alert consumers can use the label to identify goods produced under acceptable conditions.

Obviously, not all goods are equally appropriate for social labeling. Labeling works best when consumers sympathize with the ethical framework indicated in the label – when the label refers to a widely accepted human rights concern, rather than to more contested concerns. It works best for goods that are identifiable and distinct; thus, for example, it is far easier to label carpets – which go intact to the consumer – than it might be to label ball-bearings, which are rarely sold directly to consumers. And labeling may work best when it covers luxury goods, for which demand is very elastic, than when labels are attached to goods that are considered necessities; labels may be much more effective for products for which consumers have many choices, such as floor coverings, than for products that are more basic, and less substitutable. Finally, labeling implies that private regulation is required to supplement ordinary state inspections, suggesting that participants in the labeling process are meeting a higher standard than would normally be the case with goods produced in a specific region or country; labels automatically invoke some sense of monitoring, appealing to consumers partly through a suggestion that the label is applied in good faith, reflecting a sincere effort to ensure that the ethical conditions claimed in the label, represent reality (Hilowitz, 1998).

Rugmark is usually described as the outcome of a joint effort by Indian activists, international organizations like UNICEF, and German church and trade union activists seeking to help reduce child labor, but in fact, the program emerged as an initiative of the Indo-German Export Promotion Project, a program begun in 1988 as a joint German–Indian development, run through the German embassy and funded by the German government, to increase Indian export earnings, mainly from Germany and other countries of the European Union. Dietrich Kebschull (1999, p. 189) – who still served as IGEP director 10 years later – wrote that Rugmark was created in response to "otherwise well-meaning idealists," who "proposed to boycott carpet supplies from India, since only then, according to them, could the roots of child labor be removed." It was Indian carpet manufacturers, he claims, who suggested a social label as a way to protect the 'thousands of workers and their families' in the Indian carpet belt who relied on export sales for their livelihood from the threat of an international boycott: as early as 1990, he writes, manufacturers asked his program to help develop a certification system as a way to protect access to international markets for their carpets. Over the next 2 years, together with representatives from international organizations, social activists, and inputs from large department stores in Germany, Kebschull's IGEP developed a program designed to address international consumer concerns about child labor in the Indian carpet belt.

From the outset, both carpet manufacturers and the German government alike apparently insisted that the program would be self-regulating and financed by carpet exporters, rather than state-financed or controlled. Kebschull (1999, p. 204) writes, "the Government of Germany [has] repeatedly emphasized that it prefers this type of private and voluntary certification and self-effort vis-a-vis the alternative of strict and rigid government regulations." Using the social label instead of a "policing regime of fines and other punitive measures," Rugmark was designed to be "market-driven in such a way that members who still worked with child labor would no longer be able to sell their products abroad" (Kebschull, 1999, p. 195). Facing the threat of international consumer boycotts, it was hoped, Indian carpet weavers' own self-interest would lead them to eliminate child labor, in the effort to gain the smiley-face label for the carpets they planned to export.

By the end of its first decade, Rugmark had developed a straightforward monitoring system (interviews, Kebschull & Subramaniam, Delhi, 2003), incorporating most key principles described in discussions of independent monitoring. A local non-governmental organization, associated with a well-known Indian activist, Kailash Satyarthi, employed about a dozen full-time monitors, divided up into changing teams of two. Every weekday morning, each pair of monitors would receive a list of seven or eight looms they were to visit that day; monitors were never supposed to know in advance which looms they would see. Each team traveled in a separate vehicle, visiting looms that are often 30 or 60 km apart. If they found any children under 14 seated at registered looms, they checked whether the child was a relative of the weaver; Rugmark's rules allow family members to work on weaving, so long as the child is over years of age and is attending some hours of school. If the child was not a relative, the inspectors would take the child with them, usually to the Rugmark Foundation's school in Jagaspur. Weavers, meanwhile, would be warned, and repeated violations would result in non-registration. By late 2003, Rugmark India claimed to have registered 30,000 looms, carried out more than 180,000 inspections, found 800 looms employed nearly 1,500 children, and taken 166 children to its rehabilitation program. It was impossible to find information on how many weavers had actually been sanctioned (http://www.rugmarkindia.org/about/facts.htm,9/21/04).

In practice, however, Rugmark's monitoring scheme was far less effective than this tidy scheme suggests. Child labor activists have argued for over a century that 'putting out' systems like that common in the Indian rug manufacturing industry are almost impossible to monitor: household production is too dispersed, and children too easily available to 'help out' with work that is done at home, to make monitoring child labor in homework easy – and those difficulties are multiplied in India's carpet-belt. In contrast to the effort to eradicate child labor in soccerball production – where well-known multinationals worked with UNICEF to move all production into central warehouse, permitting easy monitoring of child workers – Rugmark sought to monitor children in villages separated by dozens of kilometers of dirt road, in home-based workshops that were adjacent to weavers' own houses. Although Rugmark's officers claimed that each registered loom would be inspected three times a year, the numbers suggested that the true figure is probably closer to once every 3 years. Even if inspections occurred more frequently, critics pointed to the physical characteristics of the village-based weaving workshops, arguing that in the time it takes monitors to walk from the well-marked Rugmark vehicles to the loom sheds, any children working on the looms have had plenty of time to vanish – or to polish up their claims to be family members. Exporters acknowledged in interviews (Agra, 2003) that looms were registered with Rugmark only during periods when the rugs they were weaving were specifically destined for Germany – the only consumer market where retailers had pledged to sell mainly Rugmark-labeled carpets (see also http://www.rugmarkindia.org/about/history.htm). Ten years after Rugmark was created, the number of monitoring teams had been reduced, and UNICEF had withdrawn its affiliation to the program (Pinto, interview, 2003).

In late 2002, a careful study of child labor in the Indian carpet industry suggested that although non-family child labor had diminished slightly in the Indian carpet industry overall, child labor by family members persisted, perhaps even more among Rugmark affiliates than among other weavers (Sharman, 2002). While the debate over the carpet industry had certainly attracted attention to the problem of child labor, and prompted the government's export promotion council to design and publicize its own code of conduct for the carpet industry – albeit with no apparent effort to incorporate any element of independent monitoring – Rugmark's most direct impact was on the discourse around child labor in the carpet industry: perhaps in stimulating a profusion of labels, it prompted a new awareness among consumers of the problem, and raised exporters' sense that they needed to address the issue in the workshops involved.

GUATEMALA'S COVERCO

Monitoring has a very specific history in Guatemala, linked to its long history of civil war and repression. In the mid-1990s, the former authoritarian government and a severely repressed guerrilla movement moved slowly, under enormous international pressure, into a democratic opening, overseen by a specially created United Nations' mission, MINUGUA. In the context of the slow move toward peace, non-governmental organizations, especially human rights organizations, played a key role: through the long and bloody civil war of the 1980s, human rights and labor groups had borne witness of repeated massacres and violations of human rights, and in the peace process of the 1990s, these groups became monitors of the gradual disarmament of warring militias (Jonas, 1991, 2000). Following what Keck and Sikkink (1998) describe as a 'boomerang' approach, these human rights groups appealed to international audiences, hoping to bring international pressure to bear on a Guatemalan state that seemed unwilling, or unable, to respond directly to its own citizens.

For many of these activists, Guatemala's transition from civil war to peace made visible a new set of violations: just as peace began to break out in Guatemala, new export-processing zones had sprung up around Guatemala City, often employing young women in conditions that gave meaning to the term 'sweatshop.' As the export processing zones expanded, issues of human rights clearly blurred with labor rights: poor young women, bent over lines of sewing machines for long hours in dimly lit, badly ventilated rooms, had little more reason to hope that the Guatemalan government would enforce its own labor code, than indigenous Guatemalan villagers had been able to expect protection from right-wing paramilitaries during the civil war. Labor unionists in Guatemala had long been targets of brutal paramilitary death squads (Goldston, 1989; Perez & Pablo, 1999); now, human rights activists and labor activists joined together to bring international attention to the market-driven violations of the apparel factories.

But it is important to recognize that this shift in Guatemala-based activism meshed with a larger international campaign. If the global spread of apparel industry has been central to recent critiques of globalization, it has also been central to discussions of private, voluntary regulatory efforts to improve working conditions through codes of conduct and consumer pressure. Through the 1990s and early 2000s, the apparel industry has been at the center of transnational labor activism, involving labor activists, corporate ethics campaigns, and consumer boycotts: it is central to transnational networks' efforts, the site where poor working conditions, corporate image, and independent monitoring schemes have come together.

This is not an entirely stateless process, however. American state policy, as many analysts have noted, has been key in shaping both global industry and global activism. While new innovations in communications and technologies certainly made global out-sourcing strategies possible, specific decisions about siting were shaped as much by American trade policies as by new technological openings. In the early 1980s, Nike provided an example of a new managerial approach, focusing on design and marketing rather than production (Korzeniewicz, 1994). Imitating Nike, many brands moved further and further from producing clothes in their own factories inside the United States; instead, they contracted with producers in low-wage regions to sew clothes according to the brand's specifications, leaving the brand free to concentrate on advertising and retail (Klein, 2002). Careful studies of the industry, however, repeatedly demonstrate that this shift reflects managerial attention to American trade policy, even more than: by the mid-1980s, companies had learned that they could avoid import duties by skillfully manipulating the American system of allocating apparel production quotas to different developing countries. Instead of fighting to sustain protectionist legislation, some managers became adept at locating sub-contracted production in countries with 'unused' quota, so that they could import their products back to the United States without facing tariff penalties (Collins, 2003; Gereffi, Spener, & Bair, 2002; Rosen, 2002).

As American brands sought sub-contracting relationships, local apparel industries mushroomed in export-processing zones, from Mauritius to Central America. Local entrepreneurs were not the only sub-contractors, however: smaller producers, especially from now-less-favored East Asian sites, also responded to changing American government policy and corporate strategies, hoping to gain access to lucrative American markets through sub-contracting relationships. In an aspect of the apparel industry that is rarely noted by analysts, the new commodity chain pattern involved a new set of international linkages: from the early 1990s, South Korean and Taiwanese entrepreneurs – drawn by changing American tariff policies to Central America – became middlemen in a rapidly changing industry. Between 1989 and 1991, Rosen (2002, p. 147) reports, at least 82 Korean and Taiwanese manufacturers moved to Guatemala, mainly investing in electronics and apparel factories. Almost inevitably, these new investments created new jobs, but also new factory-level conflicts, sometimes linked to language barriers and tensions over workplace cultures.

At the same time, facing the rapid decline of American production of apparel, American unionists began to raise concerns about the failure of local states to enforce their own labor laws: in the effort to attract foreign investment, especially to export-processing zones, local governments repeatedly relaxed their own labor codes, sometimes explicitly promising investors that the zones would be free of union interference. Several union campaigns sought to strengthen workers' union rights in specific Central American countries; American apparel unionists, for example, embarked on an organizing drive in the Dominican Republic, and launched a boycott campaign of London Fog and other brand names, for their failure to press Korean-owned sub-contractor to recognize a union in a Dominican Republic export-processing zone. Notably, the AFL–CIO's main efforts, however, went into getting the U.S. government to push the Dominican Republic to enforce its own labor laws (Jessup & Gordon, 2000).

This pattern was quite common: as apparel industry jobs moved off-shore, American unionists turned to the American government for help: In 1996, American Labor Secretary Robert Reich launched a new initiative, asking apparel brand names to work with American clothing unions to monitor and improve apparel factories outside the United States. These efforts, as has been widely reported, soon collapsed into bitter recriminations – largely over corporate insistence on keeping any monitoring processes confidential, in contrast to unions' concerns that only transparency would lead to improved working conditions, by creating public pressure on brands. Meanwhile, however, global activists raised public awareness of conditions in Nike's factories, while student activists on college campuses took up questions about the conditions under which licensed goods were being produced. By 2000, two separate efforts claiming to be seeking to improve conditions in the global apparel industry had emerged in the United States: the Fair Labor Association (FLA), backed by the industry and a tiny handful of human rights groups, and the Workers' Rights Consortium (WRC), supported by the American apparel union, UNITE, student activists, and labor and human rights groups (Boris, 2003; Ross, 1997; Esbenshade, 2004; Featherstone & United Students Against Sweatshops, 2002).

In 1997, a year after the signing of Guatemala's peace accords, COVERCO was founded by human rights and labor activists to try to monitor changing labor conditions – as part of an effort, as they put it, to help develop a 'culture of compliance' in a country that was emerging from authoritarian chaos. In a situation where the Guatemalan state has been unable, or unwilling, to enforce its own labor code, COVERCO was created to try to offer an alternative:

> The Commission for the Verification of Codes of Conduct (Coverco) is a Guatemalan non-profit organization dedicated to providing accurate and credible information about working conditions. Coverco conducts independent monitoring and investigations of workplace compliance with labor standards in Guatemala's major export industries – including apparel, bananas, coffee, and electricity – for multinational companies and international organizations. Objectivity, transparency, non-substitution and independence are the principle tenets of Coverco's work (http://www.coverco.org/eng, 9/21/04).

Widely cited as the kind of independent monitoring group that might enforce labor standards worldwide, the group emerged through discussions between labor and human rights activists in Guatemala – and in discussions with both Liz Claiborne, then experimenting with independent monitoring in response to increased American concern over working conditions in its sub-contractors, and the International Labor Rights Fund a labor NGO based in Washington DC which sought to develop new approaches to improving working standards internationally. By 2004, both the FLA and the WRC cited COVERCO in their materials as one of the leading monitoring agencies in Central America – although by 2004, the FLA had never asked COVERCO to monitor any factories.

COVERCO's monitoring program is highly detailed, involving training for its monitors in health and safety issues, unannounced visits, and above all, transparency in its reporting process. Paid by international brands – Liz Claiborne, Starbucks, and major banana companies – it has undertaken monitoring projects in specific industries and factories, including in Guatemala City's apparel zone. Its activists are highly respected, and even

Guatemalan trade unionists – who generally express deep reservations about independent monitoring, arguing that it undermines workers voice (interviews, Fuentes, Guatemala City, 2003) – recognize that its monitoring efforts are more consistent, more independent, and more transparent than those of other groups claiming to provide similar services.

Yet even COVERCO's own activists acknowledge the limitations to their efforts: a small, relatively underfunded NGO, it is hardly able to cover the entire apparel industry. Even more problematic, it depends on brandnames' commitment for its access to factories, as well as for its monitors' salaries. The monitoring group's efforts to maintain an independent stance limits its ability to engage directly with workers' unionization efforts, and sometimes makes it impossible for the monitors to respond to complaints – sometimes even in dire situations. Most seriously, if it finds problems in a factory, COVERCO cannot prevent its clients – the brandname corporation – from ending their contract with the sub-contractor. While COVERCO has been careful to work only with brand representatives who seem genuinely committed to improving conditions in their Guatemala sub-contractors' factories, COVERCO has no mechanism other than moral suasion to keep brands engaged in a problematic situation. Unless international unions and the Guatemalan state step in, the monitoring group has little power to intervene.

ACTUAL EXISTING MONITORING

What are the commonalities between existing monitoring schemes – and how do those patterns fit with the visions that drive public discussion of corporate codes of conduct and 'soft' global regulatory schemes? Through the comparison of these success stories, I hope to interrogate some of the underlying assumptions that run through discussions of independent labor monitoring. First, I explore similarities between the starting point of each scheme, looking at the kinds of activist network and issues that drive the program, and the extent to which these networks reflect the stateless vision of global activism that often dominate theoretical discussions. Then, I will turn to some of the patterns that can be discerned in the actual implementation of these monitoring schemes, comparing those similarities and differences with the vision embodied in discussions of global governance.

Each of these cases – Sullivan, Rugmark, and COVERCO – are cited as relatively successful examples of transnational campaigns pushing corporations to accept independent monitoring of workplace conditions, but that picture is somewhat misleading. In fact, each of these programs came as a result of local activists' efforts to make workplace-related issues visible – but in each case, the workplace issues were closely linked to a much wider agenda, having more to do with human rights issues than localized workplace grievances. Labor exploitation may have been central to apartheid as a system, but it was the larger systemic character of racial oppression that brought South Africa under an international spotlight, not segregated canteens or workplaces. Similarly, the problems of child workers in India's carpet industry were given prominence as an example of a larger problem – the forcible exploitation of bonded workers. Even in Guatemala, where workplace violations were central to the monitoring program, activists saw workplace violations as a reflection of a broader set of human rights violations, and as a reflection of the state's failure to protect its citizens more broadly.

At the same time, it is worth noting that none of these programs were initiated by local trade unions, although in several cases, local unionists were at least initially friendly to their efforts. In general, they stemmed from activist campaigns drawing on transnational themes, linked more directly to human rights issues than to labor questions. As Keck and Sikkink (1998) suggest, transnational movements have tended to achieve greater success when they appeal to direct humanitarian concerns than when they deal with complex, multifaceted problems. The anti-apartheid movement, campaigns against child labor, and even Guatemala's human-rights-as-labor-rights campaign seem to fit easily into the broader pattern they describe:

> As we look at the issues around which transnational advocacy networks have organized most effectively, we find two issue characteristics that appear most frequently: (1) issues involving bodily harm to vulnerable individuals, especially when there is a short and clear causal chain (or story) assigning responsibility; and (2) issues involving legal equality of opportunity (Keck & Sikkink, 1998, p. 27).

Racial discrimination, child labor, and the blurry line between human rights abuses and labor rights in Guatemala all make a more appealing case for international intervention than simple transgressions of labor law. This pattern is understandable. Labor violations tend to be far more specific, and far less gripping to external audience, than gross violations of human rights; indeed, as Brooks (2003) has recently written, the effort to attract international attention can prompt international activists to present workers as victims, asking them to bear witness to atrocities, much as survivors of massacres have borne witness to gross violations of human rights. But the stimulus for the monitoring programs – and, as I shall argue below, the pattern of monitoring and reporting – do not generally come from local workers themselves, but rather from well-intentioned activists, whose definition of the grievance may, in turn, be shaped more by international human rights discourse than by workplace conflicts.

Thus, it is perhaps not surprising that in each case, local activists raised issues that linked directly with ongoing international campaigns, or that their campaigns invoked credible threats of greater international sanctions. Divestment activists and South African trade unionists were obviously linked to the anti-apartheid movement; Indian child labor activists were part of a much larger campaign against child and bonded labor, especially in South Asia. Guatemalan activists responded directly to growing concern in the United States about the character of globalization, and concerns about the spread of the apparel industry to neighboring states, outside the reach of American unions or the U.S. Labor Department. Without the involvement of those larger global networks, it is arguable that activists in none of these cases could have persuaded employers to accept any form of monitoring.

It is worth noting, in contrast to the 'stateless' vision of transnational corporate regulation, that in all three cases, international networks appealed to powerful state actors, threatening state action to block goods produced under unacceptable conditions. In South Africa, the growing strength of the divestment movement was directly linked to legislative action, especially at the level of major American cities and states; most companies signed on to the Sullivan Principles only when discussions of national economic sanctions began to sound increasingly plausible. In India, the carpet industry was all-too-aware of the threat of legislative action: both the United States and Germany, two major markets for their products, were contemplating bans on goods produced by illegal child workers. In Guatemala, the U.S. Trade Representative made sure that Guatemalan apparel producers understood that access to American markets could be made contingent on showing some effort to improve sweatshop conditions. In each case, before any codes of conduct were adopted and before employers agreed to allow external monitors into the workplace, employers faced real threats that national legislation would block access to key export markets.

Following the 'boomerang' approach deployed by the human rights campaign, transnational activists appealed to their own national governments to make access to national markets contingent on improved corporate behavior internationally. This underscores, of course, the importance of local linkages with transnational efforts; without transnational campaigns, there would have been no threat of legislative action to influence corporations. But again, this pattern is quite different from the citizenship-based appeals of traditional labor campaigns: the appeal here is to transnational audiences, and to foreign states, rather than to domestic national labor enforcers.

Nevertheless, it is also true that those campaigns do not, on their own, appear to have produced corporate agreement to 'self-regulate'; far from demonstrating that monitoring efforts can be proffered as an alternative to state involvement in transnational labor issues, each of these examples can be directly linked to the threat of state enforcement – but the enforcing state is the importing state, not the state in which the production is occurring. Instead of the enforcement of citizenship rights, the boomerang operates to protect labor grievances through controlling access to international markets – limiting this boomerang mechanism to goods destined for export markets.

In a sharp contrast between the rhetoric of the ethical consumer movement and the reality, not one of these monitoring processes has been implemented as the result of individual consumer pressures. In each case, monitoring schemes came in response to organized consumers, acting collectively through institutional bodies. The anti-apartheid movement's pressure came through institutional stock-holders: church bodies and universities, all as institutional shareholders, wielded far more weight on corporate managers than individual stockholders could possibly have done. In India, the organized church movement, together with the German development agency, played a key role in shaping Rugmark's approach, first by persuading large German retailers to demand the Rugmark symbol, and then by working with Indian exporters to design and implement a regulatory scheme. In the case of the apparel industry, students have been almost as important in forcing corporate acquiescence as labor activists; but just as students in the anti-apartheid movement pushed university administrations to act as ethical institutional stockholders, students in the anti-sweatshop movement have worked effectively through university purchasing and licensing agreements, rather than simply focusing on persuading individual consumers to buy goods produced in union shops. Organized consumers, acting through institutions, carry far more weight – and are far more likely to be disciplined in their purchasing decisions – than individuals, no matter how ethical, and corporations are far more likely to respond to those organized pressures than to the threat of individual consumer boycotts.

But what of the impact of these schemes on working conditions? Through the comparison of actual existing monitoring, what similarities can we find in the character of corporate codes of conduct, and their impact on the workplace? Here, again, the record diverges markedly from the vision: instead of providing the basis for 'ratcheting up' standards at the workplace, the monitoring cases I have examined here appear more likely to demobilize international attention and to avoid further pressure to improve workers' conditions than to lead to more intense scrutiny or to a more enforceable regulatory framework.

Perhaps, the most common claim for corporate codes of conduct based on ethical consumer pressure is the assertion that codes of conduct lead to a changed corporate culture: repeatedly, proponents of transnational monitoring suggest that as managers around the world are forced to pay attention to a global code of conduct, their workplace cultures will be transformed to acknowledge and respond to workers' grievances. From South Africa, to India, to Guatemala, this claim appears to have some basis in fact: consumer pressure has clearly prompted concern for corporate image. In South Africa, multinational corporations initially insisted they had no responsibility for apartheid; after 15 years of concerted pressure, major business leaders had acknowledged an independent role in society, and began to call for an end to strict racial segregation. Similarly, in India, when activists first raised questions about child labor, leading carpet manufacturers claimed that children's 'nimble fingers' were required for knotting the best carpets; within a decade, leading manufacturers were much more likely to point out that for the highest quality carpets, only a trained adult weaver would do. And in Guatemala, apparel employers were clearly aware of international pressures to improve working conditions, especially as major brands and even the Guatemalan state began to discuss working conditions.

But was the change in discourse mirrored by changing behavior within the workplace? Here, the record is rather murkier. In South Africa, there is ample evidence to suggest that the monitoring scheme had little impact on the workplace, and even less on the overall problem that the Sullivan system was designed to address. In 1987, after the Reverend Sullivan himself publicly announced that his program had not contributed adequately toward eliminating racial discrimination, only a tiny handful of advocates – mostly, people who worked directly with the monitoring scheme, either through the accountancy firm paid to carry out Sullivan's monitoring or working on the board of the organization overseeing the principles – continued to claim its impact was meaningful (e.g., Sethi & Williams, 2000, p. 351). In India, Rugmark's impact is probably even more negligible: after 10 years of Rugmark's existence, child labor activists and trade unionists are bitterly critical of Rugmark's approach, using the same kinds of terms – 'corporate camouflage,' 'window-dressing,' and worse – that anti-apartheid activists used to describe the Sullivan system. Finally, while Guatemalan labor activists tend to be less dismissive of COVERCO's efforts, they nevertheless regularly assert that monitoring has not made an important contribution, pointing out that when monitoring has revealed problems in a sub-contractor, major brands have been more likely to cut off the contract (and lose workers' jobs) than to insist on ameliorating conditions.

Two issues seem particularly important in evaluating the impact of monitoring schemes. First, as critical activists point out in the case of each of these schemes, any consistent non-state monitoring program has been funded by corporations, usually through a levy on participating companies, but sometimes more directly through contracts between brand names and monitoring programs. This pattern of funding seems unavoidable in non-state regulatory schemes, but in each of these cases, it has caused suspicion, antagonism and angry accusations of complicity. Repeatedly, corporate funding for monitoring clouds the integrity of the process, causing, in each case, bitter division between activists who initially worked together to raise public awareness of the issue.

Second, each of these monitoring schemes seems woefully inadequate to the task it is meant to achieve. This is not surprising, of course, since only the most glaring problems have attracted the kind of global attention that engages corporate compliance. But in each case, decisions about the actual design of the monitoring process seem surprisingly arbitrary – so arbitrary that it is hard not to interpret the vagaries of each scheme as little more than an effort to offer overseas consumers vague promises, providing the cover of monitoring, in the terms of the old Brazilian saying, 'para os ingles ver' [for the English to see].

Finally, however, it is important to note that each time a monitoring scheme has been put in place, it has quickly been surrounded by a proliferation of other corporate codes of conduct – many of which have no monitoring whatsoever attached. In India, for example, the Carpet Export Promotion Council has created its own code of conduct, claiming monitoring but giving no evidence that monitoring has occurred; simultaneously, every carpet factory in the world seems to have attached 'No Child Labor' labels to their rugs, with no evidence whatsoever of its validity. Similarly, in Guatemala, the apparel export council has created its own code of conduct for the apparel industry, and published posters and guidelines in English, Spanish, and Korean, so that the industry can claim that all its companies are good corporate citizens – despite the council's apparent failure to monitor that claim (interviews, Guatemala, 2003).

This proliferation of codes and schemes has an obvious effect: by creating confusion for consumers and contractors, it undermines any likelihood that monitoring will lead to the 'ratcheting up' of conditions.

Most consumers – indeed, many activists in the ethical consumer movements – will be unable to distinguish between labels and codes.

While some proponents for a non-state approach to corporate regulation suggest that consumers will begin to insist on monitoring the monitors, these three examples do not offer much reason for optimism: in each case, companies who were unwilling to submit to even problematic monitoring schemes quickly found alternative ways to indicate some compliance with the basic thrust of the program.

And, of course, this proliferation of codes serves as a reminder that by their very structure, global codes of conduct give workers no voice in their design. In contrast to traditional workplace channels of grievance articulation, codes of conduct impose global concerns, which may not reflect the priorities of local workers themselves. Especially in cases where codes are linked to larger human rights issues, monitoring tends to emphasize the visible and the measurable; in none of these cases have independent monitoring schemes been important in efforts to construct meaningful channels at work, through which workers could articulate grievances or monitor their own conditions through appeals to external regulatory agencies.

CONCLUSION

What lessons, then, can we take from this comparison? On the negative side, there is the obvious conclusion about codes of conduct and corporate self-regulation. None of these examples offer much support for a vision of stateless global governance, where multinational companies might be monitored by independent civil society groups supported by alert consumers. Instead, they all support a more skeptical view, stressing both the limits to corporate self-regulation, and the risk that consumer pressure will be watered down by a profusion of less-meaningful codes.

Moreover, each of these cases underscore the limits of the human rights approach to global working conditions. In 'bearing witness' or making workplace grievances visible to an international community, none of these processes of monitoring have been able to incorporate real attention to developing workplace mechanisms of communication. Instead, they tend to stress human rights violations, and to draw on a larger agenda as monitors define the workplace issues that are of most concern. In order to attract international consumer attention to workers' rights, must we abandon a basic industrial relations framework?

But there are positive lessons as well, ones that resonate with the history of labor protections in the United States in the first part of the twentieth century. Historian Eileen Boris (2003) argues that throughout the early decades of the century, efforts to promote private workplace codes worked in parallel and in tandem with state efforts to regulate working conditions; although these 'hundreds of codes' worked through voluntary systems of enforcement, they gave impetus to growing state regulation.

In the same way, perhaps, each of these cases point to a similar possibility: as calls for codes of conduct and consumer boycotts spread internationally, growing awareness and concern about workplace issues might begin to create a constituency for greater regulation of work, both domestically and internationally. As each of these cases show, state involvement clearly provoked corporate self-regulation; perhaps publicity around major grievances and transnational consumer activism makes it increasingly plausible for state actors, in both exporting and importing markets, to attempt new forms of global governance. However, that conclusion also points to a somewhat different direction than most scholars and policy-makers have stressed: rather than focusing on independent, non-state action, perhaps efforts to regulate transnational working conditions should instead be focusing on bringing the state back in.

REFERENCES

Agnivesh, S. (1999a). A critique of selective western interventions and WTO. In: K. Voll (Ed.), *Against child labour: Indian and international dimensions and strategies* (pp. 31–38). New Delhi: Mosaic Books.

Agnivesh, S. (1999b). Indian child labor: Historical-contemporary review and worsening civilizational crisis. In: K. Voll (Ed.), *Against child labour: Indian and international dimensions and strategies* (pp. 147–153). New Delhi: Mosaic Books.

Ali, Kt. (1996). Social clauses and workers in Pakistan. *New Political Economy*, 1(2), 269–273.

Ayres, I., & Braithwaite, J. (1992). *Responsive regulation: Transcending the deregulation debate.* Oxford: Oxford University Press.

Blashill, J. (1972). Proper role of U.S. corporations in South Africa. *Fortune* (July), 47–54.

Blowfield, M. (1999). Ethical trade: A review of developments and issues. *Third World Quarterly*, 20, 753–770.

Boris, E. (2003). Consumers of the world unite! Campaigns against sweating, past and present. In: D. Bender & R. Greenwald (Eds), *Sweatshop USA: The American sweatshop in historical and global perspective* (pp. 203–224). New York: Routledge Press.

Braithwaite, J., & Drahos, P. (2000). *Global business regulation.* Cambridge: Cambridge University Press.

Brooks, E. (2003). The ideal sweatshop: Transnational and gender protest. In: D. Bender & R. Greenwald (Eds), *Sweatshop USA: The American sweatshop in historical and global perspective* (pp. 265–286). New York: Routledge Press.
Bulletin of Comparative Labour Relations 37. (2000). Multinational enterprises and the social challenges of the 21st century.
Chowdhury, G., & Beekman, M. (2001). Challenging child labour: Transnational activism and India's carpet industry. *Annals of the American Academy of Political and Social Sciences, 575*, 158–175.
Collins, J. (2003). *Threads: Gender, labor and power in the global apparel industry*. Chicago: University of Chicago Press.
Compa, L. (2001) Wary allies. *The American Prospect, 12*(12). http://144.92.189.173/web/view-print.ww?id = 5779
Compa, L., & Darricarrere, T. H. (1996). Private labor rights enforcement through corporate codes of conduct. In: L. Compa & S. Diamond (Eds), *Human rights, labor rights, and international trade* (pp. 181–197). Philadelphia: University of Pennsylvania Press.
Danaher, K. (1984). *In whose interest?: A guide to U.S.–South Africa relations*. Washington, DC: Institute for Policy Studies.
Della Porta, D., Kriesi, H., & Rucht, D. (Eds) (1999). *Social movements in a globalizing world*. New York: St. Martin's Press.
Esbenshade, J. (2004). *Monitoring sweatshops: Workers, consumers and the global apparel industry*. Philadelphia: Temple University Press.
Featherstone, L., & United Students Against Sweatshops. (2002). *Students against sweatshops*. London: Verso Press.
Frank, D. (1999). *Buy American: The untold story of economic nationalism*. Boston: Beacon Press.
Fung, A., O'Rourke, D., & Sabel, C. (2001). *Can we put an end to sweatshops?* Boston: Beacon Press.
Gay, K. (1998). *Child labor: A global crisis*. Brookfield, CT: The Millbrook Press.
Gereffi, G., Garcia-Johnson, R., & Sasser, E. (2001). The NGO-industrial complex. *Foreign Policy, 126*(July/August), 56–65.
Gereffi, G., Spener, D., & Bair, J. (Eds) (2002). *Free trade and uneven development: The North American apparel industry after NAFTA*. Philadelphia: Temple University Press.
Goldston, J. (1989). *Shattered hope: Guatemalan workers and the promise of democracy*. Boulder: Westview Press.
Gould, W. B., IV. (2003). Labor law for a global economy: The uneasy case for international labor standards. In: R. Flanagan & W. B. Gould IV (Eds), *International labor standards: Globalization, trade and public policy* (pp. 81–128). Stanford: Stanford University Press.
Greider, W. (1997). *One world, ready or not: The maniac logic of global capitalism*. New York: Simon & Schuster.
Guidry, J., Kennedy, M., & Zald, M. (Eds) (2000). *Globalizations and social movements: Culture, power and the transnational public sphere*. Ann Arbor: University of Michigan Press.
Harvey, P. (1996). *Rugmark after one year*. Washington, DC: ILRF Publications.
Hilowitz, J. (1998). *Labelling child labour products: A preliminary study*. Geneva: International Labour Organization. At www.ilo.org/public/english/ipec/labrep
International Labor Organization (ILO). (2004). *Child Labour: A textbook for university students*, ilo.org/public/english/standards/ipec, 10/11/04.

Jessup, D., & Gordon, M. (2000). Organizing in export-processing zones: The Bibong experience in the Dominican Republic. In: M. Gordon & L. Turner (Eds), *Transnational cooperation among labor unions* (pp. 179–201). Ithaca, NY: Cornell University Press.

Jonas, S. (1991). *The battle for Guatemala: Rebels, death squads and U.S. power*. Boulder: Westview Press.

Jonas, S. (2000). *Of centaurs and doves: Guatemala's peace process*. Boulder: Westview Press.

Kebschull, D. (1999). Philosophy and achievements of the 'Rugmark' labelling approach. In: K. Voll (Ed.), *Against child labour: Indian and international dimensions and strategies* (pp. 188–204). New Delhi: Mosaic Books.

Keck, M., & Sikkink, K. (1998). *Activists beyond borders: Advocacy networks in transnational politics*. Ithaca: Cornell University Press.

Khagram, S., Riker, J., & Sikkink, K. (Eds) (2002). *Restructuring global politics: Transnational movements, networks and norms*. Minneapolis: University of Minnesota Press.

Klein, N. (2002). *No logo* (2nd ed.). London: Picador Press.

Korzeniewicz, M. (1994). Commodity chains and marketing strategies: Nike and the global athletic footwear industry. In: G. Gereffi & M. Korzeniewicz (Eds), *Commodity chains and global capitalism* (pp. 247–265). Westport, CT: Praeger.

Massie, R. K. (1997). *Loosing the bonds: The United States and South Africa in the apartheid years*. New York: Doubleday.

O'Rourke, D. (2000). *Monitoring the monitors: A critique of price Waterhouse Coopers labor monitoring*. www.mit/orourke. September 28.

Ottaway, M. (2001). Reluctant missionaries. *Foreign Policy, 126*(July/August), 44–54.

Oxfam (2004). *Trading away our rights*. Oxford: Oxfam Campaign Reports.

Paul, K. (1987). The inadequacy of Sullivan reporting. In: S. Prakash Sethi (Ed.), *The South African quagmire* (pp. 402–412). Cambridge, MA: Ballinger.

Perez, S., & Pablo, J. (1999). *From the finca to the maquila: Labor and capitalist development in Central America*. Boulder: Westview Press.

Posner, M., & Nolan, J. (2003). Can codes of conduct play a role in promoting workers' rights? In: R. Flanagan & W. B. Gould IV (Eds), *International labor standards: Globalization, trade and public policy* (pp. 207–226). Stanford: Stanford University Press.

Prasad, M., Kimeldorf, H., Meyer, R., & Robinson, I. (2004). Consumers of the world unite: A market-based response to sweatshops. *Labor Studies Journal, 29* (3, Fall), 57–79.

Relly, G. (1986). The costs of disinvestment. *Foreign Policy, 63*, 131–146.

Rodriguez-Garavito, C. (2003). *Global governance and labor rights: Codes of conduct and anti-sweatshop struggles in global apparel factories in Mexico and Guatemala*. Master's thesis, Department of Sociology, University of Wisconsin-Madison.

Rosen, E. (2002). *Making sweatshops: The globalization of the U.S. apparel industry*. Berkeley: University of California Press.

Ross, A. (Ed.) (1997). *No sweat: Fashion, free trade and the rights of garment workers*. London: Verso Press.

Ruggie, J. G. (2003). Taking embedded liberalism global: The corporate connection. In: D. Held & M. Koenig-Archibugi (Eds), *Taming globalization: Frontiers of governance* (pp. 93–129). Cambridge: Polity Press.

Sampson, A. (1987). *Black and gold: Tycoons, revolutions and apartheid*. London: Hodder and Stoughton.

Schmidt, E. (1980). *Decoding corporate camouflage: U.S. business support for apartheid*. Washington, DC: Institute for Policy Studies.

Schoenberger, K. (2000). *Levi's children: Coming to terms with human rights in the global marketplace*. New York: Atlantic Monthly Press.

Schrage, E. (2004). *Promoting international worker rights through private voluntary initiatives: Public relations or public policy?* Iowa City: University of Illinois Center for Human Rights.

Seidman, G. (2003). Monitoring multinationals: Lessons from the anti-apartheid era. *Politics and Society, 31*(3), 381–406.

Sethi, P., & Williams, O. (2000). *Economic imperatives and ethical values in global business: The South African experience and international codes today*. Boston: Kluwer Academic Press.

Sethi, S. P., & Steidlmeier, P., with contributions by K. Paul, & P. Shrivastava. (1991). *Up against the corporate wall*. Englewood Cliffs, NJ: Prentice-Hall.

Shafir, G. (2004). Citizenship and human rights in an era of globalization. In: A. Brysk & G. Shafir (Eds), *People out of place* (pp. 11–28). New York: Routledge.

Sharman, A. (2002). Impact of social labeling on child labor in the carpet industry. *Economic and Political Weekly* (December 28), 5198–5204.

Smith, J., & Johnston, H. (Eds) (2002). *Globalization and resistance: Transnational dimensions of social movements*. New York: Rowan and Littlefield Pubs.

Spence, J. E. (1998). South Africa: A case study in human rights and sanctions. In: J. Mitchell (Ed.), *Companies in a world of conflict: NGOs, sanctions and corporate responsibility* (pp. 253–299). London: Earthscan Publications with the Royal Institute of International Affairs.

Stiglitz, J. (2002). *Globalization and its discontents*. New York: Norton Press.

University of Maryland, Program on International Policy Attitudes. (2000). *Americans on globalization: A study of public attitudes*. Available at http://www.americans-world.org/digest/global_issues/intertrade/laborstandards.cfm, 02/08/05.

Vidal, J. (2004). Fairtrade sales hit 100 million pounds a year: Ethical system goes mainstream. *The Guardian*, Saturday February 28.

Voll, K. (Ed.) (1999). *Against Child Labor*. New Delhi: Mosaic Books, Ltd.

Waddock, S. (2002). *Leading corporate citizens: Vision, values, value-added*. New York: McGraw-Hill.

Wells, D. (1999). Building transnational coordinative unionism. In: H. Juarez & S. Babson (Eds), *Confronting change: Auto labor and lean production in North America* (pp. 487–505). Detroit: Wayne State University and Universidade de Puebla.

Whittaker, A. (Ed.) (1988). *India's carpet boys: A pattern of slavery*. London: Anti-Slavery Society.

Williams, O. F. (Ed.) (2000). *Global codes of conduct: An idea whose time has come*. Illinois: Notre Dame University Press.

Websites

http://www.coverco.org/eng
http://www.rugmarkindia.org/about/facts.htm,9/21/04

Interviews

Agnivesh, Swamy, January 8, 2003, New Delhi.
Exporter (asked not to be identified), January 10, 2003, Agra.
Homero Fuentes, various interviews, May 2003, January 2005.
Kebschull, Dietrich. Director, Rugmark. January 7, 2003, New Delhi.
Pinto, Jerry. UNICEF. January 14, 2003, New Delhi.
Worker leaders of an apparel factory union (asked not to be identified by name). May 2003, Guatemala City.
Subramaniam, Sharda. Deputy director, Rugmark India. January 7, 2003, New Delhi.

PART III:
STRATEGIC QUESTIONS AND GLOBAL DEVELOPMENTS

THE POVERTY OF RESOURCE EXTRACTION

Stephen G. Bunker[†]

ABSTRACT

One of the defining characteristics of industrial capitalism is the rapid expansion of social production. This expansion requires increased use of matter and energy. Society cannot create either matter or energy, so industrial expansion in one place means that matter and energy must be extracted and transported from other places. Because social production expands through both new technologies and new products, industrial growth requires not only greater amounts, but also an increasing variety of material and energetic forms. Because these different forms of matter and energy are found in limited quantities in different parts of the world, expansion, technological innovations, and product differentiation in productive economies entail the frequent relocation of extractive economies, either because they have depleted the natural resources on which they depend or because new technologies have shifted the market. Regions which depend on exporting extracted natural resources are therefore likely to suffer from severe fluctuations in income. Capital sunk in extractive infrastructure may devalue radically. These problems limit their capacity for sustained development. Nonetheless, resource extraction figures prominently in the economic plans of many lessdeveloped nations. A growing literature addresses the economic or the political pitfalls that beset extractive economies. This essay explores their ecological roots.

SOCIETY AND NATURE

We cannot understand social production without understanding natural production. Social production requires matter and energy, which humans can neither create nor destroy, and whose transformations follow physical laws which humans cannot change.

Most analyses of development focus on the differences between the means, relations, and amounts of production and consumption in different societies. Production in society, however, is merely the transformation of matter and energy originally produced in nature. Natural production is also the transformation of matter and energy, and so differs from social production only in the sense that humans intentionally intervene in those transformations, which we call social production.

This single difference, however, though, has a series of profound and far-reaching consequences. Human intentionality is directed by social learning and information, and this information is cumulable across generations. Much of this accumulated information is technological, that is, it specifies the outcomes of particular combinations of matter and energy. Human needs and desires are expansive, so humans have used this information to direct and accelerate the transformation of matter and energy into increasing numbers and volumes of useable or exchangeable forms. Because technological information is cumulable, social productivity has increased enormously over the relatively short period since the evolution of Homo sapiens.

As more technological information has accumulated, and as this information has been directed to the transformation of an expanded amount of matter and energy into a larger mass and greater variety of products, social production has been divided into a growing number of specialized tasks. Different specialized groups produce different commodities. Within each resulting sector, smaller groups carry out different steps or processes. These processes must be coordinated in time and space.

Coordination is easier and less costly across shorter distances, so the different processes tend to locate as close to each other as possible. The resulting spatial concentration of social production not only facilitates transport and communication, it also lessens the cost to each specialized sector of the roads, canals, railroads, water pipes, drainage systems, power lines, and other infrastructure which their operation requires. Industrial and transport use of fossil fuels has greatly increased the tendency for social production to expand rapidly within relatively concentrated spaces, because these non-human energy forms allow an increased amount of matter and energy to be imported and transformed by less human labor in a bounded area.

Natural production, in contrast, is not subject to intentional direction. The kinds of information that affect natural productivity are genetically encoded through selective processes of evolution and coevolution within and between species. They are not susceptible either to social learning or cross-generational transmission except in a few limited cases, and those few cases are not technological in the sense defined above. Rather, they involve the use of a single tool or the exploitation of a particular kind of food and so are not cumulable in the same sense as social learning and technological innovation.

An even more important difference between social and natural production, though, is that production in nature occurs only within and between the metabolisms of individual organisms. A particular organism contributes to natural productivity only to the extent that it stores internally energy and matter in forms which can be consumed, transformed, and stored again by some other organism's metabolic processes. In contrast, most social production occurs outside of the individual organism's human body; human producers are not directly consumed but rather continue to manipulate matter and energy to produce desired products rather than simply to sustain and reproduce themselves physically.

Social productivity can be increased by learning and applying information about the results of energetic and material transformations. In nature, productivity can only be increased if new species add to the total amount of matter and energy transformed within an ecosystem – a bounded area defined by interaction between interdependent species (Kendeigh, 1974).

These new species can only evolve, however, if other species are already storing metabolically – that is, within the individual organisms of their members – the amounts and forms of matter and energy necessary to sustain the new species. The new species sustains itself by consuming matter and energy stored in other species. It "produces" by transforming this matter and energy into new molecular structures within its members' own organisms. This transformation requires energy, so some of the energy consumed is dissipated as heat. The consumed matter is not all perfectly absorbed; some is lost as excrement or detrita. Because some matter and energy are thus lost in each transformation, the new species itself can only produce a mass smaller than the mass made available to it by other species' production.

The new species can store and dissipate matter and energy in ways that feed back into the environment in ways that promote the growth of other species in the production chain on which it depends. The entire system, however, is finally bounded by the metabolic processes of all of the different species within it. This limits both the rate and the amount that natural production and productivity within an ecosystem can increase. Through the coevolution of multiple species, an ecosystem can become more productive, but its biomass – that is, the total amount of matter and energy produced – increases much more slowly than social production. Unlike increases in social productivity, this growth is asymptotic, that is, it tends to level off beyond a certain point (Ophuls, 1977).

The attentive reader will by now be objecting that I am trying to explain far too much with what I called the single difference between natural and social production, that is, that humans intentionally intervene in one but not in the other. Intentional intervention by itself, this reader will argue, is certainly not enough of a difference to explain why social production appears almost indefinitely and rapidly expansive while natural production expands slowly and then levels off. If both natural and social production are merely the transformation of matter and energy, why should one be able to expand so and the other not. We all know that matter and energy cannot be created or destroyed, but only transformed; why and how does society appear to escape from these bounds when nature cannot.

The answer, of course, is that natural production systems are limited to the transformation of matter and energy that occur within the bounded space of particular ecosystems. Previous transformations of matter and energy, ranging from volcanic upheavals to the far gentler and more routine photosynthetic capturing of solar energy by plants, provide the stored material and energetic forms that comprise biomass within particular ecosystems. Ongoing photosynthetic capture of solar energy by plants continues putting energy into the system. Other organisms consume and store the energy and matter combined in plants which perform photosynthesis. These organisms are themselves consumed, and the energy and matter they have stored are again transformed and stored in the organisms which consume them. This chain of transformations and storage involves an ongoing interaction between contemporary and past production. The fertility of the soil, and indeed the contours and composition of the ground that determine water flows, retention and even patterns of evapo-transpiration, are the results of previous natural production processes. Any natural production system, however, is limited to the matter and energy stored plus the incident solar energy in the bounded area of its ecosystem.

Social production systems, through the accumulation of information and the development of production and transport technologies, have been able to break beyond the bounds of particular ecosystems and to import matter and energy across these boundaries. It is for this reason that social production can expand so much more rapidly than natural production. No matter how much it expands, or how productive its technologies become, however, social production cannot create the matter and energy which it transforms, so it must import these from the natural production systems of multiple other ecosystems.

Social production systems tend to concentrate in relatively small areas. If the social production system has to import matter and energy in order to continue its expansion, and if these have to come from natural ecosystems which are not spatially concentrated in the same way, it follows that some other kind of system must emerge to export the material and energetic forms required for social production. These systems, which we will call extractive economies, are not themselves directly productive. They are social, but they cannot develop in the ways that social production systems do. First of all, they cannot concentrate spatially, because they must extract an increasing amount of matter from spatially bounded, geographically dispersed, natural production systems which are not increasing their productivity. This means that extractive economies must constantly expand into new spaces. Also, the extractive economies do not themselves determine the kinds of matter and energy which they exploit; social production systems determine that with their own technologies and market demands. Because different ecosystems produce different material and energetic forms, extractive economies must locate near the natural systems that happen to produce the forms, which are at that time required by the social production systems. This means that extractive economies cannot concentrate in relatively small areas that do not control their own location. It also means that if the production system's demands change, the extractive economy located near a particular resource loses its market or suffers a fall in prices. We will consider these problems soon, but first we must examine a related problem, resource depletion.

Production and consumption are really integral parts of the same process in natural systems. Production occurs within the metabolism of the productive organism, and the organism is consumed in the productive processes of other organisms. Natural production within an ecosystem depends as well on the physical configurations of previous productions as they are stored in the soil and as they have shaped crucial geological formations such as water systems. When extractive economies start to export matter and energy from natural systems, they necessarily reduce the matter and energy stored in the natural system. Indeed, they may actually reduce the number of direct producers if they take out living organisms, such as trees or fish. If only a limited number of older members of a species are taken out, natural production may actually increase, as there is more matter and energy available to younger members of a species, but, for reasons which will be explained later, direct producers are usually reduced at rates that diminish their capacity for reproduction. Alternately, extraction may disturb the configuration of soils and water courses by taking out sub-soil minerals. The minerals may not directly contribute to contemporary production, but the soils and water courses do.

Because the production that occurs within the metabolism of the organisms of one species becomes the matter and energy required for the production of the species that consume them, reduction of producers in one species can ramify through numerous other species within a single ecosystem, thus reducing their total productivity. If this happens, the reduction of matter and energy in an ecosystem can be far greater than the amount actually exported to the social production system. This means that the extractive economy that depends on living or self-renewing resources actually reduces the natural production on which it depends. Such an economy must constantly relocate or expand its area of operation. The problem is simpler, but just as difficult, when the extracted resource cannot renew itself in human time. In this case, the amount of minerals, fossil fuels, or other materials extracted directly and irrevocably reduces the remaining stock and so hastens the moment when the resource is exhausted.

A society that must constantly relocate faces a series of social and economic costs, which reduces its capacity to develop. In a productive economy, human labor directs some of the matter and energy it transforms into permanent structures – roads, canals, buildings, power lines, and docks, – which facilitate production, communication, and transport. Some of this infrastructure includes machines that directly heighten labor's productivity, but all of it in one way or another carries past labor into the present in ways that reduce production and marketing costs. Some of this infrastructure wears out through use and some of it is made obsolete by technological innovations; but because the social system is diversified, different parts are replaced at different times. There is seldom a need to abandon or replace the entire configuration. The relative stability of these configurations also means that social services, hospitals, schools, etc., can be built with the expectation that there will be ongoing opportunities for schooling, health services, and employment for subsequent generations.

All of this is possible because the location of social production is in large part determined by social decisions. Certainly, many cities were originally located because of particular natural advantages – fertile soils, adequate water, bays for shipping, even forests and minerals. The progressive concentration of population and economic activity, however, responds to the accumulation of multiple intentional acts to take advantage of the opportunities offered by proximity between these specialized activities. Extractive economies, however, must locate near the naturally produced resources they exploit. Extractive activities, instead of encouraging other enterprises to locate nearby, may actually diminish the economic opportunities in the region (Bunker, 1985). Extraction therefore tends to be a dead end, both economically and socially. In the following sections, I will discuss why extraction and production are separated in space, how extractive economies work, why they are different than productive economies, and why they tend to underdevelop themselves. I will leave for more extensive treatment elsewhere the obvious next questions – if extractive economies tend to underdevelop society, why do some human groups engage in them? And why do some countries deliberately promote them?

THE SPATIAL SEPARATION OF PRODUCTION AND EXTRACTION

In simple economies, extraction and production often occur in close proximity; individuals and groups typically engage in both activities. As social production expands under capitalism, both the amount and the variety of material and energetic forms consumed in its concentrated industrial loci increase. Natural production, however, does not increase or diversify at the same rate as social production. Indeed, many particular forms are naturally produced only within particular ecosystems in specific locations, and extraction usually leads to a depletion or reduction of natural products in these specific locations (Jalée, 1969; Caldwell, 1977; Bunker, 1985). Capitalist expansion can only occur, therefore, through the proliferation of dispersed extractive economies (cf. Lenin, 1965; Luxemburg, 1968). The expansion of industrial capitalist production entails, as a physical necessity, the widening spatial and temporal separation of extraction and production (Bunker, 1992, 1996). Matter and energy flow from increasingly dispersed extractive economies, whose locations are primarily determined by natural processes, to increasingly centralized productive economies whose locations are socially determined. The development of transport technologies that reduce the time and cost of bringing raw materials to industrial centers accelerates this flow and widens the cumulative distances between the many extractive and the few productive economies (Bunker & Ciccantell, 1999).

The accumulation of value, growing social complexity and power, and continuity and flexibility of physical infrastructure and social organization in the productive economy all require expanding quantities of matter and energy, which can only be gained through corresponding loss of value, social simplification, organizational instability, and infrastructural impermanence in extractive economies. The search for raw materials drove the expansion of early states and empires and extended trading networks (Ekholm & Friedman, 1982, p. 97; Diakonoff, 1969, p. 28; McNeill, 1963, pp. 71–74; Adams, 1977, pp. 165–174; Drennan, 1984; Chaudhuri, 1985, pp. 203–204). Nonetheless, with the notable exceptions of lumber for ships, metals for arms, and stones for building, most of the matter socially transformed was extracted close at hand. It was not until the conquest of the New World that extracted matter in large quantities was transported between widely distant regions, as gold and silver, cacao, animal oils, and spices fueled the surge of commerce that preceded the capitalist revolution (Bunker & Ciccantell, 1998).

Industrial capitalism makes the progressive spatial separation of extraction and production physically inevitable. Under capitalism, dominant classes systematically intervene in the organization and coordination of production for profitable exchange. Individual firms compete to lower commodity prices by substituting non-human energy for human energy. The reduced unit costs of production allow increased per capita consumption of transformed matter and energy. Expanded consumption widens and deepens the markets through which capital circulates, thus accelerating the accumulation of capital at the same time that it stimulates investment in new enterprises. New enterprises purchase more labor. Urban industrial populations grow as per capita consumption of matter and energy increases. Through these cumulative and mutually reinforcing processes, each increment in the industrial transformation and consumption of matter and energy creates the conditions for a further increase in the amounts of matter and energy required. Fossil fuels and new technologies have so reduced transport costs that a wide range of material and energetic forms once too bulky for profitable exchange can now move, in large quantities, across great distances. This, in turn, allows for tremendous increases in the mass of matter and energy transformed by industry. It also intensifies its inherent tendencies to spatial concentration.

The same forces that expand capitalist production foster its spatial concentration (Smith, 1984). The increased use of non-human energy requires an increased scale of production. This reduces the number of individual competitive firms in specific sectors, so it centralizes production spatially at the same time it concentrates entrepreneurial control. It also requires larger and more costly machines within larger and more specialized firms. The proliferation of different machines means that the "chain of labor" – the number of specialized steps or phases in the transformation of naturally produced forms into commodities – becomes longer. The different phases that result must occupy different physical spaces, so the movement of the matter and energy being transformed through this chain imposes increased transport and communication costs.

These communication, coordination, and transport costs can be reduced by proximity between the different processes within this chain, so firms tend to locate close to each other. Proximity also lowers costs by allowing for the sharing of some of the capital fixed in infrastructure – docks, streets, canals, railroads, etc. The spatial concentration of multiple firms promotes as well the urban agglomerations, which provide both labor for production and markets for commodities. In summary, expansion of social production, the concentration of ownership of the means of production, the proliferation of increasingly specialized and interdependent divisions or links in the chain of labor, and the spatial concentration of industrial production all reinforce and accelerate each other.

Expanded production entails product diversification. Social demand for particular products is necessarily finite, so expansion requires the continuous creation of new needs or demands. The mass of energy and matter and the diversity of naturally produced forms consumed thus increase together. The progressive substitution of labor by new and larger machines also requires an expanding variety of material and energy; coal instead of wood, oil instead of coal; bauxite, manganese, and chromium instead of iron. They also require more intense conversions of energy, which result in higher temperatures that can only be contained and controlled by alloys that use new combinations of minerals. The energy thus transformed must be transmitted at new efficiencies and speeds requiring, for example, the substitution of copper by more conductive metals. These material forms occur naturally in different parts of the world, so they must be extracted from an ever wider range of locations. The expanded mass and diversified forms of matter and energy consumed must be drawn from progressively more distant and disparate sources.

Because matter and energy can be imported from many ecosystems, social production can be vastly increased within a bounded space. To a lesser degree, the mix of social and natural production which comprises agriculture can be similarly intensified. Natural production, however, does not accelerate at the same pace; indeed, most extraction either depletes what is already produced or reduces productivity in ecosystems. The progressive separation of extraction and production proceeds at rates determined by the different rates and direction of change in social and in natural production, as well as by social demand for new energetic and material forms.

THE INTERNAL DYNAMIC OF EXTRACTIVE ECONOMIES

As we have seen, extractive economies must locate near the natural production systems they exploit, but once organized there, labor is directed according to the exchange-based, profit-maximizing logic of social production systems. Ecosystemic production tends to conserve energy through complex cycles of production and consumption between multiple species, but extractive economies tend to concentrate on those few material forms which provide the greatest returns to labor and capital. Because the efficiency of ecosystemic production resides in the tight cycles of production and consumption between multiple species, extractive specialization disrupts ecosystemic production far more than the extraction of an equivalent amount of matter and energy from a wider range of forms. Where species diversity and interdependence is high, as in tropical forests, the effects of extracting most members of a few species can ramify through extensive biotic chains, reducing production by several times the amounts of matter and energy actually extracted (Janzen, 1973; Richards, 1977; Bunker, 1985). Exchange-oriented extractive specialization thus maximizes ecosystemic costs in order to minimize labor and capital costs.

Specialized extractive economies develop in response to demands created by direct consumption and technological needs within the productive economy. Self-sufficient regional economies that previously exploited a wide range of natural products for their own use values start to concentrate on the extraction of the narrow range of natural products, which will provide the highest returns on external markets. In productive economies, production is intentionally directed to products for which there is a known market. In extractive economies, exportable goods are produced in nature without and beyond human intervention or intention. Their value in exchange does not direct the process of their production. Indeed, their exchange value can only be realized by removing them out of the natural system that produced it and away from the human economy, which extracted it.

This spatial separation of production, exchange and use in extractive economies critically influences the mechanisms that lead to different patterns of development in extractive and productive economies. In productive economies, where exchange value is socially and deliberately created, competition between firms to lower costs engenders increased production by increasing the scale of production. Labor benefits as goods become cheaper. Extractive economies, in contrast, cannot redirect natural production, so increase can only occur by more destructive exploitation of labor and nature. This causes a diminution of natural forces of production, and a consequent loss of both use and exchange values.

The search for profit leads to specialization in both extractive and productive economies, but the effects of specialization are very different. Specialization in a productive economy enhances labor productivity and increases the mass of socially produced goods. Specialization within an extractive economy, however, typically leads to depletion or to the disruption of the ecosystemic linkages, which sustain natural productivity and symbiotic balance. Specialization promotes flexibility in the production, and rigidity in the extraction, of exchange values. The capitalist can determine the form of the social product, and can thus direct labor to produce goods in accordance with demand. Nature's production cannot be directed; the only possible response to changing demand is to extract more or less of a particular resource.

The dynamics of scale function inversely in extractive and productive economies. The forces of production develop progressively in industrial systems because the unit costs of commodity production tend to fall as the scale of production increases. In extractive systems, unit costs tend to rise as the scale of extraction increases. Extraction usually starts by appropriating the most accessible sources. Greater amounts of any extractive commodity can be obtained only by exploiting increasingly distant or difficult sources. Although technological innovation may reduce costs of some extractive processes in the short run, unit costs of extraction continue to rise in the long run. Therefore, when extractive systems respond to increased external demand or internal pressures to increase profits, they tend to impoverish themselves (1) by depleting easily accessible non-self-renewing resources, or (2) by exploiting the most proximate self-renewing resources beyond their capacities for regeneration, thereby (3) requiring more labor and capital per unit extracted and so (4) forcing the unit cost of the extracted resources to rise so high that the development of synthetic or cultivated alternatives in other regions or the development of transport technologies that cheapen transport to more distant sources become cost effective.

The tendency for unit costs to rise is exacerbated by reduction of natural production within symbiotic chains, which include the extracted resources or which are disrupted by the process of extraction. Such disruption limits the human carrying capacity of the extracted environment, and may over time restrict the availability of labor (Bunker, 1985). It also increases the costs of reproducing labor by limiting agricultural potential in areas near the extractive enterprise. When this occurs, states and firms in productive economies seek other sources, or devise material substitutions.

Once an economy producing the raw material has been freed of the need to locate near the source of the natural product, it will tend to locate where land, labor, and infrastructure are more readily accessible and politically controllable. Technologies that cheapen access to larger, more distant sources, and successful plantation or industrial production of formerly extracted commodities, complete the cycle of extractive impoverishment and instability by introducing progressive economies of scale in new locations. The new location's competitive advantages eventually eliminate or seriously reduce the original and increasingly costly extractive economy. The lowered cost of the previously extractive raw material allows further expansion of industrial production (Bunker, 1992).

Extractive economies constitute an extreme case of what de Janvry (1981) has called dependent disarticulation. Socially articulated economies produce goods for internal consumption. The resulting acceleration of social and economic activity through linkages between wages, consumption capacity, and markets enhances returns to capital and expands production of goods. The articulation of production and consumption partially resolves the contradictions between wage costs and profits, making wage increases and social welfare expenses systemically rational. The disarticulated economy, in contrast, depends on externalmarkets and therefore lacks an internal consumption-driven accelerator to rationalize high wages and welfare costs. The spatial dispersion of extractive economies, their spatial and temporal instability, and the periodic dislocation of the labor force as more accessible resources within a region are depleted to create extreme forms of social disarticulation.

SUMMARY AND CONCLUSION

The ecological dynamics of extraction have a series of unfavorable economic outcomes. The economic and political mechanisms that underlie most of the Dutch disease and resource course explanations, though, imply social agency, and so encourage a tendency to blame the extractive victims for their own aborted development. In this final section, I show how these economic failures result from material, not social, causes.

Extractive economies necessarily locate at the most accessible sources of raw materials; depletion removes them to areas increasingly distant from existing demographic and economic centers. This raises the costs of labor recruitment, subsistence, shelter, and infrastructural development. Labor often becomes expeditionary, requiring the temporary migration of males. Demographic instability impedes the emergence of linked local economies; local sources of supply may not have time to develop fully. Because the extractive enterprise is located far from other economic activities, it often monopolizes whatever labor is locally available, further limiting the potential for other, linked economies.

Also, transport into the extractive region may be artificially cheap, as export vehicles for the extracted good would otherwise come in empty (North, 1961). Cheap transport heightens competition from externally produced goods; further restricting whatever production is already established or might emerge (see Weinstein, 1983). The extractive economy thus fosters near total dependence on imported foodstuffs and other staple goods. This further reduces the possibility of local economic linkages. The absence of linkages and the distance from demographic centers enhance control over, and exploitation of, labor, because the purchasers of labor can control the provision of labor's subsistence needs. Distance from established communities eliminates competitive demand for labor and reduces labor's ability to organize in its own defense, as there are few alternative social organizations to provide support. Even when labor manages to organize successfully, its power and its militancy are vulnerable to fluctuations and instability in the extractive enterprise and to the brutal repression, which its demographic isolation and residential homogeneity facilitate.

The same forces that disperse extractive labor into unstable, economically disarticulated, and politically isolated transitory communities also restrict the potential for significant accumulation and reinvestment of capital that might foment articulated productive economies in the region. Because the extractive sector forms enclaves removed from other economic activities, and because the infrastructure which it does develop tends to be highly specialized and located in areas, which do not offer other economic opportunities, profits tend to be invested either in warehouses or transport facilities (Watkins, 1963, 1972; Levin, 1960; Naylor, 1972) or in other regions, which offer better investment opportunities (Innis, 1956).

The tendency for unit costs to rise in extractive economies may lead to more capital investment in the extractive process itself, but this concentration of capital in removal and transport infrastructure frequently creates especially severe technological dependencies on the industrial countries. Railroads, steamships, docks, drilling rigs, pipelines, and earth-moving machinery require techniques and capitals, which extractive economies are highly unlikely to develop. The concentration of investment in export facilities instead of production- enhancing infrastructure further concentrates control over exchange and profit (see esp. Weinstein, 1983; Moran, 1974; Solberg, 1976; Blair, 1976; Cobbe, 1979; Levin, 1960; Katzmann, 1961). Alternately, excess capital accumulated from extractive exports may be invested in real estate speculation in the urban export nodes (Weinstein, 1983; Feagin, 1985; cf Harvey, 1982). This drives up urban rents and makes productive investment even less likely. This phenomenon, though recognized in the literature considerably earlier, only gained general recognition and notoriety when it was baptized "the Dutch disease" in 1991 (see Barham & Coomes, 1996; Coronil, 1997).

Some extractive economies have replicated the integration of extraction and production that characterized pre-capitalist and early capitalist economies. The potential for such development depends in part on the spatial location of the resource, in part on its natural or physical characteristics, and in part on the degree of capital concentration and intensification in the economic sector which uses or consumes the resource (North, 1961). Because of the general tendency for capital to concentrate and intensify in all productive sectors over time, and for materials to be used in more and more costly machines, these possibilities for productive economies to emerge from extraction diminish as capitalism evolves (Mandel, 1975). Capital accumulation and technological advances in productive economies also work directly to restrict such possibilities; as transport technologies improve and lower the costs for bulk movements of matter, the marginal price advantage which preliminary processing to reduce bulk provides to the extractive region is pushed back toward pure extraction (cf. de Silva, 1982, p. 78). In this sense, advancing globalization and the concentration and expansion of financial and technological power that drives it exacerbates the relative impoverishment of extractive economies and their subordination to industrial ones.

It should be clear that most of these dynamics occur beyond the power domains that the society organized around an extractive economy can control. Social scientific theories focus on social causation – whether as structure or through human agency – and so may not incorporate the non-human – material or physical constraints on the progressive development of the economics that mediate between social and natural production.

REFERENCES

Adams, W. Y. (1977). *Nubia: Corridor to Africa*. Princeton: Princeton University Press.
Barham, B., & Coomes, O. (1996). *Prosperity's promise*. Boulder: Westview Press.
Blair, J. (1976). *The control of oil*. New York: Random House.
Bunker, S. G. (1985). *Underdeveloping the Amazon: Extraction, unequal exchange, and the failure of the modern state*. Urbana: University of Illinois Press.
Bunker, S. G. (1992). Natural resources extraction and power differentials in the world economy. In: S. Ortiz & S. Lees (Eds), *Understanding economic process* (pp. 61–84). Washington, DC: University Presses of America.
Bunker, S. G. (1996). Raw materials and the global economy: Oversights and distortions in industrial ecology. *Society and Natural Resources, 9*, 419–429.
Bunker, S. G., & Ciccantell, P. (1999). Raw materials access strategies of rising Hegemons. In: W. Goldfrank (Ed.), *Ecology and the World-System*. Westport, CT: Greenwood Press.
Caldwell, M. (1977). *The wealth of some nations*. London: Zed Press.
Chaudhuri, K. N. (1985). *Trade and civilization in the Indian Ocean: An economic history from the rise of Islam to 1750*. Cambridge: Cambridge University Press.
Cobbe, J. H. (1979). *Governments and mining companies in developing countries*. Boulder, CO: Westview Press.
Coronil, F. (1997). *The magical state: Nature, money, and modernity in Venezuela*. Chicago: University of Chicago Press.
de Janvry, A. (1981). *The agrarian question and reformism in Latin America*. Baltimore: John Hopkins University Press.
de Silva, S. B. D. (1982). *The political economy of development*. London: Routledge and Kegan Paul.
Diakonoff, I. M. (1969). Main features of the economy in the monarchies of ancient Western Asia. *Ecole Practique des Hautes Etudes-Sorbonne, Congress at Colloques, 10*(3), 13–32 Paris and The Hague: Mouton.
Drennan, R. D. (1984). Long-distance movement of goods in the Mesoamerican formative and classic. *American Antiquity, 49*(1), 27–43.
Ekholm, K., & Friedman, J. (1982). Capital imperialism and exploitation in ancient world-systems. *Review, 6*(1), 87–110.
Feagin, J. R. (1985). The global context of metropolitan growth: Houston and the oil industry. *American Journal of Sociology, 90*(6), (May), 1204–1230.
Innis, H. A. (1956). *Essays in Canadian economic history*. Toronto: University of Toronto Press.
Jalée, P. (1969). *The third world in the world economy*. New York: Monthly Review Press.
Janzen, D. H. (1973). Tropical agro-eco systems. *Science, 182*, (21 December), 1212–1219.
Katzmann, M. T. (1961). Paradoxes of Amazonian development in a 'resource-starved' world. *The Journal of Developing Areas, 10*, (July), 445–460.
Kendeigh, S. C. (1974). *Ecology, with special reference to animals and man*. Englewood Cliffs, NJ: Prentice-Hall.
Lenin, V. I. (1965). *Imperialism: The highest stage of capitalism*. Peking: Foreign Languages Publishing House [1916].
Levin, J. (1960). *Export economies*. Cambridge: Harvard University Press.
Luxemburg, R. (1968). *The accumulation of capital*. New York: Monthly Review Press [1913].
Mandel, E. (1975). *Late capitalism*. London: New Left Review Editions.
McNeill, W. H. (1963). *The rise of the West*. Chicago: University of Chicago Press.

Moran, T. H. (1974). *Multinational corporations and the politics of dependence: Copper in Chile.* Princeton: Princeton University Press.

Naylor, R. T. (1972). The rise and fall of the third commercial empire of the St. Lawrence. In: G. Teeple (Ed.), *Capitalism and the National Question.* Toronto: University of Toronto Press.

North, D. C. (1961). *Economic growth of the United States, 1790–1860.* Englewood Heights, NJ: Prentice-Hall.

Ophuls, W. (1977). *Ecology and the politics of scarcity.* San Francisco: W. H. Freeman and Co.

Richards, P. W. (1977). Tropical forests and woodlands: An overview. *Agro-Ecosystems, 3,* 225–238.

Smith, N. (1984). *Uneven development: Nature, capital, and the production of space.* Oxford: Basil Blackwell.

Solberg, C. (1976). *Oil power: The rise and imminent fall of an American Empire.* New York: New American Library.

Watkins, M. (1963). A staple theory of economic growth. *Canadian Journal of Economics and Political Science, 29*(2), 141–158.

Weinstein, B. (1983). *The Amazon rubber boom: 1850–1920.* Palo Alto: Stanford University Press.

FROM COLONIALISM TO GREEN CAPITALISM: SOCIAL MOVEMENTS AND EMERGENCE OF FOOD REGIMES

Harriet Friedmann

ABSTRACT

This paper suggests that a corporate-environmental food regime is emerging as part of a larger restructuring of capitalism. Like past food regimes, it reflects specific social and political compromises, which I interpret through the social movement concept of interpretive frames. The diasporic-colonial food regime of 1870–1914 grew up in response to working class movements in Europe, and created a historically unprecedent class of commercial family farmers. When world markets collapsed, those farmers entered into new alliances, including one that led to the mercantile-industrial food regime of 1947–1973. Lineaments of a new food regime based on quality audited supply chains seems to be emerging in the space opened by impasse in international negotiations over food standards. Led by food retailers, agrofood corporations are selectively appropriating demands of environmental, food safety, animal welfare, fair trade, and other social movements that arose in the interstices of the second food regime. If it consolidates, the new food regime promises to shift the historical balance between public and private regulation, and to widen the gap between privileged and poor consumers as it deepens commodification and marginalizes existing peasants. Social movements are already regrouping and consolidation of the regime remains uncertain.

THE QUESTION: IS A NEW FOOD REGIME EMERGING?

It has been a decade and a half since scholars have recognized the unfolding crisis of the postwar international food regime, and begun to track changes that might constellate into a new food regime (Friedmann, 1994, 2005; Friedmann & McMichael, 1989; Burch & Lawrence, 2004). That crisis began in 1973. This paper suggests that an emerging regime is part of a larger restructuring of capitalism in response to "green" issues (Sandler, 1994; Campbell, 2004; Campbell & Coombes, 1999; Campbell & Liepins, 2001). The lineaments of what I call a *corporate-environmental food regime* appear in very specific and unequal compromises among social movements, states, and powerful agrofood corporations.

The corporate-environmental food regime, like past food regimes, is a specific constellation of governments, corporations, collective organizations, and individuals that allow for renewed accumulation of capital based on shared definition of social purpose by key actors (Ruggie, 1982), while marginalizing others. Like prior food regimes, it will have important and very different implications for farmers, food workers, and consumers in various parts of the world. Unlike the postwar regime, which standardized diets, it is likely to consolidate and deepen inequalities between rich and poor eaters. Like past food regimes, it will deepen commodity relations in agriculture and transform relations between farmers, food workers, and agrofood corporations.

International Food regimes are sustained but nonetheless temporary constellations of interests and relationships. They are part of larger periods of stability in relations of power and property, in the past corresponding to British and U.S. hegemony. They are above all *historical*. Since international markets in grain and livestock products began in the 19th century,[1] food regimes have been shaped by (unequal) relations among states, capitalist enterprises, and people, who migrated, bought, sold, and reshaped cultures of farming and eating within large, indeed, global constellations of power and property. Relatively stable sets of relationships fall into distinct periods, with unstable periods in between shaped by political contests over a new way forward. Emphasis on periods of global stability, and of change, distinguishes the food regime approach from other ways of understanding agrofood systems (cf. Goodman & Watts, 1997). At the same time, even at their most stable, food regimes unfold through internal tensions that eventually lead to crisis, that is, to an inability of the key relationships and practices to continue to function as before. At this point, many of the rules which had been implicit become named and contested. That is what *crisis* looks like.

In order to understand the present transformation, I shift the focus of analysis of past food regimes toward periods of restructuring instead of periods of stability. Contests over new directions have so far created new food regimes – something by no means guaranteed to continue into the future. Contests have lasted almost as long as the regimes themselves. We are due for a new food regime, if there is to be one. In order to ground analysis of an emerging regime, I refocus historical analysis on *transitions* between the first and second food regimes, and on the rise of the first. These are times of choice over alternative ways to organize power and property in land, labor and consumption. While I will not explore counter-factual trajectories – what might have happened if other actors and relationships had prevailed – this view of food in global history (Grew, 1999) attends particularly to those specific periods when several outcomes were possible. This shift in emphasis directs attention to social movements as engines of regime crisis and formation.

Social movements take a much larger role in the paradoxical unfolding of successive food regimes. On that basis, it is easier to understand how the unraveling of the food regime that was in its prime between 1947 and 1973 left specific actors in trouble, particularly farmers and consumers, and how other groups began to press new issues, particularly related to environment and health. After a quarter century of contested change, a new round of accumulation appears to be emerging in the agrofood sector, based on selective appropriation of demands by environmental movements, and including issues pressed by fair trade, consumer health, and animal welfare activists. I take the reader through the following steps: first, I describe an emerging ecological or "green" capitalism; second, I interpret social movement demands as entering into the shared perceptual *frames* that allow for food regimes to emerge, and as contributing to unfolding regime crisis by *naming* rules that were implicit while they worked; third, I retell the stories of the first and second food regimes as outcomes of social movements in contention with each other and with powerful institutions of rule and wealth; fourth, I look at environmental and other social movements that arose in the interstices of the second food regime; fifth and finally, I outline how environmental and related politics are shaping an emerging food regime as "green."

GREEN CAPITALISM?

An ecological phase of capitalism would entail a shift in rules of economic activity so that profits are renewed through less depletion of resources (which can mean lower raw material costs), less pollution (which can create demand for new technologies), and selling products that are culturally defined as environmentally superior. This would be a dramatically different "environmental regime" from the one that encouraged industrialization of agriculture and food after the Second World War. According to Sandler (1994, p. 44), an environmental regime always implicitly shapes class relations and profit-making activities, for instance, through understandings of nature, cost accounting, allowable materials and products, taxes, and consumer goods. Thus, environmental regimes always exist, even when they promote ignorance of ecosystem effects or repression of social opposition to damaging practices.

A "green" environmental regime would be one that reshapes accumulation of capital through altering production practices so as to reduce harmful environmental effects and satisfy cultural shifts in demand for "green" commodities. This possibility contrasts with the usual assumption that capitalist enterprises by their nature seek to externalize costs, such as pollution of waterways by fertilizer runoff. Similarly, changes in environmental consciousness and related changes in health, animal welfare, and trade concerns, lead to consumer demand for new kinds of commodities. In a green environmental regime, opportunities arise for technical, managerial, marketing, and input-manufacturing enterprises associated with "green" food commodities.

In agriculture, other things being equal, this could mean elimination or reduction of polluting industrial inputs. Of course, whether profits rise, fall, or stay the same depends on whether, for example, on-farm nutrients (e.g., manure or compost) are recycled on farm or purchased from another enterprise, which becomes a new source of profit. In other words, does agroecology define new production methods, leading to reduction of market activity? Or do "green" industrial farms shift demand away from agrochemical input industries and toward "organic" input industries specializing in allowable inputs (Guthman, 2004)?

A green environmental regime, and thus green capitalism, arises as a response to pressures by social movements. For example, concerns about food safety and quality by consumers and about environmental effects of industrial farming have inspired rapid growth since the early 1970s of a web of enterprises that produce, process, transport, advise, supply inputs, certify, and market "organic" foods. At the same time, the response is selective, choosing those demands that best fit with expanding market opportunities and profits. Thus, according to Guthman (2004, pp. 110–111), when "the farm crisis of the 1980s articulated with increased environmental concern and changes in consumer tastes," prospects for growth tempted many producers to shift from sustainable farming (a process and production orientation) to organic commodities (a product and marketing orientation). This in turn led to a "drive for regulatory legislation [that] effectively subsumed much of the organic movement into an organic industry."

Thus green capitalism is not a contradiction in terms. The imperative to "grow or die," Sandler (1994) argues, refers to profits not to quantities of products. Only under specific rules of land use and taxation, and only with certain cultural norms governing consumption, are profits dependent on increased resource use or externalizing costs of pollution. Parallel to the selective appropriation by the 19th century capitalism of demands for reduced exploitation – initially in the form of shorter hours of work – green capitalism can selectively appropriate demands of environmental movements for reduced pollution and depletion. Just as "a coalition of enlightened capitalists, middle-class reformers, and militant labor movements brought us not socialism but welfare capitalism" (*ibid.*, p. 49), so the coalition of environmental, consumer, and fair trade movements promises not reorganization of society around the central value of enhancing ecosystem integrity, but green capitalism. If successful, it promotes a new round of accumulation as a specific outcome of the standoff between "conventional" and "alternative" food systems. If a new regime consolidates, a new frame will make terms like these redundant; it will need no name. Challengers will seek to name it, that is, to expose its implicit workings.

The shift to a corporate-environmental food regime is, if I am correct, the most recent manifestation in agrofood production of the resilience of powerful organizations, which appropriate social movement demands to serve renewed accumulation (Scott, 1998). Before I turn to the two past regimes, I would like to introduce a language for bringing social movements more centrally into the histories.

RISE AND FALL OF FOOD REGIMES: FRAMING AND NAMING

Food regimes have so far been based on *implicit rules*. The first food regime was framed within a general rhetoric of free trade and the actual workings of the gold standard. The world wheat market that arose in the decades after 1870 was not really anyone's goal. However, vast international shipments of wheat made possible what actors really wanted to do – capitalists wanted to build railways, states of the European diaspora wanted to push back frontiers against indigenous peoples and build states to rival (and complement) those of Europe, and the poor and politically repressed of Europe wanted to find a better life in the European colonies. Wheat was the substance that gave railways income from freight, expanding states a way to hold territory against the dispossessed, and diasporic Europeans a way to make an income.

The second food regime was even more implicit. Agriculture was framed specifically not as trade for much of those commodities that crossed frontiers. Under the rubric of *aid*, an innovation of the post-World War II era that worked through a monetary system centered on the US$, commodities could be transferred without payments in the usual way. Because currencies were divided into "hard" and "soft" according to whether anyone wanted them outside the country, and after the War most currencies were soft, aid was a way to transfer commodities for soft currencies; that is, not for payment of the usual kind. These transfers benefited everyone involved at certain times. Of course, they had many of the effects of trade, but ignoring those effects and calling some transfers aid, suited powerful (and many not so powerful) interests in all the countries that mattered.

The point is that beneath the natural appearance of a working regime lie unstated assumptions that are in effect implicit rules guiding relationships, practices, and outcomes – such as which countries specialize in growing certain crops and which countries are importers. Borrowing from the social movement literature (e.g., Tarrow, 1994), I understand an enduring complex of assumptions and implicit rules as a socially constructed *frame* for interpreting reality.[2] I argue that food regimes emerge out of contests among social movements and powerful institutions, and reflect negotiated frames for instituting new rules. The relationships and practices of a regime soon come to seem natural. When the regime works really well, the consequences of actions are predictable, and it appears to work without rules.

Implicit aspects of the frame become *named*, when the regime stops working well, that is, when actions no longer have the same consequences. Arguments over alternative ways of solving problems that arise as a result take place in part over how to name aspects of the faltering regime. When names catch on, it is a sign that the regime is in crisis.

A good example is naming certain transfers of agricultural commodities, which once went under the universally approved rubric of *aid*, as *dumping*. During the 1950s and 1960s *food aid*, as I explain below, was the frame for transferring huge amounts of grain and other commodities internationally. In the 1980s, some of it came to be named "subsidized exports," which sounds very different. In 1982, I argued that "concessional aid" (the majority of U.S. aid) was in effect dumping (Friedmann, 1982). Dumping refers to sale of a commodity abroad at a price lower than in the domestic market. This clearly fit the practice of "selling" wheat and other "surplus" commodities to governments in return for "soft" or inconvertible currencies, which was how most U.S. (and later European) "aid" worked. Case studies showed that aid shipments, as one would expect dumping to do, led to a decline in domestic food production. However, the frame included a widely held belief that peasant agriculture was backward and bound to disappear. There was widespread resistance to naming aid as dumping as long as it helped the U.S. to dispose of its domestic farm surpluses, and the Third World governments to welcome the many benefits they got from accepting multiply subsidized food imports.

Only when aid became competitive did the frame become open to question. How can something as beneficial as aid be competitive? However, it was not the intellectual conundrum that caused the questioning. It was practical and dangerous conflicts between powerful states, initially the U.S. and the European Community (as it was in the 1980s). Mounting domestic food surpluses eventually appeared in Europe, because its domestic agricultural policy was similar to the U.S. in key respects, and it started to try to get rid of them in the same way. Competition between the two giants was costly and verged on what came to look like trade wars. One of the goals of the trade negotiations that began in 1986 was to reframe agriculture as trade. They succeeded in 1995, when an Agreement on Agriculture became part of the World Trade Organization (WTO). Now it is rarely denied that export subsidies constitute dumping, and the word "aid" is less often used to describe that practice. "Aid" has shifted to mean something done in emergencies, and is usually assumed to be a gift.[3]

Naming is a way that social groups challenge specific features of a waning regime. Naming emphasizes change rather than stability, in contrast to some approaches to international regimes (e.g., Hopkins, 1980; Krasner, 1983), and it does so in two ways. First, prolonged periods of confusion and experimentation, as regimes unravel and alternative interpretations and projects emerge, last as long as the regimes themselves. Second, regimes appear less as static structures (Goodman & Watts, 1997) and more as provisional compromises among some of the contending social actors, who manage to create a new interpretive frame in common. The new regime is in turn built on a historically specific set of relationships, which will over time diverge from the implicit expectations of the frame. No compromise can endure indefinitely.

Times of contention offer real choices of direction. More than one compromise is always possible. Social movements play a key role both in unfolding crisis and in emerging relations of wealth and power. The emblem of *quality standards* – which is presently reconfiguring relations among social movements, transnational corporate food supply chains, governments and international organizations – appears to be the basis for new and contending frames, and thus for one of several possible new regimes. Before arguing that a corporate-environmental food regime is emerging, I first reinterpret past food regimes with a focus on the social movements that shaped new relations of power and inequality.

WORKERS AND FARMERS: SOCIAL MOVEMENTS AND FOOD REGIMES

Each of the past two food regimes was the combined outcome of social movements intersecting with state strategies and strategies of profit-seeking corporations. Each regime unfolded for 20–30 years, and so did the crisis that followed each regime. New groups created by or in response to the old regime – workers in the first regime, and farmers in the second – organized to pursue their goals or defend their perceived interests. Their search for solutions entered into the compromises with powerful economic and political actors to shape a successor regime. Of course, the new regime rarely had all the results they had envisioned. Like states and corporations, social movements are rarely careful about what they ask for.

Colonial-Diasporic Food Regime, 1870–1914

The colonial-diasporic food regime[4] arose in the form of a world wheat market, which was the first price-setting market in basic subsistence good. It emerged from a convergence of state policies in Europe and the European diaspora. Governments in Europe, faced with popular unrest by labor, anarchist, and socialist movements, were interested in promoting emigration of troublemakers and import of cheap foods to pacify hungry citizens who remained. England was the first country intentionally to sacrifice domestic food security. It sacrificed the interests of very powerful groups – landowners and capitalist farmers, who were unable to compete with cheap

From Colonialism to Green Capitalism

imports – in favor of social stability for industrial employers and growing cities. Instead, they left to diasporic states the task of financing the transcontinental stage of the railways, along with shipping among the most dynamic capitalist sector of the era. Demand spurred rail, train, and ship industries in England, and gave another boost to industrial profits.

Even as they sought autonomy from European rule, states in America, Australia, and New Zealand embarked on projects to conquer territories inhabited by indigenous peoples. To consolidate their hold, it was crucial to link the conquered territories economically and culturally to Europe. After violently evicting indigenous peoples, expanding European diasporic states reorganized landscapes by imposing a grid of "homesteads" through railways and surveys (Crosby, 1986; Cronon, 2003, 1991). They recruited migrants to use land in a way different from both the ways of indigenous peoples and the ways of the European homeland. By organizing conquered land into a grid of potential farms and recruiting Europeans to work on them, "Neo-European" states secured territories culturally.[5]

Farmers recruited through the European diaspora were very different from colonial elites in classical colonies, such as India. While the latter found a variety of ways to mobilize the labor of colonial subjects, European settlers were fleeing economic deprivation and political persecution in Europe. They intended to establish themselves as farmers and to stay. Far from having colonial subjects to exploit, they were themselves vulnerable to powerful interests, particularly the railways, who transported first them and then their commodities. European settlers, unfamiliar with farming in new terrains or perhaps at all, grew what was asked by railways and merchants, who wanted to ship wheat and livestock products back to England and the rest of Europe. Settlers not only paid fares for themselves and their families, but steadily paid freight charges for wheat. The dependence of settlers on selling specialized wheat and livestock commodities via national railways and ports to distant markets in Europe guaranteed their attachment to expanding national economies and states.

Thus, a novel constellation of class and inter-state relations grew out of the convergent interests of industrializing European states, pressed by social unrest, and expanding states of the European diaspora. Working class movements were a key driver of the late-19th century European diaspora. Territorial expansion was a key driver of railway expansion and thus European and international profits.

The food regime created a new class of farmers dependent on export markets. Indeed, the central innovation of the colonial-diasporic food regime was the fully commercial farm based on family labor. In contrast to peasants, European diasporic settlers had to buy consumption goods and tools and were compelled to sell their products, and therefore to specialize in what was demanded. Their reliance on unpaid labor of men, women and children – exploitation of family labor – allowed them to lower costs relative to farms in England and elsewhere, including former export regions in Eastern Europe. Despite notorious exploitation of agricultural laborers, English farmers nonetheless did have to pay wages. Thus, a food regime arose on the basis of family farmers specialized in a monocultural export crop. Paradoxically, the triumph of wheat farms with unpaid family labor underpinned the first price-setting world market in a basic food staple.

The regime had the intended effect of reducing food costs to urban populations in Europe. It unfolded through a downward spiral of falling prices, crisis of European agriculture, leading to further immiseration and eviction of small farmers and agricultural workers from the countryside, and a complementary upward spiral of immigration to grain export regions in North America, temperate South America, Australia, and New Zealand. Thus, implicitly complementary policies of European and diasporic states drove the emergence and unfolding of the first international food regime. Their convergent practices created classes of family farmers, which had never existed in history, could exist only through international trade, and would suffer most from a collapse of the regime.

Environmentally, the colonial-diasporic food regime promoted mining of virgin soil, whose fertility (in the case of North America) was the outcome of eons of use by indigenous peoples and bison. The soil erosion consistently plaguing North American prairie farms can be traced back to the fragility introduced by plowing perennial grasslands (Jackson, 1984), which for a brief time (in geological measure) was able to yield crops with little labor or renewal of nutrients. The regime converted vast grassland ecosystems into "neo-European landscapes"(Crosby, 1986). These transformed landscapes, which were later naturalized as the "breadbaskets" of the world, performed apparent miracles. In place of the complex of perennial grasses, buffalo, and indigenous societies – partly through use of fire (Pyne, 2001) – which had sustained a stable ecosystem – European settlers introduced European grasses and cattle (Cronon, 1991). These "changes in the land" (Cronon, 2003) led to soil depletion, and eventually water depletion, in the very area on which large number of eaters across the ocean depended. It set the stage for industrial monocultures, which arose in the second regime to cope with environmental problems of the colonial-diasporic regime.

In contrast English High Farming, as it was called, was based on scientific principles of agronomy designed to renew soils and even to maximize long-term fertility. English farming, which went into precipitous decline after 1870, had become scientific as well as capitalist in the preceding century. High Farming has been called the most ecologically sophisticated and energy efficient farming system ever known (Bayliss-Smith, 1982). There is much to recover from its careful attention to recycling of nutrients, farm scale, and other features of ecological farming (Duncan, 1996).

Crisis of the Colonial-Diasporic Food Regime: Legacies and Alternative Possibilities

The colonial-diasporic food regime collapsed in world depression and ecological catastrophe (in North America called the "Dust Bowl") in the 1930s, only two generations after the rise of a wheat market. The key legacy of the regime was a new type and significance of farm politics. The defunct colonial-diasporic food regime left a class of wretched farmers concentrated in export-dependent regions inappropriate for European crops and agronomy. Because of their non-capitalist structure, commercial family farms responded "perversely" to falling prices (relative to economic models) by growing more. Historic limits to price falls no longer held. Many farmers had no choice but to leave the land and join the masses in search of work. Their misery complemented that of the remaining peasants and farmers of Europe. Surviving farmers formed or renewed political movements that became significant in settler countries and in Europe.

A new type of farm politics, distinct from peasant movements in other parts of the world,[6] was a legacy of the unraveling settler-colonial food regime. Farmer movements in the rising hegemonic power, the U.S., were to shape the unusual features of a later regime, but only after a crisis lasting through world economic depression and war between 1925 and 1945.

The actual configuration of the second food regime, which is the subject of the next section, was not the only one possible, or even the one that seemed most likely in the 1930s. First, in the first regime, the U.S. was not a dominant wheat exporter. The colonial-diasporic food regime created a number of new export regions, among which the U.S. was far from dominant. In fact, Punjab in the 1890s was seen by the US Department of Agriculture as its most alarming competitor. Punjab was also a settler region of the time, complete with wars (against Afghans), state-sponsored railways and laying out farms, and recruitment of settlers to grow wheat for export to Britain. Other newly colonized wheat export regions have also fallen from memory, namely Siberia and the Danube Basin (Friedmann, 1978). Second,

European colonies (later the Third World) were not dependent on food imports, but (despite variations due to climate and political changes) were largely self-provisioning and occasionally exported surpluses.[7] Third, European diets were not spread into racialized colonies of rule. The legacy of colonial interactions was culinary and agronomic diversity and creativity rather than standardization (Friedmann, 2005).

During the Depression of the 1930s, unsalable wheat stocks coexisted with hungry people. The problem was widely framed by governments during the Depression as volatile agricultural markets, which led to price instability for farmers and unstable supplies for consumers. The first solution was international, which seemed appropriate to the scale of the problem. International commodity agreements committed governments to export and import quantities within negotiated bands. Then during World War II, Allied governments tightly coordinated food supplies, including domestic regulation of agriculture for the war effort. Trade commitments during the War were understood as preliminary to national economic plans after the War. The latter reflected widely shared commitments by governments to their people to create what came to be named "welfare states," including both a minimum diet and farm stability. These took shape as a postwar plan for a World Food Board. Commitments to export and import would guide domestic economic plans.

Had wartime plans prevailed to create a World Food Board,[8] the victorious Allies would have made the Food and Agriculture Organization of the United Nations into a powerful organization, authorized by leading states to administer international agricultural commodity agreements. Yet, the World Food Board proposal, designed by the U.S. and U.K., was defeated at a meeting in Washington, DC, in 1947, only 2 years after the end of World War II, with the U.S. and Britain (under a Labour government) voting against it. This was the lost alternative for a second food regime (Friedmann, 1998).

The reasons for its defeat lie in a reframing of the interests of commercial family farmers in the U.S. in such a way that domestic farm policy precluded agreement to the World Food Board proposal. Other changes in 1947 shocked wartime agreement on postwar plans, but they do not account for the shift in this plan. A massive rupture in Allied relations occurred in 1947, when Cold War rivalry replaced cooperation between the West and the Soviet Union. Since rivalry between blocs centered on competition over delivery of high standards of living, including food, this might suggest a revision of the Proposal to stabilize food and agriculture within the Free World. Indebtedness of Britain to the U.S. for war loans marked a big change in hegemony, and allowed U.S. position to carry more weight than during the War. This explains why even a Labour Party delegation would have bowed to U.S. pressure to abandon the World Food Board. The puzzle remains why the U.S. should have reversed its policy regarding international regulation of food and agriculture.

The key to the puzzle is the particular shape of U.S. domestic farm policies during the Depression, which were continued into the postwar period and which were to limit U.S. international commitments and thus shape international trade and through them, domestic policies of other countries. U.S. farm policy was not the only type developed during the Depression and World War II. Among the many agricultural support programs created in various countries during the Depression, the one chosen was the only one that would result in government held surplus stocks. The British system of deficiency payments had the advantages of transparency and non-trade-distortion – to use phrases current in the 21st century. The government set target incomes for farmers and paid the difference between actual and target incomes out of general revenues. No surpluses accumulated anywhere, and prices to consumers were not affected. This form of subsidy was consistent with the World Food Board proposal and with liberal international trade.

By contrast, U.S. farm policy was designed not to be transparent (what were effectively subsidies were called "loans") and to raise agricultural prices rather than directly subsidizing farm incomes. An elaborate system of government purchases removed enough wheat or other specified commodities from the market to achieve target prices set by Congress. The result was surpluses held by government agencies. These put downward pressure on prices and therefore became self-perpetuating. They also required import controls to prevent farmers from all over the world sending their grain to the U.S., where prices were kept above world prices. This mercantile system of domestic agricultural policy was the achievement of the farm organizations, which were one of the three pillars of the New Deal coalition of the Democratic Party in power during the last years of the Great Depression and early postwar reconstruction.

Farm politics in the U.S., via emerging U.S. hegemony, led not only to refusal of the World Food Board, but also to a set of practices that structured the second international food regime. U.S. farm subsidies, which were unusual in their inconsistency with liberal trade, created the tail that wagged U.S. policy dogs, not only in agriculture but more widely in international trade agreements.[9] Because it was the leading economic power, all the features of the second food regime flowed from protection and dispersal of U.S. stocks. Domestic dispersal, which had begun during the Depression through "food stamps" as a form of welfare payment in kind, continued after the War but were far from adequate to the scale of the problem. Postwar monetary rules, which replaced the defunct gold standard with a dollar-based international system, allowed for a much larger outlet abroad in the form of "food aid." The most remarkable innovation of U.S. hegemony was "aid" in the form of sales of U.S. goods for "soft" currencies held by the U.S. government as "counterpart funds." Food aid was such a large proportion of all international agricultural shipments for two decades that it defined the unique feature of the second international food regime, its state-led or mercantile character.

Mercantile-Industrial Food Regime

For 25 years, the food regime that emerged after the defeat of the World Food Board in 1947 framed what seemed natural about agriculture, food, farm labor, land use, and international patterns of specialization and what was loosely called "trade." It unfolded as the expression of complementary goals of states, firms, social classes and consumers, dramatically changed patterns of international production and trade. Within the framework of "food aid," export subsidies became a defining feature of the emergent food regime. It transformed the U.S. from one among many exporters in the first food regime, to a dominant exporter. It transformed Japan and the colonies and new nations of the Third World from self-sufficient to importing countries. It transformed Europe from the dominant import region of the colonial-diasporic food regime, to a self-sufficient and eventually major export region. And it paradoxically framed the emergence of a number of giant agrofood capitals, which eventually became powerful actors, whose interests diverged from both farmers and national states. It did this through promoting industrialization of agriculture and elaboration of manufactured edible commodities sold by ever larger retail capitals.

The food regime of 1947–1973 can therefore be called *mercantile-industrial*. Its mercantile and industrial aspects contrasted sharply with the free trade and family labor of the earlier regime. The tensions among mercantile policies, family farmers, and agrofood corporations were contained for a quarter century as the food regime transformed ways of farming and of eating in all parts of the world, starting with the U.S.

Diasporic farmer movements of the 1930s forced an agenda with an unanticipated and unprecedented outcome. The diaspora that grew out of labor strife in Europe in the 1800s experienced its own crisis, when international wheat markets collapsed in the 1930s. Diasporic and European farmers demanded protection from unstable international markets, and agricultural protection took many national forms. However, it was the specific set of policies demanded by farmer movements in the U.S., which was the emerging hegemon, which shaped the next food regime. Only the particular ideology and political leverage of U.S. farmers can explain how the U.S. would introduce a form of domestic farm subsidy that led to government held surpluses and required import controls. When other states were constrained to adopt complementary domestic and trade policies, the whole regime took on a mercantile character. This took shape through a shared belief – upheld in the GATT agreement – that agricultural trade was exceptional.

Subsidized exports were a key institution of the mercantile-industrial food regime. Export subsidies originated – and to some extent continue – as "food aid." As a broader institutional innovation, foreign economic aid was based on the unique role of the dollar under the Bretton Woods monetary system. Most national currencies were not convertible to dollars, because most countries did not have sufficient export capacity to earn dollars. However, foreign aid allowed the U.S. to "sell" goods abroad in return for inconvertible (or "soft") currency of the import country.[10] This was intended to be temporary, to help countries develop export capacity so that eventually they would earn "hard" currency. In Europe, the Marshall Plan pioneered U.S. aid as a temporary – and successful – measure to rebuild trading partners, and to wean European colonies from dependence on imperial trade in favor of dollars (Wood, 1986). When Public Law 480 applied food aid in 1954 to "underdeveloped" countries – the new definition of those emerging from colonial rule – it became the foundation of the mercantile-industrial food regime.

As undisputed hegemon, the U.S. balanced its power and the wealth – which allowed it to protect its domestic policies – with the vision to foster complementary accommodations in the interests of other governments. Subsidized exports elevated the rank of the U.S. to leading export nation, and fostered a perception that it was somehow naturally a "breadbasket." European countries devastated by war accepted Marshall Aid for food, feed, and fertilizer, which set major commodity crops, especially wheat and livestock, on a path to industrial farming on the U.S. model. That aid did yield to commercial imports, especially feeds for intensive animal operations (Friedmann, 1994). The shared vision of "development" as national industrial growth encouraged Europe to agree to U.S. leadership even as their empires dissolved. Equally important, it encouraged new states created through anti-colonial struggles also to embrace U.S. leadership (Sachs, 1992; McMichael, 2004). (The Soviet bloc was separated from the west by mutual trade embargoes.) As development was almost universally understood to mean industrial growth,[11] that embrace included subsidized wheat imports from the U.S. For the Third World, however, aid did not yield to commerce but to chronic import dependence.

Food aid shipments undermined agriculture in many traditional peasant regions. Many could not compete with subsidized U.S. commodities. At their peak, the U.S. wheat shipments under PL 480 constituted more than 40 percent of international shipments. While the U.S. had actively promoted conversion to wheat diets in the early years, for instance in occupied Japan after World War II, urban elites in the Third World often embraced wheat as superior to local staples.[12] Together, these contributed to large movements of peasants to the cities.

However, neither growing dependence on food imports nor undermining farm sectors were problematic for Third World governments. First of all, within the frame of the food regime, aid shipments did not count as exports. Second, and related, agriculture and food were framed as backdrops to the main play, which was industrialization. The Third World governments needed to get labor out of "backward" farming and into the anticipated "modern" urban industries. Proletarianization was thus an explicit goal of "developing" countries, as they came to be called (after "underdeveloped" went out of fashion). Food aid helped in several ways. It substituted for domestic food supplies, helped with patronage-based state-building after independence from colonial rule, and forced people out of self-provisioning and local markets. These were all good things for what McMichael (2004) calls the Development Project.

Domestic food and agricultural policies in all parts of the world were shaped by two factors. Externally, subsidized grain and other shipments put a chronic downward pressure on world prices, even for non-recipients. Low prices required protection in import countries with the clout and desire to protect domestic agriculture, particularly Japan and European countries. Low prices also hampered export competition even by other European diasporic exporters such as Canada and Argentina.

Internally, the U.S. modeled and supported major state involvement and industrialization of agriculture. Governments in all parts of the world adopted locally suitable versions of U.S. mercantile agricultural policies. Both were encouraged by international development agencies during the 1950s and 1960s. In the Third World, industrialization of agriculture, called the Green Revolution, increased grain production and – as in the U.S. – also contributed to expulsion of farmers from the countryside. Japan, Britain, and the European Economic Community all adopted farm subsidies that were modified versions of the U.S. model (and eventually had surpluses of their own). The Common Agricultural Policy of 1957 (with specific policies defined in 1958) was the founding policy of European integration in the Treaty of Rome. During the 1950s and 1960s, these mercantile policies allowed for complementary national regulation of domestic farm sectors and agricultural trade. And within these nationally regulated spaces, agriculture and food became reorganized into industries with their own technical dynamics and the source of large profits.

The mercantile regime was also, paradoxically, *industrial*. The colonial-diasporic food regime had been led by merchant capitals, at least in agriculture; even railways took profits through shipping wheat and meat. In the mercantile-industrial food regime, large industrial firms finally become dominant within an increasingly specialized and integrated agrofood sector. Some capitalist organizations grew up to supply agriculture with machinery, chemicals, livestock feeds, veterinary medicines, and a variety of other inputs related to industrialization of agriculture. Others processed farm products as ingredients for evermore elaborate edible commodities. Still others began the long road from small specialty stores and farmers markets to giant supermarkets. These large capitalist firms sandwiched farmers between them as buyers and sellers. Farm organizations began to talk of the "cost-price" squeeze they faced between corporations with great market power. On one side were corporate sellers of chemical and mechanical farm inputs, and on the other buyers of crops and livestock as raw materials for further processing.

Paradoxically, beneath the mercantile surface of trade rules, these firms integrated production sectors transnationally. For example, the national livestock sector of Holland, which depended on imports of industrial feed grains from transnational suppliers, in a sense only appeared to be national (Friedmann, 1994). Similarly, promotion of import substitution in the Third World, for instance through the Green Revolution, actually substituted grain import dependence for dependence on industrial inputs such as tube wells and chemical fertilizers. In tandem with the growth and transnational reach of agrofood corporations, farmers became ever more specialized. Mixed crop and livestock operations, arguably important in many regions for ecological sustainability, gave way to monocropped fields and factory livestock operations. Agrofood corporations increased profits and control by lengthening commodity supply chains. Particularly to supply consumer demand for meat (a complex cultural phenomenon), monocropping of maize and soybeans as feedstuffs became the basis for much farming in the old diasporic regions. Farmers in the U.S. especially became larger and more monocultural, fewer in number, more integrated into corporate controlled supply chains, more dependent on subsidized exports, and in receipt of a shrinking share of prices.

Four changes gradually came into conflict with the practices – and the frame – of the mercantile-industrial food regime. First, Third World countries (which came to be called the South with the demise of the Cold War) were caught in a squeeze between import needs for basic foods and plummeting prices for the colonial exports they still depended on from the earlier regime. Industrial or "durable foods" increasingly found substitutes for sugar and tropical oils, which were among the most important. As reference to any ingredient label will attest, sugars have been replaced by a variety of "sweeteners," including chemicals such as aspartame, and industrial by-products such as high fructose corn syrup (which also benefits from U.S. government subsidies). Second, corporate reorganization of commodity chains accelerated the declining numbers and political resources of farmers, and "farm lobbies" came to reflect growing corporate presence even in farming. Third, transnational corporations found themselves constrained by the mercantile trading rules and domestic subsidies of the regime, and supported moves to liberalize trade.

Détente between the U.S. and the Soviet Union in the early 1970s revealed the fourth, deeply implicit framework for the mercantile-industrial food regime: the mutual trade embargo between Cold War blocs. The capitalist bloc had acted as a dam containing agrofood trade and aid. Surpluses accumulated behind the dam and had to be disposed of within it. Surplus disposal was key to the dynamics of the regime. The regime would cease to exist without surpluses and non-market – subsidized – exports that worked for both sender and recipient.

Yet, the regime was not visible as such, and surpluses simply presented themselves as a chronic problem. The U.S. saw an opportunity to sell off its surpluses for hard currency and at the same time shift geopolitical alliances through "Détente" with the Soviet Union in 1972 and 1973. The Soviet–American grain deals of those years were so huge that they cleared surplus stocks for the first time since World War II. They caused the price of wheat and other grains and oilseeds to more than triple. Food aid and even some commercial contracts – crucially a sale of soybeans to Japan – were suspended. Food import-dependent countries of the global South, which also faced soaring energy prices in the same years, began to borrow from private banks. The U.S. consumers outraged at the high meat prices started boycotts. Farmers enraged at being closed out of a share of the high prices, which were captured by trading corporations, put intense pressure on Congress. The regime fell into an acknowledged – though rarely remembered – World Food Crisis in 1974.

Crisis of the Mercantile-Industrial Food Regime: Reframing Trade

The World Food Summit of 1974 began to reveal the frame of the mercantile-industrial food regime. It was called by the Food and Agriculture Organization in Rome. The FAO, which had been marginal to the operation of the regime, had (like many specialized United Nations agencies) devoted its energies to hunger and peasant agriculture in the Third World. Suddenly, billions of people were defined as "food insecure" by the disappearance of U.S. surplus stocks and surge in world grain prices. The initial response was not to question whether markets themselves might increase vulnerability – despite the lessons of the crisis of the 1930s. It was to frame the problem as hunger, that is, people lacking food. At the first World Food Summit governments declared an "inalienable right to be free from hunger and malnutrition," and committed themselves to achieving this right universally by 1984 (FAO, 1996; Friedmann, 2004). The Summit created the World Food Council to upgrade the desultory activities of the World Food Program, the International Fund for Agricultural Development and the FAO Committee on World Food Security. The language of "food security" and "right to food" emerged from this moment. While the right to food was already mentioned in the 1948 Universal Declaration of Human Rights (Alston, 1994, pp. 206–207), food security named the absence of an automatic connection between meeting needs and agricultural production, which had been implicit in the regime frame (Lacy & Busch, 1984).

As hunger increased, export subsidies were no longer disguised. First, the aid became reframed as inconsistent with subsidized exports. Bilateral U.S. "concessional" flows dried up after the Soviet sales. Multilateral food aid institutions were upgraded. European aid expanded. A newly enriched Organization of Petroleum Exporting Countries began to use its oil revenues to give its own aid. Food aid came to be understood more explicitly as either "humanitarian" or an extension of foreign policy. Congress changed the U.S. food aid legislation to emphasize grants rather than concessional sales in the wake of revelations that allocations had been illegally redirected to the war in Vietnam.

Second, export subsidies became dangerously competitive. Once named, they led to formal attempts to include agriculture in trade agreements.

European surpluses, predictably generated by a parallel system of domestic agricultural price subsidies, had also led to subsidized exports. By the 1980s, competitive export subsidies led to a near trade war between Europe and the U.S. Their interest was to resolve this mutually destructive competition. At the same time, second rank exporters led by Argentina, Canada, and Australia formed the "Cairns Group" to press for an end to mercantile practices. New exporters of grains and soy for industrial livestock, notably Brazil, joined the effort (Friedmann, 1994). These governments had not been able to afford to subsidize their own exports,[13] and expected that an end to mercantile practices would finally give them a fair share of world exports. The major countries of what came to be called the North, therefore, agreed to try to include agriculture within trade agreements in the GATT negotiations that began in 1986. This shift was supported (somewhat ambivalently at first) by agrofood industries, which had come to experience as restrictive the mercantile framework that had nurtured their growth for more than three decades. The effort got momentum from the collapse of the Soviet bloc and the rapid privatization of assets in each country. The WTO was created in 1995, complete with an historic Agreement on Agriculture.

The mercantile-industrial food regime was over. Interests in the old regime died hard, however. The U.S. was hooked on grain exports, and its trade deficit was growing. Japan and Europe had large constituencies that defined food security as domestic sufficiency, and active farm lobbies. Mercantile trade practices did not end, nor did domestic farm subsidies. Although the North, especially through the Group of Seven industrial governments, made great strides in reframing the issue from hunger to trade,[14] the Agreement on Agriculture of the WTO remained very much an agreement in principle.

"Farm lobbies" supposedly prevented powerful governments from meeting their commitments to end domestic and export subsidies. Farm lobbies in the North were pillars of the unraveling mercantile-industrial food regime. Yet, the influence of farm organizations on national policies, which seemed formidable in the 1980s and 1990s, ultimately rested on a fragile social base. The number of farmers had fallen to a tiny percentage of the population because of the very success of the regime – price supports rewarded larger farms, and industrialization of agriculture subordinated farmers to large agricultural input and food-processing firms.

The interests of farmers (and as we shall see, consumers) became less monolithic as the regime unraveled. The U.S., despite increasing farm subsidies to unprecedented levels, was increasingly committed to policies, such as promotion of genetically modified seeds, which intensified concentration of industry power and farm size. Meanwhile, field crops had become concentrated in livestock feed grains, for both domestic and export operations. Domestic U.S. grain prices continued to fall, benefiting increasingly concentrated livestock capitals. Some grain farmers recognized that they were no longer helped by domestic subsidies, and began to identify a shared interest with farmers abroad, who continued to be hurt by the low U.S. prices. They advocated for a mix of measures to raise domestic prices (Ray, De La Torre Ugarte, & Tiller, 2003). However, the most vocal and influential voices in the official U.S. farm lobbies, which represented the largest actors interested in each specialized "commodity," had become those of agribusiness. They benefited from increasing U.S. subsidies while opposing subsidies in international organizations.

The EU began to shift in the direction of "non-trade distorting" subsidies under the rubric of "multifunctionality." This meant that farm subsidies would be redirected toward specific environmental, landscape preservation, rural community, and other "services" by farmers and away from commodity-specific subsidies. Yet, this policy was largely a tactic in negotiations with the U.S. It was designed with environmental organizations rather than farm organizations, and not particularly welcomed by farmers (Vihinen, 2004). Nonetheless, multifunctionality was a dramatic reframing of agriculture. As we shall see, it got extra purchase from food safety scares, which rocked consumer confidence in industrial agriculture. It opened new spaces in Europe, and intersected with new possibilities for reframing food and agriculture in other parts of the world.

By 2003, Europe and the U.S. still had not resolved their disagreements but found a new solidarity in face of a coherent challenge by countries of the South. In that year a coalition of leading governments of the South walked out of the WTO talks because the North remained intransigent over agricultural subsidies, both domestic and export. The three countries that led the 2003 coalition had emerged from marginal roles prior to 1974. Brazil had become a leading competitor, especially in soy exports. India shifted from leading recipient of U.S. food aid to more or less self-provisioning. China shifted from isolation to embrace Western seeds and techniques to industrialize agriculture. If the North does accede to the demands of the South, however, the results may not be as hoped by any of the protagonists. Abolishing subsidies cannot bring a new regime.

Two dominant, opposing positions remain locked into the productivist frame of the old regime. The first response to high food prices in 1974 was universal confusion about how such a reversal of "development" could have happened and framed hunger as the problem. The question was whether redistribution or increasing supply was the solution. Advocates of the right to food focused on income redistribution to widen access to commercial food. The attention to redistribution had indeed been the alternative to neoliberalism, which was particularly promoted by the G7, and would have applied not only to social classes but also to rules creating greater equality between North and South.[15] But the 1980s and 1990s saw the triumph of neoliberal policies centered on trade and finance. Advocates of free trade pinned hopes on technological change, now including genetic technologies (Runge, Senauer, Pardey, & Rosegrant, 2003).

As the trajectory of crisis in the global South followed the shift from hunger to trade, farmer movements and land reform came to the fore. In the South, significant social movements have arisen among farmers facing devastation from subsidized North imports and enforced reorientation of domestic agriculture toward exports to make government debt payments. They have pressed governments to take a stand at the WTO. Farm movements are also pressing governments to redistribute land, such as the Landless Movement in Brazil; to protect them against new threats from intellectual property claims on seeds, typical of several movements in India; and resist the pressure to redirect agriculture toward export crops to the North instead of food production.

Farm movements became international. A transnational network of farm organizations called Via Campesina was founded at a 1993 meeting in Mons, Belgium of 55 peasant and farmer organizations from 36 countries. This reframed farmers and peasants of North and South as one group, "people of the fields." It has grown quickly in its first decade, in both numbers and sophistication. Via Campesina was the culmination of national and cross-border organizing in the Americas, Europe, and Asia to oppose regional and international free-trade agreements (Edelman, 2003). Nongovernmental organizations and social movements had mounted increasingly large and lively parallel summits to many international organizations, including the World Food Summits between 1974 and 2002. Demonstrations opposing trade agreements, beginning with the Canada-US trade agreement of 1989 and extending to the North American Free Trade Agreement in 1994 and the WTO in 1999, exposed farmers and their supporters to international perspectives. Analytical and strategic discussions evolved into the Agricultural Forum parallel to the Summit of the Americas in Quebec City, Canada, in 2001, and broadened to reframe issues. Cultural and biological diversity, gender equality, dietary effects on health, ecological effects of farming systems, appropriate technologies, farmers' knowledge, and fair trade, joined classical issues of farmers' rights, land reform, agricultural labor, hunger, and social justice in the World Social Forums in Porto Alegre, Brazil and Mumbai, India, and then in the regional social fora it spun off (Friedmann, 2002). From these gatherings emerged a rough consensus on a reframing concept: *food sovereignty*.[16]

Between 1974 and the turn of the century, old institutions had ceased to work as before or – especially in the South – even to exist. Changes in food aid, farm subsidies and marketing boards, and consumer food subsidies led to a panoply of contests over how to reframe issues. These contests, however, took place in the midst of a wider loss of confidence in many parts of the world in the merits of the agrofood system created by the mercantile-industrial food regime. A new regime seems to be emerging not from attempts to restore elements of the past, but from a range of cross-cutting alliances and issues linking food and agriculture to new issues. These include quality, safety, biological and cultural diversity, intellectual property, animal welfare, environmental pollution, energy use, and gender and racial inequalities. The most important of these fall under the broad category of environment.

ANTECEDENTS TO GREEN CAPITALISM

New issues brought food and agriculture, which had been marginal to public consciousness and administered by separate branches of government, to a contentious center in the politics of the North. Environmental criticism of industrial agriculture began at the pinnacle of the mercantile-industrial food regime. Rachel Carson's *Silent Spring*, often credited with launching the environmental movement in the U.S., documented the effects of pesticides on what later came to be called "biological diversity." Yet, agriculture was far from the center of early environmental institutions. Air pollution was the first unifying issue of newly created national environmental ministries in the years after the first international conference on the environment in Stockholm in 1972. However, in the 1960s and 1970s, concerns about food additives and pesticide residues came to the fore. As more consumers were supplied by the industrial food system in the 1980s and 1990s, environmental and consumer movements took up issues related to food safety and food quality in response to outbreaks of diseases such as *E. coli* and BSE. Challenges to industrial agrofood practices also arose from animal rights activists. A large international movement opposed genetically engineered seeds, which were announced and rapidly introduced into maize and soy fields around the world in the 1990s.

"Organic" and local farms, which had begun to experiment with agroecology and a revival of cooking during the 1960s and 1970s, were always interesting to large food corporations. A game of naming played out around the terms *natural, health*, and *organic*. Corporate manufacturers (and later fast-food corporations) rightly considered the terms an implicit criticism of their own products as unnatural, unhealthy, and not organic (often *chemical*). At the same time, they were alert to market trends. A massive wave of mergers and consolidations swept the U.S. and the world in the 1980s. Some of the new giants, such as Beatrice Foods and General Foods, purchased some of the more successful alternative food producers in California and integrated their product lines to supply the growing network of "health" food stores across the continent. Retail corporations, whose power in the food system grew in tandem with increasing consumer anxieties, developed their own brands, which often claimed to raise quality and environmental standards, even as they displaced brand loyalty to old manufacturing corporations. These early experiments with "niche" product lines allowed corporate brands to appropriate the words *healthy* and *natural*, which came to adorn even the most extraordinarily reconstituted edible commodities. Indeed, at the end of the trend, candy bars with vitamins added are sold as "functional" foods claimed to promote health better than freshly prepared balanced meals.

Organic, however, was more sensitive because it related to farming. Farmers and farm lobbies joined agribusiness interests in rejecting the criticism of chemical-intensive industrial farming. As the sector grew in response to demand, certification became a complex political issue, both among farmers and at various levels of government. By the time it began to be resolved nationally in the 1990s (Guthman, 2004), international conflicts over food safety, including farm techniques, had become part of trade conflicts. The European Union and Japan refused imports of products from livestock treated with hormones and genetically modified foods and seeds. The conflict with exporting countries – the U.S. and the new Cairns Group at the WTO – overlapped with trade conflicts already described in previous sections.

In the South, the mercantile-industrial food regime had brought the Green Revolution and industrial agriculture. It simplified agro-ecosystems to increase production of basic food staples, such as rice in Asia and potatoes in the Andes. It marginalized rural communities based on mixed farming cultures and threatened loss of both indigenous cultivars and knowledge. The crisis of the mercantile-industrial food regime reversed this classical project of import substitution via industrial farming. International pressure to collect debts, which consolidated under the term "structural adjustment" in the 1980s, insisted on shifting to exports and removing government regulation, especially farm and food subsidies, and import restrictions. In many places, agriculture shifted from domestic food production to "non-traditional" exports such as fruits, vegetables, and flowers (as well as re-emphasizing "traditional" exports of coffee, sugar, and other tropical crops introduced by the colonial-diasporic food regime). Cattle production moved into tropical forest ecosystems to provide beef for industrial chains extending to cooked hamburgers. Social movements arose that linked classical issues of land, labor, and livelihood to new ones: displacement of indigenous peoples, protection of indigenous knowledge and cultivars, and agroecology (McMichael, 2005b).

By 2001, when the first World Social Forum brought together social movements from North and South, common understandings began to emerge of the inter-relationships among biological and cultural diversity and the threat posed by industrial farming. In North and South, experiments proliferate in growing food in ecologically sensitive ways and relinking consumption in municipal regions and protecting, reviving or creating regional food cultures. The "Slow Food" movement creates "convivia" to revive ecological and pleasurable eating, and more recently "presidia" to protect the diversity of cultivars, livestock, and local techniques. Indigenous farmers are playing increasingly effective roles in the larger movement of small farmers in Via Campesina.[17] Building on several decades of international feminist dialogues, women play a large and self-conscious role in many of these movements. If the past is a guide, some of the demands of these movements will inspire a new food regime and partly shape it, probably with unexpected results (Friedmann, 2001). In the wings, capital is ever ready to appropriate what works.

LINEAMENTS OF A CORPORATE-ENVIRONMENTAL FOOD REGIME

A convergence of environmental politics and retail-led reorganization of food supply chains suggests the emergence of a *corporate-environmental food regime*. The emergent regime, as I see it, consists of two differentiated ways of organizing food supply chains, roughly corresponding to increasingly transnational classes of rich and poor consumers. Both are led by private capitals, sometimes the same firms selling quality and cheap commodities to different classes of consumers. In the U.S., the two supermarket chains defining the two class markets are Whole Foods (a stunning appropriation of a 1960s counter-cultural term)[18] and Walmart. In Europe, by contrast, a single consortium coordinates a massive transnational organization of quality audited supply chains; however, the fact that these are constructed by private capitals, and not by government policies, opens the door to Walmart or small entrepreneurs catering to low-income consumers in the future. While the U.S. and Europe remain the largest markets, the rise of privileged consumers in large countries of the global South and China, and the reach of agricultural supply chains into the fields of the global South, raise questions about new articulations between interstate relations and agricultural land and labor.

The lead by private capitals is the outcome of a continuing impasse among governments of the North in international organizations. Although the WTO Agreement on Agriculture in 1995 reflected the determination of the EU and U.S. (and other powerful states) to resolve their trade disputes, these had already been overtaken by food standards issues.[19] These were to be negotiated in Codex Alimentarius, a joint committee of the World Health Organization and the Food and Agriculture Organization, which after 1995 would be enforceable by a WTO disputes tribunal. Whether specific "Sanitary and Phyto-Sanitary" measures by national states were to be treated as hidden import restrictions was to be arbitrated through governmental challenges brought to the new WTO tribunal. The U.S. successfully challenged EU rules banning any beef treated with hormones, resulting in annual penalties of $180,000,000. In this context, the EU decision not to renew its moratorium on genetically modified foods – which pitted wide public support against intransigent opposition by export governments – was made in the shadow of a threatened U.S. challenge. The decision indicates acceptance of a different configuration; public standards will be lower, as the EU drops its international insistence on higher standards, but new measures, particularly "traceability," support private sector initiatives to negotiate and enforce their own, higher than public standards.

Pressure to yield national standards to trade agreements is amplified by the pressure for the North to present a unified front against a resurgent South. The first crisis of the WTO in 1999 in Seattle simply delayed negotiations on an Agreement on Agriculture. The second crisis came in Cancun in 2003, when major governments of the South vetoed further concessions until the North met its existing commitments on subsidies. Within 4 years, the main cleavage had shifted from U.S.–EU to North–South. Conflicts over national standards would not be easy to resolve at the WTO.

Action has quietly moved to private capital. Regulation has historically helped food manufacturers by creating trust among consumers and clear rules for producers. The question is whether transnational agrofood corporations can effectively regulate themselves. I once answered in negative (Friedmann, 1994). Now I can qualify that answer. They have the capacity to organize supply chains that cross many national borders as private transnational supply chains, and to create, enforce, and "audit" (governments would call it "inspect") producers, shippers, and handlers along the chain. Yet, they still need inter-governmental standards to set a floor for their activities. Thus, in contrast to the 19th century national regulation, which forced private interests to raise standards above what the market allowed, the "quality" commodities offered to privileged consumers are being constructed *above* the floor set by international organizations.

Governments of North and South are for different reasons embracing *minimal inter-governmental* standards. As the EU drops its *state-level* commitment to specific "quality" standards such as hormone-free animal products and ban on genetically modified foods, it abandons government standards as public and universal. Instead, private capitals, which operate outside the jurisdiction of inter-state agreements, create their own carefully regulated supply chains containing just those *higher* standards that cannot be sustained in inter-governmental negotiations. Of course, the lower public sector standard invites importation and even local production of commodities meeting minimal standards for low-end consumers. Supply chains for both quality and minimal standard commodities cross many and changing frontiers. They are supported by uniform inter-governmental standards even when private audits require additional standards. As a result, faltering international organizations, including the WTO, are being outflanked by *private* transformations of agrofood supply chains in response to social movements of consumers, environmentalists, and others.

There were national precedents for a new configuration of public and private standards. In the 1980s and 1990s, U.S. national controversies over public certification of "organics" pitted large-scale "corporate" growers against adherents to "holistic" principles from which the term derived in the 1970s. Increasing market opportunities had attracted farmers with little commitment to principles of the social movement, with regard either to ecosystem integrity or even less to labor standards (Guthman, 2004, pp. 51–53). Moreover, the proliferation of certification bodies created confusion, and in the face of inter-governmental failures to resolve it, corporations began to shift the terrain.

Corporate supply chains, more than social movement supply chains they appropriated, depend on some kind of certification. According to Raynolds (2003, p. 737), "The rising importance of mainstream retailers and food corporation in Northern organic markets is reinforcing the position of big producers in Latin America able to guarantee large continuous supplies of standardized goods." The standards applied by corporate supply chains are an elaborate set of specifications applied to all links in the chain, abstracting from local environmental (and labor) conditions that originally informed organic and fair trade movements. They press against the small producers and trade organizations still adhering to those principles. Campbell (2004, Campbell & Coombe, 1999) calls this a form of "green protectionism" by the North, forcing higher national standards, e.g., in New Zealand, to give way to those dictated by private supply chains ending in rich Northern consumers.

Corporations have selectively responded to consumer demand (a privatized expression of demands by health and environmental movements) with audited supply chains delivering "identity preservation" and "traceability" from seed (or embryo) to plate. Thus, U.S.-based Cargill corporation is reorganizing to contract for specialty audited lines of formerly standard products. A recent innovation is to sell off its Brazilian subsidiaries that grew oranges and processed them into frozen orange juice. Instead, it is contracting Brazilian companies Citrosuco and Cutrale to supply oranges with specific characteristics, such as those picked from a tree with a "certain age," comparing the taste differences to those among grapevines. It is similarly investing in ingredients for "functional foods," claimed to offer specifically engineered health effects. Cargill is selling a product called CoroWise, made from plant sterols "that might help reduce cholesterol."[20]

A more far-reaching innovation has emerged in Europe, where public consensus could not result in public policy because of Cairns Group and U.S. intransigence at the WTO. By 1999, private capitals in Europe, anticipating the imminent expiration of the ban on genetically modified foods yet perceiving that consumers would continue to want a guarantee of "quality," organized an innovative consortium of private retailers, manufacturers, private certifying bodies, and others representing perceived consumer interests, to negotiate their own "quality" standards. Led by supermarket chains, EUREP-GAP ("Euro-Retailer Produce Working Group-Good Agricultural Practice") is a consortium of enterprises including food manufacturers, restaurant and catering chains, and credentialing and auditing bodies, that requires documentation at every stage of production and transport that an elaborate set of rules has been followed. EUREP-GAP sets standards according to their own interpretation of social movement issues. The website states:

> In responding to the demands of consumers, retailers and their global suppliers have created and implemented a series of sector specific farm certification standards. The aim is to ensure integrity, transparency and harmonisation of global agricultural standards. This includes the requirements for safe food that is produced respecting worker health, safety and welfare, environmental and animal welfare issues.[21]

Yet, this combination of basic public regulation underpinning higher private standards differentiates citizens – all of whom benefit equally from public regulation – into consumers – only some of whom can afford expensive quality standards. Neither the industrial food system nor the growing numbers of poor are going away; indeed, standard edible commodities are produced by some of the same corporations involved in constructing quality audited food chains. For example, both Codex Alimentarius and EUREP-GAP are now deciding standards for animal production, including feeds for intensive livestock. If Codex allows genetically modified feed grains (especially if it permits no labeling), while EUREP-GAP requires audits guaranteeing use of GM-free feeds, the combination of public and private standards would create conditions for distinct "rich" and "poor" supply chains in animal products.

The new mix of private and inter-governmental regulation will have significant effects on inter-state power. Private power may weaken rival national farm lobbies. Whatever mix of residual popular strength and large corporate influence keeps U.S. farm lobbies together, they are likely to fragment in face of EUREP-GAP temptations. If European retailers were to offer premium prices for, say, beef fed with non-genetically modified feeds, some U.S. farmers would likely respond. They would therefore increase demand for segregated, identity-preserved feeds. Segregated supply chains for organic soy already exist. Thus, intransigent U.S. and Cairns Group refusal to be required to segregate by international bodies[22] would no longer be bolstered by a solidary farm bloc. EUREP holds training workshops for auditors all over the world, including the U.S.

The third food regime also takes place against the backdrop of declining U.S. hegemony. One mechanism of decline, which I documented elsewhere (Friedmann, 1994), is that rising states are able to be flexible while hegemons are locked in to existing investments, geographies, alliances, and institutions. In the early stages of crisis in the late 1970s, Brazil and Japan formed a new trade link that shifted patterns in the mercantile-industrial food regime and made Brazil a major exporter. The form of investment was also distinct, consisting of joint ventures with both states and national capitals, and locating soy processing in Brazil. Similarly, EUREP represents an innovative approach to international supply chains and quality assurance that is likely to put its members at an advantage relative to U.S. corporations. While U.S. Department of Agriculture inspectors enforce quality standards, for instance in the booming export region of Sao Francisco in Brazil, by locating government inspectors at the port, EUREP requires each firm in the supply chain to document (and invest in labor, equipment, and organization) every stage of the life and travel of each mango, and trains auditors to check (Cavalcanti, 2004). The detail of the U.S. standards is consequently lower, and Whole Foods, for example, has to arrange its own quality audits for a much smaller supply chain.

As emerging power (perhaps even eventual hegemonic successor), China has already had massive effects. Vast plantings of genetically modified soybeans (and cotton) took place in a short time, giving China a boost in the latest phase of industrial agriculture and undermining international efforts to oppose GM crops. China's imports of GM soybeans gave Argentina an option to the European and Japanese markets, which resisted GM soy throughout the 1990s. The Chinese outlet, plus smuggling of outlawed seeds across the border, undermined Brazil's ban on GM crops, which has since expired. On the quality side, China has developed an entire exotic sector of tomatoes, which it exports as paste (Pritchard & Burch, 2003). As China's proportionally small, but absolutely large class of privileged consumers emerges, it is likely that it will affect quality supply chains as well.[23]

The South has been the laboratory for elements of the corporate-environmental food regime. Structural adjustment policies, which systematically attacked all aspects of the state-centered development in universal favor until the 1970s, paved the way for both global markets in edible commodities and transnational quality supply chains. Exports of fresh fruits and vegetables and of livestock products have been well established in many countries. Increasingly centralized private supply chains set national and local regions in competition with each other to sell mangoes or green beans. Some areas are now emerging as major quality export sites, such as Northeastern Brazil, South Africa, and New Zealand.

At the same time, as sites get locked in through elaborate technologies of quality control and documentation, their bargaining power may increase. Quality requirements, which selectively take up fair trade and other social justice and environmental demands, actually meet some of the old demands for development. For instance, documentation requires that agricultural workers be literate, and upgrades what have been marginal occupations. Yet, in the short run it means that a tractor driver, who cannot write, or work with computers, loses his job. Social justice requirements can include hiring a proportion of women, which is a good thing, but the standard format and external authority may play havoc with local social and family relations.[24]

National states continue to play a key role in regulating food and agriculture – private capital alone cannot regulate conditions of production, such as land use and labor markets, or of consumption, such as food safety. As agrofood systems restructure transnationally, international organizations such as the WTO and UN institutions are proving indispensable even as their role is subordinated to the private sector. International rules will determine standards in governments of the South – to the extent that national regulatory capacity allows for enforcement. Challenges to inequality among states are directed not to private corporations or consortia, but to Codex Alimentarius. This already burdened international organization is thus trying to take on the burden through a "trust fund" to which qualified governments of the South may apply for relatively small sums of money to help them develop "capacity" to administer international standards.

Even if some labor standards improve, both quality and standard commodities deepen longstanding processes that dispossess and marginalize peasants and agrarian communities, and create more poor consumers and more people without stable incomes to consume at all. Workers in large agricultural export operations in northern Mexico do not easily find ways to grow or buy either the tomatoes they produce for export or the beans and corn they once grew or bought in local markets (Barndt, 2002). They are now switching not to commercial *burritos* (a traditional meal of corn and beans) but to manufactured "Chinese" soups.[25] It is unlikely that the vast majority of Chinese rapidly entering food markets will demand or be offered "quality" foods of the kind organized by EUREP-GAP, at least for a long time. At the same time, EUREP-GAP includes MacDonald's of Germany. As long as income inequality remains the same or worsens, cuisines of the poor are likely to be based on standard edible commodities. While the rise of "quality" agrofood systems may herald a new "green capitalism," it may serve only privileged consumers within a food regime rife with new contradictions.

NO CONCLUSION: THE CONTEST CONTINUES

The emerging corporate-environmental food regime is already contested by the very movements it draws on, because many health and environmental problems, and most social problems, cannot be reduced to consumer demand. In place of a conclusion, I offer some speculative forays into how my picture of global restructuring of capital and classes fits with Lang and Heasman's (2004) analysis of conflicting paradigms for the future of food. These paradigms help to interpret initial, promising moves by social and environmental movements, whose projects are being appropriated and distorted by powerful capitals and states.

Lang and Heasman name the industrial aspect of mercantile-industrial food as a Productionist paradigm. It is dying. Two "paradigms" are vying to succeed it. Each offers distinct and opposing solutions to inherited health and environmental problems. The "Life Sciences Integrated paradigm" focuses on individual disease predispositions and crop characteristics, and privileges the biochemical, genetic approach linking specialized sciences with centralized industries. The "Ecologically Integrated paradigm," by contrast, builds on the holistic science of ecosystems and human health, and asserts an intrinsic link between the two. It elevates the public sector, which is the way that citizens manage their collective needs.

The mercantile aspect of the dying food regime invites us to interpret the two paradigms on a global scale. The Life Sciences Integrated paradigm offers engineered foods containing vitamins and other synthetic nutrients. These will complement the distinct foods offered to high- and low-end consumers. Plants and animals engineered to require fewer environmentally dangerous chemicals and toxins (so far, more have been engineered to tolerate larger doses of herbicides) are designed to improve productivity to feed low-end consumers. And bureaucratically organized and centrally monitored corporate supply chains transform selected aspects of the ecological model into transnationally sourced high-end commodities. The corporate-environmental food regime encapsulates two distinct corporate strategies for privileged and cash-poor customers across the globe. Therefore, the distinction between fresh, relatively unprocessed, and low-chemical input products on one side, and highly engineered edible commodities composed of denatured and recombined ingredients on the other, describes two complementary systems within a single emerging food regime.

My analysis of the emerging corporate-environmental food regime suggests interpreting the Ecologically Integrated paradigm at multiple scales, including the global. Lang and Heasman's concept of *ecological public health* names an emergent project to reclaim political spaces within which citizens relate to one another and to the places they inhabit in common. This can already be seen at all levels of scale, from municipal food security projects in tension with transnational supply chains, to international organizations in tension with one another and with private firms over the relative weight of environmental (and health) versus trade concerns in regulating agrofood relations. Social movements are already regrouping in a variety of ways – from the Food Alliance in the U.S. which brands ecologically sensitive, regional foods, to the Slow Food Foundation for Biodiversity, which creates a global network for private groups and local governments to brand typical products, and to develop and exchange their seeds and skills.[26] Both reassert the deeper meanings of agroecology and community in ways that do not reject markets but rather seek to "multiply niches" as an alternative strategy to expansion of one set of products and procedures at the expense of all others (Fonte & Boccia, 2004).

The tension at the heart of the emerging corporate-environmental food regime is thus coming into view: states, firms, social movements, and citizens are entering a new political era characterized by a struggle over the relative weight of private, public, and self-organized institutions. The key issue, therefore, for food and agriculture, and for reshaping governance at all scales, is democracy. That implies rethinking the meaning of *public*. Ecological public health must encompass the biosphere. An unequal contest is under way over the restructuring international institutions. Whether there will be a public sphere at the global level depends in part on the outcome of struggles between governments and non-governmental organizations promoting the Life Sciences Integrated paradigm, and those promoting the Ecologically Integrated paradigm. It is not known how irreparable is the damage to human and ecosystem health and environment of the mercantile-industrial food regime, nor whether it can be corrected or will be worsened by the emerging corporate-environmental food regime. The unfolding of another hierarchical regime based on accumulation of capital may not be the only, necessary, or even stable future. Integrated networks may offer a democratic and sustainable alternative. Much depends on whether and how democracy can find cosmopolitan[27] expression.

NOTES

1. Earlier markets in sugar, coffee, tea, etc. reshaped vast agro-ecosystems, labor systems, cultures, and diets, and their legacies are part of the story. See the oeuvre of Sidney Mintz, e.g. (1985). However, the point of entry is after the expansion of European rule and cultures, including transformation of exotic landscapes and diets according to European ideas and practices, to the period of price-setting world markets in wheat and other "settler" foods (Friedmann, 1978; Cronon, 1991).

2. Of course, the social movement literature focuses on how movements frame grievances about powerful institutions. The negotiation is mainly within the movement, of course in relation to experiences of challenging powerful groups. I am

adapting the term to express something closer to *hegemony*, but because it applies only to a food regime, and not to the larger context, I prefer the more limited term *frame*.

3. The implication of the word is still that shipments are charitable gifts, and the word is powerful. In fact, even much emergency aid is "tied," that is, it requires recipients to use money "donated" to buy commodities from the donor. Critics such as Oxfam International have argued against this practice for a long time but have not succeeded in undermining the frame on this point.

4. Diaspora is a Greek word literally meaning the dispersal of seeds. It is used metaphorically to refer to the spread of cultural colonies from a homeland, which may still exist or existed only in the past. Jews have used this word for a long time. Africans spread across the earth, originally through the slave trade, adopted it later. Now it is widely used for any group. In application to Europeans opens more nuanced ways of thinking about inter-cultural relations than the traditional (and usually implicit) assumption that cultures correspond to state or have specific class belongings (see Cohen, 1997). Similar recruitment of setters created what could be called farming diasporas in Northwest British India (now Pakistan), Siberia, and the Danube Basin. The first was not European, and the diasporic farmers of the second two are not usually treated that way, but perhaps should be. Thanks to Tony Weis for suggesting the term diaspora to describe the founding process of the first food regime.

5. The phrase from Alfred Crosby (1986) refers to the transformation of landscapes and mix of species with the joint invasion of humans and their companion species, wanted and unwanted, from Europe. I have tried to incorporate cultural aspects inextricably linked with species, especially in agriculture and cuisines, with the concept of "biocultural diaspora" (Friedmann, 2005).

6. Although sharecroppers of the South shared many characteristics of peasantries and entered into populist politics of the late-19th century and the farm politics of the New Deal coalition. Race politics complicated the story as much as relations to landlords and markets.

7. The immense suffering from famines in certain peripheral regions of the colonial-diasporic food regime resulted from colonial disorganization of old coping systems and climatic cycles (Davis, 2001).

8. War often provides the occasion for massive institutional change (Arrighi, 1994; Ikenberry, 2001).

9. Inconsistency with domestic Agricultural Commodity Programs was a key reason that the International Trade Organization agreement, signed in Havana in 1948, was not ratified by Congress. Instead, the General Agreement on Tariffs and Trade, which was meant to be temporary until the ITO came into effect, became permanent, and included a clause – at the behest of the U.S. – excluding agriculture from trade negotiations. This lasted through several "rounds" of the GATT. Including agriculture was a goal of the last Uruguay Round and culminated in the Agreement on Agriculture of the WTO.

10. These payments in national currencies, called counterpart funds, could only be used in the country itself. Thus, the word "aid" is appropriate in the sense that the U.S. accepted "soft" currencies in return for its goods, and in the case of Marshall Aid particularly, used those currencies to assist in the rebuilding of national

industries, including export capacity. Thus about a decade and a half after World War II, most countries of Europe were exporting enough to make their currencies convertible into dollars.

11. The leading exception was Gandhi, who led the Indian independence movement and believed in self-reliance in all sectors. However, the government was formed by believers in industrial development, including Nehru, the first prime minister and leader of the emerging non-aligned movement ("third world").

12. Earlier movements toward a "world cuisine" were industrial (Goody, 1982, pp. 175–190). The shift of basic staple is more clearly a feature of the intersection between ideas of modernity and U.S. hegemony.

13. Nonetheless, the U.S. has consistently attacked the Canadian Wheat Board, which holds a legal monopoly of wheat and some other grains destined for export, as inconsistent with "free markets."

14. The Group of Seven industrial nations attempted collectively to manage the growing rivalry among international currencies that had supplanted dollar supremacy in the 1970s; the footloose speculative capital released after the Thatcher and Reagan governments removed capital controls in the 1980s; and the transfer in the 1980s and 1990s to the Third World and former Soviet bloc governments of full responsibility for bad loans made to them by private banks to during the energy and food crises of the 1970s – the "debt crisis."

15. The challenge originated in the late-1960s and culminated in the early-1970s as "The New International Economic Order." Its institutional expression was the United Nations Conference on Trade and Development, formed in 1967, whose passage through the neoliberal era may offer partial support to a voice for the South in a new regime, along with other UN agencies, particularly the Convention on Biodiversity (Bartlett & Friedmann, in press). In the North, it was the Brandt Commission, which supported a sort of global Keynesian solution to the impasses of the 1970s.

16. Sometimes also as food democracy.

17. http://www.viacampesina.org/. See McMichael (2005a).

18. A popular joke is to call it "Whole Paycheck."

19. The Agreement on Agriculture relegated all quality issues to two categories, called Sanitary and Phyto-Sanitary measures and Technical Barriers to Trade, which would allow governments to make exceptions to the general principle of unrestricted trade. The agreement specified Codex Alimentarius, an obscure agency of FAO and the World Health Organization, as the arbiter of standards enforceable by the WTO (see Bartlett & Friedmann, in press).

20. www.cargill.com, 2/7/04, and Cargill press release reported in *Star-Tribune*, 10/7/04, both cited in *The Ram's Horn*, 222, July 2004, 2–3.

21. http://www.eurep.org/ Accessed September 4, 2004.

22. Most recently at the meeting of technical experts on traceability on the Convention on Biodiversity in Montreal, March 2005.

23. As a personal complaint, Canadian cherry prices have skyrocketed, I am told by local merchants, because of Japanese demand.

24. These examples come from Salete Cavalcanti, personal communication.

25. Victor Heurta of Equipo Puebla, personal communication, June 2004.

26. www.slowfoodfoundation.com

27. A promising vision comes out of part of the experience of European renegotiation of sovereignty (e.g., Archibugi, Held, & Kohler, 1998).

REFERENCES

Alston, P. (1994). International law and the right to food. In: B. Harriss-White & R. Hoffenberg (Eds), *Food: Multidisciplinary perspectives*. Oxford: Blackwell.
Archibugi, D., Held, D., & Kohler, M. (1998). *Re-imagining political community: Studies in cosmopolitan democracy*. Stanford: Stanford University Press.
Arrighi, G. (1994). *The long twentieth century: Money, power, and the origins of our times*. London: Verso.
Barndt, D. (2002). *Tangled routes: Women, work, and globalization on the tomato trail*. Lanham, MD: Rowman and Littlefield.
Bartlett, D., & Friedmann, H. (in press). Discourse and structure in the governance of genetically modified foods: Disempowering civil society. In: J. Kirton & P. Hajnal (Eds), *Sustainability, civil society, and international governance: Local, North American and global perspectives*. Ashgate.
Bayliss-Smith, T. (1982). *The ecology of agricultural systems*. London: Cambridge University Press.
Burch, D., & Lawrence, G. (2004). Supermarket own brands, supply chains and the changing agri-food system: The UK experience. Paper presented at the Agri-food XI Conference, Australian National University, Canberra, 9–11 June. *International Journal of Sociology of Agriculture and Food*, 2005. (forthcoming).
Campbell, H. (2004). Green protectionism part 2: EUREP-GAP, agri-food systems governance and the decline of organic exporting from New Zealand. *World congress of the international rural sociological association*, Trondheim, Norway, July 25–30.
Campbell, H., & Coombes, B. (1999). "Green protectionism" and organic food exporting from New Zealand: Crisis experiments in the breakdown of fordist trade and agricultural policies. *Rural Sociology, 64*(2), 302–319.
Campbell, H., & Liepins, R. (2001). Naming organics: Understanding organic standards in New Zealand as a discursive field. *Sociologia Ruralis, 41*(1), 21–39.
Cavalcanti, J. S. B. (2004). The dynamics of local development: From hunger to quality food, cases from Northeastern Brazil. *Symposium on local development strategies in food supply chains, XI World congress of rural sociology*, Trondheim, Norway, July 29.
Cohen, R. (1997). *Global diasporas: An introduction*. Seattle: University of Washington Press.
Cronon, W. (1991). *Nature's metropolis: Chicago and the great West*. NY: W.W. Norton.
Cronon, W. (2003). *Changes in the land: Indians, colonists, and the ecology of New England*. NewYork: Hill and Wang.
Crosby, A. (1986). *Ecological imperialism*. London: Cambridge University Press.
Davis, M. (2001). *Late Victorian holocausts*. London: Verso.
Duncan, C. (1996). *The centrality of agriculture*. Montreal: McGill-Queens University Press.
Edelman, M. (2003). Transnational peasant and farmer movements and networks. In: M. Kaldor, H. Anheier & M. Glasius (Eds), *Global civil society yearbook 2003* (pp. 185–220). Oxford: Oxford University Press.
Fonte, M., & Boccia, F. (2004). Local rural development in food supply chains: Small Producers and big actors. *XI world congress of rural sociology*, Trondheim, Norway, July 29.

Food and Agriculture Organization (FAO). (1996). *World food summit*. Rome. http://www.fao.org/wfs/index_en.htm
Friedmann, H. (1978). World market state, and family farm: Social bases of household production in the era of wage labour. *Comparative Studies in Society and History, 20*(4), 545–586.
Friedmann, H. (1982). The political economy of food: The rise and fall of the postwar international food order. In: M. Burawoy & T. Skocpol (Eds), *Marxist inquiries: Studies of labour, class and states. American Journal of Sociology, 88*(Suppl.), S248–S286.
Friedmann, H. (1994). International relations of food. In: B. Harriss-White & R. Hoffenberg (Eds), *Food: Multidisciplinary perspectives*. Oxford: Blackwell (also New Left Review, 197, January/February 1993, 29–57).
Friedmann, H. (1998). A sustainable world food economy. In: R. Keil, D. V. J. Bell, L. Fawcett & P. Penz (Eds), *Political ecology: Global and local* (pp. 87–101). London: Routledge.
Friedmann, H. (2001). The world social forum at Porto Alegre and the people's summit at Quebec City: A view from the ground. *Studies in Political Economy, 66*, 85–105.
Friedmann, H. (2004). Feeding the empire: The pathologies of globalized agriculture. In: C. Leys & L. Panitch (Eds), *The empire reloaded: socialist register 2005* (pp. 207–225). London: Merlin Press.
Friedmann, H. (2005). Modernity and the hamburger: Cattle and wheat in ecological and culinary change. Presented at the colloquium in agrarian studies, Yale University, January 14. http://www.yale.edu/agrarianstudies/papers/Hamburger.pdf
Friedmann, H., & McMichael, P. (1989). Agriculture and the state system: The rise and decline of national agriculture. *Sociologia Ruralis, 19*(2), 93–117.
Goodman, D., & Watts, M. (1997). *Globalising agriculture*. London: Routledge.
Goody, J. (1982). *Cooking, cuisine and class: A study in comparative sociology*. Cambridge: Cambridge University Press.
Grew, R. (Ed.) (1999). *Food in global history*. Boulder: Westview.
Guthman, J. (2004). *Agrarian dreams: The paradox of organic farming in California*. Berkeley: University of California.
Hopkins, R. F. (1980). *Global food interdependence: Challenge to United States policy*. NY: Columbia University Press.
Ikenberry, J. (2001). *After victory: Strategic restraint, and the rebuilding of order after major wars*. Princeton: Princeton University Press.
Jackson, W. (1984). Introduction. In: W. Jackson, W. Berry & B. Coleman (Eds), *Meeting the expectations of the land*. San Francisco: North Point Press.
Krasner, S. (1983). Structural causes and regime consequences: Regimes as intervening variables. In: S. Krasner, (Ed.), *International regimes* (pp. 1–22, 355–368). Ithaca: Cornell University Press.
Lacy, W. B., & Busch, L. (1984). *Food security in the United States*. Boulder, CO: Westview.
Lang, T., & Heasman, M. (2004). *Food wars: Public health and the battle for mouths minds and markets*. London: Earthscan.
McMichael, P. (2004). *Development and social change: A global analysis* (3rd ed.). Thousand Oaks: Pine Forge.
McMichael, P. (2005a). Globalization. In: T. Janoski, R. Alford, A. Hicks & M. Schwartz (Eds), *A handbook of political sociology: States, civil societies and globalization*. New York: Cambridge University Press.
McMichael, P. (2005b). Global development and the corporate food regime. This volume.

Mintz, S. (1985). *Sweetness and power*. New York: Viking.
Pritchard, B., & Burch, D. (2003). *Agrifood globalization in perspective: International restructuring in the processing tomato industry*. Aldershot: Ashgate.
Pyne, S. (2001). *Fire: A brief history*. Washington, DC: University of Washington Press.
Ray, D. E., De La Torre Ugarte, D. G., & Tiller, K. J. (2003). *Rethinking US agricultural policy: Changing course to secure farmer livelihoods worldwide*. University of Tennessee: Agricultural Policy Analysis Center http://www.agpolicy.org/blueprint.html
Raynolds, L. (2003). The globalization of organic agro-food networks. *World Development, 32*(5), 725–743.
Ruggie, J. (1982). International regimes, transactions, and change: Embedded liberalism in the postwar economic order. *International Organization, 36*(2), 139–174.
Runge, G. F., Senauer, B., Pardey, P. G., & Rosegrant, M. W. (2003). *Ending hunger in our lifetime: Food security and globalization*. Johns Hopkins University Press.
Sachs, W. (Ed.) (1992). *The development dictionary: A guide to knowledge as power*. London: Zed.
Sandler, B. (1994). Grow or die: Marxist theories of capitalism and the environment. *Rethinking Marxism, 7*(2), 38–57.
Scott, J. C. (1998). *Seeing like a state: How certain schemes to improve the human condition have failed*. New Haven: Yale University Press.
Tarrow, S. (1994). *Power in movement: Social movements, collective action, and politics*. Cambridge: Cambridge University Press.
Vihinen, H. (2004). Panel on multifunctional agriculture. *XI World congress of rural sociology*, Trondheim, Norway, July 30.
Wood, R. (1986). *From Marshall plan to debt crisis: Foreign aid and development choices in the world economy*. Berkeley: University of California.

GLOBAL DEVELOPMENT AND THE CORPORATE FOOD REGIME

Philip McMichael

ABSTRACT

The corporate food regime is presented here as a vector of the project of global development. As such, it expresses not only the social and ecological contradictions of capitalism, but also the world-historical conjuncture in which the deployment of price and credit relations are key mechanisms of 'accumulation through dispossession.' The global displacement of peasant cultures of provision by dumping, the supermarket revolution, and conversion of land for agro-exports, incubate 'food sovereignty' movements expressing alternative relationships to the land, farming and food.

INTRODUCTION

The concept of 'global development,' informing the Doha Round, is premised on the political reconstruction of agriculture as a *world* economic sector. In 2001, the U.S. Secretary of Agriculture, Ann Veneman, envisioned a 'global agriculture (where) future agriculture policies must be market-oriented...they must integrate agriculture into the global economy, not insulate us from it' (quoted in IUF, 2002, p. 4). Such reference to a 'global agriculture' is a discursive construct embedded in the political narrative of globalization, as a progressive realization of economic liberalization. The narrative is prescriptive, but not inevitable. And yet, while agricultural trade remains the center of political controversy in the WTO, the seemingly irresolvable nature of these trade rules will continue to realize this narrative.

Meanwhile, Vía Campesina, the transnational peasant coalition, observes that the "massive movement of food around the world is forcing the increased movement of people." Notwithstanding the profound impacts of human displacement on such a growing scale, the juxtaposition of new circuits of food and labor represents a historic moment in the reproduction of capitalism through mechanisms of 'accumulation by dispossession.' The latter is both an originating and a self-propelling dynamic, where capital expands through the release of assets, whether new or over-valued: "[w]hat accumulation by dispossession does is to release a set of assets (including labour power) at very low (and in some instances zero) cost. Over-accumulated capital can seize hold of such assets and immediately turn them to profitable use" (Harvey, 2003, p. 149).

In the context of corporate globalization, 'accumulation by dispossession' operates through *general* mechanisms of structural adjustment, which devalue and privatize assets across the global South, as well as through *particular* mechanisms of displacement of peasant agriculture, as a world agriculture emerges. Here, local provisioning is subjected to the combined pressures of dumping of Northern food surpluses, an agro-industrial supermarket revolution, and the appropriation of land for agro-exporting. That is, through economic liberalization, new food circuits relentlessly displace small farmers into an expanding circuit of casual labor, flexibly employed when employed at all. Thus, a global labor reserve, and (displaced/released) cultures of provision, represent new opportunities for accumulation in a global project of 'development.'

This chapter proceeds by examining the institutional tensions in the Doha Development Round associated with the pursuit of global development, via the corporate food regime. While the rhetoric of development frames the WTO Ministerial meetings since the Doha Ministerial in 2001, the practice of global development is filtered through the competitive relations among (unequal) states. And these competitive relations are increasingly governed by the corporate pursuit of 'comparative advantage' across the state system. The latter is decisive in constructing a world agriculture, generating the new circuits of labor fueling 'global development.'

The corporate food regime is a key vector of the project of global development. This project is characterized by the global de-regulation of financial relations, calibrating monetary value by credit (rather than labor) relations – as practiced through the privatizing disciplines internalized by indebted states, the corporatization of agriculture and agro-exports, and a world-scale casualization of labor (McMichael, 1999). The corporate food regime exemplifies, and underpins, these trends, through the determination of a world price for agricultural commodities strikingly divorced from cost.

It is one thing to subject agriculture to the price form, but quite another, through *political* means, to artificially depress agricultural prices through a food regime of overproduction and dumping. While the postwar U.S.-centered food regime managed overproduction to serve targeted Third World markets, the world price of the corporate food regime is universalized through liberalization (currency devaluation, reduced farm supports, and corporatization of markets), rendering farmers everywhere vulnerable to dispossession as a precondition of the construction of a world agriculture.

THE DOHA MINISTERIAL AS A DEVELOPMENT INITIATIVE

The designation of the WTO Ministerial in Doha (2001) as the 'development round' responded to concerns in the global South that 'globalization' was not meeting its promise. Accordingly, the Doha Development Agenda Round aimed to strengthen globalization as an inclusive force. Naming it a development round recalls the legitimizing function of development discourse in moments of intensified global inequality, like the era of decolonization (Escobar, 1995). It also reminds us that calling the new round 'development' simultaneously promises *and* proscribes.

The Doha Round proposed to facilitate new trade-offs for the global South, whereby further de-regulation of Southern economies would be matched with possible Northern concessions. These concessions were:

1. Freer trade, e.g., improved access to Northern agricultural markets, and reduction of Northern subsidies of farmer and agro-exports.
2. Qualification of WTO protocols, e.g., public health emergencies overriding specifications of TRIPs for trade in pharmaceuticals.
3. Management of liberalization of services to enable participation by Southern countries in service trade.
4. Reinforcement of Special and Differential Treatment provisions to address food security and rural development needs of Southern countries.

5. Technical assistance and capacity building schemes for the global South, especially for the 'least developed countries.'

As it happened, the development round was stillborn, because of institutional inertia, concessions by Northern states to corporate lobbies (e.g., the pharmaceutical industry), and lack of capacity in Southern states to address and/or implement reforms. In the run-up to the Cancun Ministerial in September 2003, the Northern states adopted a more aggressive stance, reformulating the Doha Round as an opportunity to impose a corporate agenda of equal domestic treatment of foreign corporations, notably in private investment in public services, in return for Northern action in ending farm subsidies. However, where the latter decoupled subsidies from farm prices, removing farm assistance to the WTO's 'non-trade-distorting' Green Box (as part of the Agreement on Agriculture), the Northern states, and especially the EU, disingenuously retained the capacity to dump cheap farm produce onto the world market.

The combination of the Europeans' attempt to reintroduce the Singapore agenda regarding a global investment treaty, and the North's avoidance of the dumping question, crystallized a counter-mobilization in Cancun (September 2003) of the global South, represented by the so-called G-20 (the Southern equivalent of the Cairns Group of agro-exporting states). Since Cancun, while trade negotiations have slowed if not stalled, the parties have regrouped – the U.S. around bilateral negotiations, the G-20 around regional agreements, and the Europeans around CAP reforms offset by progress in 'trade' in services, via the GATS. At the same time, the EU and the U.S. have made attempts to co-opt the leaders of the G-20, Brazil and India (Wiggerthale, 2004, p. 20).

Revival of the Doha Round pivots on agriculture, whose centrality to Doha is reflected in its contentiousness. New negotiations in 2004 involved a revision of the pre-Cancun agreement struck between the EU and the U.S., including counter-proposals by the G20 (Oxford Analytica, 2004). The focus of the new March text included the three key, original issues of market access, export subsidies, and domestic support policies. The subsequent 'July Package' contained a commitment to end export subsidies, but over at least a decade. Meanwhile, additional demands from the global South, led by the newly empowered G-33 (exporters dedicated to protecting their domestic markets), for a 'Development Box,' to sanction subsidies supporting agriculture which is farmer-driven rather than trade-driven (surplus dumping) gained little ground (Khor, 2004, p. 3). While agricultural reform is central, it unfolds in piecemeal fashion, with the EU making what it considers concessions in decoupling farm payments from commodity prices (though without ending overproduction), and successful WTO litigation by Brazil on U.S. cotton subsidies, which have wrought havoc on African producers.

In short, Doha concentrates international tensions and the contradictory relations which constitute 'development.' Currently, Doha claims further global deregulation as the premise of development. Historically, Doha replicates the GATT Uruguay Round of the 1980s, which aimed to liberalize agriculture and services (then banking, insurance, and telecommunications) in which the North held a competitive advantage. At the time the global South was skeptical, as its cheaper exports of steel products, footwear, electronic products, and agricultural products were limited by Northern protections. India and Brazil led the resistance to broadening GATT, but Northern pressure and the promise of open markets, including agricultural markets, tipped the balance (Adams, 1993, pp. 196–197). When GATT became the WTO, the liberalizing Agreement on Agriculture was the *quid pro quo* for the global South's acceptance of TRIPs and TRIMs, which "soon proved to be a double threat to food security and sovereignty in the developing world" (Wallach & Woodall, 2004, p. 193).

The Doha Round continues this dance, disingenuously representing GATS 2000 as a trade agreement, which demands openness to 'cross-border' provision of services (by TNCs) as a condition for opening EU and U.S. markets in garments, textiles, and agricultural products (Wallach, 2003). Oxfam's Kevin Watkins (2002, p. 21) argues this replays the Uruguay Round, when the global North offered market access in return for protection of TNC patents (costing the South $40 billion in technology rents). He maintains that while the game has changed, the rules are the same: "The West buys your bananas and shirts if you give its banks and insurance companies unrestricted access to your markets."

Offering perspective on the terms in, and means by, which Doha addresses agricultural reform, Vía Campesina, noted: "The negotiations on agriculture still seem to be a fight between the 'corporate elephants of the agro-industry' represented by the European Union, the United States and the Cairns group instead of negotiation on how to come to fair, equitable trade relations that give protection to domestic food production and consumption and the world's environment" (quoted in Wallach & Woodall, 2004, p. 215). Sophia Murphy (2004, p. 4) suggests "the U.S. and the EU are fighting what is likely to be a losing battle to maintain their export share in world agricultural markets". Subsidizing their farmers is a short-term, and increasingly untenable, tactic in the world market where countries like Brazil, Argentina, Russia, China, and India can offer cheaper farm commodities to transnational agribusinesses concerned with reducing costs and accessing emerging markets of middle class consumers in these countries. She concludes: "While the U.S., E.U. and Cairns Group/G20 fight with each other over who will get (or keep) the investment of transnational agribusiness, most developing countries [notably in sub-Saharan Africa] are left on the sidelines" (*idem*).

LINEAGES OF A CORPORATE FOOD REGIME

The losing battle within the global North nevertheless conditions the construction of a 'world agriculture.' The combined dumping of subsidized food surpluses and growing agribusiness access to land, labor, and markets in the global South clears the way for corporate-driven food supply chains binding together a (selective) global consumer class. I examine this historic process via the concept of the 'food regime.'[1]

Food regime analysis has centered on distinguishing specific political–economic organization of food production and consumption relations during the periods of British and U.S. hegemony (Friedmann, 1987; Friedmann & McMichael, 1989). As Harriet Friedmann (2005, p. 129) puts it, "Free trade in agriculture, key to British hegemony, gave way under U.S. hegemony to managed agriculture within the Free World". The point of such a distinction is to account for the particular developments in agriculture associated with each regime. In the second half of the nineteenth century, the British-centered world market encouraged the incubation of industrial agriculture in settler states geared to supplying cheap foodstuffs for a proletarianizing Europe. Through the devices of the U.S.-aid program of the mid-twentieth century, surplus foods and green revolution technologies from the First World entered the urban markets and the agrarian sectors of the Third World, respectively.

The continuities across these two eras were the progressive industrialization and specialization of agricultures (alongside tropical export agricultures originating in colonialism), and a project of state-building, proceeding from the settler colonies to the ex-colonies, as European empires collapsed and the development era took shape. But there the similarities end. In fact, these periods reveal quite distinct principles with respect to food and capitalism.

The first period was anchored in Britain's model of 'free trade imperialism,' the deployment of a policy of economic liberalism to gain access to the economies and colonial empires of its rival European states, and thereby consolidate British commercial dominance in the world economy. The City of London and the sterling/gold standard facilitated capital's first world market, especially in channeling investment to the 'peripheries' of the world economy given the protectionism of European rivals (McMichael, 2005a, pp. 11–27). Within these global circuits the "first price-governed market" in food emerged, anchored in the U.S. frontier of family farming, which produced low-cost wheat relative to that produced on capitalist farms in Europe (Friedmann, 2005, p. 125, 1978). Cheap foodstuffs from the colonies (from sugar to grains) sustained capital's primitive wage-relation in Europe, where elites remained committed to restricted consumption for the proletariat (Mintz, 1986; Halperin, 2004, p. 91).

The second period, characterized as "embedded liberalism" (Ruggie, 1982, but see Lacher, 1999), was governed by a series of social protections, from policies of full employment, through fixed monetary exchanges, to managed farm sectors. Farshad Araghi (2003, p. 51) views this as an "aid-based food order of an exceptionally reformist period of world capitalism" rather than as a 'food regime of capital.' The question here concerns both history and intentionality. Historically, Britain formed its free trade empire spatially through incorporation of new lands and resources, politically through backstopping the gold standard (as an instrument of economic liberalism), and temporally through manipulating countries' sterling balances in London to deepen the circulation of capital. The U.S., by contrast, was not concerned with outmanoeuvring economic rivals, so much as containing the Soviet empire. Accordingly, it reconstructed the capitalist world order "not through formal empire, but rather through the reconstitution of states as integral elements of an informal American empire" (Panitch & Gindin, 2004, p. 17). Central to this objective was political legitimation via the 'development project:' a state-building process in the Free World via economic and military aid, with the U.S. model of consumption as the ultimate, phenomenal, goal of development (McMichael, 2004a).

This model, represented as the endpoint of development (Rostow, 1960), was historically particular to the U.S. as one of a set of (mainly settler) states lacking a landed aristocracy, which might restrict domestic markets and consumption levels for the working poor (Halperin, 2004, p. 280). In addition, the Fordist response to the Great Depression in the U.S. promoted mass production via mass consumption (Halperin, 2004, p. 282). The 'inner-directedness' of this dynamic model, integrating agriculture and industry, facilitated the incorporation of food consumption relations into an intensified capital accumulation in the postwar period, and distinguished the U.S. model of modernity (Friedmann & McMichael, 1989). Following the British imperial legacy, 'beefing up' (steak *and* fast-food hamburger) was the dietary form in which modernity was represented (Rifkin, 1992). Historically, it was a product of a 'managed agriculture,' depending on commodity stabilization programs and public support for capital-intensive agriculture, and expressed in mounting food surpluses (a model also adopted in Europe, stimulated by Marshall Plan aid).

The food aid regime was a solution to the overproduction of agricultural commodities within a heavily protected U.S. farm sector, offering food at concessional prices as aid to friendly Third World regimes on the Cold War perimeter. Local, counterpart funds generated through this program promoted agribusiness and adoption of western diets (Friedmann, 1982). Thus, the *Pax Americana* centered on states as guarantors of markets. Agricultural commodity prices remained relatively stable during this period of publicly regulated trade in foodstuffs (Tubiana, 1989). Hegemony was achieved through the development project, which was also a vehicle for the 'freedom of enterprise' associated with the reach of the U.S. multinational corporation (Arrighi, 1982).

The distinctiveness of these food regimes lay in the instrumental role of food in securing global hegemony – in the first, Britain's 'workshop of the world' project linked the fortunes of an emergent industrial capitalism to expanding cheap food supply chains across the world; in the second, the United States used food politically to create alliances and markets for its agribusiness. The model of accumulation differed markedly across these two eras.

The point is not to *hypostatize* 'food regimes.' They constitute a lens on broader relations in the political history of capital. They express, simultaneously, forms of geo-political ordering and, related, forms of accumulation, and they are vectors of power. In the first, British hegemony, premised on 'gunboat diplomacy' and a sophisticated financial architecture centered on London, constructed a price-governed world market through which food resources were developed in, and appropriated from, 'European peripheries' to cheapen labor costs (Friedmann, 1978; Luxemburg, 1963; Davis, 2001). In the second, U.S. informal empire balanced the historic commitment to the social contract with containment-driven state-building, legitimized through the aid regime of the development project. Food's role was to subsidize, simultaneously, the First World social contract and Third World urban-industrial development.

The difference *across* the two 'food regimes' was the realization of First World citizenship and Third World independence. This emerged through the crisis of the British model (Polanyi, 1957), social transformation precipitated by ensuing warfare in Europe (Halperin, 2004), the collapse of

European empires, and the completion of the state's system – championed by the rising power of the U.S. and its model of accumulation anchored in national economic integration. Through these successive food regimes, the relations of production and consumption of food expressed the distinct moments in the political history of capital.

The 'corporate food regime' is yet another moment. It carries legacies of the previous food regimes, nevertheless expressing a new moment in the political history of capital. The political decomposition of citizenship and of national sovereignty, via the neo-liberal 'globalization project,' reverse the political gains ('welfare' and 'development' states) associated with the period of U.S. hegemony, facilitating an unprecedented conversion of agriculture across the world to supply a relatively affluent global consumer class. The vehicle of this corporate-driven process is the WTO's Agreement on Agriculture, which, as above, institutionalizes a distinctive form of economic liberalism geared to deepening market relations via the privatization of states.

The distinguishing mark of the corporate food regime as a new moment in world capitalism lies in the politics of neo-liberalism. As argued elsewhere, the 'globalization project' emerged to resolve the crisis of the 'development project,' in which the financial relations associated with the rise of transnational corporations and banks, and offshore money markets, were constrained by the social and spatial limits of the national state and its charge of civic protection (McMichael, 2004a). The 1980s debt crisis of the Third World revealed a world-economic crisis generated by over-reaching: of the U.S. dollar, transnational bank lending, and borrowing by Third World states. In this atmosphere of crisis, investors chose financial instruments over productive investments and firms relocated manufacturing to Third World export processing zones.

This was enabled by the new 'conditions' of structural adjustment, and the dumping of cheap foodstuffs (lowering wage costs), stemming from the breaching of the U.S.-centered food regime in the 1970s. Here, U.S. détente with the Soviet Union was marked by massive U.S. grain shipments to the Soviet Union, opening the door to an escalating trade war with Europe in commercial food exporting (Friedmann, 2005, pp. 132–133). Behind the protections of the Common Agricultural Policy (CAP), Europe had achieved self-sufficiency by the 1970s, in the form of an imported (U.S.) model of industrial agriculture producing surpluses of butter, milk, cereals, and beef. With the French government proclaiming 'Produce to export: agriculture is France's green petrol' (Bové & Dufour, 2001, p. 148), and the U.S. committed to agro-exporting as a rear-guard 'green power' strategy expressing hegemonic decline (Revel & Riboud, 1986), intensified competition for world market outlets via agro-export dumping shaped the transition from developmentalism to globalism.

Agro-export dumping undermined the U.S.-centered food regime's system of stable prices and managed disposal of food surpluses. World agricultural prices fell from a mean of 100 in 1975 to 61 by 1989 – a 39 percent decline. Bearing less and less relation to the cost of production, which included increasingly expensive farm subsidies, price volatility and decline brought the agro-exporting states to the 1986 GATT Uruguay Round (1986), declaring "an urgent need to bring more discipline and predictability to world agricultural trade" (quoted in Watkins, 1991, p. 44). The outcome of this round was the signing of the Agreement on Agriculture in the newly founded WTO, 1995, and the institutionalization of the corporate food regime.

ORIGINS OF 'FOOD SOVEREIGNTY'

As a lens on the political history of capital, the 'food regime' embodies the tensions of periods of world ordering. In this sense, the food regime is not a political–economic order, as such, rather it is a vehicle of a contradictory conjuncture, governed by the 'double movement' of accumulation/legitimation. The British-centered food regime embodied the tensions associated with the demands for citizenship and decolonization, realized in the subsequent U.S.-centered food regime, which modeled the possibilities of each via economic nationalism. The U.S.-centered regime, in turn, embodied the tensions associated with social protectionism, as the principle of 'freedom of enterprise,' central to the U.S. informal empire, undermined economic nationalism (Arrighi, 1982; Lacher, 1999; Friedmann & McMichael, 1989). Resolution via economic transnationalism has been institutionalized in the governance mechanisms of the multilateral institutions, led by the WTO. Here, the *corporate* food regime embodies the tensions between a trajectory of 'world agriculture' and cultural survival, expressed in the politics of 'food sovereignty.'

The current political conjuncture is the culmination of a long-term imperial trajectory – not simply the conversion of the non-European world to export monocultures, but also the power relation consigning the peoples of the colonized hinterlands to an unseen, racialized underconsumption that has become the condition for metropolitan development and overconsumption. In this trajectory, the appropriation of agricultural resources for capitalist consumption relations (encompassing regions of capitalist modernity in much of the global North and parts of the global South) is realized through an expanding foundation of human impoverishment and displacement, and the marginalization of agrarian/food cultures. This much the generic capitalist dynamic of accumulation/dispossession would predict.

What is distinctive about this conjuncture is how dispossession is accomplished. Briefly, where the 'development project' socialized security, the 'globalization project' privatizes security. These phases both represent political solutions to material needs. But Third World material needs under the development project were already the result of colonial-induced social catastrophes. Mike Davis (2001) has documented, for example, how empire dismantled village grain reserve systems in the non-European world, by commodifying grain and transforming it into an export product.

The insecurities attending colonialism animated the twentieth-century decolonization movement. However, despite Frantz Fanon's (1967), warnings in the execution of the development project across the postcolonial world: "Instead of the state being used as an instrument of development, development became an instrument of the state's legitimacy" (Bose, 1997, p. 34). In other words, while all states were officially charged, under the UN system, with implementing the social contract, most ruling elites saw that as an opportunity to centralize power and thereby progressively undermine the viability of cultural forms of security in the name of development. To this end, they prosecuted cash cropping with World Bank funding, prioritized industrialization as the centerpiece of development, promoted mechanisms of urban bias for political purposes, dam-building, and imported cheap foodstuffs via the food aid regime. The managed construction of the Third World (urban) consumer paralleled the decimation of peasant agriculture. Each confirmed the central tenets of the development vision: that the western consumption pattern was a universal desire and peasants were historical remnants destined to disappear.

The development project incorporated post–colonial states into a universal system of national accounting methods, standardizing the measurement of material well-being (GNP), and the 'externalization' of a variety of environmental degradations and social catastrophes. Only monetized transactions were counted as productive, devaluing subsistence, cooperative labor, indigenous culture, seed saving, and managing the commons as unproductive, marginalized and undeveloped activity. As a consequence, the world's rural population decreased by some 25 percent in the second half of the twentieth century with the steady displacement of peasant cultures (Hobsbawm, 1992, p. 56; Araghi, 1995, 1999).

It is important to stress that this process is not simply the realization of the development narrative – a preordained movement of rural populations into an increasingly urbanized wage-labor force – but the displacement of biodiversity, customary forms of knowledge and moral economy. This historic rupture accounts for the emergence of 'food sovereignty' as an alternative to the productivist paradigm, which measures food security in the quantitative/monetized terms of market transactions. Food sovereignty is as much a cultural, as a material, principle. How this rupture came to express itself in the 'food sovereignty' paradigm depended on the de-legitimization of development.

The development honeymoon lasted at most for three decades (ca 1950–1980). The so-called 'lost decade' of the 1980s was a key turning point, as the management of the debt crisis heralded three profound changes in the global political economy. First, the deployment by the debt managers (IMF, World Bank, G-7) of structural adjustment conditions across much of the Third World punctured the 'developmentalist illusion' (Arrighi, 1990). States, compelled to adopt neo-classical economic solutions, reversed course on the social contract. Second, on a world scale, neo-liberalism reinforced a financialization of capital, away from productive investment toward securitization and business mergers and takeovers. Third, international power relations were recast in terms of the North/South axis, rather than containment politics legitimized by developmentalism.

The debt regime began the institutionalization of the 'globalization project,' via the WTO, as the mother of all trade agreements (though not the father, given the virulence of NAFTA, for example). During this transition from a collapsing development, and emerging globalization, project, the Agreement on Agriculture sprung from the Uruguay Round's movement to reform farm sectors and agricultural trade. Consistent with the neo-classical agenda, 'food security' came to be redefined, and institutionalized, in the WTO as an inter-national market relation. That is, in spite of the asymmetry between the Northern and Southern agricultural labor force percentages – 4 percent, versus 30–70 percent, respectively (Kwa, 2002), a system of 'free trade' in agricultural products was installed to privatize food security as a global, corporate relation.

PRIVATIZATION OF FOOD SECURITY VIA THE CORPORATE FOOD REGIME

The shift in the 'site' of food security from the nation-state to the world market was engineered during the Uruguay Round (1986–1994), anticipating the WTO's Agreement on Agriculture (1995). Under this agreement, states no longer have the right to food self-sufficiency as a national strategy. The WTO's minimum import rule requires all member states to allow imports of food up to at least 5 percent of the volume of domestic consumption – despite Article 25 (1) of the UN's Universal Declaration of Human Rights, and Article 11 of the International Covenant on Economic, Social, and Cultural Rights, which viewed "the right of peoples to exercise sovereignty over their natural wealth and resources" as essential to the realization of human rights (Desmarais, 2003, p. 148).

On the face of it, states appear to have been trumped by the WTO, exposing their domestic food markets to the grain traders. French Farmers' Confederation leader, Jose Bové declares this is a "totalitarian exercise" that allows the TNCs to force domestic producers "to submit to their logic" (Bové & Dufour, 2001, p. 137). Nevertheless, the logic of subordinating agriculture to the corporate model is not synonymous with a stateless world food market.

In the first place, the U.S. introduced a redefinition of food security as "best provided through a smooth-functioning world market" (quoted in Ritchie, 1993, fn 25) into the Uruguay Round in order to secure a competitive advantage for U.S. agribusiness via the GATT, and subsequently the WTO's Agreement on Agriculture. Second, and related, the WTO retains this mercantilist imprint in managing asymmetrical agricultural relations, founded in an unequal state system. Third, corporate agriculture's trajectory is governed by historic divisions of labor and current financial mergers that centralize agribusiness capital. Unlike industry or services, the capitalization of agriculture retains important spatial dimensions, expressed politically in Northern agribusiness lobbies and farm sector policies geared to producing (and dumping) food surpluses.

Thus, in Europe food self-sufficiency was the initial postwar goal, shaping Common Market policies in 1957, and into the 1960s. In return for the right to protect large-scale staple food production (cereals, milk, beef, sugar), the EEC agreed to import U.S. soya beans for European livestock in the Kennedy Round of 1962–1967 (Herman & Kuper, 2003, p. 5). Bové notes: 'The arrival of the first soya beans in French ports, not subject to any Customs duties, signaled the start of agricultural industrialization" (Bové & Dufour, 2001, p. 61). Cheap imported soya beans, complementing local maize grains and silage, underwrote a global livestock complex (cf. Friedmann, 1993). This in turn drove a CAP (1962) geared to guaranteed high internal prices and the overproduction of cereals, generating food surpluses and their untidy dumping on the world market. CAP management of overproduction involved establishing production quotas, reducing the farm population by 90 percent, and hastening corporate monocultures (Herman & Kuper, 2003, pp. 10–11). Moving to manage overproduction internationally, the U.S. Agriculture Secretary, John Block, observed in 1986: "the idea that developing countries should feed themselves is an anachronism from a bygone era. They could better ensure their food security by relying on U.S. agricultural products, which are available in most cases at lower cost" (quoted in Schaeffer, 1995, p. 268).

This form of global 'food security' is accomplished through the political construction of commodity prices. In 1986, U.S. corn dumping forced Zimbabwe's grain marketing board to cut domestic producers prices almost in half and to reduce its purchase quota from these producers (Watkins, 1991, p. 43). A decade later, in 1996, politicization of price was key to NAFTA – in 8 months the domestic price of Mexican maize fell almost 50 percent, "converging with the world price 12 years earlier than envisaged" (Herman & Kuper, 2003, p. 72). In 2002, the average price below the cost of production of various U.S. agribusiness exports was 43 percent for wheat, 25 percent for soybeans, 13 percent for corn, and 35 percent for rice (IATP, 2004, p. 3).

The political determination of world agricultural commodity prices emerged through the Uruguay Round negotiations, which sought to stem the escalation of farm subsidies and manage the crisis of overproduction arising from the U.S. and European Community agricultural policies (Dawkins, 1999). Anticipating the outcome of the Round, in 1992 (by the 'McSharry reform') the EU began switching from its original CAP farm price support policies to U.S.-style government subsidies (Dawkins, 1999). Replacing a guaranteed price with direct payments introduced the 'world price' to European producers, stimulating rather than eliminating surpluses (Herman & Kuper, 2003, pp. 27–28), and synchronizing EU policy with that of the U.S. in favoring traders over producers.

The preference given to the price form disempowers farmers, and empowers agribusiness, across the world. In the North, traders and processors purchase commodities through farm contracts at low prices unrelated to production costs. For processors, artificially cheapened corn subsidizes 'supersizing' in the fast food industry (Manning, 2004, p. 43). For traders, low commodity prices enable commodity dumping in the world market (assisted by export subsidies, especially European), forcing local prices down at the expense of small farmers. The resulting, or potential for, low-cost agricultural production in the global South in turn enables global sourcing by agribusiness to exert further downward pressure on Northern farmers.

The result has been a mass exodus from farming in North, and South. It is accomplished by depressed prices and the competitive advantage of intensive agriculture integrated into agribusiness, and favored by a system of asymmetrical farm supports. Privileging the price form facilitated the restructuring of Northern farm sectors, dominated by corporate agriculture.[2]

Synchronization of Northern farm policy anticipated the WTO's Agreement on Agriculture. Despite the rhetoric of free trade, the Northern agenda is realized through a corporate-mercantilist comparative advantage in a highly unequal world market. The Agreement on Agriculture was designed to open agricultural markets through minimum import requirements and tariff and producer subsidy reductions. Southern states signed on in the hopes of improving their foreign currency income from expanded agro-exports (under the imperative of servicing foreign debt). But the effect was to open markets for northern products, strengthening the position of the global North in the international division of labor in agriculture (Pistorius & van Wijk, 1999, pp. 110–111). From 1970–2000, declines in the world percentage of agri-exports from Africa (10 to 3 percent), Latin America and the Caribbean (14 to 12 percent), and the 'Least Developed Countries' (5 to 1 percent), contrasted with a Northern increase from 64 to 71 percent (FAOSTAT, 2004).

Within the rules set by the WTO, delinked from the UN Charter's provisions for economic and cultural (food) sovereignty, growing food dependencies fulfilled the global vision of 'food security.' National health, social, and environmental regulations are assumed to restrict trade, and, therefore, were required by the WTO to be translated into visible and quantifiable tariffs, then subject to reduction over time. In addition, a subsidy hierarchy was constructed, where subsidies were consigned to 'boxes,' arranged according to degree of protectionist effect (Herman & Kuper, 2003, pp. 35–36). The box system works to the advantage of the Northern states, which routinely consign decoupled farm support payments to the 'non-trade-distorting' Green Box. The CAP, in particular, justifies such an arrangement through a 'rural development' initiative prepared for the 1999 WTO Ministerial, whereby direct farm payments support the 'multifunctionality' of agriculture.

Besides allowing for a bait and switch operation to hide Northern subsidies, the box system also disadvantages Southern states, which lack the resources for (decoupled) farm support programs. The combination of reduction of customs duties via 'tarrification' and protection of expanding farm subsidies via 'boxes,' has constructed a regulatory system that transfers resources from public to private hands in the North, and exports food dependency (and insecurity) to the South via dumping.[3] Already in the mid-1990s, half of the foreign exchange of the FAO's 88 low-income food deficit countries went to food imports (LeQuesne, 1997). The destabilizing effects of intensified export dumping, and Northern agricultural subsidies, frame Doha and the geo-political tensions expressed at Cancun.

While the WTO is composed of member states, the very asymmetry of the state system privileges corporate solutions in the implementation of rules. For instance, the recent CAP reform, introducing 'multifunctionality' as a method of renaming the decoupling of farm subsidies to reward agriculture's non-remunerative services (environment, space, rural habitation, food safety, and animal welfare) and making the CAP WTO-compliant, "paves the way for the end of any policy of market management" and allows "beneficiaries of decoupled subsidies to produce without restraints (other than those of a phony ecology), to produce what they want and eventually to change their production every year" (Herman & Kuper, 2003, p. 84). The logical extension of this reform is the 'de-localization' of agricultural production to preserve the European environment, while importing food from offshore regions with low wages and weak environmental regulations – as the Doux group, the foremost French and European poultry producer, accomplished by purchasing Frangosul, the fourth largest poultry producer in Brazil, where production costs undercut those in France by two-thirds (*ibid.*, pp. 21–22). De-localization is part of the global sourcing strategy of U.S. corporations (Blank, 1998; Public Citizen, 2001), a movement confirmed by the recent migration of failing U.S. soy farmers to Brazil's expanding and low-cost Matto Grosso region.

The WTO policy eliminating 'market management' of agriculture shifts priorities from public interest in producing use-values for domestic provisioning, to private/public encouragement of producing exchange-values to expand profits and export revenues. Liberalization is the means to this end – either through de-coupling, which supports Northern agribusiness with public monies, or through reduction of Southern protections – opening economies to food importing and/or agribusiness offshore investment. Legitimized by the discourse of food security, its privatization conditions an emerging *world* agriculture subordinated to capital.[4]

WORLD AGRICULTURE AND EMPIRE

Historically, the movement of capital involves the progressive subordination of agriculture, as an attempt to resolve agro-ecological crises stemming from the 'metabolic rift,' in a deepening of the rupture in nutrient cycling between countryside and city (Moore, 2000, p. 123). Across the former food regimes, subordination occurred within the framework of the nation-state, whether via the national/colonial state nexus, or the national/neo-colonial state nexus. The WTO, as the material expression of the state/capital nexus, continues this process of subordination by capital on behalf of its member states.

The WTO is not a state, rather a disembodied, and unrepresentative, executive, but on a world scale. Comprised of member states, the WTO not only instrumentalizes the competitive and hierarchical relations among those states (cf. Buttel, 2003), but it also denies civil society full representation. In these terms, the Cancun impasse expressed opposition to Northern hypocrisy by Southern states, disenfranchised by WTO procedures and overwhelmed by the material consequences in the erosion of their domestic farm sectors. But, ironically, the G-20's call for greater market access expresses at one and the same time a formal demand for equivalence in trade opportunities, and yet a substantive complicity in the movement toward a world agriculture based in agro-exporting (Peine & McMichael, 2005).

G-20 complicity expresses the logic of the Agreement on Agriculture, namely to complete the liberalization of trade relations as the condition for a world agriculture. But a world agriculture involves more than an intensifying system of food swapping across national boundaries. It is premised on the green revolution principle of 'appropriation,' the progressive removal of components of agricultural production from the control of the farmer via intervention in natural processes (Goodman, Sorj, & Wilkinson, 1987), starting with bio-engineered seeds, and complemented with a range of chemical and mechanical inputs and specialized agricultural inputs (e.g., livestock feed).

Green, and subsequently, gene revolution technologies deepen the elimination of biodiversity, seed saving, and local knowledge via agro-industrial monocultures. Bio-engineering has transformed the crop development industry[5] through the concentration and centralization of agri-chemical corporations (Pistorius & van Wijk, 1999), and the corporate 'gene giants' already account for more than one-third of the global seed market and 100 percent of the transgenic seed market (Shiva, 2000, p. 9). Deploying the discourse of intellectual property rights, the biotechnology industry seeks to institutionalize gene patenting, through the WTO's TRIPs protocol,[6] as a key to elaborating a world agriculture, premised on the elimination of *extant* agricultures and agro-ecologies through the privatization of knowledge – a principal feature of the corporate food regime.

The abstraction from ecology and local entitlements associated with a world agriculture privileges the production of inputs for food processors, agri-chemical companies or global retailers. Agro-industrialization, delivering agriculture to an array of input industries (from energy through fertilizer to animal feed), consolidates a specialization process whereby "[I]n intensive farming the object is to adapt the soil to the crop, never the other way round" (Bové & Dufour, 2001, p. 67), also a movement of abstraction anticipating a world agriculture. While this movement of abstraction is associated with the history of the agricultural frontiers of European capitalism (Friedmann, 2000; Moore, 2000), its completion as a world agriculture is prefigured in the biological and socio-economic blueprints of the gene revolution and the WTO's Agreement on Agriculture.

The concept of a 'world agriculture' refers, not to the entirety of agriculture across the earth, but to a transnational space of corporate agricultural and food relations integrated by commodity circuits. Justin Rosenberg terms this space 'the empire of civil society': a politically managed "material integration of social reproduction across borders" involving "the extraction and relaying of surpluses" (Rosenberg, 2001, pp. 134–135, 131). But the material integration of social reproduction across borders is not simply a space of globalized commodity flows creating new interdependencies – an immanent tendency in the history of capital. Rather, beyond Rosenberg's formulation, a world agriculture resembles Hardt and Negri's (2000, p. xv) emergent concept of 'Empire,' characterized by the removal of boundaries – either spatial or temporal (implicit in the process of abstraction), and, most significantly, a "paradigmatic form of biopower", where capital reconstitutes humans through reconstituting the natural order, in the name of food security and peace. This is particularly the case for agricultural workers, more than half of whom are women, and who comprise a third of the 1.3 billion people actively engaged in agricultural production (half of the world's labor force), concentrated in the global South, and as high as 80 percent of the workforce in some countries (IUF, 2002, p. 3).

Deborah Barndt's (1997) representation of one set of increasingly common conditions of social reproduction of the agricultural labor force in corporate agriculture captures this process:

> [T]he only Mexican inputs are the land, the sun, and the workers.... The South has been the source of the seeds, while the North has the biotechnology to alter agro-export production also denies them participation in subsistence agriculture, especially since the peso crisis in 1995, which has forced migrant workers to move to even more scattered work sites. They now travel most of the year – with little time to grow food on their own plots in their home communities...[W]ith this loss of control comes a spiritual loss, and a

loss of a knowledge of seeds, of organic fertilizers and pesticides, of sustainable practices such as crop rotation or leaving the land fallow for a year—practices that had maintained the land for millennia (1997, pp. 59–62).

Such abstraction of agriculture through its incorporation and reproduction within global capital circuits imparts a 'food from nowhere' character to the corporate food regime (Bové & Dufour, 2001, p. 55). At the core of this process is the appropriation of farming, via the expulsion of rural populations through land dispossession and concentration, as farming is rendered unviable by withdrawal of public supports and exposure to a world price, or the conversion of farmers to contract farming or hired/plantation/migrant labor, depending on context and crop. Mexico, the home of maize, has been so transformed by liberalization and NAFTA into a food deficit country, and forced to import yellow corn from the U.S. at the expense of almost 2 million *campesinos,* unable to compete with corn price falls on the order of 70 percent (Carlsen, 2003; Oxfam, 2003). In Brazil, price falls for staple crops like rice and beans render small farming increasingly nonviable, exacerbating a swelling rural exodus and rising urban unemployment (Cassel & Patel, 2003); while in China recent liberalization associated with WTO accession has accelerated a swelling rural migrant population that overwhelms urban job markets, coinciding with the shrinking of state enterprises (Eisenburger & Patel, 2003). In a 1997 FAO study of 16 Southern countries, reporting the dispossession of at least 20–30 million people, the overall impact of liberalization was identified with: "...a general trend towards the concentration of farms, in a wide crosssection of countries. While this led to increased productivity and competitiveness with positive results, in the virtual absence of safety nets the process also marginalized small producers and added to unemployment and poverty" (Madeley, 2000; p. 75).

Loss of land, livelihood, and knowledge constitute the core of cultural displacement and dispossession. But empire, as the corporate food regime, emerges through related forms of dispossession, notably of local food markets and cuisines – such as displacement in Mexico of inexpensive white maize tortillas by yellow corn tortillas manufactured at triple the price (Bensinger, 2003; Oxfam, 2003, p. 19). Analytically, the construction of a world agriculture involves 'accumulation by dispossession' (Harvey, 2003). While this process is both secular and cyclical, the neo-liberal project focuses the expansion of profit on the release or privatization of (public) assets. Here, the global integration of social reproduction is effected through the appropriation of farming and informal provisioning (wet markets, street vendors, and the commons). These processes eliminate *extant* systems of provisioning, converting them to inputs for the corporate food regime's proliferating supply chains.

Land expropriation may be the original form of 'accumulation by dispossession,' but the realization of the corporate food regime involves a deeper, and broader, reconstitution of material culture, centered on biopolitical mechanisms. Thus, the global fast food industry, grossing $110 billion a year in the U.S., provides cheap and unhealthy convenience foods, based on the appropriation of home-cooking activities and knowledges (cf. Friedmann, 1999). The supermarket revolution in the global South (Reardon, Timmer, Barrett, & Berdegue, 2003) intensifies the combination of food processing and retailing accumulation, incorporating small or independent producers and local markets and street vending into new corporate circuits and biopolitical relations.

In the 1990s, supermarkets expanded their reach in Latin American countries from 15–30 percent to 50–70 percent of national retail sales – a growth rate five times that in the U.S., and accelerating now across Asia. In Latin America, firms, including Ahold, Carrefour, and Wal-Mart, comprise 70–80 percent of the top five supermarket chains, centralizing procurement from farmers across the region (and their own global processing plants), and serving regional consumers (Regmi & Gehlhar, 2005). In a case study of Guatemala, where supermarkets now control 35 percent of food retailing, it was reported that "their sudden appearance has brought unanticipated and daunting challenges to millions of struggling, small farmers" – especially tenuous relations in the absence of binding contractual agreements, rewarded only if they consistently meet new quality standards, but subject to declining prices as retailers have virtually unlimited suppliers (Dugger, 2004). Meanwhile, urban diets converge on a narrowing base of staple grains, increasing consumption of animal protein, edible oils, salt and sugar, and declining dietary fiber, as consumption of brand name processed and store-bought foods rises, contributing to an increasing prevalence of non-communicable (dietary) diseases and obesity (Kennedy, Nantel, & Shetty, 2004, p. 14).

Corporate circuits frame the global transformation of social, biopolitical and ecological relations. Thus, the director-general of the Centre for International Forestry Research (Cifor) noted: "In the 1970s and the 1980s most of the meat from the Amazon was being produced by small ranchers selling to local slaughterhouses. Very large commercial ranchers linked to supermarkets are now targeting the whole of Brazil and the global market" (quoted in Vidal, 2004, p. 3). Huge ranching operations organized by European supermarkets now dominate the beef export market (75 percent of

Brazil's beef exports flow to Europe and the Middle East). At the same time, corporate-led factory farming is transforming the food sector – currently targeting Argentina, Brazil, China, India, Mexico, Pakistan, the Philippines, South Africa, Taiwan, and Thailand. Asia, whose global consumer class outstrips that of North America and Europe combined, leads the livestock revolution (French, 2004, p. 148). Two thirds of the global expansion of meat consumption is in the global South, sourced with Brazilian soybeans. As a Chinese middle class emerges, China has shifted from a net exporter of soybeans to the world's largest importer of whole soybeans and oils – even Brazilian pastures are converted to soyfields, pushing cattle herds deeper into the Amazon (Rohter, 2003, p. 3). In this way, biopolitical dynamics are expressed in dietary and ecological transformations.

Neo-liberal discourse represents the material integration of social reproduction as an expansion of market efficiencies through freedom of trade and enterprise. However, it is premised on the deployment of the price weapon, through dumping, to undermine local farming and incorporate local consumption relations into global circuits, as well as on agro-exporting, via structural adjustment measures, to displace publicly entitled foods. Given the extent of displacement and dispossession, what is being socially reproduced? The contradictory relations of the corporate food regime. The paradox of this food regime is that at the same time as it represents global integration as the condition for food security, it immiserates populations, including its own labor force. The perverse consequence of global market integration is the export of deprivation, as 'free' markets exclude and/or starve populations dispossessed through their implementation. In turn, dispossessed populations function as reserve labor, lowering wages and offering the possibility of labor casualization throughout the corporate empire.

More than simply a cumulative agro-ecological crisis (Moore, 2000), the corporate food regime is also realized through social crisis. For example, neo-liberal policies introduced in 1991 threaten India's tens of millions of small farmers, the livelihood source of 75 percent of the population. In 2000, the Indian Ministry of Agriculture observed: "The growth in agriculture has slackened during the 1990s. Agriculture has become a relatively unrewarding profession due to an unfavourable price regime and low value addition, causing abandoning of farming and migration from rural areas" (quoted in Paringaux, 2000, p. 4). Corporate seed prices have inflated tenfold, cheap imports (notably of rice and vegetable oils) have undercut local farmers and processors, and policies promoting agro-exports of high-value commodities like farmed shrimp, flowers, and meat in the name of food security increase human insecurities. Every dollar of foreign exchange earned on meat exports destroys 15 dollars' worth of ecological capital stemming from the use of farm animals in sustainable agriculture, according to Vandana Shiva (2000, p. 14). In other words, a condition for the social reproduction of affluence is cultural displacement and unsustainable ecologies.

Is this an inevitable condition? Certainly not: the global integration of social reproduction is an immanent, rather than an absolute, process, in tendency and scope. The corporate food regime is a political construct, and its beneficiaries constitute only about a quarter of the world's population, despite the widening effects of social exclusion, through the appropriation of resources (material, intellectual, and spiritual), and the privatization of public goods. At the same time, these effects generate the conditions for overcoming the social and ecological crisis of the corporate food regime, in resistance movements dedicated to the social re-embedding of markets. Ultimately, the trajectory of the corporate food regime is constituted through resistances: both protective (e.g., environmentalism) and proactive, where 'food sovereignty' posits an alternative global moral economy.

THE FOOD SOVEREIGNTY MOVEMENT

Food sovereignty represents an alternative principle to food security, as currently defined by the corporate food regime. But it is not the antithesis of food security, rather, food sovereignty is a premise for genuine food security, since "food is first and foremost a source of nutrition and only secondarily an item of trade" (Vía Campesina, 2002, p. 8).

In the terms of the corporate food regime, 'food security' is to be achieved through trade, rather than through a strategy of self-sufficiency. The chairman of Cargill put it recently like this: "There is a mistaken belief that the greatest agricultural need in the developing world is to develop the capacity to grow food for local consumption. This is misguided. Countries should produce what they produce best – and trade" (quoted in Lynas, 2001). This definition frames the WTO's Agreement on Agriculture.

In this context, the concept of 'food sovereignty' was developed by the international farmers' movement, Vía Campesina, and introduced into public debate during the 1996 World Food Summit. Vía Campesina defines food sovereignty in the following way:

> In order to guarantee the independence and food sovereignty of all of the world's peoples, it is essential that food be produced through diversified, farmer-based production systems. Food sovereignty is the right of peoples to define their own agriculture and food policies, to protect and regulate domestic agricultural production and trade in

order to achieve sustainable development objectives, to determine the extent to which they want to be self reliant, and to restrict the dumping of products in their markets. Food sovereignty does not negate trade, but rather, it promotes the formulation of trade policies and practices that serve the rights of peoples to safe, healthy and ecologically sustainable production (Vía Campesina, 2001).

It is important to emphasize that trade is not ruled out, under the Vía Campesina vision, rather it is a question of the regime under which trade occurs. The anti-capitalist resistance represented by the Vía Campesina does not reject the global for the local, rather it redefines the global in terms appropriate to democratic conditions of food production and distribution. As Judit Bodnar emphasizes in her interpretation of the conflict between the French Farmers' Confederation and MacDonalds in 1999, Jose Bové and his followers destroy transgenic corn produced by global firms "not because the seeds are produced by 'others' but because of the way they are produced" (Bodnar, 2003, p. 141). Under the slogan of 'the world is not for sale,' Bové and the Vía Campesina emphasize two central premises: first, that the international tensions surrounding the politics of food ultimately derive not from conflict between governments, but that between models of production and rural development – "a conflict that exists in both the North and the South" (Vía Campesina, 2003, p. 5); and second, that the struggle is global but decentralized in content and leadership. Bové articulates the latter point as follows:

> The strength of this global movement is precisely that it differs from place to place.... The world is a complex place, and it would be a mistake to look for a single answer to complex and different phenomena. We have to provide answers at different levels – not just the international level, but local and national levels too (Bové & Dufour, 2001, p. 168).

Embedded in this quote is the 'global' vision represented by the Vía Campesina, namely that an alternative modernity depends on rejecting the WTO/corporate move to privatize modernity and erase (shared) local knowledges (cf. Desmarais, 2003), and on reinstating "the right of peoples, communities and countries to define their own agricultural, labour, fishing, food and land policies which are ecologically, socially, economically and culturally appropriate to their unique circumstances" (quoted in Ainger, 2003, p. 11). Bodnar's study emphasizes that, despite Bové's relative privilege in producing the internationally traded Roquefort cheese, as an artisan he represents a production model that appeals to farmers and consumers worldwide, striving for transparent production and distribution in opposition to the mass production model of industrial agriculture. In addition, the model elevates democratic economy and fair trade principles, as essential to a global civil society, over the reactionary "link between land and nation" (Bodnar, 2003, pp. 141–143).

On the other side of the world, this sentiment echoes through another constituent of the Vía Campesina, the landless-workers' movement in Brazil, where exports of coffee, sugar, poultry, cacao, orange juice concentrate, and soy and corn destined for livestock in the global North leave behind 44 million chronically hungry Brazilians – as Candido Grzybowski (2004), director of IBASE in Rio de Janeiro, observed:

> Probably in Brazil there exists no greater taboo than that centuries-old question, the agrarian question. But there is no question that is more current because it is not limited to the countryside itself, to its population.... The modernity of the MST consists in questioning us about this, about the past of our agrarian origins and about the future in the use of our natural resources, with the question of land at the center.... We are, of the large countries of the world, the least demographically dense, the most privileged in terms of natural resources – land, water, biodiversity – and at the same time, the most unequal and tragically, the most predatory. For how long, in the name of an even more narrow vision, will we be able to maintain the right to act on this part of Planet Earth in a way that is so socially and ecologically irresponsible?

This appeal to a global movement against the uniformity of the corporate trade regime, in the interests of the future sustainability of the social and natural world, proceeds from an analysis of the power base of the neo-liberal model. First, the Vía Campesina argues that a world market of agricultural products is non-existent, rather, the corporate food regime, accounting for 10 percent of world agricultural production, is:

> an international trade of surpluses of milk, cereals and meat dumped primarily by the E.U., the U.S. and other members of the CAIRNS group. Behind the faces of national trade negotiators are powerful TNCs such as Monsanto and Cargill who are the real beneficiaries of domestic subsidies and supports, international trade negotiations and the global manipulations of trade regimes (2001, p. 6).

Second, agro-industrialization is being rapidly globalized through the mobility of financial capital, and its ability to rapidly concentrate, centralize, and coordinate global agribusiness operations. According to Joao Stedile of the MST, world agriculture is dominated by 10 TNCs, such as Monsanto, Bayer, Cargill, Nestle, Syngenta, BASF, Novartis, and ADM, operating in and across distinct sectors related to agricultural production, and controlling commercial agriculture, agrobusiness, the agro-toxins, and seeds: "now capital is not content to buy labor and hold land as private property, but it also wants to turn knowledge, technology, farm technologies and seeds into private property" to increase productivity per acre, with the goal of developing a food model based in the unification of eating habits across the world

(Vía Campesina, 2004c, p. 2). The power relation in the corporate food regime is expressed in the Vía Campesina (2004b, p. 3) claim that "multinational corporations want to manipulate our crops to be able to control all of the food chain around the world, requiring us to stop producing food and start consuming their products".

The mechanism realizing this world agriculture is the neo-liberal model, institutionalized in the WTO and structural adjustment policies. As the Vía Campesina's website observes:

> The specialisation of production in regions that can export at lowest costs, importation of agricultural products at prices below the cost of production in the importing country, the agreement by the WTO of public support that allows the rich countries to export at prices below their cost of production, is destroying food sovereignty in all regions. Prices called global, are artificial and result in dumping. They are disconnected from the reality of production. Many countries are forced to export because of their debt and the structural adjustment programs imposed by the IMF and the World Bank (http://ns.rds.org.hn/via/).

Within this context, the Vía Campesina reformulates the crisis of the corporate food regime, critiquing unequivocally the *representation* of the Cancun standoff as a North–South conflict. Maintaining that the real conflict is "between centralized, corporate-driven, export-oriented, industrial agriculture versus decentralized, peasant- and family farm-based sustainable production primarily oriented towards domestic markets," – a conflict invisibilized in global trade negotiations – the Vía Campesina (1999, p. 3) argues the WTO is a "totally inappropriate institution for democratic decision-making" regarding food sovereignty and social and ecological sustainability, should get out of agriculture. Through this critique the Vía Campesina separates itself from the 'freer trade' bid by the G-20, which it views as promoting agro-export interests in the South at the expense of the majority of domestic producers:

> they too are demanding the abolition of 'trade distorting' subsidies and more access to markets, both in the North and in the South, without acknowledging that it is in fact the unbalanced focus on exports and corporate interests which is the main problem.... Increased liberalization and generalized market access will serve only to strengthen the grip of multinational agribusiness cartels, deepening the problems of poverty and social exclusion of millions of people in the world (2003, p. 5).

The Vía Campesina opposes the WTO's neo-liberal project of constructing a world agriculture based in 'comparative advantage,' because it is not about strategies of regional differentiation so much as about corporate global sourcing strategies, premised on the existence of a reserve army of cheap labor. Noting that "the massive movement of food around the world is forcing the increased movement of people," the Vía Campesina offers a new paradigm based in self-reliance at the national or community scale, as the anchor of an alternative globalization. Here, food sovereignty depends on access to credit, land and fair prices to be set via rules negotiated in a reformed UN and alternative multilateral institutions such as a Convention on Food Sovereignty and Trade in Food and Agriculture, an International Court of Justice, a World Commission on Sustainable Agriculture and Food Sovereignty, and so forth (2001, p. 8). As Bové asks, "Why should the global market escape the rule of international law or human rights conventions passed by the United Nations?" (Bové & Dufour, 2001, p. 165). The premise, of course, is "the active participation of farmers' movements in defining agricultural and food policies within a democratic framework." The specificity of this politics is that, while the consumer movement has discovered that "eating has become a political act," articulating the health/transparency relations of food, Vía Campesina adds the social/ecological and historical dimension: "producing quality products for our own people has also become a political act...this touches our very identities as citizens of this world" (www.ns.rds.org.hn/via/).

In sum, the coherence of the Vía Campesina vision, uncompromising in its relationship with the growth paradigm of neo-liberalism, and with NGOs and multilateral institutions (Desmarais, 2003), constitutes a distinctive politics of modernity rooted in a global moral economy. Echoing the early twentieth-century argument by Peter Kropotkin that the preminent social question is the 'question of bread,' Amory Starr (2001) proposes that the global anti-capitalist movement for 'diversity' is best summarized as 'agricultural:'

> encompassing first world farmers seeking market protection, farmers resisting genetic engineering, indigenous sovereignty movements seeking to control land and practices, sustainable development, localist economic visions, and third world peasant movements reacting to the failures of urbanization and neoliberalism by insisting on rights to land and subsistence. These movements have a variety of relationships to political economy, formal democracy and existing nations. But none imagines that growth, modernization or technology provide answers to their problems; indeed they see corporate technology as economically and ecologically dangerous (2001, p. 224).

And just as Starr characterizes the core of the anti-corporate globalization movement as centered on agricultural issues, so the Vía Campesina can be viewed as the core of the resistance to the corporate food regime by articulating that which it seeks to eliminate. There are many strands of resistance to the corporate food regime, from environmentalists through seed savers to community supported agricultures, but the Vía Campesina's unique method of uniting the diversity of agrarian producers across the world unifies a heterogeneous resistance in which social, economic, cultural, and environmental relations feature in different configurations across the world.

GLOBAL CAPITALISM AND THE CORPORATE FOOD REGIME

The phenomenal dynamics of the corporate food regime, namely global dispossession of farmers, reorganization of food supply chains, and centralization of agri-food relations, express the immanence of capital and its drive to deepen commodity relations. The question is how these dynamics also specify the world-historical conjuncture? The answer lies in the politics of the corporate empire, that is, how a reconfigured state system accommodates the strategy of corporate globalization, centered on a U.S. imperial strategy.

The origins of corporate globalization stem from the de-regulation of financial relations in the 1970s, as a U.S. strategy to unburden itself of rising claims on the dollar, relocate debt to weaker states in the currency hierarchy, and reassert U.S. power within an emergent neo-liberal framework (Helleiner, 1996, pp. 111–119). Decoupling the dollar from gold in the early 1970s allowed currencies to float, and facilitated a rapid expansion of the offshore dollar market and global banking institutions. The era of 'financialization' expressed a hegemonic crisis (Arrighi, 1994; Panitch & Gindin, 2004) as the U.S. state moved to reconstitute its power through eliminating capital controls, and laying the conditions for gaining access to global savings by liberalizing capital markets, with lowered trade and investment barriers benefiting U.S. transnational corporations. This strategy was the condition of and for a counter-mobilization of capital to disorganize labor, globally. It shaped a general reconstitution of states, via structural adjustment and free trade agreements, to institutionalize 'financialization' in the WTO and GATS protocols, and, more recently, has governed U.S. 'preemptive' neo-liberal development policies for 'failing' states (Soederberg, 2004; Panitch & Gindin, 2004).

Financial liberalization encouraged securitization (tradable debt) and the proliferation of a variety of financial instruments, creating new money out of expected future income. As argued elsewhere, under this regime the value of money is determined increasingly by its ability to command credit, rather than by creating value through the wage relation (McMichael, 2000).

This is consistent with Harvey's concept of 'accumulation by dispossession,' where capital expands through releasing, and centralizing, assets. The decomposition of the wage relation (casualization) is directly related to the decomposition of the nation-state, as capital undermines its foundation in a wage–labor order (embedded in the modern social-democratic state) by seeking to evade or weaken organized labor through access to a world market in labor. Since the wage form no longer *governs* valorization, various forms of labor are valorized directly through political/non-market mechanisms as corporate globalization reconstitutes its labor force on world scale, through dispossession, casual contracts, and the recursive 'race to the bottom' dynamic. The reproduction of money, via global financial relations, supplants capitalism's earlier focus on the reproduction of wage–labor in the consolidation of the nation-state.

An emergent 'world agriculture' is premised on three key dynamics. First is the reconstitution of capital through financialization, such that corporate strategies intensify vertical integration (from seed to supermarket) with flexible horizontal mergers and alliances, on a global scale. Vía Campesina has noted that agri-power no longer resides in control over land, rather it resides in the relations that surround agricultural production – those that "control loans, materials supply, the dissemination of new technologies, such as transgenic products, on the one hand, and those that control national and international product warehousing systems, transportation, distribution and retail sales to the consumer, on the other hand, have real power" (Vía Campesina, 2004a, p. 5). As Burch and Lawrence (2005) have shown, one pertinent form of this reconstitution is the rise of highly innovative and flexible (generic) 'own brand' agri-food manufacturers serving supermarket chains (with specialty foods, including home meal replacements, organic foods, functional foods and prepared dietary products) and challenging the independence of brand-based manufacturing capital in the supply chain stemming from the so-called Fordist era.

Second, the privatization of states via the relations of financialization, including WTO trade and investment rules, reconstitutes capital on a global scale, and the transformation of food security into a private relation (McMichael, 2004b). Under this dynamic, agricultural protections mutate from a public food security/self-sufficiency goal into a goal of subsidizing corporate agriculture, agro-exporting, and global sourcing, facilitated by the power relations within the WTO, as well as currency devaluations induced by structural-adjustment policies in the global South.

Third, the priority given to the reproduction of money has specific political and social consequences. The preservation of money value increasingly governs institutional politics in global and national arenas, generalizing a cycle of liberalization and crisis management through structural adjustment, at the expense of sustained social policies. Globally, the casualization of labor through redundancy and flexibility practices is linked to, and conditioned by, peasant expropriation. This reserve army of labor, within a transnational space governed by WTO principles of liberalization, is the foundation for capitalist development on a global scale.

CONCLUSION

The argument of this chapter is that the 'food regime' is a vector of social reproduction of capital on a world scale. As such, it expresses the genetic structure of capitalism in the accumulation/dispossession dynamic, and the political structure insofar as states govern transnational circuits of food, and their role in subsidizing the wage relation. Nonetheless geo-politics and the accumulation/legitimation dialectic order the political history of capitalism in distinct ways. The moment of world capitalism that defines the corporate food regime is realized through the construction of a world agriculture. The discursive element of this construction is akin to Cameron and Palan's (2004, p. 15) "imagined economies of globalization", where authority and sovereignty no longer inhabit the same space. These imagined economies inhabit "different normative and cognitive spaces whereby the boundaries of the state ... are rendered multiple, complex and dynamic" (*ibid.*, pp. 15–17), and while they have an ontological force, "their importance lies less in what they describe than in what they narrate. In representing a dynamic respatialization of social and economic relations, the discourses of globalization and exclusion posit the immanent development of new spatial forms to which policy-makers, industrialists, jurists and ordinary people must adapt" (*ibid.*, p. 20). Such construction of a world agriculture serves to legitimize this transnational circuit and its assault on peasant cultures, as a condition for global food security.

The immanence of a world agriculture is ultimately shaped by the world-historical conjuncture, which I specify via analytical comparison. Polanyi viewed the institution of the self-regulating market as an attempt to commodify land, labor and money, and the protectionist movement as a counter-movement of regulation of each of these social substances. The counter-movement involved a cumulative politics of nation-state formation, whereby labor legislation, agrarian protectionism, and central banking attempted to re-embed the market in society. But this was a nineteenth and early twentieth-century double movement that configured the modern welfare/development state (McMichael, 2005b). In the twenty-first century, this trinity no longer operates through the same double movement. Rather, the regulation of money is no longer vested in the state per se, but in instrumentalities such as the IMF, whose task has become a generalized imperative to reproduce (corporate) money through expending labor and land across the world with decreasing regard for their sustainability. The construction of a world agriculture, deepening the instrumental use, misuse, and abandonment of natural and social resources, unfolds within this general imperative.

Arguably, the food sovereignty movement is the most direct symptom of this socio-ecological crisis, especially insofar as it embodies a diversity of responses corresponding to the re-spatialization of social and economic relations in the corporate food regime. As an expression of the corporate food regime, it reveals both the immanent, *and* the historical, conditions governing the politics of capitalist development in the twenty-first century. That is, in the crisis of the Doha Round, the discourse of development is most clearly framed by the dialectic of 'food security' versus 'food sovereignty.'

NOTES

1. In relation to Harriet Friedmann's chapter in this volume, which reworks the 'food regime' concept in politico-normative terms, I offer a complementary use of the food regime as a vector of the social reproduction of capital on a world scale, and as a lens focusing on the social fact of dispossession. While a 'price-governed market' is the common feature of food regimes, the construction of this relationship is specific to the historical conjuncture in which each operates.

2. By the mid-1990s, 80 percent of farm subsidies in the OECD countries concentrated on the largest 20 percent of (corporate) farms, rendering small farmers increasingly vulnerable to the vicissitudes of a de-regulated (and increasingly privately managed) global market for agricultural products. U.S. farm income declined by almost 50 percent between 1996 and 1999 (Gorelick, 2000, pp. 28–30), and Europe lost half of its full-time equivalent agricultural employment between 1980 and 2001, with the equivalent of 1 million farm jobs disappearing in the latter half of the 1990s (Herman & Kuper, 2003, pp. 29–40).

3. Dumping was institutionalized within the WTO, via what is know as the 'Blair House Agreement,' concerning exports, negotiated between the U.S. and the E.U. The agreement "tied reductions in both domestic support and export subsidies to baseline levels of 1986, when stocks and subsidies were at their peak, thus giving both the E.U and the U.S. ample flexibility in meeting their obligations," and established a 'peace clause' regarding action against farm support programs and export subsidies (Dawkins, 1999). The legitimation of export subsidies (for 25 of 132 WTO members)

perversely allowed the U.S. and the E.U to intensify export dumping such that "just 3 (members) are responsible for 93% of all subsidized wheat exports and just 2 of them are responsible for subsidizing 94% of butter and 80% of beef exports" (Dawkins, 1999).

4. Thus, in 2001, President Bush proclaimed, on the eve of the WTO Doha Ministerial, 'I want America to feed the world… It starts with having an administration committed to knocking down barriers to trade, and we are' (quoted in IUF 2002, p. 4). The associated U.S. vision of a 'global agriculture' is premised on the superiority of a corporate-dominated world market for foodstuffs over domestic food systems (Peine & McMichael, 2005).

5. "Typically, a crop development conglomerate is organized around one OECD-based transnational enterprise (TNE), rooted in the chemical, pharmaceutical, or food processing industry. This TNE maintains a network of linkages with one or more plant breeding firms, new biology firms, genomics and software firms, and also with public research institutes. The nature of the linkages is diverse and varies from temporary research collaboration to complete take-overs" (Pistorius & van Wijk, 1999, p. 118).

6. The TRIPs protocol requires states to regulate biological resources, whether through patenting or an effective *sui generis* system, deriving from the 1992 Convention on Biological Diversity. Although the protocol is yet to be universally implemented, states choosing the latter path remain under pressure to market their genetic resources for foreign exchange (McMichael, 2003, pp. 183–184).

REFERENCES

Adams, N. (1993). *Worlds apart. The North–South divide and the international system.* London: Zed.

Ainger, K. (2003). The new peasants' revolt. *New Internationalist, 353*, 9–13.

Araghi, F. (1995). Global de-peasantization, 1945–1990. *Sociological Quarterly, 36*(2), 337–368.

Araghi, F. (1999). The great global enclosure of our times: Peasants and the agrarian Question at the end of the twentieth century. In: F. Magdoff, J. B. Foster & F. H. Buttel (Eds), *Hungry for profit: The agribusiness threat to farmers, food and the environment* (pp. 145–160). New York: Monthly Review Press.

Araghi, F. (2003). Food regimes and the production of value: Some methodological issues. *Journal of Peasant Studies, 30*(2), 41–70.

Arrighi, G. (1982). The crisis of U.S. hegemony. In: S. Amin, G. Arrighi, A. G. Frank & I. Wallerstein (Eds), *Dynamics of Global Crisis.* New York: Monthly Review Press.

Arrighi, G. (1990). The developmentalist illusion: A reconceptualization of the semi-periphery. In: W. G. Martin (Ed.), *Semiperipheral states in the world-economy* (pp. 11–42). Westport, CT: Greenwood Press.

Arrighi, G. (1994). *The long twentieth century. Money, power, and the origins of our times.* London: Verso.

Barndt, D. (1997). Bio/cultural diversity and equity in post-NAFTA Mexico (Or: Tomasita comes North while Big Mac goes South). In: J. Drydyk & P. Penz (Eds), *Global justice, global democracy* (pp. 55–69). Winnipeg: Fernwood Publishing.

Bensinger, K. (2003). Mexican corn comes a cropper. *The Washington Times*, September 9.

Blank, S. (1998). *The end of agriculture in the American portfolio.* Westport, CT: Quorum Books.
Bodnar, J. (2003). Roquefort vs Big Mac: Globalization and its others. *Archives in European. Sociology, XLIV, 1,* 133–144.
Bose, S. (1997). Instruments and idioms of colonial and national development: India's historical experience in comparative perspective. In: F. Cooper & R. Packard (Eds), *International development and the social sciences* (pp. 45–63). Berkeley: University of California Press.
Bové, J., & Dufour, F. (2001). *The world is not for sale.* London: Verso.
Burch, D., & Lawrence, G. (2005). Supermarket own brands, supply chains and the changing agri-food system: The UK experience. *International Journal of Sociology of Agriculture and Food, 13*(1), 1–17.
Buttel, F. H. (2003). The global politics of GEOs. The Achilles' Heel of the globalization regime? In: R. S. Schurmann & D. D. T. Kelso (Eds), *Engineering trouble. Biotechnology and its discontents.* Berkeley: University of California Press.
Cameron, A., & Palan, R. (2004). *The imagined economies of globalization.* London: Sage.
Carlsen, L. (2003). The Mexican farmers' movement: Exposing the myths of free trade. *Americas program policy report.* Silver City (NM): Interhemispheric Resource Center. Available at: www.americaspolicy.org
Cassel, A., & Patel, R. (2003). Agricultural trade liberalization and Brazil's rural poor: Consolidating inequality. *Food First Policy Brief.* August.
Davis, M. (2001). *Late Victorian holocausts. El Nino famines and the making of the third world.* London: Verso.
Dawkins, K. (1999). Agricultural prices and trade policy: Evaluating and correcting the Uruguay round agreement on agriculture. *UNCTAD* Paper, Geneva, December 12–14.
Desmarais, A. A. (2003). *The Vía Campesina: Peasants resisting globalization.* Unpublished Ph.D. dissertation, Geography, University of Calgary.
Dugger, C. W. (2004) Supermarket giants crush central American farmers. *New York Times,* December 28, pp. A1, A10.
Eisenburger, M., & Patel, R. (2003). Agricultural liberalization in China: Curbing the State and creating cheap labor. *Food First Policy Brief,* September.
Escobar, A. (1995). *Encountering development: The making and unmaking of the third world.* Princeton: Princeton University Press.
Fanon, F. (1967). *The wretched of the earth.* Harmondsworth: Penguin.
FAOSTAT. (2004). www.fao.org
French, H. (2004). Linking globalization, consumption, and governance. In: L. Starke (Ed.), *State of the world, 2004: The consumer society.* Washington, DC: The WorldWatch Institute.
Friedmann, H. (1982). The political economy of food: The rise and fall of the postwar international food order. *American Journal of Sociology, 88S,* 248–286.
Friedmann, H. (1987). Family farms and international food regimes. In: T. Shanin (Ed.), *Peasants and peasant societies* (pp. 258–276). Oxford: Basil Blackwell.
Friedmann, H. (1993). The political economy of food: A global crisis. *New Left Review, 197,* 27–59.
Friedmann, H. (1999). Remaking 'traditions:' How we eat, what we eat and the changing political economy of food. In: D. Barndt (Ed.), *Women working the NAFTA food chain.* Toronto: Second Story Press.
Friedmann, H. (2000). What on earth is the modern world-system? Food-getting and territory in the modern era and beyond. *Journal of World-System Research, VI*(2), 480–515.

Friedmann, H. (2005). Feeding the empire: The pathologies of globalized agriculture. In: L. Panitch & C. Leys (Eds), *The empire reloaded Socialist register 2005* (pp. 124–143). London: Merlin Press.

Friedmann, H., & McMichael, P. (1989). Agriculture and the state system: The rise and fall of national agricultures, 1870 to the present. *Sociologia Ruralis, XXIX*(2), 93–117.

Goodman, D., Sorj, B., & Wilkinson, J. (1987). *From farming to biotechnology*. Oxford: Basil Blackwell.

Gorelick, S. (2000). Facing the farm crisis. *The Ecologist, 30*(4), 28–32.

Grzybowski, C. (2004). *Taboo in the countryside. Thank you, MST*. IBASE, Rio de Janeiro, April 19.

Halperin, S. (2004). *War and social change in modern Europe. The great transformation revisited*. Cambridge: Cambridge University Press.

Hardt, M., & Negri, A. (2000). *Empire*. Cambridge, MA. & London: Harvard University Press.

Harvey, D. (2003). *The new imperialism*. Oxford: Oxford University Press.

Helleiner, E. (1996). *States and the reemergence of global finance: From Bretton Woods to the 1990s*. Ithaca: Cornell University Press.

Herman, P., & Kuper, R. (2003). *Food for thought. towards a future for farming*. London: Pluto Press.

Hobsbawm, E. (1992). The crisis of today's ideologies. *New Left Review, 192*, 55–64.

IATP. (2004). *United States dumping on world agricultural markets*. Minneapolis: Institute for Agriculture and Trade Policy. www.tradeobservatory.org

IUF. (2002). *The WTO and the world food system: A trade union approach*. Geneva: International Union of Food, Agricultural, Hotel, Restaurant, Catering, Tobacco and Allied Workers' Associations.

Kennedy, G., Nantel, G., & Shetty, P. (2004). Globalization of food systems in developing countries: A synthesis of country case studies. In: *Globalization of food systems in developing countries: Impact on food security and nutrition*. (pp. 1–26). Rome: FAO.

Khor, M. (2004). *Comments on the WTO's Geneva 'July 2004 Package'*. TWN Briefing Paper, 22, August.

Kwa, A. (2002). Development box: Can it adequately address the agricultural crisis in developing countries? *Focus on the global South*, April 15. Posted by wto-info@iatp.org

Lacher, H. (1999). Embedded liberalism, disembedded markets: Reconceptualizating the *pax Americana*. *New Political Economy, 4*(3), 343–360.

LeQuesne, C. (1997). *The world trade organisation and food security*. Talk to UK Food Group, July 15.

Luxemburg, R. (1963). *The accumulation of capital*. London: Routledge & Kegan Paul.

Lynas, M. (2001). Selling starvation. *Corporate Watch, 7*(Spring).

Madeley, J. (2000). *Hungry for trade*. London & New York: Zed Books.

Manning, R. (2004). The oil we eat. *Harpers Magazine*, February, pp. 37–45.

McMichael, P. (1999). The global crisis of wage labour. *Studies in Political Economy, 58*, 11–40.

McMichael, P. (2000). World-systems analysis, globalization, and incorporated omparison. *Journal of World-Systems Research, VI*(3), 668–690.

McMichael, P. (2003). Food security and social reproduction: Issues and contradictions. In: I. Bakker & S. Gill (Eds), *Power, production and social reproduction*. New York: Palgrave Macmillan.

McMichael, P. (2004a). *Development and social change. A global perspective*. Thousand Oaks: Pine Forge Press.

McMichael, P. (2004b). Biotechnology and food security: Profiting on insecurity? In: L. Beneria & S. Bisnath (Eds), *Global tensions. Challenges and opportunities in the world economy*. New York & London: Routledge.
McMichael, P. (2005a). *Settlers and the agrarian question[1984]*. Cambridge: Cambridge University Press.
McMichael, P. (2005b). Globalization. In: T. Janoski, R. Alford, A. Hicks & M. Schwartz (Eds), *A handbook of political sociology: States, civil societies and globalization*. New York: Cambridge University Press.
Mintz, S. (1986). *Sweetness and power*. New York: Vintage.
Moore, J. W. (2000). Environmental crises and the metabolic rift in world-historical perspective. *Organization & Environment*, *13*(2), 123–157.
Murphy, S. (2004). *Agricultural trade: Time for a new framework*. Presentation at Oxford University, June 8–9.
Oxfam. (2003). *Dumping without borders: How U.S. agricultural policies are destroying the livelihoods of Mexican corn farmers*. Oxfam Briefing Paper #50.
Oxford Analytica. (2004). Doha round hangs on farm talks. *Oxford Analytica*, February 20. www.oxan.com
Panitch, L., & Gindin, S. (2004). Global capitalism and American empire. In: L. Panitch & C. Leys (Eds), *The new imperial challenge: Socialist register 2004*. London: Merlin Press.
Paringaux, R.-P. (2000). The deliberate destruction of agriculture. India: Free markets, empty bellies. *Le Monde Diplomatique*, September 1–9.
Peine, E., & McMichael, P. (2005). Globalization and governance. In: V. Higgins & G. Lawrence (Eds), *Agricultural regulation*. London: Routledge.
Pistorius, R., & van Wijk, J. (1999). *The exploitation of plant genetic information. Political strategies in crop development*. Oxon: CABI Publishing.
Polanyi, K. (1957). *The great transformation*. Boston: Beacon Press.
Public Citizen. (2001). Down on the farm: NAFTA's seven-year war on farmers and ranchers in the U.S., Canada and Mexico. June 26. Public Citizen: Washington, DC. www.citizen.org/documents/ACFF2.pdf
Reardon, T., Timmer, C. P., Barrett, C. B., & Berdegue, J. (2003). The rise of supermarkets in Africa, Asia and Latin America. *American Journal of Agricultural Economics*, *85*(5), 1140–1146.
Regmi, A., & Gehlhar, M. (2005). Processed food trade pressured by evolving global supply chains. *Amber Waves (Economic Research Service/USDA)*, *3*(1), 12–19.
Revel, A., & Riboud, C. (1986). *American green power*. Baltimore: Johns Hopkins University Press.
Rifkin, J. (1992). *Beyond beef. The rise and fall of the cattle culture*. New York: Penguin.
Rohter, L. (2003). Relentless foe of the Amazon jungle: Soybeans. *New York Times*, September 17, p. 3.
Rosenberg, J. (2001). *The empire of civil society*. London & New York: Verso.
Rostow, W. W. (1960). *The stages of economic growth*. Cambridge: Cambridge University Press.
Ruggie, J. (1982). International regimes, transactions and change: Embedded liberalism in the post-war order. *International Organization*, *36*(3), 379–415.
Schaeffer, R. (1995). Free trade agreements: Their impact on agriculture and the environment. In: P. McMichael (Ed.), *Food and agrarian orders in the world-economy*. Westport, CT: Greenwood Press.

Shiva, V. (2000). *Stolen harvest. The hijacking of the global food supply.* Boston: South End Press.
Soederberg, S. (2004). American empire and 'excluded states': The millenium challenge account and the shift to pre-emptive development. *Third World Quarterly, 25*(2), 279–302.
Starr, A. (2001). *Naming the enemy. Anti-corporate movements confront globalization.* London & New York: Zed Books.
Tubiana, L. (1989). World trade in agricultural products: From global regulation to market fragmentation. In: D. Goodman & M. Redclift (Eds), *The international farm crisis.* New York: St. Martin's Press.
Vía Campesina. (1999). *Seattle declaration: Take WTO out of agriculture.* December 3. www.viacampesina.org/welcome_english.php3
Vía Campesina. (2001). *Our world is not for sale. Priority to peoples' food sovereignty.* Bulletin, November 1. www.viacampesina.org/welcome_english.php3
Vía Campesina. (2002). *Proposals of Vía Campesina for sustainable, farmer based agricultural production.* Bulletin, August. www.viacampesina.org/welcome_english.php3
Vía Campesina. (2003). *Statement on agriculture after Cancun.* Bulletin, December 15.www.viacampesina.org/welcome_english.php3
Vía Campesina. (2004a). *Announcement world forum on agrarian reform.* March 3. www.viacampesina.org/welcome_english.php3
Vía Campesina. (2004b). *Rejection of the FAO agreements.* Bulletin 3, June 17. www.viacampesina.org/welcome_english.php3
Vía Campesina. (2004c). *The domination of capital over agriculture.* Bulletin 4, June 18. www.viacampesina.org/welcome_english.php3
Vidal, J. (2004). Demand for beef speeds destruction of Amazon forest. *Guardian Weekly, 3*(April), 8–14.
Wallach, L. (2003). *What the WTO didn't want you to know.* Retrieved, March 8.
Wallach, L., & Woodall, P. (2004). *Whose trade organization?* New York and London: The New Press.
Watkins, K. (1991). Agriculture and food security in the GATT Uruguay round. *Review of African Political Economy, 50,* 38–50.
Watkins, K. (2002). Money talks. *Guardian Weekly, 21*(May), 9–15.
Wiggerthale, M. (2004). *Liberalisation of agricultural trade – the way forward for sustainable development? Global Issue Paper,* X, Heinrich Böll Foundation, November.

SHIFTING STRATEGIES OF SOVEREIGNTY: BRAZIL AND THE POLITICS OF GLOBALIZATION

Sara Schoonmaker

ABSTRACT

This chapter explores Lula's internationalist strategy toward the politics of globalization, which involves building alliances within the Common Market of the South (Mercosur) and between Mercosur and the European Union. It compares Lula's internationalism with the earlier nationalist Brazilian informatics policy as shifting strategies of sovereignty, highlighting their differences as interventions in the politics of globalization. In the process, it explores the changing conditions of globalization and assesses the potential of Lula's strategy as an alternative to the dominant neoliberal globalization form.

Since his election as Brazilian president in December 2002, Luiz Inácio Lula da Silva intervened in the politics of globalization in controversial and complex ways, primarily in the context of participating in three sets of negotiations over free-trade agreements. He co-chaired talks on the Free Trade Area of the Americas (FTAA) with the U.S., sought to strengthen and expand relationships among Latin American governments in the

Common Market of the South (Mercosur), and was a key leader of the Group of 22 alliance among delegates from the global South in the World Trade Organization (WTO). In each of these venues, Lula challenged the dominant form of neoliberal globalization, designed to open markets around the world to global capital. He developed a strategy to transform free-trade negotiations by forging an alternative culture of globalization, or an emergent moral economy, centered on the issues of combating global hunger and poverty. Lula's strategy reflected key contours of contemporary struggles over the politics of globalization, including struggles between countries from the global North and South over the political, economic and cultural conditions for development, as well as struggles between groups united in their opposition to the dominant form of neoliberal globalization but divided over the strategies to put their opposition into practice.

Lula thus developed a strategy to respond to changing dynamics in the politics of globalization. That strategy was particularly relevant for the Brazilian government, since it was rooted in a history of Brazilian government intervention to promote national economic and political sovereignty. One notable example of such intervention was the informatics policy begun in 1976. This policy was designed to combat what Brazil and other governments in the global South viewed as a new form of information dependency, based on their lack of development of technological, industrial and scientific capacities in computer manufacturing and software. The informatics policy targeted the development of computer and software industries as key sectors influencing Brazil's ability to compete in the global economy. It sparked trade wars with the U.S. government in the mid-1980s, when President Reagan charged that its restrictions on foreign investment in Brazil represented unfair trade practices against the U.S. firms. Indeed, the controversies and struggles that arose over the Brazilian informatics policy were grounded in the Brazilian government's strategy of opposing the U.S. government efforts to promote free trade and protecting its local industry from competition from foreign capital.

Decades later, Lula used a markedly different strategy to continue this struggle to promote Brazilian economic and political sovereignty. He raised the stakes in the politics of globalization, pursuing an internationalist vision of solidarity among Latin American governments and other nations in the global South to advocate for human rights for the world's poor. This chapter will compare Lula's internationalism with the informatics policy as shifting strategies of sovereignty, highlighting their differences as interventions in the politics of globalization and assessing the potential of Lula's strategy as an alternative to neoliberal globalization.

GLOBALIZATION, DISCOURSE AND STRATEGIES OF SOVEREIGNTY

Under contemporary conditions of globalization, states interact with a range of powerful transnational bodies, including international trade regimes like the WTO and FTAA. As Held (2000, p. 398) argues, "states deploy their sovereignty and autonomy as bargaining chips in negotiations involving coordination and collaboration across shifting transnational and international networks." Indeed, the power of international networks and regimes like the WTO and FTAA are part of an increase in regional and global governance that states must address as they engage in trade and development in the global economy. Since these non-state actors exercise major influence in the politics of globalization, states face pressures to develop a strategy to engage with them. Globalization thus transforms the conditions for states to exercise power, leading states to "become central in initiating new kinds of transnational collaboration, from the emergence of different forms of military alliances to the advancement of human rights regimes" (Held, 2000, p. 397).

Lula's strategy of sovereignty exemplifies such an approach, emphasizing the centrality of the state as initiator of transnational alliances. Indeed, it focused on strengthening collaboration between states in the global South to negotiate not only with powerful states, but also with non-state actors like the FTAA, the WTO and MERCOSUR. Lula shifted away from Brazil's historic emphasis on national government intervention to an internationalist strategy rooted in alliance building, pursuing sovereignty beyond the boundaries of national borders as a way to more effectively confront powerful international interests in the politics of globalization. This strategy fits with Held's (2000, p. 399) argument that under contemporary conditions of globalization, "the idea of a political community of fate – of a self-determining collectivity – can no longer be meaningfully located within the boundaries of a single nation-state alone."

Indeed, Lula pursued sovereignty through an internationalist vision rather than a nationalist one. This approach was apt since he sought to advocate broadly for human rights for the poor, not just within Brazil, but also within the global South as a whole (and particularly in Latin America). He used innovative discursive strategies as central elements in his struggle against the dominant form of neoliberal globalization. He rearticulated the discourse of free trade in a distinct way to fight for cultural values that have been historically juxtaposed to free trade and the dominance of global capital, emphasizing the social implications of trade in terms of hunger and inequality on an international scale. Through this politically astute approach grounded in alternative cultural values, Lula joined the discourse of free trade with the discourse about global hunger and the social exclusion of the world's poor from economic development.

In this process, Lula engaged in what Williams (1977, p. 126) called an emergent alternative approach, involving "new meanings and values, new practices, new relationships and kinds of relationships...which are substantially alternative or oppositional" to the dominant form. Indeed, Lula framed his advocacy for free trade as a struggle for the rights of farmers and the poor in the global South, to be waged by forming new relationships among Latin American governments in the Common Market of the South (Mercosur), the FTAA and among delegates from the global South in the WTO. Drawing on Williams (1977), I conceptualize Lula's strategy for sovereignty as emergent internationalism.

These new alliances are a vital part of Lula's shifting strategy of sovereignty, through which the Brazilian government rearticulates its opposition to neoliberal globalization in a new and politically skillful way. This approach is particularly fitting in the context of the "reconfiguration of political power," where states face a proliferation of regional and international forms of governance (Held, 2000, p. 394). In order to understand the meaning and implications of this strategy compared to the informatics strategy pursued in the 1970s and 1980s, I theorize globalization as a multifaceted process, where economic and political conditions and practices are inextricably bound up with cultural and discursive ones. In the process, I highlight the dynamic changeable and multidimensional nature of globalization and the political struggles to shape it.

Building on Schoonmaker (2002), I conceptualize globalization as a complex, multidimensional process involving the simultaneous interaction of economic, political, cultural and discursive practices. This post-structural political economy perspective illuminates the importance of the cultural and discursive dimensions of globalization through which key meanings of the economic and political conditions of globalization are interpreted and defined.

For example, Gibson-Graham (1996, p. 120) conceptualizes globalization as "a discourse, that is, as a language of domination, a tightly scripted narrative of differential power." In discourse, actors exercise power through the use of language as they struggle over how to define the conditions for economic and political practices. Theorizing globalization as a discourse thus involves appreciating the ways that these political and economic practices are constituted and contested through struggles over language and definitions of the terms and conditions for operating in the global political economy. As Foucault argues, "it is in discourse that power and knowledge are joined together" (1978, p. 100).

Analyzing the discursive dimension of globalization makes it possible to identify how relations of power are constituted in language as well as in action, and particularly in the complex interaction between the two. In the first volume of *The History of Sexuality*, Foucault emphasizes the importance of understanding that "[d]iscourse transmits and produces power; it reinforces it, but also undermines and exposes it, renders it fragile and makes it possible to thwart it" (1978, p. 101). Discourses are articulated through a complex, unstable process where they have multiple meanings for multiple interests. Discourse can thus be an instrument for exercising power, a point at which we see the effects of power as well as a starting point for strategies to oppose and resist power (Schoonmaker, 2002).

Foucault provides guidelines for how to conduct such a discursive analysis, which are useful in understanding the discourse of globalization. He argues that the theorist must reconstruct the

> multiplicity of discursive elements...with the things said and those concealed, the enunciations required and those forbidden...; with the variants and different effects – according to who is speaking, his position of power, the institutional context in which he happens to be situated – that it implies; and with the shifts and reutilizations of identical formulas for contrary objectives that it also includes (1978, p. 100).

Such a theoretical reconstruction sheds light on the power struggle involved as Lula challenged the dominant neoliberal discourse of globalization with a discourse of sovereignty and on the potential for using the sovereignty discourse to create an alternative strategy.

DISCURSIVE STRUGGLES OVER FREE TRADE AND NATIONAL SOVEREIGNTY

The "discursive elements" (Foucault, 1978, p. 100) of the neoliberal globalization discourse involve four key assumptions. The first is economic determinism, where an objective economic logic determines market operations and leads markets to expand on a global scale. Second, free trade is viewed as most conducive for operation in the global system, since eradicating the so-called "barriers to trade," allows "free" access to trade and markets for those parties most rationally equipped to participate. Third, the state is viewed as an impediment to the rational operation of these objective market forces. Finally, there is an ahistorical assumption that the expansion of global trade and production is a novel, unprecedented development (Schoonmaker, 2002).

Since the mid-1940s, the U.S. government championed various versions of a free-trade discourse in its negotiations over international trade and development, which coalesced into a fully articulated neoliberal globalization discourse during struggles over the General Agreement on Tariffs and Trade (GATT) during the 1980s. In trade debates during the 1970s and 1980s, Brazil led other countries in the global South to struggle against the discourse of free trade with an oppositional discourse of national sovereignty. The sovereignty discourse was based on nationalist cultural values that viewed national governments as the rightful arbiters of trade and development policy, in a global context characterized by historical relations of power between former colonies and colonial powers. This discourse recognized the rights of governments in the global South to implement protections to promote the growth of local industry and technology.

Brazil and India led the opposition to the neoliberal globalization discourse in debates over whether to expand the GATT into a regime governing trade in services as well as goods, using these trade negotiations as a vehicle to resist the domination of markets in the global South by global capital. They lost this struggle with the inclusion of services trade within the GATT and the eventual consolidation of the WTO as the global neoliberal trade regime replacing the GATT, when the Uruguay Round of negotiations concluded in 1995 (Cowhey & Aronson, 1989; Nicolaides, 1989; Marconini, 1990; Schoonmaker, 2002).

During the 1970s and 1980s, the Brazilian government fought a simultaneous, protracted struggle to implement its informatics strategy and promote national development of its information technology sector. This sector was targeted for its potential to promote productivity in an array of industries, due to the integration of information technology into a diverse field of economic processes. Given the large size of the Brazilian market, as well as a highly trained pool of scientists and engineers with expertise in information technology, this sector held the promise of promoting national development in a cutting edge field. Informatics policy proponents also argued that the policy could help decrease Brazilian dependency on computer imports, which grew 600 percent between 1969 and 1974, comprising Brazil's third largest manufactured import and costing approximately $100 million in foreign exchange (Evans, 1995, 1986).

Indeed, the Brazilian informatics policy was a cardinal example of a nationalist development strategy and its conflicts with the dominant neoliberal globalization discourse. The cornerstone of this strategy, and its defining feature as an economic nationalist approach, was the concept of the "market reserve," which was rooted in nationalist cultural values that defined the market as part of Brazil's national patrimony that should be protected by the government to promote local economic development. The market reserve policy was established in 1976 and then extended for 8 more years in 1984 through the National Informatics Law. It prohibited multinational corporations with home bases outside Brazil from investing in markets for mini- and personal computers and restricting foreign imports and the acquisition of foreign technologies (Adler, 1987; Schoonmaker, 2002).

The nationalist form of the informatics policy, rooted in its strategy of pursuing national sovereignty by restricting the access of foreign capital to Brazilian markets, threatened the U.S. government. In 1985, President Reagan responded to this perceived threat by initiating an investigation of Brazilian informatics for potentially violating the interests of the U.S. firms under Section 301 of the 1974 Trade Act.

The reasons for this investigation were complex and largely symbolic, rather than a response to short-term economic interests. Indeed, the U.S. computer-related exports to Brazil rose by 146 percent between 1979 and 1985, compared with a 138 percent increase in such exports worldwide. The U.S. government concerns with Brazilian informatics thus extended beyond the traditional focus on exports that motivates trade disputes. As a State Department official testified before Congress, "[i]t seems that Brazil, despite its rapid growth, still sees itself as an underdeveloped country, a developing country, which needs to utilize what we call infant industry policies in order to nurture its growth.... We are concerned in fact that other developing countries not emulate Brail's approach to development" (U.S. House Committee on Energy and Commerce, 1988, pp. 22–23).

In the interviews I conducted with Brazilian business executives involved with the informatics policy's development and implementation, they underscored the symbolic nature of the policy's perceived "threat" to the U.S. government. They noted that the overtly nationalist character of the policy made it a target for trade conflicts, since the U.S. government disliked the notion of Brazil being a nationalist model for other governments in the global South (Ripper, 1990, interview; Fregni, 1990, interview). Indeed, U.S. computer transnationals doing business in Brazil developed a working relationship with the Brazilian government under the conditions of the policy, and executives in these firms expressed concerns that U.S. trade pressures might disturb this arrangement (Gomes, 1992, interview).

The Reagan administration's investigation of Brazilian informatics sparked a trade war with the Brazilian government. It unleashed a complicated array of national and international pressures that eventually led to the demise of the informatics policy and the Brazilian government's support for nationalist approaches to economic development. From 1990 until 2001, the Collor and Cardoso administrations dismantled the informatics policy as part of a broader process of opening Brazilian markets in response to the constraints of neoliberal globalization. During this period, the Brazilian government accommodated the neoliberal globalization model by advocating free trade and opening Brazilian markets to foreign trade and investment. Its use of both the free trade and neoliberal globalization discourses paralleled the use of those discourses by the U.S. government and transnational corporations seeking access to Brazilian and other markets in the global South. The advocacy of free trade by this range of international actors was thus an integral part of the broader advocacy of the neoliberal globalization model (Schoonmaker, 2002).

During his candidacy for and presidency of Brazil since 2002, Lula ruptured this fusion of the free trade and neoliberal globalization discourses. In a bold and politically insightful move, Lula used the free-trade discourse to rearticulate the Brazilian strategy to defend national sovereignty by opposing neoliberal globalization. He understood the free-trade discourse as a key element of the neoliberal globalization discourse used by the U.S. government since the post-war period. Drawing upon its symbolic power, he creatively rearticulated the free-trade discourse, combining it with elements from the sovereignty discourse to oppose the domination of markets in the global South by the U.S. and European economic and political interests. In the process, Lula developed an internationalist, yet regionally based, strategy linking Brazil's struggle for sovereignty with other Latin American countries and with the poor people in all parts of the world. As an alternative to neoliberal globalization, this strategy was markedly different from the informatics strategy. The key contrasts between these two alternatives lay in their underlying values and their stance with respect to trade politics and negotiations.

BROADENING THE SCOPE: INCORPORATING ALTERNATIVE VALUES INTO TRADE AND DEVELOPMENT POLICY

Lula's new strategy of sovereignty involved a shift from a nationalist to an internationalist form of development and trade policy. As discussed above, the informatics policy was oriented virtually exclusively toward the Brazilian market, as a nationalist strategy to develop computer manufacturing and software as key industrial sectors to compete in the global economy. By contrast, Lula pursued an internationalist strategy designed to promote Brazilian sovereignty by shifting its policy focus from the national to the international arena in the struggles over trade and development politics.

Central to this internationalist shift was Lula's incorporation of alternative values into negotiations over trade and development. As mentioned above, Lula's strategy is what Williams (1977, p. 124) called an emergent alternative to the dominant, involving the development of new practices, values, relationships and kinds of relationships that the dominant form "neglects, undervalues, opposes, represses, or even cannot recognize." Indeed, Lula's emergent internationalism emphasized the eradication of hunger on a global scale as a central theme in his discourse on development and trade policy, a theme completely absent from, and thus truly unrecognized, by the dominant neoliberal globalization discourse.

Indeed, this dominant discourse is based upon the assumption that markets operate efficiently to allocate resources so that social welfare will be maximized at the national as well as international levels. Markets are viewed as neutral, objective forces that work to the benefit of all, rather than fostering the interests of one class or social group at the expense of others (Epstein, Graham, & Nembhard, 1993). The global expansion of markets, crafted through free-trade agreements such as the WTO and the FTAA, is thus viewed as a way to foster conditions for prosperity on an international scale.

Such expansion, however, has been shown to exacerbate problems of global inequality with respect to the distribution of income, which has become more unequal since the 1970s and had dire consequences for the world's poor (Hirst & Thompson, 1999). Free-trade regimes create conditions, where transnational corporations exercise substantial power over markets. In the agricultural sector, this has led to an international system of trade and production geared toward the export-oriented crops produced by corporate agriculture, rather than toward small producers catering to local needs. Crops like strawberries and cut flowers are grown on large industrial farms and exported to affluent consumers, and livestock are fed large quantities of grain that could otherwise be used to feed the poor (http://www.globalpolicy.org/socecon/hunger/economy/).

According to a report by Action Aid International, the interests of small farmers in the global South are damaged in three key ways by such transnational corporate control. First, market concentration drives down prices for staples such as wheat, coffee and tea, which provides short-term benefits for consumers but hurts small producers, who grow these crops, and find it difficult to compete with large corporations that enjoy lower operating costs due to economies of scale. For example, Monsanto controls 90 percent of the world grain trade and manages 91 percent of the market for genetically modified seeds. Second, small farmers are hurt, when agribusinesses raise the prices of agricultural inputs or form price-fixing cartels, again depressing prices for the products of small farmers and making it difficult for them to enter markets. Finally, agribusinesses set standards for participation in supply chains for fruit, vegetables and other products that small, poor farmers are unable to meet (http://www.globalpolicy.org/socecon/tncs/2005/01powerhungry.pdf).

In addition to its damaging effects on the interests of small farmers, the expansion of free trade is linked to environmental problems and the complex economic, political and military conflicts involved with what President Bush calls the "war on terror." The growth of world trade involves expanding processes of both production and consumption, leading to increasing traffic in workers, natural resources and other factors of production, as well as the consumption of fossil fuels required to transport them. Such growth is often accompanied by lax environmental regulations allowing corporations to consume the raw materials available in one area of the world and then freely move their operations to another (Brennan, 2003). As Brennan (2003, p. 35) argues, "[t]he impetus to expand (and find the fuel to maintain) transportation and telecommunications networks was a common cause of twentieth-century war...that...will also feature in the twenty-first century." The U.S.-led war and occupation of Iraq supports Brennan's (2003) emphasis upon the connections between the neoliberal expansion of trade and production and the drive to gain access to natural resources as integrally linked causes of twenty-first century war making.

Lula made a similar point when he raised the issue of world hunger in international debates over trade and development, employing the discourse of combating terrorism and weapons of mass destruction that emerged in the years following the September 11 attacks. He argued that "hunger in itself is a weapon of mass destruction" that kills 11 children every minute, a fact virtually unrecognized in previous political speeches about the war on terror (http://www.brazil.org.uk/page.php?cid = 1812).

Despite the multiple links between the dominant model of neoliberal globalization and global inequality, these connections were not effectively articulated in the discourse over trade until Lula brought them to the forefront. In the 2 years following his election, Lula consistently raised the problem of hunger in international fora such as the World Forum, the G-8 Summit, the United Nations General Assembly, and the Summit of the Americas. In a speech entitled "Making Globalisation Work for All," given at an international conference on globalization held at the HM Treasury in London in February 2004, Lula exhorted participants to "muster the political will" to fund programs in the global South that would contribute to eradicating hunger, such as worker training, health care and education (http://www.brazil.org.uk/page.php?cid = 1812). He emphasized "the fight against hunger as a central pillar in the struggle against exclusion and international inequality, as well as a crucial step on the road to greater social justice, sustainable growth, human development and peace..." (http://www.brazil.org.uk/page.php?cid = 1812). This integration of the struggle to eradicate hunger as a centerpiece of international negotiations over trade and development, rather than as a side issue to be dealt with separately from the main agenda, was a crucial element of Lula's internationalist strategy for sovereignty.

Indeed, the emergent alternative nature of this new internationalist strategy was rooted in Lula's insistence upon viewing global trade and development within the context of power relations between countries in the global North and South and upon raising those inequalities in discussions at a range of international fora. In a speech at the United Nations General Assembly in September 2004, Lula emphasized these power relations by discussing hunger and inequality as part of the legacy of colonialism. He stated that 125 of today's 191 nations were

> subjected to the oppression of a few powers, which originally occupied less than 2% of the globe. The end of colonialism confirms, in the political arena, the right of peoples to self-determination... Political transformation, however, has not been transposed to the economic and social fields. And history shows this will not happen spontaneously (http://www.brazil.org.uk/page.php?cid = 1887).

Lula noted that the current per capita income of the world's wealthiest country (U.S.) was 80 times greater than that of the poorest country, dramatically more unequal than in 1820, when it was five times greater. Problems of global inequality increased even in the last 10 years, as per capita income fell in 54 countries: the number of children starving to death grew in 14 countries, life expectancy decreased in 34 countries and lack of basic sanitation killed more children than all the military conflicts since the second World War (http://www.brazil.org.uk/page.php?cid = 1887).

In his speeches about trade and development, Lula thus emphasized the ethical, as well as economic, problems involved with the effects of the neoliberal globalization model on global inequality. He brought hunger back in to the discourse on trade and development, integrating values of social justice into these debates. These efforts fit with political economists Hirst and Thompson's (1999, p. 75) call to recognize the ethical dimension of global inequalities in income and trade, stating that

> [t]here are good ethical arguments against this situation. Its consequences for the living conditions, life expectancy and security of the world's poor are obvious. It should not be *allowed* to go on and we should do something about it urgently as a matter of *conscience*. Ethics, however, have rarely moved economists, Western policy-makers and company executives: they need other rationales in terms of economic and business opportunities. (Emphasis in original).

Hirst and Thompson (1999, p. 76) provide some of these rationales, such as economic and security problems that may arise, when two-thirds of the world's population is excluded systematically from the prosperity enjoyed by the "already employed and successful in the wealthy 14 percent of the world and a few client states." Indeed, what the Bush administration and its allies perceive as "threats to national security" and the "war on terror" arose in a global context fraught with inequalities and tensions between the world's rich and poor.

Lula provided further rationales for economists and policy-makers in the global North to consider hunger and inequality in the context of negotiations over global trade and development, arguing that such negotiations will not be successful unless they are broadened to include these issues crucial to the global South. Lula thus integrated alternative values of considering the effects of trade on hunger and inequality as a political tactic both to pressure representatives from the global North and to mobilize those from the global South.

Lula's strategy was rooted in an oppositional stance toward the dominant neoliberal globalization model, particularly within the FTAA and the WTO, and its links to inequality and hunger in the global South. Opposition to the neoliberal globalization model appealed to a diverse range of constituencies within Brazil, including the poor, landless movements, and large sectors of Brazilian business and agriculture as well as with the international *alter-mondialiste* movement.[1] For example, the Central Unica de Trabalhadores (CUT), Brazil's major industrial union, actively mobilized against the FTAA. Lula thus attempted to build alliances among local capital, labor and the poor around their common interests in opposing neoliberal globalization, and particularly the interests of the U.S. and other representatives from the global North within the FTAA and the WTO.

This strategy was complicated, however, since Lula did not reject free-trade agreements outright as the more radical groups and movements advocated. By contrast, he expressed a commitment to participate in the FTAA and the WTO, albeit through a process of struggle to transform them. The contradictory nature of his strategy created tensions between Lula and his allies to the left. These tensions coincided with other political struggles in Brazil, where Lula failed to fulfill his electoral promises to address inequalities in income, education and health care as the top priorities of his administration. Instead, Lula strove to balance competing interests in Congress to build a coalition to pursue a much more limited agenda, including social security reform designed to increase the contributions of government workers and limit retirement benefits to future workers, tax reform designed to increase efficiency and reduce tax competition between Brazilian states and fiscal conservatism and efforts to retain foreign investment within the country. During his first 2 years in office, Lula thus struggled to maintain his Workers' Party's (PT) traditional support base among workers, particularly unionists and the poor, and a range of social movements. (Helfand, 2004; Chu, 2005). As Gleber Naime, PT organization secretary, stated, "These two years we've demonstrated our capacity to govern.... And the changes may not be as far-reaching as we want them to be, but they're what's been possible" (Chu, 2005, p. A3).

Lula's struggle to balance the desire for far-reaching changes with what appears politically possible extends from conflicts within Brazil to the international sphere. This struggle is particularly evident in Lula's participation in the World Social Forum (WSF), a gathering of diverse participants in the broader *altermondialiste* movement held annually since 2001. In 2003, a newly elected Lula was welcomed as a celebrity at the WSF, where the participants largely embraced his opposition to neoliberal globalization and advocacy for the poor in the global South. By 2005, however, leftist activists and academics at the WSF critiqued Lula for attempting to build support for his government by "repackaging neo-liberalism as the way to help the world's poor." (http://www.zmag.org/content/showarticle.cfm?SectionID=1&ItemID=7197).

Lula's engagement with the neoliberal model in the WTO and the FTAA is more complex, however, than such a "repackaging" process suggests. The strategy of participating in free-trade negotiations with the intention to transform them is fraught with contradictions that could undermine or derail it and is certainly not guaranteed to promote alternative values of combating global hunger and poverty. This strategy is an attempt, however flawed and problematic, to make choices, to navigate the conflicting interests involved with power relations between countries in the global North and South, within an institutional context of free-trade regimes freighted with the legacy of colonialism and the economic and political power of the North.

In making this attempt, Lula at times sounds like a hypocrite, a political pragmatist, who will say whatever it takes to score political points and win short-term victories. For example, Lula sounded such a note, when he addressed the issue of world hunger in a speech to the Mercosur-EU Business Forum in October of 2003. He stated that it would be ineffective to "play the poverty card" in such negotiations, because in business, "no one respects someone who arrives hanging his head in a submissive way. It's necessary to have pride because if you don't respect yourself, the other side in the negotiations won't respect you either" (http://www.brazil.org.uk/page.php?cid=1766). This statement implies that confronting countries in the global North with hard questions of global inequality, hunger and social injustice is merely a "card" to be played at the most advantageous moment and that such a gesture involves an act of submission rather than pride or defiance. This statement is loaded with possible meanings, given its disjuncture with Lula's other public appeals to honor alternative values in the context of free-trade agreements. It signifies the complex, fractured nature of Lula's venture to integrate alternative values that, as Williams (1977) argues is characteristic of the dominant form, are neglected, undervalued, opposed, repressed and unrecognized by the neoliberal globalization discourse. It raises questions about how one can speak a repressed, unrecognizable language while undertaking communication with the powerful.

Indeed, the contradictory nature of Lula's strategy is underscored by the rest of his 2003 speech to the Mercosur-EU Business Forum. After noting the ineffectuality of "playing the poverty card," he described his approach as developing partnerships with governments that were willing to strike mutually acceptable terms, where each government gave up something that made it worthwhile for the other to make a counteroffer. In the case of Mercosur's negotiations with the European Union (EU), he urged his European counterparts to add additional agricultural products to the negotiating process, since those were of most interest to Brazil. He noted the importance of understanding "that international trade is still a long way from being a relationship between equal partners. It needs to be liberalized in such a way as not to extend or reinforce the inequality existing between countries" (http://www.brazil.org.uk/page.php?cid=1766).

In the end, Lula thus called on his trading partners in the global North to recognize the inequalities of power involved with their relationship and to move toward trade agreements that would counteract them. In order to address the problem of global hunger in the context of international trade and development negotiations, Lula's emergent internationalism thus involved both attempting, in flawed and contradictory ways, to articulate alternative values in the discourse on trade and development, and building new kinds of relationships between Brazil and its trading partners.

FROM NATIONAL TO INTERNATIONAL POLICY: DEVELOPING INTERNATIONAL ALLIANCES

The importance of these new relationships attests to the changing conditions of globalization that have transformed the prospects for sovereignty and undermined the viability of the traditional form of economic nationalism based on states acting alone to promote their country's economic development (Held, 2000). Lula responded to these changed conditions by pursuing an internationalist strategy to strengthen and extend the Common Market of the South (Mercosur) beyond its current membership of Brazil, Argentina, Paraguay and Uruguay. He advocated strengthening Mercosur's regional presence as a trading bloc by expanding it to include Chile and Bolivia as full members, and eventually the rest of the Andean Community (Downie, 2003). During his first year in office, Lula engaged in extensive outreach to South American governments in an effort to foster these new regional alliances. On trips to Peru and Colombia, he encouraged greater cooperation between these Andean Pact countries and their historic rivals in Mercosur (Greider & Rapoza, 2003). Such efforts were not new in and of themselves, since they resonated with earlier efforts by the Brazilian government to bolster South American trade alliances. The alternative nature of Lula's strategy, however, was shaped by the historical context of the rise of the EU, which Lula viewed as an example of the economic and political benefits to be gained by building these new forms of alliances extending beyond the nation state.

Lula pursued the development of such alliances at Mercosur's meeting in Paraguay in June 2003. The Brazilian contingent presented a program to promote Latin American unity and bargaining power in relationship to the U.S. and other governments in the global North by developing Mercosur based on the model of the EU (Downie, 2003). They emphasized the connections between trade relationships and the complex social and political conditions involved with the broader process of development, advocating the growth of Mercosur's political, social and cultural programs. Such changes would involve expanding Mercosur's purview beyond its traditional focus on trade relationships. They are still in the negotiating stage, however, these changes suggest the potential to institutionalize new forms of cooperation to address common concerns in the Latin American region from improving the quality of life for the poor to providing a stronger alliance to work through the United Nations and the Security Council to address international conflicts and threats to human rights. Such new forms of cooperation are examples of the "transnational collaboration" that Held (2000, p. 397) views as key to navigating the current conditions of globalization. Indeed, these alliances could provide a stronger institutional base for Latin American governments to challenge the dominant neoliberal globalization form.

The centerpiece of Lula's strategy to develop this institutional base was to strengthen and expand Mercosur as a Latin American trading bloc. To further international economic and political cooperation among Mercosur trading partners, the Brazilian contingent advocated the development of Customs Union and Common Market programs at the June 2003 meeting. It proposed that the members should consider following the example of the EU to create a Mercosur parliament as well as establishing a Monetary Institute to develop a single regional currency. These programs might involve developing new trade partnerships and negotiating new trade agreements with the EU, India, South Africa and South Korea (Angrisani, 2003).

Lula's strategy for sovereignty thus involved an emergent internationalism, emphasizing the development of new alliances and relationships among Latin American nations extending from trade and development policy to social, political and cultural programs. This internationalist vision was grounded primarily in the effort to strengthen and expand Mercosur using the model of the EU, which Lula described as a "paradigm for integration" (http://www.brazil.org.uk/page.php?cid = 1766). It responded to the changed conditions of globalization theorized by Held (2000), where sovereignty involved building new forms of cooperation beyond the bounds of the nation state.

The move to expand Mercosur, however, also occurred within a context of Brazilian and Argentine dominance within that bloc, where those countries pursued individual interests through domestic decrees if they were unable to forge a regional consensus. Similar to the above discussion, Lula's strategy for sovereignty was complicated. Relationships in Mercosur were fraught with tensions arising from the history of difficulties in implementing regional accords, which would need to be addressed in the process of building increased cooperation (Angrisani, 2003).

Lula's emergent internationalist strategy for sovereignty thus viewed the EU as a potential model for building transnational alliances to pursue Latin American sovereignty under contemporary conditions of globalization. He engaged in the politics of globalization by intensive alliance building, both within Mercosur and by strengthening political and economic ties between Mercosur and the EU, which was Brazil's principal trading partner and source of foreign investment. Lula articulated the importance of these multidimensional relationships in a speech at the Mercosur-EU Business Forum in October 2003, stating, "[o]ur affinity with Europe is also historical, cultural and political. We see the world in a similar way. All of this forms a solid base that we must value, and on which we must build a closer relationship that is more profitable for both blocs." (http://www.brazil.org.uk/page.php?cid = 1766).

In the geopolitical context of the Bush administration's policy of preemptive war and continuing occupation of Iraq, and of widespread international opposition to those policies, Lula's remarks underscored the political significance of his emergent internationalist strategy to strengthen alliances between Mercosur and the EU. Such alliances provided a potential counterweight to the power of the U.S. in trade negotiations in the WTO and the FTAA, which could bolster Brazil's position in the politics of globalization. These alliances were also freighted with tensions, however, since Lula engaged in struggles with the EU as well.

SHIFTING NEGOTIATING STRATEGIES: FREE-TRADE DISCOURSE AND EMERGENT INTERNATIONALISM

In addition to formulating trade and development policy by strengthening international alliances, Lula crafted a new negotiating strategy to engage in trade politics, breaking from the earlier informatics strategy closing the market to foreign capital to promote economic development and national sovereignty. In the new era, the Lula administration demanded that the U.S. and EU open markets in the global North to exports from the global South. Instead of using the sovereignty discourse to defend the rights of governments in the global South to close their markets, Lula thus employed the free-trade discourse to push for open markets in the global North.

This skillful discursive strategy sharpened the North–South conflict in the politics of globalization by highlighting ways that governments and corporations based in the global North failed to comply with their own calls for free trade, and in the process, hurt the economic interests of farmers and industrialists in the global South. The goal of this emergent struggle over trade politics was to promote sovereignty and development in the South. Lula articulated alternative values, however, to frame this development as a human rights issue to advocate for the world's poor.

Lula thus used the free-trade discourse in an innovative way: to call for a new moral economy that infused questions of social justice with those of economic development and trade. As discussed above, this strategy did not involve merely "repackaging neo-liberalism as the way to help the world's poor" (http://www.zmag.org/content/showarticle.cfm?SectionID = 1&ItemID = 7197). By contrast, Lula pinpointed the inequalities between countries in the global North and South within the existing neoliberal trade regime of the WTO, as well as ongoing discussions over the FTAA. He emphasized the inconsistent application of free-trade principles to favor the U.S. and EU, particularly in the area of agricultural subsidies. For example, at the Mercosur-EU Business Forum he stated, "What we want is equality of opportunity, which is to say unimpeded access to markets and an end to abusive restrictions that distort international trade to the detriment, most of all, of developing countries. The billion-dollar agricultural subsidies have created veritable trade apartheid" (http://www.brazil.org.uk/page.php?cid = 1766).

Lula's powerful metaphor of "trade apartheid" further signifies the sharpening of the North–South conflicts over the politics of globalization, even in the context of his strategy to strengthen transnational alliances between Brazil, Mercosur and the EU. Through this language, Lula highlights the inextricable connections between what the dominant neoliberal discourse views as "objective" processes of economic development and the structural conditions of race and class inequality that make such development possible.

Struggles over "trade apartheid" were particularly acute in the area of agriculture, where the U.S. and EU governments maintained subsidies that hurt agricultural interests in the South. The Lula administration used the WTO as an institutional framework to attack these trade policies, using the discourse of free trade, speaking the language of the dominant neoliberal discourse in an effort to undermine it.

It filed a complaint with the WTO, noting that the U.S. government's cotton subsidies were particularly important to Brazil as the world's fifth largest cotton producer. In this complaint, the Brazilian government charged that between 1999 and 2003, the U.S. used $12.47 billion of subsidies to American farmers to retain its position as the world's second-largest cotton grower and largest cotton exporter. In April 2004, a WTO panel decided in favor of Brazil, finding that these subsidies artificially lowered international cotton prices and damaged the interests of farmers from the global South. In March 2005, the WTO appellate body upheld that ruling, paving the way for further challenges to subsidies in the global North that undermine the interests of farmers in the global South (Becker, 2005; Sequera, 2004).[2]

These events highlight the importance of trade negotiations as a terrain for the struggle over the politics of globalization. The Brazilian government effectively employed the free-trade discourse as a tactic to wage these struggles. These successes do not, however, reveal that single states pursue strategies for sovereignty primarily by acting alone. Indeed, the above WTO complaint was further evidence of the Brazilian government's effective emphasis on alliance building, since it was joined by Argentina, Australia, Benin, Canada, Chad, China, the European Community, India, New Zealand, Pakistan, Paraguay, Taiwan and Venezuela (Becker, 2005).

In a similar vein, the Brazilian government engaged in extensive, and sometimes tense, negotiations with other governments to define the issues to be covered within the FTAA and the WTO. Lula fought for a particular position with respect to those definitions, however, the multilateral nature of these institutional contexts required him to negotiate the content of those positions and build alliances in order to put them into practice. Due to the contrasting politics of globalization in each venue, the FTAA involved a greater emphasis on negotiation and the WTO on alliance building.

With respect to the FTAA, Lula sought to limit the scope of the issues discussed, and thus marginalize it as a venue for trade negotiations, due to the dominance of the U.S. government in that context (Brazil News, 2003). Toward that end, Lula advocated a weaker FTAA that would cover whatever issues were not addressed within the WTO or bilateral negotiations; such as standards, technical issues like rules of origin, competition policy and harmonization. By contrast, the U.S. government favored a broader scope of negotiations for the FTAA, which would expand its purview to include the questions of opening markets in services and government procurement, as well as strengthening roles on investment and intellectual property. It pressured Latin American governments to support its position by threatening to forego the FTAA in place of bilateral arrangements with individual governments, or smaller groups of governments, willing to cooperate with its free-trade agenda.

In this context, a range of Latin American governments supported the U.S. call to widen the FTAA's purview to include questions of opening markets in services, government procurement, investment and intellectual property. Smaller Caribbean economies were relatively unconcerned about the Brazilian government's charge that a strong FTAA would increase competition from U.S. industry. Indeed, they were primarily interested in negotiating access to U.S. markets. Colombia, Peru and 10 other Latin American governments supported the U.S. position as a way to solidify their existing trade preferences with the U.S. government and avoid the prospect of being excluded from the FTAA, as the U.S. government had threatened (Brazil news, 2003, The Economist, 2003).

In the wake of U.S. government pressures and the compliance by other Latin American governments to the U.S. position, Lula continued to oppose the broader version of the FTAA. On the basis of the free-trade discourse, such an agreement would prohibit domestic-content policies, which have been used historically by governments in the global South to promote economic development. The Brazilian government has used such policies since the 1950s to promote the transfer of technology and the development of local industries, including informatics. Under such an application of the free-trade discourse within the FTAA, the Brazilian government would not be allowed to require transnational corporations selling their products within Brazil to include a percentage of domestically manufactured parts. By outlawing such policies as impediments to free trade, the FTAA would deny the Brazilian government one of its key tools for encouraging industrial growth, potentially fostering greater dependence on the U.S. capital in the process. Such a version of the FTAA would strengthen the process of neoliberal globalization by supporting the interests of transnational corporations in challenging national regulations that impede their access to global markets.

In a similar vein, the current version of the FTAA gives corporations the power to sue national and local governments over health and safety regulations as restraints of free trade. And the Bush administration is pushing Latin American governments to accept a degree of patent protection for transnational corporations that even the WTO has refused. According to a study by the Center for Economic and Policy Research, Brazil's net losses from increased royalties and licensing fees would outweigh the benefits from increased trade (Gourevitch, 2002).

These impacts on Brazilian development help explain why the Lula administration continues to struggle to limit the purview of the FTAA, and highlights the stakes involved with the FTAA negotiations for the broader neoliberal globalization agenda. Indeed, supporting the free-trade discourse within the institutional context of the FTAA involves supporting the dominant neoliberal globalization model of opening markets around the world to global capital and creating obstacles for states in the global South to enact policies to shape conditions of economic development. These implications contrast markedly with Lula's use of the free-trade discourse discussed above, to pressure governments in the global North to open markets to those in the global South.

Lula's broader strategy of emergent internationalism involves a series of interrelated elements in the sphere of trade politics. His negotiating strategy on the FTAA is linked to his efforts to finalize a free-trade agreement between Mercosur and the EU by the end of 2004. Lula highlighted these connections in a speech to farmers at an agricultural conference, noting that reducing tariffs and quotas between these two trading blocs would "improve Brazil's position for the FTAA, so we're not exclusively subjected to U.S. economic pressure" (www.latimes.com/business/investing/wire/sns-ap-brazil-europe,0,193650.story?coll = sns-ap-investing-headlines).

Such an EU-Mercosur deal could increase Lula's willingness to include agricultural issues in the FTAA negotiations, rather than relegating disputes over agricultural subsidies and tariffs to the WTO. It would strengthen the Brazilian government's prospects for pursuing its emergent internationalist strategy within the institutional context of both of these trade accords. As Lula stated in a speech to the Mercosur-E.U. Business Forum, "Brazil wants to negotiate [the FTAA]...What we don't want is to be defeated in the FTAA...because we want to defend our economy, our industry, our agriculture, our trade, our jobs and our sovereignty." (http://www.brazil.org.uk/page.php?cid = 1766).

Lula thus employed distinct strategies to pursue the overarching goal of sovereignty in different institutional venues. Since the U.S. government dominated the FTAA negotiations, he sought to limit the scope of those talks and bolster Brazil's position by forming an agreement with the EU. In the WTO negotiations, he emphasized alliance building to pressure governments in the global North to open their markets to the global South.

Lula initiated a dialogue with South Africa and India, sparking the formation of the Group of 22 (G-22) alliance of delegations from 22 countries at the WTO meetings in Cancún, Mexico in September of 2003. The G-22 voiced opposition to the neoliberal trade agenda within the WTO, critiquing it for perpetuating world hunger and inequality, as well as a lack of technological development and cooperation to benefit countries in the global South. The G-22 successfully challenged the neoliberal globalization agenda at Cancún. The WTO talks collapsed, since neither the G-22 nor the U.S. government and its allies would make sufficient concessions to warrant continued negotiations.

Yashwant Sinha, the Indian Finance Minister, explained the significance of the G-22 alliance, stating, "We have thought enough about South-South cooperation and we have reached this stage now where we want to give it a concrete shape" (Greider & Rapoza, 2003, p. 11). Lula echoed similar themes in his speech at a parliamentary meeting on the FTAA in October of 2003, where he described the creation of the G-22 as an "extraordinary new political phenomenon, not because of what was achieved there, but because, for the first time, a group of countries sharing certain similarities in terms of their economies and their social problems discovered it was necessary to unite in order to try to make the rich countries open up a little space for us" (http://www.brazil.org.uk/page.php?cid=1764).

In this speech, Lula used the free-trade discourse to articulate his strategy for sovereignty by expressing his support for free trade and advocating Latin American countries having policies in common to push for access to markets in the global North. In the process, Lula exposed the U.S. and EU efforts to define neoliberal trade regimes in terms favorable to their economic interests. He articulated the conflicting interests between the U.S., the EU, and governments in the global South. He argued that the U.S. and the EU have dominated world trade debates and asserted their economic interests at the expense of farmers, a range of business sectors, the middle classes and the poor in the global South. He emphasized the importance of understanding that trade politics are about more than economic interests, since conditions of international trade are powerful forces shaping social issues of hunger and inequality on a global scale (http://www.brazil.org.uk/page.php?cid=1764).

Lula's use of the free-trade discourse was a politically creative and astute strategy to struggle for economic and political sovereignty for countries in the global South. It fit with Foucault's (1978, p. 100) argument that we "must not imagine a world of discourse divided between accepted discourse and excluded discourse, or between the dominant discourse and the dominated one; but as a multiplicity of discursive elements that can come into play in various strategies." Indeed, the advocacy of free trade was a vital discursive element used in distinct, opposing ways in the strategies of the Brazilian and U.S. governments during negotiations over the WTO and the FTAA in the early 2000s.

Lula's remarks highlighted the importance of developing political unity among countries from the global South to acknowledge and defend their common economic and social interests in the context of neoliberal globalization, however, they misrepresented the novelty of the G-22 alliance. This alliance was not the "first time" that countries from the global South with common economic and social problems united to defend common interests in struggles with the global North (http://www.brazil.org.uk/page.php?cid=1764).

Indeed, there was a vital history of alliance formation by governments in the global South to forge alternatives to the neoliberal globalization agenda. In 1955, the Non-Aligned Movement of Asian and African governments called on the powers of the global North to recognize their concerns that the dominant model of economic development subverted their ability to make economic, political and social choices. In 1974, the G-77 Third World states proposed radical changes to strengthen their position in global trade and development by creating a New International Economic Order (NIEO). These changes included increased transfer of technology, improved access to international financing and terms of trade for mining and agricultural products, as well as opening markets in the global North to industrial exports from the global South (McMichael, 2004). This last demand reveals the historical roots of contemporary struggles over the politics of globalization, and particularly Lula's strategy to use the free-trade discourse to pursue sovereignty for the global South.

Brazil and India's leadership of the alliance within the WTO was reminiscent of a struggle in the 1980s. From 1984 to 1986, Brazil and India led a group of 10 delegations (the G-10) from the global South to oppose U.S. government efforts to expand the purview of the neoliberal GATTrade from the regulation of trade in goods to trade in services. These delegations represented Argentina, Cuba, Egypt, Nicaragua, Nigeria, Peru, Tanzania and Yugoslavia. They favored greater government control over services, and were concerned that being pressured to open their markets in areas like banking and insurance would exacerbate their comparative disadvantages in the services fields.

By contrast, the U.S. delegation led a group including Canada, the United Kingdom, Sweden and Japan to push for incorporating the regulation of services trade directly under the GATT trade regime, and accomplishing this shift at a rapid pace. The U.S. government pressured the members of the G-10 by threatening to withdraw their tariff preferences unless they changed their positions and supported inclusion of services trade within the GATT. Schoonmaker (2002, p. 63) described the reaction of the Reagan administration to this struggle; quoting Clayton Yeutter, the U.S. Trade Representative, who stated that "[w]e simply cannot afford to have a handful of countries, responsible for 5 percent of world trade, dictate the destiny of a large number of countries who deal with 95 percent of that trade." After intensive and protracted negotiations culminating at the end of 1988, the

U.S. government and its allies successfully established the GATT as the international regime governing trade in services. Its neoliberal regime promoting free trade in goods, opening markets throughout the world to global capital, was extended to cover the expanding markets for trade in services (Schoonmaker, 2002; Aronson & Cowhey, 1984; Nicolaides, 1989; Bhalla, 1990; Marconini, 1990; Kakabadse, 1987).

The Bush administration employed similar tactics in response to the G-22's efforts at the WTO meetings almost two decades later. Robert Zoellick, the U.S. Trade Representative, characterized the collapse of the WTO talks in Cancún as the fault of the intransigent G-22 delegations. Roundly criticizing Brazil as the leader of the alliance of "won't do" countries, he stated that the U.S. government would "move towards free trade with can-do countries" (http://www.investmentwatch.org/articles/ft11january2004.html). Similar to the actions during the GATT negotiations, U.S. Trade Representative Zoellick stated that the U.S. would make "advances on multiple fronts" (The Economist, 2003, p. 35) by cutting off bilateral trade negotiations with "won't do" countries remaining within the former G-22 alliance and formulating either bilateral or regional alliances with "can-do" countries. In a similar vein, Charles Grassley, the chairman of the Senate Finance Committee, expressed doubts that any member of the G-22 would be able to negotiate a bilateral trade deal with the U.S. government (The Economist, 2003, p. 35).

Tensions between the U.S. and Brazilian governments flared in the wake of the WTO talks' collapse. The *Folha de São Paulo*, a major Brazilian newspaper, accused the U.S. Trade Representative Zoellick of making "an open declaration of war against Brazil" (Greider & Rapoza, 2003, p. 12). Brazilian foreign minister Celso Amorim critiqued the U.S. Trade Representative Zoellick for "making threats" against U.S. trading partners in the WTO (The Economist, 2003, p. 35). In an interview with a *Newsweek* reporter, Amorim stated that the delegates were "making progress and ready to negotiate amendments on agricultural subsidies" (http://www.brazil.org.uk/page.php?cid=1759) when the U.S. and other Western nations insisted on discussing rules concerning government procurement, competitiveness and trade financing, the so-called "Singapore issues." In Amorim's view, "[n]o one benefits by saying, 'OK, now we will only pursue bilateral trade agreements.' There is no substitute for the WTO" (http://www.brazil.org.uk/page.php?cid=1759). Indeed, Amorim viewed Cancún as a victory for Brazil, since

> [w]e were able to cut our losses...the proposal by the United States and European Union, would have meant greatly scaling back expectations from previous talks in Doha. The Brazilian delegation decided that the limited gains...were not worth it. This was not

obstruction. It was a deliberate position. And if we all take care not to let ourselves get carried away by emotions, we have the basis to continue negotiating. We achieved a political victory. Despite the initial resistance, we were treated as a legitimate negotiating party, not as a grouplet of countries over in the corner shouting and creating obstacles (http://www.brazil.org.uk/page.php?cid=1759).

This victory, however significant, was a single battle in a longer struggle to forge an alternative to the neoliberal globalization agenda. As such, this victory sparked resistance and conflict. The U.S. government pressures in the wake of Cancún shook the alliance of delegates from the global South. In the weeks following the united stand against the neoliberal trade agenda, the Group of 22 shrunk to 12 members. Central American and Caribbean governments left the coalition after they were threatened with the loss of trade preferences with the U.S. government. Peru, Colombia, Paraguay and Uruguay soon followed. Colombian President Alvaro Uribe expressed hopes that his government would enter negotiations over a bilateral trade deal in the wake of that decision (Greider & Rapoza, 2003; The Economist, 2003).

Despite these effects of the U.S. pressure on small countries more vulnerable to losing their ties to the U.S. markets, the initial formation of the G-22 highlighted the breadth of opposition to the neoliberal trade agenda championed by the U.S. government. Federico Cuello, former WTO ambassador from the Dominican Republic, stated that "Brazil embodies the hope of countries like the Dominican Republic, showing that you can still have dignity at the negotiating table... . I doubt that Lula, who has massive public support and a top-notch Cabinet, will be intimidated" (Greider & Rapoza, 2003, p. 12). The fact that delegations left the G-22 revealed their vulnerability to political pressure. The prospects for resistance to the neoliberal trade agenda remained, however, as Lula and his allies from the global South continued to strategize their next moves.

Indeed, the U.S. government was far from wholly successful at stifling the opposition. Five months after Cancún, in the context of national and international resistance to the U.S. government's neoliberal agenda, the Bush administration shifted to a more conciliatory stance. The U.S. Trade Representative Zoellick characterized the U.S. government as trying to "reach out to developing countries" http://www.investmentwatch.org/articles/ft11january2004.html) by addressing the issues of agriculture and investment, as well as backing a candidate from the global South as incoming chair of the WTO general council. Zoellick expressed this pacificatory stance by stating that "[w]e're trying to provide constructive leadership" (http://www.investmentwatch.org/articles/ft11january2004.html) rather than dictating the terms for global trade talks. He crafted a letter, "trying to make some suggestions without crossing the line of creating controversy over specifics," suggesting options for how to proceed with the WTO talks (http://www.investmentwatch.org/articles/ft11january2004.html).

Zoellick's remarks suggested that he recognized the depth of the conflicts between its position and that of the delegations from the global South, as well as the unlikelihood of resolving them in time to complete the talks by the original deadline of January 2005. Indeed, the change in the U.S. government's position supported Lula's characterization of the G-22 as an "extraordinary new political phenomenon" (http://www.brazil.org.uk/page.php?cid=1764). What was extraordinary about the G-22, however, was not the process of alliance building among delegates from the global South to articulate their interests in a global trade forum. The unusual quality of this alliance was its success in pressuring the U.S. government to make concessions both in terms of specific trade issues and in terms of the overall process and timetable of the trade negotiations. For example, the U.S. Trade Representative Zoellick expressed his willingness to reconsider the timing of reductions in industrial and agricultural tariffs, as well as particular demands by African delegations to reduce cotton subsidies (Alden & Barber, 2004).

The Bush administration's changed negotiating stance revealed the extent of U.S. interests in concluding the Doha round of the WTO talks. As Held (2000) argued, transnational networks and regimes have become increasingly important under contemporary conditions of globalization; so important that even dominant states like the U.S. must engage with them. Such engagement is particularly vital on trade issues like agricultural subsidies that involve changing the trade policies of a wide range of government. Indeed, Jagdish Bhagwati (2004), a Columbia economist and External Advisor to the Director General of the WTO, argued that multilateral trade negotiations were the only effective way to address such issues. Bhagwati (2004) criticized the G-22 for their unwillingness to reduce their own restrictions on agricultural trade, and was equally judgmental of the U.S. government for negotiating bilateral deals in the wake of the Cancún talks' collapse. He viewed this collapse as "a stepping stone to a successful conclusion of the Doha round," however, since none of the parties involved could successfully meet their objectives without this multilateral forum (Bhagwati, 2004, p. 52).

As discussed above, Brazilian Foreign Minister Celso Amorim expressed a similar view of the importance of multilateral trade negotiations as indispensable for resolving issues such as trade in agriculture. Minister

Amorim had a vision of the importance of alliances between delegations from the global South as a vital part of these negotiations, however, which differed from Bhagwati's (2004) view that it is necessary to work within the multilateral structure of the WTO to forge accords including so many parties. Bhagwati (2004) thus emphasized the constraints of structural forms, while Amorim highlighted the relationships between participants as a shifting, dynamic force shaping the negotiating process. Indeed, decades of participating in multilateral trade negotiations never guaranteed governments from the global South that their interests would prevail in the final agreements. The prospects for pursuing these interests were forged through ongoing processes of struggle and alliance building. The difference between Bhagwati's (2004) and Amorim's views was revealed in Amorim's comments after WTO negotiations resumed in Geneva in August 2004; where he cited a "new dynamic within the WTO.... This new multipolarity is important because without it the notion of a 'multilateral' trade system, represented by the WTO, would be a fiction" (http://www.brazil.org.uk/page/php?cid=1877).

True multilateralism, or "multipolarity," thus required active participation by delegations from the global South. This multipolar dynamic arose with the reemergence of the G-22 at Geneva. They made proposals and won inclusion of an agreement by all 147 members of the WTO to eliminate agricultural export subsidies. This agreement reflected the continuing vitality of the G-22 alliance as a force pressing the interests of governments in the global South within the WTO. Its success was limited, however, since no decision was made about when the elimination of subsidies would begin or how this process would be implemented (http://www.brazzil.com/2004/html/articles/aug04/p105aug04.htm). The struggle to open agricultural markets in the global North to farmers from the global South thus continued to infuse trade debates and the politics of globalization.

CONCLUSION

The Brazilian government's shifting strategies of sovereignty, from a nationalist effort to restrict access to Brazilian markets in the informatics sector in the 1970s and the 1980s to an internationalist struggle to open markets in the global North to agricultural products in the early 2000s, reveal key dynamics in the process of globalization. Indeed, the informatics strategy involved pursuing national development, and a long-range vision of national sovereignty through greater local control over conditions of development, by fighting the neoliberal globalization project of opening markets around the world to global capital. This earlier strategy employed a discourse of national sovereignty and an oppositional stance toward the U.S. government and its efforts to promote the neoliberal agenda. Decades later, however, conditions of globalization are characterized by the increasing importance of international actors and the difficulty of pursuing sovereignty through nation states acting alone (Held, 2000). In this changed context, Lula initiated a politically insightful and creative process of crafting a strategy that retained the broad commitment to sovereignty, both within Brazil and throughout nations in the global South, by rearticulating these nationalist goals in internationalist terms.

Lula's emergent internationalism stressed economic development as multidimensional, inextricably linked to cultural norms and forged through political and discursive processes. In his speeches to various international audiences, from the European Union Business Forum to Parliamentary Meetings on the FTAA, Lula highlighted the implications of trade and development policy for conditions of global inequality and particularly for the world's poor. His call to craft a trade and development agenda that would eradicate hunger as a weapon of mass destruction demanded inventive experimentation from all parties involved in international negotiations such as the FTAA and the WTO.

Such an approach is emergent, in Williams' (1977) terms, because it involves the development of new practices, values, relationships and kinds of relationships that are repressed, opposed, and indeed, unrecognizable by the dominant form. It contradicts the dominant neoliberal view that markets operate according to objective economic laws that must be obeyed to ensure the efficient functioning of the global economy. By contrast, Lula's emergent internationalism views cultural norms as embedded in all trade and development policy decisions; thus emphasizing a cultural, normative dimension to economic policies and practices that the dominant neoliberal model cannot recognize or support. Indeed, if trade and development policies are assumed to be governed by objective laws outside cultural influence, then a normative approach such as Lula advocates is inconceivable and repressed. Lula's emergent approach calls on policymakers to make the norms upon which their strategies are based explicit by facing their implications for the world's poor. This stance resonates with social groups and movements both within Brazil and in the broader *altermondialiste* movement, although potential allies on the left critique Lula for "repackaging neo-liberalism as the way to help the world's poor." (http://www.zmag.org/content/showarticle.cfm?SectionID=1&ItemID=7197).

Lula's strategy for sovereignty was more complicated, however, involving both the use of the free-trade discourse combined with alliance-building in the institutional context of the WTO, and the struggle against that discourse in the U.S.-dominated FTAA. Through this complex and contradictory strategy, Lula demonstrated that, under contemporary conditions of globalization, traditionally nationalist goals of economic and political sovereignty can more effectively be pursued through an internationalist strategy of alliance building among governments in the global South. Such a strategy creates possibilities for governments in the global South to both increase their trade with each other and forge alliances to demand access to markets in the global North. These alliances created the dynamic of multipolarity within the WTO, where the G-22 is struggling to transform the agenda to benefit economic interests in the global South.

The consequences of this struggle, and of Lula's emergent internationalism, remain to be seen. The G-22's actions at Cancún and Geneva suggest, however, that the strategy of pressing governments in the global North to open their markets to the global South can catalyze alliances between these historically disenfranchised populations, creating conditions to pursue their sovereignty in dynamic, venturesome ways. By infusing trade debates with questions about their implications for social justice and the world's poor, and thus calling for a new moral economy, Lula's emergent internationalism makes a vital contribution to this process.

NOTES

1. The French term *altermondialiste* conjures images of people building alternative worlds, which are not adequately captured by the English translation as the anti-globalization movement.

2. In a similar vein, the WTO issued a preliminary ruling that the EU's 75% tariff on salted chicken imports from Brazil was protectionist (http://oglobo.globo.com/online/default/asp).

ACKNOWLEDGMENTS

I would like to thank Philip McMichael for his valuable comments and Michael Thoeresz for his research assistance on this project.

REFERENCES

Adler, E. (1987). *The power of ideology: The quest for technological autonomy in Argentina and Brazil.* Berkeley: University of California Press.

Alden, E., & Barber, L. (2004). U.S. adopts softer touch in trade negotiations. *Financial Times,* January 11.

Angrisani, L. (2003). More Latin, less America? Creating a free trade area of the Americas. *The National Interest,* (Fall), 77–84.

Aronson, J., & Cowhey, P. (1984). *Trade in services: A case for open markets.* Washington, DC: American Enterprise Institute.

Becker, E. (2005). U.S. loses final ruling on subsidies for cotton. *The New York Times,* March 3.

Bhagwati, J. (2004). Don't cry for Cancún. *Foreign Affairs,* January/February, 52–63.

Bhalla, S. (1990). India. In: K. Sauvant & P. Messerlin (Eds), *The Uruguay round: Services in the world economy* (pp. 188–196). Washington, DC: World Bank.

Brazil News. (2003). FTAA co-chairs search for ways to make progress in negotiations. *Brazil News, 4*(5), 2.

Brennan, T. (2003). *Globalization and its terrors: Daily life in the West.* London: Routledge.

Chu, H. (2005). Ruling party in Brazil at a crossroads. *The Los Angeles Times,* February 21, p. A3.

Cowhey, P., & Aronson, J. (1989). Global diplomacy and national policy options for telecommunications. In: P. Cowhey, J. Aronson & G. Szekely (Eds), *Changing Networks: Mexico's Telecommunications Options* (pp. 51–78). San Diego: Center for U.S.-Mexican Studies.

Downie, A. (2003). Brazil seeking stronger ties. *The MiamiHerald,* September 13, C1.

Epstein, G., Graham, J., & Nembhard, J. (Eds) (1993). *Creating a new world economy: Forces of change and plans for action.* Philadelphia: Temple University Press.

Evans, P. (1986). State, capital, and the transformation of dependence: The Brazilian computer case. *World Development, 14*(2), 791–808.

Evans, P. (1995). *Embedded autonomy: States and industrial transformation.* Princeton: Princeton University Press.

Foucault, M. (1978). In: R. Hurley (Trans.), *The history of sexuality. volume I: An introduction.* New York: Vintage Books.

Fregni, E. (1990). Interview by author. São Paulo.

Gibson-Graham, J. K. (1996). *The end of capitalism (as we knew it).* Oxford: Blackwell Publishers.

Gomes, R. (pseudonym). (1992). Interview by author. Rio de Janeiro.

Gourevitch, A. (2002). Lula's rules. *American Prospect, 13*(21), 19–20.

Greider, W., & Rapoza, K. (2003). Lula raises the stakes. *The Nation,* December 1, pp. 11–17.

Held, D. (2000). Regulating globalization? the reinvention of politics. *International Sociology, 15*(2), 394–408.

Helfand, S. (2004). Brazil under Lula: The first sixteen months. Paper presented at Latin American studies colloquium series, University of Redlands.

Hirst, P., & Thompson, G. (1999). *Globalization in question.* Malden, Mass: Blackwell.

Kakabadse, M. (1987). *International trade in services: Prospects for liberalisation in the 1990s.* London: Croom Helm.

Marconini, M. (1990). The Uruguay round negotiations on services: An overview. In: K. Sauvant & P. Messerlin (Eds), *The Uruguay round: Services in the world economy* (pp. 19–26). Washington, DC: World Bank.
McMichael, P. (2004). *Development and social change: A global perspective*. Thousand Oaks, CA: Pine Forge.
Nicolaides, P. (1989). *Liberalizing services trade: Strategies for success*. London: Royal Institute of International Affairs.
Ripper, M. (1990). Interview by author. Rio de Janeiro.
Schoonmaker, S. (2002). *High-tech trade wars: U.S.–Brazilian conflicts in the global economy*. Pittsburgh: University of Pittsburgh Press.
Sequera, V. S. (2004). American trade bloc to cement accord. *Financial News*, April 30.
The Economist (2003). Trade in the Americas: Much wind and little light. *The Economist*, October 16, p. 35–36.
U.S. House Committee on Energy and Commerce. (1988). Hearing on informatics trade problems with brazil before the subcommittee on commerce, consumer protection, and competitiveness of the committee on energy and commerce. 100th Cong., 1st sess., 15 July 1987. Washington, DC: U.S. Government Printing Office.
Williams, R. (1977). *Marxism and Literature*. Oxford: Oxford University Press.

SET UP A CONTINUATION ORDER TODAY!

Did you know that you can set up a continuation order on all Elsevier-JAI series and have each new volume sent directly to you upon publication? For details on how to set up a **continuation order**, contact your nearest regional sales office listed below.

To view related series in Sociology, please visit:

www.elsevier.com/sociology

The Americas
Customer Service Department
11830 Westline Industrial Drive
St. Louis, MO 63146
USA
US customers:
Tel: +1 800 545 2522 (Toll-free number)
Fax: +1 800 535 9935
For Customers outside US:
Tel: +1 800 460 3110 (Toll-free number).
Fax: +1 314 453 7095
usbkinfo@elsevier.com

Europe, Middle East & Africa
Customer Service Department
Linacre House
Jordan Hill
Oxford OX2 8DP
UK
Tel: +44 (0) 1865 474140
Fax: +44 (0) 1865 474141
eurobkinfo@elsevier.com

Japan
Customer Service Department
2F Higashi Azabu, 1 Chome Bldg
1-9-15 Higashi Azabu, Minato-ku
Tokyo 106-0044
Japan
Tel: +81 3 3589 6370
Fax: +81 3 3589 6371
books@elsevierjapan.com

APAC
Customer Service Department
3 Killiney Road #08-01
Winsland House I
Singapore 239519
Tel: +65 6349 0222
Fax: +65 6733 1510
asiainfo@elsevier.com

Australia & New Zealand
Customer Service Department
30-52 Smidmore Street
Marrickville, New South Wales 2204
Australia
Tel: +61 (02) 9517 8999
Fax: +61 (02) 9517 2249
service@elsevier.com.au

30% Discount for Authors on All Books!

A 30% discount is available to Elsevier book and journal contributors on all books *(except multi-volume reference works).*

To claim your discount, full payment is required with your order, which must be sent directly to the publisher at the nearest regional sales office above.